Britain Since 1700

Britain Since 1700

R. J. COOTES

LONGMAN

LONGMAN GROUP LIMITED
London

Associated companies, branches and representatives
throughout the world

© Longman Group Ltd 1968

First published 1968
Eighth impression 1975

ISBN 0 582 20501 8

Printed in Great Britain by Jarrold & Sons Ltd, Norwich

Contents

Preface

The requirements of pupils studying modern British History for the Certificate of Secondary Education have largely determined the range of vocabulary and the selection of material found in this volume. To give pupils something substantial to get their teeth into, the social and economic aspects in particular are dealt with at greater length than is customary at this level. Nevertheless, there has been no attempt to achieve an encyclopaedic coverage of the period. This book is designed to provide the *focus* for a course, since it is assumed that teachers will want to use all kinds of additional material with their classes.

It is hoped that some of the suggestions in the Further Study sections will prove helpful not only to teachers but to pupils engaged on independent projects. Simplicity of style and language were important factors in recommending books for further reading. However, on topics where there is a large volume of suitable material many admirable books were squeezed out for lack of space. Apologies are due to the authors and publishers concerned.

Eighth Printing, 1975. The opportunity has been taken to bring up to date many of the facts and figures in the closing chapters. At the same time nearly a hundred books and filmstrips have been added to the Further Study sections.

I should like to thank my collaborator, Mr L. E. Snellgrove, for all his help and encouragement; Mrs Madeleine Gunny, for her sterling work on the illustrations; Dr W. A. Armstrong and Mr P. Isaac for their valuable advice; several members of Longman's staff, whose assistance has gone far beyond their normal course of duty, and, not least, my wife, who suggested numerous improvements to the text.

RICHARD J. COOTES

Acknowledgements

The authors and publisher are grateful to the following for permission to reproduce photographs:

Aerofilms and Aero Pictorial Ltd. 50/51, 168, 312, 316; The Associated Press Ltd. 331; British Aircraft Corporation 324 (right); British Hovercraft Corporation 322/323 (bottom); British Motor Corporation 257; British Museum 16, 113; British Railway Board 320/321; British Rail (Western Region) 152; Camera Press Ltd. 306 (bottom), 307, 309, 311, 320, 328, 330; Canada House 327; Canadian Pacific 224; J. Allan Cash 329 (bottom); Central Press Photos Ltd. 335; Co-operative Union Ltd. 143; Esso Ltd. 317; John R. Freeman 65, 66, 75, 79, 83, 89, 96, 102; Ford of Britain 318; Fox Photos Ltd. 279; General Post Office 100; Greater London Council Photo Library 220; James Hall 136/7; Hawker Siddeley Photo News 324 (left); The John Hilleson Agency Ltd. 302/303; Imperial War Museum 298, 300/301, 301; International Business Machines 318/319; Keystone Press Agency Ltd. 284 (bottom), 306 (top), 307, 308, 310, 322/323 (top), 333, 338; Mansell Collection 12 (bottom), 14/15 (bottom), 18/19, 20 (top), 21 (bottom), 30 (top), 34 (bottom), 35 (bottom), 37, 40/41, 43, 46, 47, 57, 82, 90, 93, 97, 99, 114/115, 118, 123, 129, 158/159, 178, 211 (top), 230, 242, 243, 248, 249, 259, 262, 270, 272, 276, 277, 280; Eric de Mare 64/5, 73, 98, 105, 153, 176; The Mitchell Library, Glasgow 24; National Coal Board 315; National Library of Ireland 234/5; National Portrait Gallery 64 (top); National Union of Railwaymen 205; Nottingham Public Libraries 126; Paul Popper Ltd. 275, 329 (top); *Punch* 110, 180, 284; Radio Times Hulton Picture Library 12/13 (top), 15 (top), 17 (bottom), 25, 26, 31 (bottom), 34 (top), 36, 39, 42, 52, 56, 61, 68, 72, 94, 108, 109, 111, 116, 122, 124, 125, 129 (top) and (middle), 131, 134, 135, 138, 139, 141, 144, 155, 156, 160, 161, 163, 164, 166, 167, 169, 171, 173, 178, 181, 188, 190, 191, 196, 199, 203, 207, 208, 210/211, 212, 214, 216, 218, 222, 225, 227, 228, 231, 232, 236, 239, 241, 243, 245, 246, 247, 250, 254/255, 260, 263, 264/265, 265, 271, 273, 274/275, 283, 285, 286, 289, 291, 292, 295, 296, 303, 304/305; Rolls-Royce 255; Science Museum *frontispiece,* 52/53, 63, 76/77, 78, 85, 86, 87, 146, 147, 148, 150, 154, 157, 159, 175, 182, 254, 256; The Trustees of Sir John Soane's Museum 22/23; Society for Promoting Christian Knowledge 45, 256/257; Trades Union Congress 200; University of Reading, Museum of English Rural Life 54/55, 240; Josiah Wedgwood & Sons Ltd. 88; The Wellcome Historical Medical Museum 184/185, 186, 187, 192, 193, 194/195, 213; York City Engineer's Office 261, 290.

We have been unable to trace the copyright owners of the following photographs and apologise for any infringement of copyright: 126, 129 (bottom), 137, 144, 172, 336.

1 Villagers and Townsmen
England in the early eighteenth century

If we travelled back through time to the England of some two and a half centuries ago, we would find none of the familiar features of mid twentieth-century life. It was like a different world. There were few towns, and, by our standards, these were very small and quiet. There were no mechanical forms of transport and hardly any proper roads. Factories were almost unheard of. The people dressed altogether differently, ate different kinds of food and lived in homes which we would regard as rough, dirty and smelly. Even their favourite sports and pastimes were, for the most part, totally foreign to us. The great majority of the people lived in remote villages or small market towns, farming the land or working in the village trades. It was a way of life which resembled that of the later Middle Ages more closely than that of our own day.

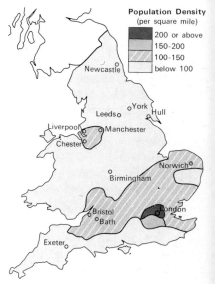

England in the Early
Eighteenth Century

Population

England and Wales at the beginning of the eighteenth century were inhabited by about $5\frac{1}{2}$ million people — much less than the population of present day London. We have no exact figures because the first official census was not carried out until 1801, but we can guess fairly accurately on the basis of parish registers and other surviving documents. Roughly a third of the total population lived in south-eastern England. The most densely inhabited area stretched roughly from the mouth of the Severn to below the Thames estuary in the south and the Wash in the north. This was understandable in an age when agriculture was the chief occupation, for these lands are among the most fertile in the British Isles. They also enjoy a relatively warm climate and are not excessively hilly, like many of the Northern and Western counties.

The people of the eighteenth century had much larger families than we do today. But, because they did not live so long, the total population increased only slowly — especially up to about 1750. Killing diseases like smallpox, dysentery, consumption and typhus fevers were widespread. They did most damage among the poor, whose defences against illness were weakened by shortage of food, inadequate shelter and, in some cases, excessive drinking. In the period 1720–50, cheap gin was consumed in great quantities, especially in the London area. By 1750 a quarter of the houses in the slum district around Holborn were gin shops! Parliament was forced to take action. In 1751 the tax on spirits was greatly increased and their sale by distillers and shopkeepers was strictly controlled.

Although the poor were most exposed to disease, the general lack of sanitation and medical knowledge meant that even the wealthiest citizens were quite likely to suffer sudden and early death. Queen Anne (1702–14) had seventeen children, yet none of them reached maturity. The 'death rate' — the number of deaths per thousand per year — fell sharply in the second half of the eighteenth century. Consequently the population of England and Wales reached 9 million by 1801. This rapid increase was due to better living conditions and, to a lesser extent, improved medical treatment — both of which checked disease and ill-health. The medical profession in general was becoming slightly more scientific, and midwifery in particular was greatly improved by the work of a Scotsman, Dr William Smellie.

Farming and the countryside

The village was still the main centre of English life. A large majority of the population was engaged in agriculture and in rural crafts, like those of the blacksmith, carpenter, wheelwright, thatcher and miller. The village community was very self-sufficient. Few of its inhabitants ever had cause to travel beyond the nearest market town, where they sold their surplus produce and bought shoes, clothes, or anything which might be difficult to obtain in the village. All the main items in the countryman's diet were produced locally. Cereals were the chief crop — wheat, rye, barley or oats — from which bread was baked and ale was brewed. The other principal products of agriculture, apart from wool, were meat and dairy produce and, in some areas, fruit and vegetables. However, meat was something of a luxury among ordinary folk, unless they were fortunate enough to own a cow or a pig.

Most farmers were **smallholders,** with anything up to twenty acres of land. Some of them, together with their families, combined

Above: A wealthy supper party

Left: A gathering of poor people

farming with other employment in the home, especially the making of woollen cloth. They lived in roughly built houses of timber, brick or stone according to which building materials were readily available in the area. Most of the houses in the village were clustered together round the parish church and village inn, along the main highway. Inside they were simply furnished, with strong tables, chairs and stools. Smallholders did without carpets, curtains, upholstered furniture and many other things which we would regard as necessities in our own homes. In the evening, light was provided by dimly burning candles. **Labourers,** working for wages, were normally found on the larger farms, where there was too much work for one family to cope with. They often lived in wooden or mud-walled shacks, where the whole family slept in one room.

Very little of the land was actually owned by those who farmed it. Most smallholders rented their land from members of the nobility and gentry, though there was, in addition, quite a large class of **freeholders.** Because they had property of their own, most yeoman freeholders occupied a position in the social scale above that of the tenant farmer. It was an age when social power and prestige depended very largely on ownership of land. Thus **the nobility** dominated the highest political offices and held the top positions in the Church and in the army and navy. Some of these aristocratic families had thousands of acres, scattered over a wide area. The Duke of Newcastle had an income of £40,000 a year from estates in twelve counties. Successful merchants, bankers and businessmen were keen to invest their wealth in land, for this was the only sure way of gaining acceptance in the higher ranks of society.

Next to the nobility in the social scale came the gentry — the major landowners in each county who were not of noble birth. In the village, the chief landowner was called **the squire.** Although he was a Justice of the Peace and often active in politics, he was usually just like an ordinary villager in his speech and manners. The greater part of many a squire's life was devoted to fox-hunting, good food and strong ale. His home—the Hall—probably seemed like a palace to most of the villagers, but it was bare and uncomfortable by modern standards. Only the best rooms had carpets and few, if any, had curtains. Seats were usually straight-backed chairs, stools and benches. The house was so draughty that the family slept in box-beds with built-up sides. Outside there were stables and farm buildings and possibly a coach-house — but coaches could only be used in fine weather, because of the poor state of the roads.

Next to the squire, the most important individual in the village was **the parson.** Although many people attended church more from social custom than religious conviction, it was still a far more religious age than our own. The parish church was at the very centre of village life. When he was not attending to the needs of his parishioners, the parson usually farmed his own small plot of land, called the glebe. In addition, he received a 'tithe' (tenth) of the produce of all the other farms in the parish. Frequently the parson's income from the Church was so small that he relied on the glebe and the tithe to make ends meet.

Towns and town life

Towns were few and far between and very small by present day standards, except for **London.** With a population of over half a million, it was more than ten times larger than any other town in Britain and it dominated English life even more than it does today. In London all degrees of splendour and squalor were to be found — everything from brutal ignorance to great intellect.

In the fashionable streets and squares to the **west** of the City lived those engaged in business and government, the professions and the arts. Merchants, bankers, lawyers, doctors, writers and politicians rubbed shoulders with the wealthier country gentlemen, who normally took up residence in their town-houses during the 'social season'. The main centres of social life were the **coffee-houses** where everything from business to political gossip was carried on, amid clouds of tobacco smoke. Political and religious groups each had their favourite coffee-houses, and these later grew into exclusive clubs. Edward **Lloyd's** coffee-house in Lombard Street was the meeting-place for merchants and sea-captains. There they heard shipping news and arranged insurance on cargo and vessels. So much business was done at Lloyd's that before long it became the centre of the world's shipping insurance.

In contrast, the narrow streets, courts and alleys of the **East End** were the home of London's poor. Dockers, seamen and all kinds of other workers lived in filthy, overcrowded dwellings, surrounded by open sewers and back-garden cesspools. The streets overflowed with the rubbish that was thrown into them from every house, shop and workplace. In the absence of a police force, vice and crime flourished. No one went out after dark except on very urgent business, for daytime pickpockets became thieves and murderers at nightfall. Disease was even more common than crime. More than half the children born in the East End died under the age of five. Those who survived lived in constant fear of the epidemics which swept through the poorer districts from time to time.

London's most crowded highway was the **River Thames.** Passenger traffic jostled with the cargo boats, for, until Westminster Bridge was opened (1750) London Bridge provided the only road across the river. The Pool of London was the centre of the nation's shipping. It handled most of the European, Mediterranean and African trade, some of the sugar and tobacco from the American and West Indian colonies, and practically all the trade with India and the Far East. In addition, almost every English county supplied London with food and raw materials, mostly by sea. In return, London sent foreign imports all over the kingdom and also the products of its own industries, for it was not only a port but an important manufacturing centre. Some of the most skilled workmen in Britain were employed in the capital, in the manufacture of a wide range of luxury goods and in shipbuilding, sugar-refining, calico-printing and furniture-making.

The largest **towns outside London** were Norwich (a market town and the centre of the East Anglian cloth trade) and Bristol (the major western port). North of the Border, Edinburgh, the seat of Scottish Government and the centre of the country's social life, was

View of London in the 1780s

Bath—centre of fashionable living

about the same size. However, important as these towns were, it is unlikely that any of them contained as many as 50,000 inhabitants. Other towns were a great deal smaller. Some of those that are the biggest today were then either small ports or centres of small-scale domestic industry — for example, Birmingham (metal trades); Newcastle (coal and the Baltic trade); Liverpool (transatlantic trade); Hull (Baltic trade and shipbuilding); Leeds and Manchester (centres of the textile trades of Yorkshire and South Lancashire). It is doubtful if any of them had a population exceeding 10,000 in 1700.

Some of the largest towns had little or no connection with industry or overseas trade. Places like York, Exeter and Chester were important regional centres of social life as well as being markets for the surrounding countryside. They attracted many of the 'lesser gentry' who could not afford to keep town-houses in London. When the Assizes and Quarter Sessions were held, these towns enjoyed a brief 'season', during which numerous social functions took place — balls, musical recitals, card parties and even plays performed by travelling theatrical companies. But the main centre of fashionable living, outside London, was **Bath.** It was a small, unattractive town before **Richard Nash,** a

Pit Ticket

man of fashion, went there (1705) and began to organise it as a pleasure resort. His insistence on the highest standards of dress and manners earned him the name of 'Beau' (French for fine or handsome). As Master of Ceremonies, Nash engaged an orchestra and arranged plays, balls, parties, and gambling sessions. He even had the streets paved so they would not be out of keeping with the terraces of stately houses, which were fast replacing the shambles of the old town.

In spite of their outward show of gracefulness and refinement, the upper classes had many coarse and unpleasant habits. They spat, swore, picked their teeth in public, washed infrequently and ate and drank far too much. They gambled for high stakes, usually for want of anything better to do; and the violent arguments that often resulted could lead to deadly duels with swords and pistols. It was an age of violence and also of brutality. All classes of the population revelled in bloodthirsty sports and spectacles. The sufferings of animals were regarded as great entertainment, especially bull- and bear-baiting and cock-fighting. In London large crowds followed the procession of condemned criminals from Newgate Gaol to the gallows at Tyburn (along present day Oxford Street). The well-to-do hired rooms in houses overlooking the scaffold to give them a better view of the hangings. Equally popular were visits to watch the antics of the chained lunatics at Bethlem Hospital — usually shortened to 'Bedlam', a word we still use today.

The extremes of wealth and poverty were much more sharply defined in the town than in the village. The poorer quarters of the larger provincial towns were as wretched as the East End of London. People lived in waterlogged cellars, crowded into ramshackle wooden huts, or overran large houses together with several other families. Well-to-do townspeople, on the other hand, enjoyed more luxuries and comforts than their counterparts in the countryside, as well as a more varied social life. Through their closer contact with London and the other centres of trade and fashionable living, they found it easier to get luxuries like imported spices, tea and sugar, and domestic items like china plates and silver cutlery which were rarely seen on the wealthiest village table.

A public execution at Tyburn

Stonemasons at work

The Age of the Craftsman

The village rather than the town was the centre of English industry in the early eighteenth century. Mining and quarrying, timber-cutting, iron-smelting and a wide range of manufacturing industries were scattered around the countryside. Most trades were carried on in the home, but there were a few examples of large-scale industry, for example the naval dockyards on the Thames and the south coast, where the Crown employed hundreds of shipwrights, carpenters, smiths and nail-makers. Even in 1700 the industries of England and Wales were probably more advanced than those of any other country in the world. There was always a large surplus available for export, while very few manufactured goods needed to be imported.

Woollen cloth manufacture had been England's chief industry since the early Middle Ages, and the main source of exports. English cloth was sold all over Europe, and in India, Africa and America. To represent its great importance in English history, the Lord Chancellor still sits on a woolsack in the House of Lords. Cloth was made in almost every county where sheep were reared, but there were three main areas. In the West Riding of Yorkshire, where most of the work was done in sheds attached to farms, a large proportion of the cheaper, coarser cloth was made. Most of the fine cloth came from the West Country and East Anglia, where the industry was organised on a larger scale. Clothiers often employed their own salesmen, clerks and craftsmen, though the main processes of spinning and weaving were usually carried out in the nearby villages.

Iron was mined and smelted in areas where timber was readily available, for charcoal was used as fuel in the blast-furnace. The manufacture of **metal goods** was centred around Birmingham and the West Midlands, as it is today, and Sheffield was already well

known for its cutlery. **Coal-mining** was a long-established industry in the North-East of England, particularly in the Newcastle area. Other mining districts, like South Wales (coal), Cornwall (tin, lead and copper) and Cheshire (salt) were less developed, partly because of the lack of suitable **transport** facilities. Navigable rivers were few and far between, and it was difficult to move bulky goods overland because of the lack of proper roads. This was one of the reasons why practically all industry in the early eighteenth century was on a small scale. Until means of transport were improved, it would remain very difficult to sell goods in large quantities outside the locality in which they were produced.

In the early years of the century, steam-engines began to be used for pumping water out of mines. But, apart from this, and a limited use of water-wheels driven by fast-flowing streams, all forms of industry depended largely upon human strength and skill. The normal method of entry into a trade was to serve a long and thorough apprenticeship. The apprentice became part of his master's 'family' and, if he was lucky, he would be given some general education in addition to skilled training. It was an age of craftsmanship, when art was still an essential part of industry. Many goods made in this period are highly valued today for their quality of workmanship; especially china and glassware, silver plate and furniture.

Further study

The main aspects of English life introduced in this chapter are dealt with more fully later in the book. Nevertheless, the following publications will be helpful in gaining a better knowledge of the period:

General accounts

D. Lindsay and E. S. Washington, *A Portrait of Britain, 1688–1851* (O.U.P.) Chapter 4

T. K. Derry and T. L. Jarman, *The Making of Modern Britain* (Murray) Chapters 1–3

Roger Hart, *English Life in the Eighteenth Century* (Wayland, English Life series)

J.R.C. Yglesias, *Georgian England* (Longman, Focus on History series)

Special topics

In Longman's Then and There series:

J. Dymoke, *London in the Eighteenth Century*

H. Green, *Village Life in the Eighteenth Century*

E. J. Sheppard, *Bath in the Eighteenth Century*

The Orange Shelf of Ginn's History Bookshelves, ed. C. B. Firth, contains six titles on Georgian England, of which the following three are especially helpful at this stage: *Life in a Country House, Life in a Village* and *A Trip to a Watering Place.*

Filmstrips

Life in Early Georgian Times (Common Ground, Longman)

Social Life in the Eighteenth Century (Hulton)

2 Partners in Power

Crown, Parliament and the Union with Scotland

Nowadays the Queen reigns, but she does not *rule*. The important decisions of government are made by Members of Parliament — the people's elected representatives. In the early eighteenth century, however, the monarch was far from being a mere figurehead. The Crown and the Houses of Parliament were *partners in power.* On the one hand, the **King** was expected to give real leadership; to choose his own ministers and to pursue his own policy, especially in foreign affairs. On the other hand, there were important restrictions on royal power. The greatest of these was the King's dependence on **Parliament** for his income. This 'power of the purse' gave M.P.s an opportunity to resist the policy of the King if they considered it to be unjustified. The day-to-day expenditure of the sovereign was covered by the Civil List, which was granted annually. But extra money for things like the upkeep of the army and navy had to be voted separately by the Commons.

Queen Anne

Although the King was free to appoint what **ministers** he liked, in practice his choice was often limited by the need to select men who could command the support of Parliament. The three most important ministers were the First Lord of the Treasury (Chancellor of the Exchequer) who controlled finance, and the two Secretaries of State in charge of foreign and home affairs. The amount of personal influence enjoyed by the King varied considerably from one reign to the next — depending on his personality and skill and his relations with his ministers and with Parliament. **William III** (1688–1702) was an experienced statesman and, throughout his reign, he was firmly in command of the Government. He controlled foreign affairs in particular with little reference to Parliament. But **Queen Anne** (1702–14) found there was a great deal of government business that she was unable to handle personally. She was forced to rely on her ministers much more than William had done.

The Hanoverian succession

All of Anne's seventeen children died before she became Queen. Thus she was destined to be the last in the line of Stuart monarchs who had reigned both in England and Scotland since 1603. She had a half-brother, James Edward Stuart, but he was barred from the throne because he was a Catholic. Their father, James II, had been deposed in the Revolution of 1688 for the same religious beliefs. Therefore, on Anne's death, the succession fell upon a German prince, George of Hanover. **George I** (1714–27) had two important points in his favour. He was a Protestant and he was a great-grandson of James I, which made him next in line to the throne. But in almost every other respect he was unsuited to his new position. He was already fifty-four years old, could not speak English, and knew very little about the government, laws and customs of his new kingdom. To make matters worse, he was rather stupid!

During the reigns of William and Anne, a kind of **cabinet** of about a dozen of the most important ministers had met two or three times a week to discuss the affairs of government with the sovereign. George I was unable to enter into such discussions, partly because he could not speak the language. Within three years he stopped attending altogether and a different kind of 'inner cabinet' began to develop. It consisted of six or seven of the most powerful ministers, and met in private. Although the King was not included, his permission was required before each issue could be discussed and no decisions were final without his consent. By the reign of George II, the inner cabinet was well established and in command of most of the important affairs of government. This was the forerunner of the modern Cabinet.

When the King gave up attending the meetings of his ministers, it was natural that one of the inner cabinet should, by common consent, take the lead in discussion and act as the main link with the Crown. As time went on, he became the first or **'prime' minister** — although the title was not an official one until 1905. The first real prime minister was **Sir Robert Walpole,** who was Leader of the Government from 1721 to 1742, although he never used the title himself. Walpole, a Norfolk squire, had a great gift for managing men and getting them to do his will. For the best part of twenty years, he carried out a policy of peace abroad and financial reform at home which was rarely challenged by the Crown, Parliament or his fellow ministers.

Parliament and the people

Ever since the Middle Ages, Parliament had consisted of two separate Houses — the Lords and the Commons. In the early eighteenth century, the membership of the **House of Lords** (under 200) was about a fifth of its present size, yet it had much more power and influence than it has today. Most of the important ministers were peers. The 513 members of the **Commons** (558 after 1707) were elected — but by a very small proportion of the population. Britain was far from being a 'democracy', where voting rights are distributed equally among the adult population. The right to vote was a privilege enjoyed by about 250,000 of the most influential male citizens. No women were allowed to vote before 1918.

Members of Parliament were not paid. They had to have a private income from their property. Thus the Commons, as well as the Lords, was dominated by the landowning classes — although many M.P.s had other interests, in trade, banking and the like. At first sight it may seem strange that they were prepared to devote their time to politics without being paid, but this is precisely what Local Government councillors do today. They want to make sure that their interests and opinions are considered before any decisions are taken. In an age when the great majority of the people had no proper schooling, many M.P.s felt it was their duty, as educated and responsible citizens, to play a part in governing the country. Besides, the wealthier

Sir Robert Walpole

they were the more they had to lose if the nation was governed badly and taxes were unwisely spent.

In present day parliamentary **elections,** the country is divided up into roughly equal portions (constituencies) each of which returns one M.P. In this period, however, members stood for either counties or boroughs. In each county, all freeholders with property worth at least forty shillings a year could vote, and two members were elected. The remaining seats — well over 400 of them — belonged to the boroughs. Their distribution bore no relation to the density of population. While places like Leeds, Manchester, Birmingham and Sheffield had no seats at all, scores of hamlets and villages, mostly in the South, returned one or two members each. The boroughs in the five south-western counties together accounted for a quarter of all M.P.s. **'Rotten'** (decayed) **boroughs** like Sarum in Wiltshire and Castle Rising in Norfolk — once busy with markets and local trades — had declined and become farmland. Nevertheless, they continued to return their M.P.s. Voting rights varied enormously from one borough to the next. In about a dozen, including Westminster, almost every man voted; in others, only the 'freemen' of the trade guilds were the electors.

Most of the candidates called themselves either 'Whigs' or 'Tories', to indicate their views on major issues like the Church and the monarchy. But **political parties** in this period were loosely organised and did not control politics like they do today. Elections were not decided by making speeches but by wealth and influence. There was no secret ballot. Thus it was easy for candidates to bribe or bully the electors, for they could check the poll books afterwards to see how the votes were cast. Vast sums of money were spent in buying votes, and the result of an election often depended on which candidates could offer the biggest bribes. Many boroughs were 'in the pocket' of a local landowner (usually called **pocket boroughs**). In other words, one man owned enough property to be able to control the votes of the majority of the electorate. He could often 'arrange' the election without anyone daring to oppose him or the candidates of his choice. When this happened there was no need for any voting, for the number of candidates did not exceed the number of seats available.

No reform of this unfair and corrupt electoral system was achieved before 1832 (see Chapter 11). The nobility and the gentry had a monopoly of political power and saw no reason why they should risk losing it.

'Open voting' in an eighteenth century election

Scotland in the early eighteenth century

At the beginning of our period, the English and the Scots generally regarded each other as foreigners. They had been ruled by the same monarch since 1603, when James VI of Scotland became James I of England, but they had little else in common. They had separate parliaments and different systems of religion, law and education. The appalling condition of the Great North Road, which was often impassable in winter, meant London and Edinburgh were, at the very best, almost a week's journey apart. This further reduced the pos-

sibility of contact between the two peoples who were, for the most part, suspicious and ignorant of each other.

Scotland was much less wealthy than its southern neighbour. Its **agriculture** was very backward, and frequently unable to support the small population of about 1 million. Thousands died of starvation if the harvest failed, as it did each year from 1696 to 1702, when the crops were continually spoiled by bad weather. Oats were the basic crop, along with barley for making scones and ale. Though many animals were reared, the people ate very little meat. Most of their sheep and cattle had to be sold over the border to pay for essential imports. Scottish **industry** was as backward as its agriculture in this period. Very few manufactured goods were home-produced, with the exception of woollen cloth. **Overseas trade** was confined to Ireland and the Continent, especially Norway and Holland, which took small quantities of salmon, coal, salt and lead. It was all on a very small scale. The merchants of Glasgow, the largest port, had only fifteen

The port of Glasgow in the early eighteenth century

trading vessels between them in 1700.

Most **peasant farmers** lived in extreme poverty. Their clothes were rough, their children barefooted, and their tiny homes of turf or stone lacked floors, chimneys and glass windows. The **lairds** (land-owners) reflected the poverty of their tenants. Their houses were usually bare and cheerless, and their whole way of life was devoid of luxury, in contrast to that of the English gentry. The extravagant social life of some of the English towns had no parallel in Scotland; with the possible exception of Edinburgh, the headquarters of Scottish government, law and religion. Yet, even in the capital, the strict religious code forbade all dances and theatrical shows.

The Act of Union and the Jacobites

The eighteenth century began with relations between England and Scotland strained to breaking-point. The dethroning of James II (1688) had been bitterly opposed by many Scots, especially the Catholics in the Highlands. It therefore came as no surprise when, in 1703, the Scottish Parliament declared that it would choose its own monarch when Anne died. Continued hostility and complete separation were not, however, in the best interests of either country. If only they could settle their quarrels they would have much to gain from closer co-operation. England was at war with France, whose long-standing friendship with Scotland (the 'auld alliance') might now take the shape of an invasion of French troops across the Border. If Scotland agreed to a closer connection with England, which would safeguard the latter from overland attack, she might, in return, be allowed a share in the valuable English colonial trade.

Representatives of both Governments met to discuss their differences, and wisely decided that both sides would benefit if the

The start of the 'Forty-five' rebellion: Bonnie Prince Charlie lands at Moidart in western Scotland

Parliaments and commercial systems of the two countries were united. By the **Act of Union (1707)** England and Scotland became Great Britain. From then on they both used the same currency and paid the same taxes. The Scots sent forty-five M.P.s to the Commons and sixteen peers to the Lords. Most important of all for Scotland, its merchants enjoyed free trade with England and the English colonies. The Churches and legal systems of the two countries were so different that it was thought best to let them remain separate, as they still are today. It took some years for the two peoples to learn to trust and understand each other. In the meantime some hostility continued. News of the Union was greeted in Glasgow and Edinburgh with riots and demonstrations in the streets, and, before long, Scotsmen were involved in two rebellions against the Crown.

Many Highlanders remained loyal to the descendants of the deposed James II. They were called **Jacobites,** from the Latin word Jacobus—meaning James. In 1715 they rose in rebellion, hoping to make James Edward Stuart king. But, even before he arrived from the Continent to lead them, they began to drift back to the hills after an indecisive battle at **Sheriff Muir,** near Stirling.

Thirty years later, another Jacobite rebellion proved more serious. James Edward's son, **Bonnie Prince Charlie,** landed on the west coast of Scotland (July 1745) and quickly gathered support on his march to Edinburgh. He proclaimed his father king, defeated a government army at the Battle of Prestonpans and marched into England with 5000 men. But he failed to rally support among English Catholics, so that by the time he reached Derby (December) only 300 new recruits had joined him. Reluctantly, he turned back, soon to be pursued by the army of the Duke of Cumberland—George II's son. The last remnants of the Jacobite army were massacred at

Fierce fighting during the Battle of Prestonpans, near Edinburgh (September 1745)

the Battle of **Culloden Moor** (April 1746), a few miles from Inverness. Although Charles escaped to France at the end of the year, the Stuart cause was finally dead.

Culloden was the last real battle to be fought on British soil. The rebels who escaped from the field were ruthlessly tracked down and put to the sword or hanged. Nevertheless, when all the bitterness of the rebellion had died down, Scotland entered upon a happier and more prosperous age. The Government broke up the clan system in the Highlands, but raised Highland regiments for the British army, to divert the energies of the clansmen. These did great service in future wars. The building of the first roads through the Highlands, which began after the 1715 Rebellion, brought the spread of Lowland influence into areas which had previously been isolated from the mainstream of civilisation. Agriculture was greatly improved, largely due to the enclosing of the land with walls and hedges. Before the end of the century, Scottish farmers, engineers, doctors, painters and writers had travelled into England and made great names for themselves.

Most important of all, the opening of the English colonial trade to Scottish merchants after 1707 was, by the middle of the century, having a great effect on the standard of life of the people. Many of the imported cargoes of cotton, sugar and tobacco from America and the West Indies were re-exported to the Continent, at considerable profit. This transatlantic trade led to the rapid growth of Glasgow and the western ports and the development of industry on Clydeside. Glasgow began to rival Liverpool in its size and in the richness of its trade. Its tiny merchant fleet of 15 ships in 1700 had risen to 400 in the last years of the century. Meanwhile, cotton manufacture was developing rapidly in the villages of Lanark, Renfrew and Ayr; and in the east, around Perth and Dundee, the linen industry was also growing, to supply the new overseas markets. It is, therefore, not surprising that Scottish opposition to the Union had almost disappeared by the second half of the eighteenth century.

Timeline

1688	Revolution. James II deposed.
1688–1702	William III and Mary II.
1702–14	Queen Anne.
1707	Act of Union.
1714–27	George I.
1715	First Jacobite Rebellion.
1721–42	Walpole leader of the Government.
1727–60	George II.
1745	Second Jacobite Rebellion.

Further study

Details of Parliamentary Reforms in the nineteenth and twentieth centuries can be found in Chapters 11, 17 and 20.

General accounts
D. Lindsay and E. S. Washington, *A Portrait of Britain, 1688–1851* (O.U.P.) Chapters 1, 2, 3 and 5
Denis Richards and Anthony Quick, *Britain, 1714–1851* (Longmans) Chapter 2

Special topics
The Fifteen and the Forty-Five and *The Massacre at Glencoe* (Cape, Jackdaw series nos. 15, 110) contain collections of contemporary documents, compiled for use in schools.
Longman's Then and There series includes:
J. Addy, *Parliamentary Elections and Reform*, pp. 1–44
H. Shapiro, *John Wilkes and Parliament*
W. Stevenson, *The Jacobite Rising of 1745*
N. Stephenson, *Scotland and the Treaty of Union*
Alexander Ross (Ed.), *Changing Scotland, 1760–1820* (Sourcebook)

G. R. Kesteven, *The Forty-Five Rebellion* (Chatto & Windus)

Filmstrips
Sir Robert Walpole (Common Ground)
The Jacobite Rising, 1745 (Hulton)
The Hanoverian Dynasty (Unicorn Head)
Changing Scotland, 1760–1820 (Longman, Then and There Filmstrips)

3 Wealth across the Seas

Colonies and trade

'Trade is the wealth of the world', said the novelist Daniel Defoe in 1728. 'Trade makes the difference as to rich and poor, between one nation and another.' Defoe was right, for trade with the colonies was an important basis of England's growing prosperity in this period. But, although English merchants were among the wealthiest in Europe, they did not have things all their own way. The other sea-faring nations of Western Europe, especially France, Holland, Spain and Portugal, had long been rivals in the building up of trading empires in Asia, Africa and the Americas. Each country looked upon its colonies and trading posts as its own exclusive property, and foreign merchants were kept out. This explains the willingness of the Scots to unite with England (1707) for they had no colonies of their own and could only be admitted to the rich English trade if the two countries joined together as Great Britain.

The British Empire in 1713

The colonial nations of Western Europe were frequently at war with each other in the eighteenth century, especially the two greatest rivals—Britain and France. Hostilities were not confined to land battles. The side with the greatest naval strength usually tried to capture the colonies of the enemy, in the hope of retaining some of them in the peace treaty. Britain was in a fortunate position because, from the beginning of the century, its navy was the most powerful in the Western world. As a result, when George I came from Hanover (1714) his new kingdom was already the foremost colonial power. A series of land and sea wars against Louis XIV of France had just been concluded by the **Treaty of Utrecht (1713)** which greatly increased Britain's overseas possessions and trading rights, at the expense of France and Spain.

The centre of British colonising activity was North America and the Caribbean. Since the early seventeenth century, increasing numbers of Englishmen had emigrated to make new homes on the east coast of North America. Twelve of the famous **Thirteen Colonies** were already established there before 1700. The thirteenth, Georgia, was founded early in George II's reign (1733) and named after the King. Many of the early American settlers had been escaping from religious persecution at home—like the Pilgrim Fathers (1621)—but they maintained their link with 'the mother country'. The Governor and certain other officials in each colony were appointed by the Crown. In addition, each colony had its own elected assembly, which voted taxes. Whatever the reason for their original foundation, all the Thirteen Colonies were looked upon in Britain as actual or possible sources of wealth. They provided markets for the sale of British manufactures, and sent in return tobacco, dyestuffs, coffee

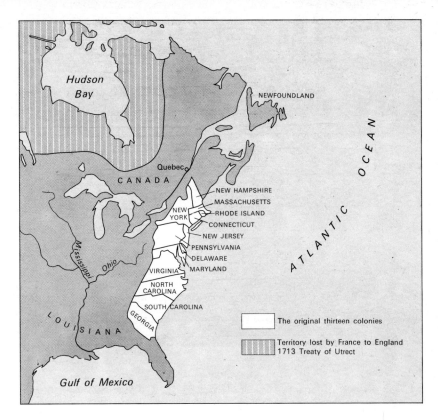

The Thirteen Colonies

and rice (from the south) and pig iron, timber and tar (from the north).

North of the Thirteen Colonies, in present day Canada, lay the territories surrendered by France at the Treaty of Utrecht. **Newfoundland** and **Nova Scotia** were centres of fishing, and the area around **Hudson Bay** supported a valuable fur trade. These lands were, for the most part, too bleak and uninviting to attract much settlement; but fishermen and fur-trappers put up with the harsh climate because trading prospects were good. Fifteen hundred miles and more to the south were the **West Indies.** Barbados, Jamaica, the Leeward Islands and the Bahamas, together with some of the islands in the later Windward group, and Bermuda in the Atlantic, made up 'the brightest jewel in the British Crown'. They were particularly valuable to Britain because they produced crops which would not grow in a European climate. Vast quantities of sugar (some of which was made into rum and molasses) and raw cotton, were shipped to Britain from the slave-worked plantations in the Caribbean.

The British empire in the New World was mainly one of settlement and plantation. *Colonisation* (the setting up of communities dependent on the mother country) was necessary to create trade where previously there had been none. However, in many other parts of the world, it was sufficient merely to establish **trading posts.** For example, in India and the Far East, valuable commodities were already being produced by the local inhabitants long before European

traders arrived on the scene. The **East India Company,** which was founded in England (1600) to trade with this area, did not establish colonies. It contented itself with 'factories' (trading stations) on the Indian coast at Calcutta, Madras, Bombay and Surat. From these bases, the Company's ships brought back silk and printed cottons, coffee, pepper and spices, indigo and saltpetre. By 1700 the Company had a foothold in China, at Canton, from which increasing quantities of tea were imported.

A number of other British trading companies had bases overseas— including the Hudson's Bay Company (1690); the short-lived South Sea Company (1711) which collapsed in a financial crisis known as the 'South Sea Bubble' (1720—21) and the Royal African Company. The last, which played an important part in the English slave trade, had forts and trading posts along the west coast of Africa—especially in the Gold Coast (present day Ghana).

There were, in addition, a number of British territories which served as naval bases and thus helped in the protection of the Empire. The two most recently acquired were **Gibraltar** (1704) and **Minorca** (1708) in the Mediterranean—both won from Spain and retained in the Treaty of Utrecht.

The slave trade

Slavery, which was a central feature of British colonial history, was as old as civilisation itself. The Pharaohs of Ancient Egypt used slave labour to build the pyramids, and the great empires of Greece and Rome were built on slavery. But the slave trade in our period was of a very special kind. It involved the shipping of Negroes from West Africa across the Atlantic to the New World, where they were sold

Surat: an early trading post of the East India Company

to the owners of plantations. This trade was started in the early sixteenth century by the Spanish and the Portuguese. They were the first to establish colonies in the New World, but, in the process, they almost exterminated the native populations, especially in the West Indies, by their brutality and the diseases they passed on. As a result, they began to import Negroes to do their work for them in their new colonies.

Realising the great fortunes that could be made from the sale of shiploads of Negroes, English seamen soon broke the Spanish and Portuguese monopoly of the slave traffic. One of the first and most famous of these was Sir John Hawkins, whose first slaving voyage was in 1562. From then on, the English share of the slave trade increased rapidly, assisted by the declining power of Spain and Portugal in the seventeenth century. Eventually, as part of the Treaty of Utrecht, Spain sold England a monopoly of the slave trade with the Spanish colonies in the New World. In the next twenty years 150,000 Negroes were shipped to the English and Spanish colonies. Still the demand went on increasing, so that by 1770 more than 100,000 slaves were traded *each year,* half of them in British ships. Bristol had been the centre of the British slave traffic in the early eighteenth century, but by about 1800 the merchants of Liverpool controlled six-sevenths of the trade and were among the richest men in the kingdom.

The early traders worked on a small scale, gaining the protection and assistance of the 'head men' in the native villages by giving them presents. Before long, however, the volume of trade was so great that European agents built coastal forts from which the collection of

Negroes being chained on board a slaving ship

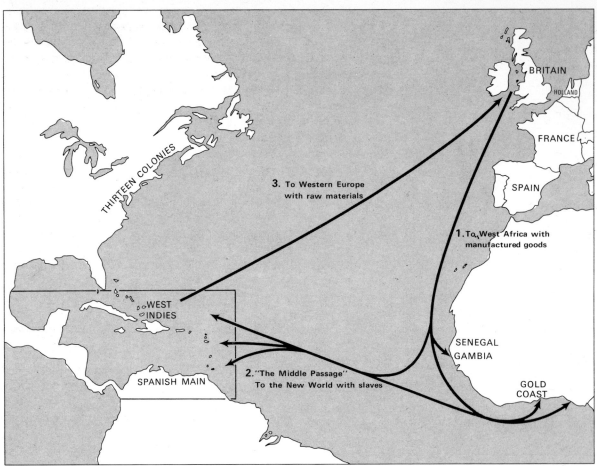

THIRTEEN COLONIES

BRITAIN

HOLLAND

FRANCE

SPAIN

3. To Western Europe
with raw materials

1. To West Africa with
manufactured goods

WEST
INDIES

SENEGAL
GAMBIA

GOLD
COAST

2. "The Middle Passage"
To the New World with slaves

SPANISH MAIN

The Triangular Trade

slaves from the interior could be supervised. Many of the slaves were criminals or prisoners from the numerous tribal wars. The chieftains would probably have cut their throats if they had not been able to trade them. The slave traders offered this as an excuse whenever they were accused of cruelty. But before the Anti-Slavery movement of the late eighteenth century (see Chapter 11) remarkably few voices were raised in protest against the slave traffic. Many traders sincerely believed that they were helping the Negroes by giving them a chance to become Christians and to escape from the primitive life in the 'dark continent' of Africa.

The slave traffic was part of a larger enterprise—the **Triangular Trade**—so called because it involved three connected voyages. On the first of these, manufactured goods were taken to Africa. Cargoes of cloth, guns, hardware—especially pots and pans—beads, rings and ornaments, spirits and tobacco were exchanged for slaves. Then followed the 'middle passage' across the Atlantic—the second of the three voyages which made up the 'trade triangle'. The wretched slaves, chained below deck, were often packed shoulder-to-shoulder to fill every available space, so that in the likely event of epidemic disease breaking out they died by the score. Unless great care was taken, up to a quarter of the precious cargo might be dead before the three months' passage was over. On arrival in the New World, the slaves were sold, usually by auction, and the ships were reloaded with local produce. Barring accidents, all that now remained was the third stage—the return voyage home, with money and a rich cargo into the bargain.

The 'Laws of Trade'

Trade was the concern of the Government as well as individual colonists and merchants. British colonies, like those of other European nations, were *possessions,* not independent territories. Their defence and much of their administration was paid for out of British taxes. Thus Parliament felt it had a right to control the trade of the colonies to ensure that Britain—and Britain alone—gained the maximum benefit from them. Since the mid seventeenth century, a series of **Navigation Acts,** otherwise known as the 'Laws of Trade', had regulated British shipping and colonial trade in the interests of the mother country.

The original Navigation Acts of 1651, 1660 and 1663 were subject to frequent alterations in the course of time, but there remained three basic principles governing all colonial trade in this period:

1. *All trade to and from British colonies had to be carried in British or colonial ships.* This was intended to encourage the growth of the British shipping industry and the training of large numbers of seamen who could defend the country in time of war.
2. *British colonies had to purchase all their manufactured goods via Britain.* The development of British industry was thereby assisted by having guaranteed markets overseas.
3. *British colonies were prevented from sending certain commodities, like sugar, tobacco, cotton and rice, to any countries outside the Empire.* This resulted in a valuable **re-export trade.** The British people could not themselves consume more than a small proportion of the produce of the colonies. Vast surpluses were therefore available for re-export to the Continent, at a handsome profit.

The 'Laws of Trade' thus gave the colonies the task of producing commodities which Britain could not—for example, sugar, cotton and tobacco, all of which required a warm climate. In addition, the colonies were forbidden from competing with the mother country in the production of manufactured goods. The industries of Britain served the whole Empire. Woollen cloth was the chief export, followed by all kinds of metal goods, hardware and cutlery. Small quantities of coal, lead, tin and copper were also exported. The Government further encouraged the development of British industry through its financial policies. Sir Robert Walpole, for example, in the 1720s and 1730s, removed customs duties on British exports and on imported raw materials, like cotton, which were necessary to supply manufacturing industries. At the same time, he discouraged imports of foreign manufactures by keeping high duties on them

A smuggler pursued by the customs officer

which artificially raised their price to the British buyer.

In spite of the growing volume of trade with the colonies, more than half the total of British exports in the eighteenth century went to the Continent. However, re-exports of colonial commodities were an important part of this trade—much of which was concentrated on the ports of Antwerp, Amsterdam, Rotterdam and Hamburg. The Portuguese ports of Lisbon and Oporto also handled much British trade, especially after the Methuen Treaty (1703) with Portugal. This brought about an increase in the export of British cloth to Portugal, in return for a reduction of a third on the British import duty on Portuguese wines. As a general rule, however, Britain tried to avoid importing goods from Europe, especially if the colonies were capable of producing them. Nevertheless, most of the essential naval supplies—pitch, tar, hemp, timber and bar iron—came from Scandinavia and the Baltic ports. The northern colonies of America sent some timber, tar and pig iron, but not enough to meet Britain's needs.

Large quantities of goods from Europe and elsewhere entered

'Clive of India'

Britain illegally—for the eighteenth century was a Golden Age for the smuggler. There were so many complicated trade regulations that they could not be enforced effectively. In any case, the duties on imported luxury articles were so high that **smuggling** was exceptionally profitable. In 1733 it was estimated that as much as a third of the total trade with France and Holland was smuggled. French wine and brandy, tea from China, and tobacco from America were the main items in this illegal trade. The understaffed revenue authorities found it very difficult to catch the culprits, for smugglers were very popular and were protected by the public. Smuggling went on almost unchecked until customs duties were reduced to a level which made it no longer a profitable risk. William Pitt's ministry made an important start in this direction after 1784 (see Chapter 14).

War and discovery, 1739–83

The peace of 1713 was little more than a pause in the colonial rivalries of the European sea powers. Between 1739 and 1783, Britain was involved in three major wars on land and sea. Her major opponent in each case was France. So many colonies changed hands in these years that the British empire of the late eighteenth century was vastly different from that of 1713. Walpole, for most of the 1720s and 1730s, kept Britain out of expensive foreign wars. He believed peace was essential for prosperity—but many City merchants and businessmen disagreed. They saw no reason to avoid war, for they were confident that British naval superiority would lead to the capture of valuable overseas territories. Their views were strongly represented in Parliament, and they further influenced government policy through their close contacts with several of the King's ministers.

In 1739, the 'commercial interest' had its way. Britain went to war with Spain, over trading disputes in the Caribbean. Great hostility towards Spain had been aroused by a certain Captain Jenkins, who showed M.P.s an ear which he claimed had been torn off by Spaniards. In this situation, Walpole's pleas for peace were ignored. Within a year a full-scale European war had broken out over the disputed succession to the Austrian throne. The **War of the Austrian Succession (1740–48)** spread to India, North America and the High Seas, where the main struggle was between Britain and France. No clear victor emerged from the Anglo-French contest, however, until the **Seven Years War (1756–63)**. It saw the rise to power of one of the greatest war statesmen in British history—**William Pitt,** later Earl of Chatham. From 1757 to 1761 he dominated the Government, in spite of George II's dislike of him, and saw much of the French overseas empire destroyed.

Britain dominated the seas and captured West Indian islands and West African trading posts from France. Even more important, through the efforts of **Robert Clive,** an East India Company clerk who became a general, French power in south-east India was broken. Clive's great victory at Plassey (1757) laid the foundations for future British supremacy over the whole of India.

In North America, France controlled the great fertile plain of the

William Pitt, Earl of Chatham

Declaration of Independence

In Congress, July 4th, 1776.

The Unanimous Declaration of the Thirteen United States of America.

WHEN, in the course of human events, it becomes necessary for one people to dissolve the political bands which have connected them with another, and to assume among the powers of the earth, the separate and equal station to which the laws of nature and of nature's God entitle them, a decent respect to the opinions of mankind requires that they should declare the causes which impel them to the separation.

We hold these truths to be self-evident — that all men are created equal, that they are endowed by their CREATOR, with certain unalienable rights; that among these are life, liberty, and the pursuit of happiness. That to secure these rights, governments are instituted among men, deriving their just powers from the consent of the governed, that whenever any form of government becomes destructive of these ends, it is the right of the people to alter or to abolish it, and to institute new government, laying its foundation on such principles, and organizing its powers in such form, as to them shall seem most likely to effect their safety and happiness. Prudence, indeed, will dictate, that governments long established, should not be changed for light and transient causes; and, accordingly, all experience has shown that mankind are more disposed to suffer, while evils are sufferable, than to right themselves by abolishing the forms to which they are accustomed. But when a long train of abuses and usurpations, pursuing invariably the same object, evinces a design to reduce them under absolute despotism, it is their right, it is their duty, to throw off such government, and to provide new guards for their future security. Such has been the patient sufferance of these colonies; and such is now the necessity which constrains them to alter their former systems of government. The history of the present king of Great Britain, is a history of repeated injuries and usurpations, all having in direct object the establishment of an absolute tyranny over these states. To prove this, let facts be submitted to a candid world.

He has refused his assent to laws, the most wholesome and necessary for the public good.

He has forbidden his governors to pass laws of immediate and pressing importance, unless suspended in their operation till his assent should be obtained; and when so suspended he has utterly neglected to attend to them.

He has refused to pass other laws, for the accommodation of large districts of people, unless those people would relinquish the right of representation in the legislature — a right inestimable to them, and formidable to tyrants only.

He has called together legislative bodies, at places unusual, uncomfortable, and distant from the depository of their public records, for the sole purpose of fatiguing them into compliance with his measures.

He has dissolved representative houses, repeatedly, for opposing with manly firmness his invasions on the rights of the people.

He has refused, for a long time after such dissolutions, to cause others to be elected; whereby the legislative powers, incapable of annihilation, have returned to the people at large, for their exercise, the state remaining, in the meantime, exposed to all the dangers of invasion from without, and convulsions within.

He has endeavoured to prevent the population of these states; for that purpose obstructing the laws for naturalization of foreigners; refusing to pass others to encourage their migrations hither, and raising the conditions of new appropriations of lands.

He has obstructed the administration of justice, by refusing his assent to laws, for establishing judiciary powers.

He has made judges dependant on his will alone for the tenure of their offices, and the amount and payment of their salaries.

He has erected a multitude of new offices, and sent hither swarms of officers, to harass our people, and eat out their substance.

He has kept among us, in time of peace, standing armies, without the consent of our legislatures.

He has affected to render the military independent of, and superior to, the civil power.

He has combined with others to subject us to a jurisdiction, foreign to our constitution, and unacknowledged by our laws, giving his assent to their acts of pretended legislation.

For quartering large bodies of armed troops among us:

For protecting them, by a mock trial, from punishment for any murders which they should commit on the inhabitants of these states:

For cutting off our trade with all parts of the world:

For imposing taxes on us without our consent:

For depriving us, in many cases, of the benefits of trial by jury:

For transporting us beyond seas, to be tried for pretended offences:

For abolishing the free system of English laws in a neighboring province, establishing therein an arbitrary government, and enlarging its boundaries, so as to render it at once an example and fit instrument for introducing the same absolute rule into these colonies:

For taking away our charters, abolishing our most valuable laws, and altering fundamentally the forms of our governments:

For suspending our own legislatures, and declaring themselves invested with power to legislate for us in all cases whatsoever.

He has abdicated government here, by declaring us out of his protection, and waging war against us.

He has plundered our seas, ravaged our coasts, burnt our towns, and destroyed the lives of our people.

He is at this time, transporting large armies of foreign mercenaries to complete the works of death, desolation, and tyranny, already begun, with circumstances of cruelty and perfidy scarcely paralleled in the most barbarous ages, and totally unworthy the head of a civilized nation.

He has constrained our fellow-citizens, taken captive on the high seas, to bear arms against their country, to become the executioners of their friends and brethren, or to fall themselves by their hands.

He has excited domestic insurrections among us, and has endeavoured to bring on the inhabitants of our frontiers, the merciless Indian savages, whose known rule of warfare is an undistinguished destruction of all ages, sexes, and conditions.

In every stage of these oppressions, we have petitioned for redress in the most humble terms: our repeated petitions have been answered only by repeated injury. A prince whose character is thus marked by every act which may define a tyrant, is unfit to be the ruler of a free people.

Nor have we been wanting in attention to our British brethren. We have warned them from time to time of attempts by their legislature, to extend an unwarrantable jurisdiction over us. We have reminded them of the circumstances of our emigration and settlement here. We have appealed to their native justice and magnanimity, and we have conjured them by the ties of our common kindred to disavow these usurpations, which would inevitably interrupt our connections and correspondence. They, too, have been deaf to the voice of justice and consanguinity. We must, therefore, acquiesce in the necessity which denounces our separation, and hold them, as we hold the rest of mankind — enemies in war — in peace, friends.

We, therefore, the representatives of the United States of America, in general congress assembled, appealing to the SUPREME JUDGE of the world for the rectitude of our intentions, do, in the name and by the authority of the good people of these colonies, solemnly publish and declare, that these United Colonies are, and of right ought to be, free and independent states — That they are absolved from all allegiance to the British crown, and that all political connexion between them and the state of Great Britain is, and ought to be, totally dissolved; and that, as free and independent states, they have full power to levy war, conclude peace, contract alliances, establish commerce, and to do all other acts and things which independent states may of right do. And for the support of this declaration, with a firm reliance on the protection of DIVINE PROVIDENCE we mutually pledge to each other our lives, our fortunes, and our sacred honor.

Th Jefferson

Benj. Harrison

Th. Nelson jr

Matthew Thornton

Rob Morris

Benjamin Rush

Benj. Franklin

John Morton

Edward Rutledge

Thos. Heyward junr.

Thomas Lynch junr.

Arthur Middleton

Caesar Rodney

Geo Read

Tho. M. Kean

John Adams

Robt Treat Paine

Elbridge Gerry

Step Hopkins

Wm. Ellery

Roger Sherman

Sam'el Huntington

Wm Williams

Oliver Wolcott

Rich'd Stockton

Jno Witherspoon

Fras Hopkinson

John Hart

Abra Clark

John Hancock

Button Gwinnett

Lyman Hall

Geo Walton

Wm Hooper

Joseph Hewes

John Penn

Wm Paca

Thos Stone

Gro Taylor

James Wilson

Geo Ross

Samuel Chase

George Wythe

Richard Henry Lee

Josiah Bartlett

Wm Whipple

Sam'l Adams

William Ellery

Charles Carroll of Carrollton

Francis Lightfoot Lee

Carter Braxton

Geo Clymer

Jas Smith

General James Wolfe

interior, from which she planned to keep the Thirteen Colonies penned into the coastlands. Pitt had other ideas, and ordered an all-out attack on Canada (1758). It was a brilliant success for the skilful young generals he put in command. **James Wolfe's** capture of Quebec (1759) which cost him his life, led to the collapse of the French empire in North America. In the **Treaty of Paris (1763)** Britain kept, among other things, Canada and all of North America down to the Mississippi.

Britain was riding on the crest of a wave—but a shock was in store. The **Thirteen Colonies,** the backbone of the American empire, were becoming increasingly restless under British rule. They objected to being taxed by a Parliament, 3000 miles away, in which they were not represented. They complained of the restrictions put upon them by the Laws of Trade. Before 1763 they had needed British military protection against the French, but now they could stand on their own feet. George III and his ministers foolishly ignored the mounting opposition in the colonies. They continued to keep a British army in North America, even though the colonists thought it no longer necessary and hated paying taxes to support it. What began as a quarrel soon grew into a full-scale revolutionary war. The Thirteen Colonies banded together and made their famous **Declaration of Independence** on 4 July 1776. Helped by France and Spain, who joined the rebels to gain revenge on Britain, they forced the Crown to recognise their independence in 1783.

Together with the loss of the Thirteen Colonies, Britain was forced to return some of its previous gains from France and Spain, including Florida, Minorca and the West African trading centre of Senegal (won in the Seven Years War). Nevertheless, in spite of this setback, trade with the new United States of America was soon greater than ever before, and important additions to the Empire were made in other parts of the world. Since the Seven Years War, Britain had established many new trading posts and naval stations; taken firm control of India and, above all, brought a whole new continent under the Crown. **Captain James Cook** claimed both **Australia** and **New Zealand** for Britain in 1770. They had been discovered by a Spaniard and a Dutchman in the seventeenth century, but their coasts had never been fully explored before Cook's voyage. At first, the Government only seemed interested in Australia as a place to send convicts. But in the nineteenth century their great value to Britain as lands for settlement and trade began to be realised.

Timeline

1703	Methuen Treaty.
1713	Treaty of Utrecht.
1720–21	South Sea Bubble.
1739	'War of Jenkins' Ear.'
1740–48	War of Austrian Succession.
1756–63	Seven Years War.
1757	Battle of Plassey (Clive).
1759	Battle of Quebec (Wolfe).
1763	Treaty of Paris.

Left: The Thirteen Colonies' Declaration of Independence, 4 July 1776

1770   Cook claims Australia and New Zealand.
1776–83 American Revolution.

Further study
The story of the British empire continues in Chapter 19.

Project
On two blank outline maps of the world, show the extent of Britain's overseas possessions:
a. In 1713, after the Treaty of Utrecht.
b. In 1783, after the American Revolution.
These, taken together, will provide an excellent summary of the dramatic changes that took place in the space of only seventy years.

General accounts
D. Lindsay and E. S. Washington, *A Portrait of Britain, 1688–1851* (O.U.P.) Chapters 7, 8 and 10
Denis Richards and Anthony Quick, *Britain, 1714–1851* (Longmans) Chapters 3 and 5

Special topics
The Jackdaw series (Cape) contains detailed material on:
The Slave Trade and Its Abolition, no. 12
The American Revolution, no. 14
The South Sea Bubble, no. 19
The Voyages of Captain Cook, no. 20
Wolfe at Quebec, no. 23
Clive of India, no. 52
Longman's Then and There series includes:
C. Clarke, *The American Revolution, 1775–83*
B. Martin, *John Newton and the Slave Trade*
Norman Nichol, *Glasgow and the Tobacco Lords*
B. Williams, *The Struggle for Canada*
D. W. Sylvester, *Captain Cook and the Pacific*
D. Sylvester, *Clive in India*
J. West, *A Captain in the Navy of Queen Anne*

G. R. Kesteven, *The Loss of the American Colonies* (Chatto & Windus, Studies in English History)
T. I. Williams, *James Cook and World Navigation* (Priory Press)
N. Wymer, Lives of Great Men and Women (O.U.P.):
Vol. 2, *Great Explorers* for Captain Cook
Vol. 5, *Soldiers and Sailors* for James Wolfe and Robert Clive
Captain Cook and the South Pacific (Cassell, Caravel Book)

Filmstrips
The Hudson's Bay Company (Unicorn Head: in colour)
Clive, Captain Cook, and William Pitt, Earl of Chatham (Common Ground, Lives of Famous Men and Women)
History of the United States, Parts 2 and 3 (Visual Information Service)

4 Faith and Charity
Religion and social improvement

In 1700 the British people could look back on almost 200 years of great religious activity and enthusiasm. But this, in turn, had resulted in much cruelty and bitterness. The period of religious conflict really began when Henry VIII (1509–47) broke away from the Roman Catholic Church and declared himself head of a separate Church of England. Before long, the new English (or Anglican) Church found itself in opposition not only to the Catholics but to other groups of Protestants called Puritans. These rejected many of its doctrines and practices and established separate Nonconformist Churches. Both the Catholic and Nonconformist minorities were persecuted by the Anglicans. They were fined, imprisoned and put to death for their beliefs. When they gained the upper hand, as the Catholics did in the reign of Mary (1553–8) or the Puritans at the end of the great Civil War (1642–9) they were quick to take revenge on the Anglicans. Instead of uniting men in love, religion seemed to be dividing them in hate.

The Church of England in the eighteenth century
In 1688 James II was deposed, mainly because of his Catholic beliefs. But, instead of leading to more religious upheaval, the 1688 Revolution proved to be a turning-point. It was followed by a **Toleration Act (1689)** which allowed Nonconformists to worship freely in their own meeting houses and chapels. Although Catholics were not

An assembly of Quakers (Nonconformists) in London

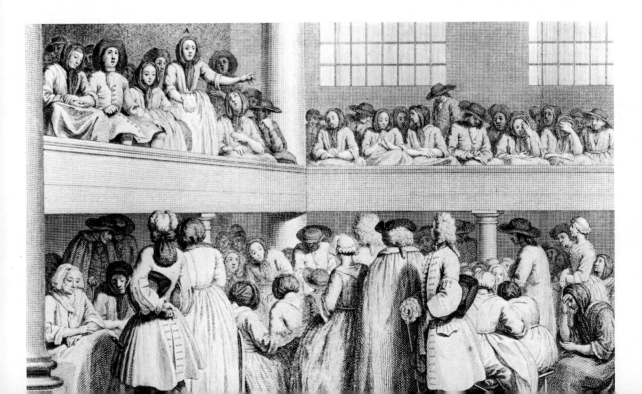

included in the Act, in practice they too had freedom of worship so long as they kept to themselves and did not try to convert others. Thus the eighteenth century saw a strong movement away from the religious conflicts of the past. Instead of emigrating to the American colonies, increasing numbers of Nonconformists stayed at home and played a vital part in the progress and prosperity of the nation.

Not only were people more tolerant of each other's beliefs in the eighteenth century, many of them also felt that to be openly *enthusiastic* about religion was dangerous for the peace and harmony of the kingdom. As a result, the Church of England in particular became a less powerful force in people's daily lives. The aristocracy and the gentry, the great majority of whom were Anglicans, continued to accept the teachings of their Church and attended services every Sunday. But they were more casual than they had been in the past. Few of them made any serious attempt to live strictly according to the principles of the Church. Sir Robert Walpole really spoke for them all when he said 'I am no saint'.

The same was true of many Church leaders. The highest positions in the Anglican Church frequently depended upon party politics. Because archbishops and bishops sat in the House of Lords, the Government tried to appoint men whose support could be relied upon in Parliament. Competition for positions carrying the most power and the greatest income became the main interest of many churchmen—who neglected their religious duties as a result. **Pluralists,** with more than one appointment, were common. They drew incomes from several parishes, which they rarely visited, and paid curates small salaries to administer them in their absence.

Standards of conduct among the clergy in general were falling. Even parsons who lived in their parishes were likely to devote much of their lives to fox-hunting, drinking and other worldly pleasures. This state of affairs was partly the fault of the universities, whose main task in this period was to train the clergy. Both Oxford and Cambridge had become centres of corruption and laziness. Degrees were awarded almost automatically—often to men of bad character and great ignorance.

Needless to say, not all clergymen neglected their religious duties. In particular, a large proportion of village parsons were devoted to their parishioners and led virtuous and useful lives. Nevertheless, in spite of their good intentions, few of them had any real understanding of the needs of common people. They were mainly aristocratic in outlook; many of them being younger sons of landowning families. They mixed with the gentry on equal terms but taught their humble parishioners that it was their Christian duty to know their place and respect their betters. Religion in this form was hardly likely to appeal to the growing manufacturing and mining communities of Britain. In any case, these areas were usually ignored by the Church, since most of them fell outside the traditional distribution of parishes. By the middle of the century there were scores of growing industrial villages and town suburbs without any church or priest. Cut off from the rest of the community, these people needed a new Christian crusade if religion was to have any meaning in their lives.

An Anglican service

John Wesley and the Methodists

The much-needed revival in the Church is linked with the life of **John Wesley (1703–91)** a clergyman's son from Epworth in North Lincolnshire. He had a rare combination of talents which made him one of the most remarkable Englishmen of modern times. Not only was he a great preacher, capable of reducing the most hostile audience to tears and tremblings; he was also a gifted organiser who set on foot an immense movement and personally supervised every detail of its administration.

After a strict religious upbringing, in which his mother set out to 'break his will' and develop in him regular habits of hard work and prayer, he went to Oxford University to prepare to become a clergyman. It was there that he and his brother Charles formed a **Holy Club**—together with George Whitfield, later a famous preacher, and thirteen others. The members cut themselves off from the pleasure-seeking activities of the majority of the students and devoted themselves to study, prayer and charitable deeds. They also indulged in periods of 'self-sacrifice' which made such severe demands on them that one member actually died! For example, sometimes, at night, they laid down in the winter frost for hours on end. All the Club's activities were done to a strict timetable. It was this methodical routine which caused fellow students to refer to them as 'Methodists', a nickname which was revived in later years.

Like most great religious leaders, John Wesley continually felt dissatisfied with himself. He failed to settle down as an Anglican minister, and in 1736 he went to the new American colony of Georgia. There he met a group of German Protestants called **Moravians.** Their beliefs and practices, which were like those of the early Christians, greatly impressed him. After returning to England he attended the Moravian meeting house in London. It was there, in May 1738, that he went through a strange experience which altered the course of his life. He described his 'conversion', as it is often called, in these words: 'I felt my heart strangely warmed. I felt that I did trust in Christ . . . and an assurance was given me that He had taken *my* sins, even *mine,* and saved me from the law of sin and death.'

From that moment on, Wesley dedicated his life to passing on to others his belief in personal salvation through Christ. He spent the next fifty-three years travelling and preaching. In that time he covered almost a quarter of a million miles and preached over 40,000 sermons—an average of more than two a day.

Wesley had no desire to form a separate Church. He accepted Anglican doctrines and always regarded his efforts as an extra activity *within* the Church. But he soon found that very few of his fellow clergymen were willing to let him speak from their pulpits. They distrusted his great fire and enthusiasm. He had no alternative but to preach in the open air, thus ignoring the rule of the Church of England which forbade the holding of services other than in properly consecrated buildings.

Wesley's aim was 'to spread scriptural holiness throughout the land'. This meant, above all, travelling to areas neglected by the

Church of England and speaking to tradesmen, miners, factory hands, fishermen and agricultural labourers, many of whom had never before heard the Christian message. Needless to say, his reception was not always favourable, especially in the early years. On occasions, Wesley and his fellow preachers were attacked with stones and almost lynched by mobs. But nothing could stop him. In the end the power of his sermons won over the most aggressive audiences. In contrast to the mild, easy-going sermons of most parish clergymen, Wesley appealed directly to the emotions. He called upon his hearers to repent and begin a new life, and he often spoke of death and the torments of Hell. The effect was sometimes quite frightening. Wesley recorded in his diary that one of his audiences 'exceedingly trembled and quaked . . . and began to call upon God with strong cries and tears'.

In the circumstances of eighteenth-century life, when the average mother saw several of her babies die in their first years, death was closer and somehow more real. People were therefore greatly moved

Wesley meets an unfriendly reception at Wednesbury, near Birmingham

Opposite: Wesley in his later years

by Wesley's promise of salvation—it gave them a new purpose in life and made the hardships of their daily existence more bearable. The emotional impact of Methodist meetings was greatly increased by the mass-singing of hymns. Most of them were written by **Charles Wesley,** who is said to have composed more than 6,500 altogether. Many are still firm favourites today, like 'Hark, the herald angels sing!' and 'Rejoice, the Lord is King'.

John Wesley could do more than inspire men, he could organise them. All converts were formed into permanent congregations with clearly-defined sets of rules. The basic unit was the local 'class', consisting of about a dozen members from the same neighbourhood. They met weekly to pray and to help each other to overcome temptation. A number of classes made up a 'society'. The eventual aim of each society was to build a proper chapel where services could be held. To this end, 'stewards' were appointed to collect weekly contributions from all members. By 1784 there were already 356 Methodist chapels—mostly in areas where there were no churches, so as to avoid competition with the Church of England. Preachers were appointed to look after each society and to give sermons and lead the hymn-singing. Most of them came from the same social background as the people they served. What they lacked in education they tried to make up for in the power of their leadership and the strength of their religious devotion.

Wesley expected his followers to be Anglicans and attend normal church services in addition to their Methodist meetings. But most Church of England leaders would not co-operate with him. In 1784 the Bishop of London refused Wesley's request that two ministers should be specially ordained to lead the Methodists in America. Wesley was forced to do it himself, an act which led to a complete break with the Church of England and the formation of a separate **Methodist Church** soon after his death. By 1815 there were nearly a quarter of a million Methodists in Britain, and almost as many in the U.S.A. Today it is one of the largest Protestant Churches, with millions of members scattered throughout every English-speaking country. It has certainly lived up to Wesley's famous motto: 'The world is my parish.'

The importance of Wesley

The Methodist movement drew its main support from the 'common people'. It gave a new self-respect to hundreds of thousands of underprivileged citizens and made them thrifty, sober and hard-working. In fact, these 'Methodist virtues' soon became more widely accepted and thus played an important part in Britain's growing prosperity. Wesley's work had important political effects as well. Many of the working men who led the early trade unions and fought for Parliamentary reform in the early nineteenth century gained valuable experience of public speaking in Methodist chapels. Also, by giving the poor real hope of a better life in the world to come, Wesley encouraged them to put up with their hardships and reject violence or revolution as a way out. Thus, indirectly, the Methodist movement may have reduced the possibility of the British people

following the example of the French Revolution of 1789 (see Chapter 10).

Wesley's teaching not only helped to prevent revolution, it encouraged peaceful reform. He was one of the first to organise Sunday schools for poor children—although it must be admitted that he had a very narrow view of what should be taught in them. He considered knowledge of the Bible to be sufficient for such children and insisted that they should never be idle. His rather narrow-minded views and superstitious beliefs came out in the books which he wrote to provide himself with money to support his religious activities. They were published at prices within the reach of ordinary people and covered a wide range of subjects, including religion, history, grammar, physics and medicine. About medicine he was particularly ignorant. Most of his remedies for ailments were nothing more than folklore, like swallowing three pounds of mercury to 'untwist a gut'!

Nevertheless, Wesley did give great encouragement to charitable works and social improvements in general. He was one of the first public figures to speak out against the evils of the slave trade. He strongly supported the campaign for reforming the prisons, led by his friend John Howard. At his London headquarters he opened a dispensary where the poor could get free medicine and medical advice. By the end of his life, his attitude to religion was shared by a large group of clergy and laymen *within* the Church of England. The **Evangelicals,** as they were called, firmly believed that it was a Christian's duty to help the less fortunate. They included men like William Wilberforce, leader of the movement to abolish slavery. The Evangelicals played a major part in the social reforms of the first half of the nineteenth century (see Chapter 11).

Charity schools and the Foundling Hospital

Methodists claimed the Church of England was 'out of touch' with the common people. Although this was true of the majority of Anglicans, there were important exceptions. Throughout this period, *all* kinds of Christians, working individually and in groups, tried to bring about improvements in social conditions. A good example was the provision of schools for children from poor families. There was no compulsory system of free state education in the eighteenth century— nor, indeed, before the last quarter of the nineteenth century (see Chapter 18). In the meantime most of the children from families that could not afford the fees of private or grammar schools never learned to read or write. Usually, their only hope was to get a place in a **charity school.**

Charity schools existed in some areas in the seventeenth century, but progress was slow before the foundation of the **Society for the Promotion of Christian Knowledge (1699).** Through this organisation the Church of England encouraged parishes to raise local subscriptions towards building and maintaining schools for the poor. Financial support came mostly from the clergy and wealthy landowners, but many tradesmen and others contributed as well. By the end of George I's reign (1727) there were over 20,000 children

The bare interior of a charity school

attending Church of England charity schools. Many of the teachers were clergymen, and the curriculum was based on Scripture, but the pupils were also taught reading and writing and were sometimes given a grounding in a useful trade. The Charity Schools movement was the first organised attempt to provide education for the poor. By the 1780s, it was reinforced by the building of **Sunday schools** – especially in the growing manufacturing areas like South Lancashire. For children working six days a week, Sunday was the only time available for schooling.

Thomas Coram (1668–1751) was a wealthy sea-captain and a devoutly religious man who devoted much of his long life to helping the poor. Walking through the docklands of East London, he had been shocked by the sight of dead children lying by the roadside. He decided to do something about it and began to raise funds to build a hospital for 'foundling' (deserted) children. There they could be restored to health and given a basic education before being apprenticed to a tradesman. Some of the greatest men of the time helped him, including Handel, who donated an organ, and the

artist Hogarth, who gave paintings to be sold. By 1741 the **Foundling Hospital** was opened. So great was the need for it that for several years it was continuously overcrowded.

The state of the prisons

The appalling conditions of prison life began to attract the attention of an increasing number of social reformers in this period. Eighteenth century prisons were not normally used as places of punishment. They were supposed to be temporary lodgings, where suspects awaited trial, where debtors were detained until they settled their debts, and where convicts were held before going to the gallows or to the ships which transported them to the colonies. There were no separate cells. All prisoners, from innocent suspects to the most desperate criminals, were herded together in filthy, overcrowded buildings which were themselves breeding grounds of crime. Gaolers were not paid— they lived on money and goods extracted from the inmates. They charged fees for everything, even bread and water. Wealthy prisoners could get almost anything they wanted, including liquor, if they were prepared to pay inflated prices. On the other hand, the penniless were roughly treated. Gaolers often stole their clothes and left them just a blanket to cover themselves with.

Debtors' prisons were the greatest scandal of all. Inmates were

Inquiry into the Fleet
prison, 1729

detained until they paid their debts in full—yet they had no chance of earning money. If friends could not help them, they had to beg from strangers. For this purpose, they were sometimes led in chains through the streets or put in barred cages built into the outside wall of the prison. Needles to say, much of what they received found its way into the pockets of the gaolers.

In 1729, largely through the efforts of **General James Oglethorpe,** a distinguished soldier, a special Commons Committee investigated two of the most notorious debtors' prisons—the Fleet and Marshalsea—where torture of prisoners had been reported. Some amazingly corrupt practices were revealed. For example, the Warden of the Fleet Prison, who paid £5000 to get the appointment, made a large income from selling prisoners their freedom. When no direct action resulted from the inquiry, Oglethorpe pursued a scheme of his own. With the aid of a parliamentary grant, he established the new American colony of **Georgia** (1733) and arranged for many of the early settlers to be debtors straight from gaol.

The most famous prison reformer of the eighteenth century was **John Howard** (1726–90) a Bedfordshire magistrate. In the 1770s, at a personal cost of £30,000, he carried out a detailed investigation of a number of English prisons, including the notorious Newgate gaol in London. When it was published (1777) under the title *The State of the Prisons in England and Wales,* its evidence of appalling corruption and misery shocked public opinion. Howard's recommendations included regular payment of gaolers, better sanitation and ventilation, clean clothing and bedding, and provision of workshops and chapels for the prisoners. These things are taken for granted today, but in Howard's lifetime they were revolutionary suggestions. It was not until after his death that Parliament even began the task of reforming prisons and prison life.

Humanitarians like Coram, Oglethorpe and Howard only scratched the surface of poverty, misery and neglect. They, and others like them, toiled alone. In this period it was not considered the duty of governments to interfere in social life, even to prevent suffering. Nevertheless, their pioneering work helped to make the public more aware of some of the greatest social evils. It paved the way for an 'Age of Reform' in the nineteenth century, when later generations of humanitarians like William Wilberforce, Elizabeth Fry and Lord Shaftesbury got Parliament to intervene and tackle some of the worst social abuses (see Chapter 11). Like the reformers that followed them, the 'pioneers' of the eighteenth century were all men of strong religious conviction. They, together with John Wesley and the Methodists, brought the Church and its teachings much more into the lives of the poorest and most unfortunate people.

Timeline
1689 Toleration Act.
1699 Society for the Promotion of Christian Knowledge.
1738 John Wesley's 'conversion'.
1741 Foundling Hospital opened.
1777 *The State of the Prisons* – John Howard.
1784 Wesley ordains his own ministers.

Further study
For later developments in the Church see Chapter 20.

Project
Make a collection of hymns written by Charles Wesley (and possibly other Methodists too). Pay special attention to the words, bearing in mind the circumstances in which they were first sung.

General accounts
D. Marshall, *John Wesley* (O.U.P., Clarendon Biographies)
S. Reed Brett, *John Wesley* (A. and C. Black). Contains many quotations from Wesley's own Journal.
R. J. Unstead, *The Rise of Great Britain* (A. and C. Black). Chapter 6 is based on the famous diary of the Reverend James Woodforde (1740–1803).

Special topic
There is no better introduction to prison life than the sections of Daniel Defoe's novel *Moll Flanders* which describe life in London's Newgate gaol in the early eighteenth century.

Filmstrips
John Wesley (Common Ground, Lives of Famous Men and Women)
John Wesley (Religious Films: in colour)

5 The Changing Face of the Countryside
Agricultural Revolution

Many pages of history books are filled with the deeds of a few politicians, soldiers, sailors and the like—but the lives of the remainder of the population, though not so glamorous, were devoted to no less important matters. Farming was the main occupation of the British in the eighteenth century, and the same was true of all the peoples of the world at that time. The village and its agriculture was the backbone of the nation. Therefore changes in farming methods could, if widely adopted, affect the lives of millions. In the eighteenth and early nineteenth centuries there were agricultural changes in plenty. So great was their effect that we apply to them the term 'revolution'—a word normally used to describe events as dramatic as the overthrow of governments.

The 'open field' village

Around 1700 more than half the cultivated land was still being farmed in 'open fields', as it had been since the Middle Ages. Villages, especially in the Midlands and the South, were surrounded by three great, hedgeless fields which contained all the arable (plough) land. These fields were divided up into separate **strips,** which were shared out among the villagers—like present day allotments—according to the amount of land they owned or rented. Traditional methods of ploughing had fixed the size of strips. A 'furrow long' (furlong) of 220 yards was about as far as a team of oxen could plough before resting and turning round. The width of the average strip was about twenty-two yards, so its area was roughly an acre. The separate strips making up each family's total holding were scattered about the fields so that good soil could be evenly distributed.

Each family cultivated its own land, but it was in the interests of everyone to do some of the work on a community basis. Thus families ploughed the fields in groups, each contributing a share to the ploughing team—usually one of the oxen. Two of the fields were normally devoted to corn crops—rye, barley, oats or wheat. The third remained **fallow** (left unsown after ploughing) so that its soil could recover its richness after two consecutive years of cultivation. Thus the fallow period came to each field in rotation, one year out of three, which meant that only two-thirds of the arable land was cultivated at any time. In addition to the three fields, there were commons and wastelands, on which the villagers' livestock grazed in the summer; and meadows, which provided hay for their winter feed.

The open field method of farming was probably started in Britain by the Anglo-Saxon settlers in the fifth century, but we cannot be sure. Some historians think it existed in Britain before the time of

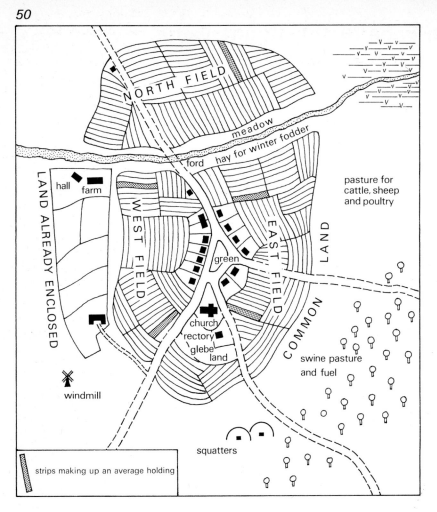

Plan of an open field village

Christ. It was found in many parts of Europe in the eighteenth century, by which time it had also been introduced into the New World by the early colonists. Aerial photographs show something very close to open field farming even today in the heart of savage New Guinea. Its long history is understandable, because it was an ideal basis for the simple community life of the countryside before the modern industrial age. It made possible the sharing out of each new piece of land as it was brought into cultivation. Above all, it allowed for co-operative ploughing, which was necessary in an age when few families owned either a plough or sufficient oxen to make up a ploughing team.

Nevertheless, open field farming had its drawbacks as well. It was wasteful of land. The fallow field produced nothing, and, even in the other fields, land was wasted on numerous paths and cart tracks and often by grass spaces or 'balks' which separated one strip from another. It was wasteful of labour, for the fallow field had to be ploughed even though it was not sown. It was also wasteful of time. Families continually travelled from one part of the village to another to cultivate their scattered strips. The raising of livestock was greatly

View of the village of Laxton, in Nottinghamshire, where open field cultivation is still carried on

handicapped by the open field system. Animals mingled together on the commons and wasteland, spreading diseases and making selective breeding impossible. There was rarely enough hay to feed all the animals in winter, so many had to be killed off in the autumn and their meat salted. Those that were carried through to the spring were so weak and undersized on their scanty diet of hay that they often had to be carried into the fields when grazing was resumed.

Strip farmers harvesting their crops.

The open field system had always been a barrier to the introduction of new methods, because it was necessary for the entire village to agree to any changes. For example, one family could not grow turnips while all the others were growing barley because, after the grain was harvested, cattle were allowed to graze on the stubble and they would eat the growing turnips! Therefore each family had to keep exact time with its neighbours in ploughing, sowing and reaping the crops. The difficulty of experimenting with new methods had not mattered so much in previous centuries. Then the main concern of the people had been to produce enough for their *own* needs ('subsistence' farming). However, by the eighteenth century, the old methods were incapable of producing enough food for the rapidly growing towns. The decline of the open field village, which began long before 1700, was therefore accelerated.

New methods and 'improving landlords'

Interest in experimental farming had been aroused by seventeenth century travellers to the Continent. They had been impressed by the advances made in countries like Holland, where good agricultural

land was too scarce to be wasted by outdated methods of cultivation. By the mid eighteenth century, the search for improvement in Britain was further encouraged by the need to feed a quickly growing population. The urgency of the problem can be seen in the fact that the population almost *doubled* in the reign of George III (1760–1820). Most of the increase was in the towns, which depended entirely on the surplus produce of the countryside. Landlords saw that they could make handsome profits if they could find ways of producing a greater surplus for sale. To increase the productivity of their land they had to convert open fields into separate, *enclosed* units (if this had not already been done) so that the latest farming techniques could be used without hindrance.

Many 'improvers' published accounts of their experiments—most of them of doubtful value. One of the best known of the earlier writers was **Jethro Tull** (1674–1741). On his Berkshire estates he applied some of the methods he had observed abroad, especially in the French vineyards, and described them in *The New Horse-Hoeing Husbandry* (1731). Tull believed that fallow periods could be cut out altogether if the soil was properly ploughed and then regularly hoed while the crops were growing. He invented a **horse-drawn hoe** which penetrated deeper into the ground than the old-fashioned harrow, so that the roots were kept moist and harmful weeds were cleared.

Tull, along with many other farmers, was very critical of the old-fashioned method of sowing seed by 'broadcasting' (throwing it in handfuls on to the ploughed land). The wastefulness of broadcasting is well summed up in the following little verse:

'Sow four grains in a row,
One for the pigeon, one for the crow,
One to rot and one to grow.'

Jethro Tull and his seed drill

Tull's answer was to invent a horse-drawn **seed-drill**, which sowed seeds in rows at a regular depth. With the aid of his new implements, he claimed he could double his crops using only a third of the previous quantity of seed. However, Tull's ideas, attractive as they seemed, had no lasting effect on British agriculture. His seed-drill never worked properly, and many of his theories were unsound, including his opposition to the use of manure. His importance was almost certainly exaggerated by later agricultural writers.

There were other ways of avoiding wasteful fallows, apart from those suggested by Tull. Some enterprising farmers, in the seventeenth century, had copied the Dutch method of growing corn and root crops alternately on the same land. **Roots,** such as turnips and swedes, take their nourishment from the soil at a deeper level than grain crops. Therefore, they can be grown straight after corn and still leave the upper soil refreshed for another corn crop in the following year. Turnips had for centuries only been thought of as a food for human beings, but some continental farmers had begun to grow them for cattle fodder. This greatly interested **Sir Richard Weston,** a Royalist refugee in Holland during the period of Cromwell's republic in the 1650s. On his return to England, Weston developed a *four*-course rotation, including turnips and clover, which made the fallow year unnecessary. Clover enriched the soil while at the same time providing a valuable addition to the diet of livestock.

The growing of roots and artificial grasses like clover between years of corn crops was already established in some parts of Britain before 1700, usually on enclosed farms. But the idea was really popularised by Charles, **Lord Townshend** (1674–1738), a diplomat turned farmer. 'Turnip' Townshend, as he was called in his later years, had a long and distinguished career in politics. As a Minister of State he played a vital part in negotiating both the Union with Scotland (1707) and the Treaty of Utrecht (1713). But he retired suddenly from political life in 1730, after a quarrel with Walpole, and concentrated on farming his estates at Raynham in Norfolk.

Townshend began by improving the quality of the soil, much of which was sandy swamp. By draining it and adding manure and marl (a mixture of clay and lime) he turned it into rich, cultivable land. Instead of the old 'three-course rotation' of autumn corn, spring corn and fallow, he alternated turnips and clover with corn crops, as Weston had done. This **Norfolk four-course rotation** of turnips, barley or oats, clover and wheat made the production of cattle fodder an important part of arable farming. Other farmers used Townshend's methods and found they produced so much animal feed that their livestock no longer had to be slaughtered in the autumn. Fresh meat could now be eaten all the year round, replacing salted meat during the winter months.

A more plentiful supply of winter feed made it possible to breed better quality **livestock.** But a good diet could never be sufficient in itself. Separate enclosed pastures were required, instead of the old commons and wastelands, so that different breeds of animals could be isolated from each other. In enclosures, breeding could be carefully controlled and the spread of disease greatly reduced; and the stock would be prevented from taking the flesh off their bones by unnecessary wandering. Improvements along these lines spread rapidly in the late eighteenth and early nineteenth centuries, and stock-breeding became a specialised art. The greatest improver in this branch of agriculture was **Robert Bakewell** (1725–95) of Dishley in Leicestershire, who took over his father's 440-acre farm in 1760.

Sheep- and cattle-farmers had previously concentrated on producing wool and milk, but Bakewell aimed to produce high quality meat as well. He selected the finest existing types of livestock and experimented with cross-breeding. Before long he succeeded in greatly increasing the amount of flesh on those parts of the animals which yielded the most expensive cuts. His most famous breed was the **New Leicester** sheep, but he also produced new breeds of longhorn cattle and farm horses. Visitors came from all over Britain and the Continent to see his model farm. They admired the cleanliness of the stalls and sheds and the excellence of Bakewell's feeding methods. In 1700 animals had been small and stringy, but by 1800 better care and selective breeding sometimes produced beasts which weighed from two to three times heavier than those a

Bakewell's *New Leicester* sheep

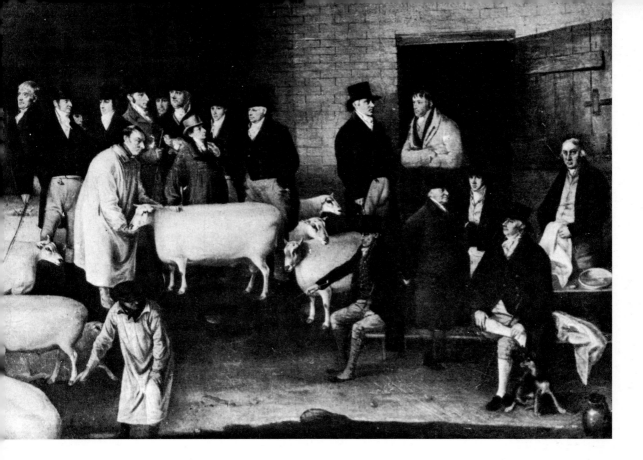

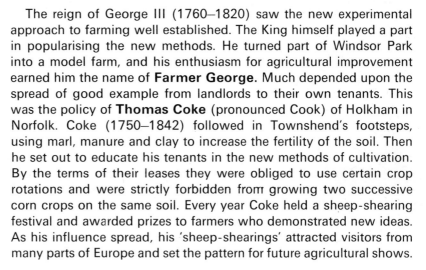

Leicestershire rams,
painted shortly after
Robert Bakewell's death

century earlier. In exceptional cases, figures like these were recorded:

Average weight of stock at Smithfield Market (London)

	1710	1795
Oxen	370 lb	800 lb
Calves	50 lb	150 lb
Sheep	38 lb	80 lb

The reign of George III (1760–1820) saw the new experimental approach to farming well established. The King himself played a part in popularising the new methods. He turned part of Windsor Park into a model farm, and his enthusiasm for agricultural improvement earned him the name of **Farmer George**. Much depended upon the spread of good example from landlords to their own tenants. This was the policy of **Thomas Coke** (pronounced Cook) of Holkham in Norfolk. Coke (1750–1842) followed in Townshend's footsteps, using marl, manure and clay to increase the fertility of the soil. Then he set out to educate his tenants in the new methods of cultivation. By the terms of their leases they were obliged to use certain crop rotations and were strictly forbidden from growing two successive corn crops on the same soil. Every year Coke held a sheep-shearing festival and awarded prizes to farmers who demonstrated new ideas. As his influence spread, his 'sheep-shearings' attracted visitors from many parts of Europe and set the pattern for future agricultural shows.

The spread of enclosure

Improvements in soil preparation, crop rotation and stock-breeding went hand-in-hand with **enclosure** of the open fields. In fact, it was the process of enclosure which, more than any other single factor, changed the face of the countryside and brought about a 'revolution' in British agriculture. When land was enclosed, the open fields, commons and wastelands were converted into a number of separate compact farms by means of fences, hedges and ditches. It was not a new idea. Ever since the Middle Ages various kinds of enclosures had been carried out, often for the purpose of sheep-farming. But not until the eighteenth century did enclosure of arable land become standard farming practice.

Up to about 1740 enclosure normally took place as a result of general agreement among the villagers. If the whole village was owned by one landlord it was even simpler. However, as the century progressed, there remained many landlords who were keen to enclose their land but were prevented from doing so by the opposition of smallholders. The latter feared they would not be able to farm their land on their own, and they were reluctant to give up their right to use the common pasture. Landlords sometimes overcame stubborn smallholders by buying up their land, but this could be a long and expensive process. They grew impatient and began to seek private Acts of Parliament which made enclosure compulsory, so long as a sufficient proportion of the landowners were in favour.

To obtain an Enclosure Act, the owners of at least four-fifths of the land of the village had to send a petition to Parliament. The squire, the parson and three or four others often made up the necessary proportion of landowners, even though they were a tiny fraction of the total village population. When the Bill had been passed by Parliament —usually a formality—a group of **Parliamentary Commissioners** visited the village. They investigated all claims to a share of the land, settled disputes, and eventually produced a map showing each landowner's allocation and the position of roads and paths. It seemed a fair procedure, but it worked to the advantage of wealthy landlords and often ignored the wishes of scores of smallholders. Many villagers had no legal documents to prove their ownership of land and had their claims ignored by the Commissioners as a result. Even if they could prove ownership, they were often unable to afford the expense of hedging and ditching and their share of the Commissioners' fees. They were forced to sell out to the highest bidder.

As the following table shows, the pace of parliamentary enclosure quickened after 1760, reaching its peak during the long wars against France (1793–1815) when high food prices were an added incentive to landlords (see Chapter 10).

Parliamentary Enclosure Acts

1751–60	156	1781–90	287
1761–70	424	1791–1800	506
1771–80	642	1801–10	906

After about 1810 much of the work was done and the number of Enclosure Acts began to fall. By the mid nineteenth century, open field villages had become a rarity—a picturesque survival from the past. The Agricultural Revolution was almost complete, and nearly everywhere the countryside had taken on its modern appearance of a 'patchwork quilt' of neatly fenced farms.

Some results of enclosure

Enclosure, and the new farming methods that went with it, brought about great changes in the **diet** of the average family. Not only was a greater quantity of food produced, but also a wider variety. More vegetables were grown, including potatoes, which became a basic part of the diet in this period. Improvements in the care of livestock resulted in more milk and dairy produce and fresh instead of salted meat in winter. In general, enclosure of the open fields was essential if British farming was to keep up with the times. By the end of the eighteenth century, the growth of industrial towns made it necessary for agriculture to be run much more on 'business' lines—in the same way as iron, coal or textiles. Even after the land was enclosed, the bigger landlords still tried to buy out the smaller ones so as to increase the scale of their operations.

As often happens when traditional ways of life are upset, many poor people suffered. Those who had no land or were forced to sell out had lost their 'little piece of England', and with it much of their security and self-respect. There were **anti-enclosure riots** among the landless poor, in spite of the harsh punishments, such as death or transportation, inflicted on the ringleaders.

This conflict between agricultural improvement and social distress can be seen in the works of **Arthur Young** (1741–1820), the leading agricultural writer and journalist of the period. From 1767 onwards, he travelled widely in England and on the Continent, carefully noting improvements and their effects. He edited a journal, *The Annals of Agriculture,* from 1784, and helped to set up the Board of Agriculture (1793) of which he became Secretary. 'The first business of all improvement is enclosure,' he said, and he did all he could to encourage it. But he had to admit that enclosures also brought much hardship. 'By nineteen out of twenty enclosure bills the poor are injured,' he said. He was critical of the way great landowners used their power in Parliament to force enclosure on the poor, and thought greater efforts should have been made to look after the dispossessed.

The loss of grazing rights on the commons and wastelands was a severe blow to the poorer villagers. These pastures, where they often kept a cow and a few geese or poultry, were almost as valuable to them as the strips they cultivated. They were sometimes given tiny plots of land in return, but these were too small to be of much value. Their plight is neatly summed up in the following verse (quoted by Arthur Young):

'Tis bad enough in man or woman to steal a goose from off a common. But surely he's without excuse who steals the common from the goose.

Therefore enclosure, by concentrating the ownership of land into fewer hands, greatly increased the class of **landless labourers.**

Arthur Young

Left: Farm workers in the early nineteenth century

Where industrial towns were within easy reach, they sometimes left the land and went to work in factories; but most of them, especially in the South, stayed to become wage labourers on the new enclosed estates. In spite of the growing agricultural prosperity, their wages were pitifully low and often had to be made up to the necessary minimum level out of the parish rates.

Timeline

1730–38	'Turnip' Townshend at Raynham.
1731	Jethro Tull's *New Horse-Hoeing Husbandry*.
1760–95	Robert Bakewell at Dishley.
1760–1820	'Farmer George' III.
1767	Arthur Young begins his tours.
1793	Board of Agriculture established.
1801–10	Peak period of Parliamentary Enclosure.

Further study

The important effects of the French Wars of 1793–1815 on British farming, and the influence of enclosure on the operation of the Poor Law, are dealt with in the last section of Chapter 10.

Visit

The village of Laxton in Nottinghamshire—about three miles off the Great North Road (A1) near Tuxford—continues, under the Ministry of Agriculture, to use the medieval open field system of cultivation. (For those who cannot get to Laxton, there is a nineteen-minute Rank motion picture about it which can be hired.)

General accounts

J. Addy, *The Agrarian Revolution* (Longmans' Then and There series) contains some contemporary material and has a separate section on enclosure in Sheffield.

Stella Davies, *Living Through the Industrial Revolution* (Routledge) Chapter 7 is especially useful on Robert Bakewell and Thomas Coke.

I. Tenen, *This England, 1714–1960* (Macmillan) pp. 45–64 and 152–65

Special topic

The Deserted Village, a poem by Oliver Goldsmith (available in many anthologies). But remember that enclosure in general did *not* lead to rural depopulation. It brought more *arable* land into cultivation than ever before—and arable farming requires a large labour force. The population was increasing in both the town *and* the countryside in this period.

Filmstrips

Agriculture and the Land, Parts 1 and 2 (Common Ground)
The Agrarian and Industrial Revolution (Educational Productions)
The Agrarian Revolution (Longman, Then and There Filmstrips)

6 Textiles and the Coming of Factories
Industrial Revolution 1

While the movement to enclose the land and use new farming methods was at its height, a similar turning-point was reached in the history of manufacture. In previous centuries most industries had been centred round the home—in villages or small towns. Families usually owned their own traditional tools (like hammers and files in the metal trades) or simple, hand-worked machines (like spinning-wheels and handlooms in cloth-making). However, before the end of the eighteenth century all this had begun to change. New techniques of manufacture and the use of machines powered by water-wheels and steam-engines resulted in the organisation of industry on a big scale—in 'factories', where many workers could be collected together in one place. As the Machine Age advanced, so the population became increasingly concentrated in towns, especially in the coalfield districts of the Midlands and the North of England, South Wales, and the Central Lowlands of Scotland.

These changes came earliest and quickest in certain branches of the textile industry—especially cotton and silk—and in trades like hardware, pottery and chemical manufacture. Nevertheless, factory industry did not become widespread, even in textiles, before the mid nineteenth century. In this chapter and in the two which follow, some of the major developments in British industry before 1850 will be described. But, first of all, we must try to discover why it was *Britain*, rather than any other country, which had the world's first 'Industrial Revolution'.

Britain leads the way
Conditions in the United Kingdom were especially suitable for the rapid growth of industry in the eighteenth century. There were large deposits of coal and iron ore, and plenty of fast-flowing streams for water power. No part of Britain is very far from either the sea or a navigable river—an important factor before transport was mechanised.

'The Industrial Revolution'

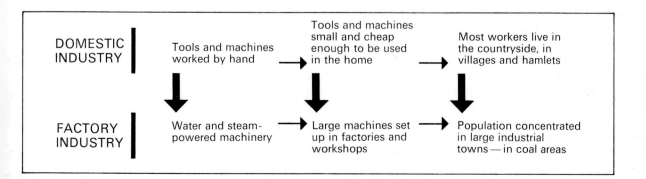

Moreover, the effect of the warm North Atlantic Drift on the climate means that these vital trade routes do not freeze in winter.

Since the end of the Civil War (1649) Britain has enjoyed almost uninterrupted **peace at home,** and has suffered far less from political and religious disputes than any other European country. The last major battle to be fought on British soil (Culloden, 1746) saw the end of the last full-scale rebellion against the Government (see Chapter 2). The rapid expansion of **trade,** from the mid seventeenth century onwards, was assisted by the absence of internal customs duties. In continental countries, like France, each separate province taxed goods passing across its frontiers—thus increasing their price even before they reached market. In Britain, on the other hand, goods travelling *within* the kingdom could not be taxed. Thus England, Wales and Scotland (after 1707) together made up probably the largest 'free trade' area in Europe.

The growth of the overseas trading empire in this period brought much **wealth** into Britain (see Chapter 3). As a result, merchants were able to influence industry. They wanted more and more goods to sell and were often prepared to find the money to finance new manufacturing processes. The Bank of England (established 1694) and hundreds of country banks, which sprang up during the eighteenth century, brought together people's savings and made some of them available for industrial development. The colonies provided additional markets for the expanding output of manufactured goods.

The remarkable **rise in population** was another factor of great importance. It meant a steadily increasing labour force and, at the same time, more customers to absorb the rising output of manufactured goods. The figures speak for themselves:

Population of Britain (excluding Ireland)

1760 (estimated)	8,000,000
1801 (census)	10,500,000
1821 (census)	14,000,000
1861 (census)	23,000,000

Thus the population *trebled* in the century after 1760—when the Industrial Revolution was at its height. This was mainly due to a rapid fall in the death-rate, particularly among infants and children under five. Cleaner water, a better diet, greater medical skill and improved methods of midwifery were probably the most important reasons. However, cheaper fuel for domestic heating, the spread of cheap cotton clothing (easier to wash and therefore healthier) and the increase in brick-built houses all played a part.

Textiles before the 'Factory Age'

The manufacture of **woollen cloth** had long been Britain's chief industry, and remained so until the end of the eighteenth century (see Chapter 1). The cloth trade was usually organised by wealthy merchant 'clothiers'. They bought the raw wool, supervised every stage of manufacture and then sold the finished material. Some skilled tasks, like the finishing processes of fulling and bleaching, required equipment which was too big for the house. They had to be

Hand wheel spinning

performed in special workshops, often in the towns. Some of these were so large that they were already half way to being factories.

On the other hand, spinning and weaving—the two most important processes—were carried on domestically. **Spinning** involved joining the short 'staples' of wool (previously separated from the mass by a process called carding) into a continuous thread or yarn. It was mostly done by women and girls, often part-time; unlike **weaving,** which was a full-time occupation for a man. The loom, on which yarn was woven into cloth, was frequently owned and hired out by the clothier.

The woollen cloth trade, in spite of being Britain's major industry, was not the first to develop factory methods of production. Almost the reverse happened in practice. It was the newer textile trades, especially silk and cotton, which proved most capable of introducing technical changes in the eighteenth century. The woollen cloth industry was held back by a number of factors. The use of new processes was restricted by old-fashioned rules and regulations; it was difficult to increase the supply of raw wool before the development of Australian sheep-farming in the nineteenth century, and wool was more difficult to twist and stretch on a machine than fibres like cotton.

The first genuine factory for the production of textile goods was in the **silk** industry. It was built by two brothers, **John and Thomas Lombe,** on an island in the river Derwent at Derby (1721). Silk does not require spinning—this has already been done by the silk-worms.

To produce a thread for weaving it has to be unwound and twisted ('thrown'). The silk-throwing machines used by the Lombe brothers were based on designs obtained secretly from Italy. Their five-storeyed mill, 400 feet long, was driven by a huge water-wheel and employed 300 workers. Other silk manufacturers followed their example, so that, by about 1760, silk-throwing was well established as a factory industry, in North Cheshire, around Stockport and Macclesfield. Nevertheless, it would be very misleading to regard these developments as the start of the 'Factory Age' in textiles. Silk remained a minor industry in Britain, unable to rival the products of France and Italy, where raw silk was in abundant supply. It was not until the successful introduction of power-driven machinery into the cotton industry, around 1770, that the 'revolution' in textiles really began.

The **cotton** industry was slow to develop in Britain, mainly because the raw material has to be imported. Cotton was expensive and difficult to obtain before the setting up of plantations in the West Indies and the American mainland. In the early eighteenth century, the art of spinning strong cotton yarn had not yet been learned. It was usually mixed with wool or linen to produce fustian. **South Lanca-shire** was already the centre of the cotton trade, and it has remained so, for several good reasons. It had a first-rate port in Liverpool, which became the main centre of the Atlantic trade by the end of the eighteenth century. Each year Liverpool handled thousands of tons of 'white gold' from the New World. The swift-flowing Pennine streams provided water power before the age of steam, and later on Lancashire's coal supplies were well able to satisfy the demands of the steam-engine. In addition, the mild, damp climate is ideal for handling cotton thread, which breaks easily in a dry atmosphere.

At the start of our period, manufacturing processes in all the textile trades were slow and laborious. But improvements were gradually being made in the weaving and finishing stages. The handloom in particular was becoming more efficient, and each weaver required five or six spinners to keep him supplied with yarn. This disproportion was greatly increased by the invention of the **flying shuttle** (1733). It was the work of **John Kay** (1704–79) a weaver from Lancashire who was working for a Colchester clothier. Previously, the shuttle (containing the 'weft' or cross-thread) had been thrown *by hand* across the loom, on which the 'warp' (longways thread) was stretched. This meant the width of cloth one man could weave, without an assistant, was limited by the length of his arms. Kay found a way of striking the shuttle to and fro with two wooden hammers which were attached by cords to a lever. In the words of his patent: 'The weaver . . . by a small pull at the cord . . . moves the said new invented shuttle from side to side to pleasure.'

Broadcloth could now be woven without the help of an assistant to catch and return the shuttle, and the whole weaving process was greatly speeded up. But Kay made little money out of his idea. Many manufacturers were glad to use his invention but refused to pay him for it. Worse still, he suffered the bitter hostility of his fellow weavers. They claimed he was trying to put them out of business, and went so far as to wreck his house (1753). He fled to France, where he died in poverty. The flying shuttle was not widely used until after 1760, when it was improved with a device called a **drop-box,** invented by Kay's son **Robert Kay.** The original invention only wove plain cloth, but the drop-box held several shuttles, loaded with yarns of different colours. By bringing the box to different levels, simple pattern-weaving could be done without having to fit different shuttles by hand each time a change of colour was needed.

The mechanisation of cotton-spinning

The flying shuttle, by speeding up weaving, further increased the shortage of yarn. Unless a quicker method of spinning could be found many weavers would have little or no work to do. But, as the old saying goes, *'necessity is the mother of invention'.* The problem of the shortage of yarn soon produced a crop of spinning-machines and, with them, the beginnings of a large-scale factory industry.

The first, a 'roller-spinning' device, patented by **Lewis Paul** in 1738, was a near miss. It had two sets of rollers which travelled at different speeds and thus drew out the thread to the right thickness before it was wound off on spindles. Five of them were installed in the first cotton-spinning mill in history—at Northampton in the 1740s—but they proved to be frail and unreliable. It was not until the main principles of Paul's machine were taken up by later inventors that roller-spinning became profitable.

In the 1760s, when the widespread popularity of the flying shuttle began, two highly successful spinning-machines were produced within the space of three years. The first, known as the **spinning-jenny,** was the work of **James Hargreaves,** a carpenter and weaver from Blackburn. It was a straightforward development of the

Replica of James Hargreaves' 'spinning-jenny' (1765)

principle of the spinning-wheel, except that one workman could spin several threads at once, simply by turning a handle. The first models had eight spindles, operated by a single wheel. But before long water-powered jennies with eighty spindles or more were built and housed in factories and large workshops. Within thirty years over 20,000 jennies were in use, practically all of them in the cotton industry. Hargreaves suffered the fate of several early textile inventors when his house and machinery were smashed by angry hand-spinners (1767). But he enjoyed better fortune after moving to Nottingham.

At the time Hargreaves left Blackburn, ten miles away in Preston **Richard Arkwright** (1732–92) was beginning a career in textiles that would make him famous in the history of British industry. He was not really an inventor. He was a clever businessman who rearranged and combined the inventions of others. When he heard of the great need for a spinning-machine, he was a hair-dealer and ex-barber with no mechanical training. But that did not stop him. In 1768, with the help of a clock-maker, he supervised the construction of a spinning-machine called the **water frame.** It closely resembled Paul's unsuccessful machine; except that it had four pairs of rollers instead of two to stretch the thread and press the fibres together. Probably the main difference between the two machines was that Arkwright's gave the yarn a firmer twist as it was wound off the rollers.

Unlike the jenny, the water frame was too difficult to operate by hand. It needed the power of a water-wheel. As a result, it led directly to the setting up of factories. Because Arkwright's machine led the breakaway from the old 'domestic system', he is usually regarded as 'the founder of the modern factory system'. With his gift for organisation and his tremendous drive and energy, he was not content simply to take out a patent for the water frame. He wanted his own factories. He went to Nottingham to raise money, and eventually got the support of a wealthy stocking-manufacturer, Jedediah Strutt. In 1771 he set up his first successful mill, at **Cromford,** near Derby, where the river Derwent runs swiftly through a narrow gorge. More mills followed, not only in Derbyshire but in Lancashire, where the largest employed 600 workers. He eventually collected a knighthood and half a million pounds in profits!

The jenny and the water frame revolutionised cotton-spinning— but both had limitations. Jenny-spun yarn was fine in texture but too weak to make satisfactory warp (longways thread). The water frame produced yarn which was strong but rather too coarse to make cloth of the highest quality. **Samuel Crompton** (1753–1827) a weaver and spinner from Bolton, overcame this problem with his **spinning-mule** (1779). Just as an ordinary mule is a cross between a horse and a donkey, so Crompton's mule combined features of both the jenny and the water frame to produce strong yarn of fine quality.

Crompton was the complete opposite of Arkwright. He was an inventor of great skill, but was totally lacking in business ability. While others made fortunes out of his invention, he died a poor man, in spite of a parliamentary grant of £5000 in 1812, most of which he

Sir Richard Arkwright

Opposite: A mule spinning factory in the nineteenth century

Below: The mill at Cromford, newly restored

used to pay off debts. The first mules were hand-operated and could be used at home. By the 1790s large water- and steam-powered versions were built, with as many as 400 spindles. These gradually replaced the jennies and water frames. British cotton cloth, made of mass-produced yarn, now rivalled in quality the best calicoes and muslins of the East. Both the name 'mule' and its basic principles are still found in modern spinning-machinery.

The transfer of cotton-spinning from the home to the factory was almost complete by 1800, much to the regret of the poor country folk who had previously relied on part-time domestic spinning as an extra source of income. There were two main stages in the growth of the industry. During the first or 'water power stage', mills were set up in remote parts of the Lancashire and Derbyshire hills, where rushing streams could easily be dammed to create artificial waterfalls. In the second stage, beginning with the introduction of steam power in 1785, the industry became concentrated in the coalfield towns of Lancashire and the Central Lowlands of Scotland. Lancashire was by far the more important. By 1800 it was the second richest and most populated county in the kingdom, after Middlesex. By that time, great quantities of cotton goods were being used by all classes. 'As for the ladies', said a pamphlet of 1782, 'they wear scarcely anything now but cotton, calicoes, muslin or silks. . . . We have scarcely any woollens now about our beds but blankets.'

The power loom

While spinning was being revolutionised, weaving continued to be a domestic handicraft. It was more difficult to apply water or steam power to the handloom, because of its complicated movements. Machines introduced from the Continent, like the Dutch 'swivel loom', were only satisfactory for the weaving of ribbons; and attempts to apply stocking-knitting machines to cloth-weaving all failed.

Nineteenth century power loom

Meanwhile, the weavers prospered. Whereas previously there had not been enough yarn to keep them all busy, now there was more than they could use. They were so much in demand that in Bolton, at the end of the century, they walked about the streets with £5 notes stuck in their hat-bands.

But the great prosperity of the handloom weavers was short-lived. A talented clergyman named **Edmund Cartwright** (1743–1823) became interested in the idea of a **power loom,** following a conversation with some Manchester manufacturers. They told him of the great need for a mechanical loom but claimed it was impossible to make one. Although Cartwright was not a mechanic, he decided to try to prove them wrong and paid a blacksmith and a carpenter to help him. His first machine (patented in 1785) was very clumsy and needed two strong men to work it; but he was on the right track. By 1789 he had produced a loom driven by a Watt steam-engine (see Chapter 8) which could weave any kind of plain cloth. All operations previously done by hand or foot could now be performed mechanically and the weaver's task was reduced to that of repairing broken threads. Cartwright, like others before him, made little profit from his invention. Therefore, in recognition of his services to British industry, Parliament granted him £10,000 in 1809 and he retired to a farm in Kent.

The handloom weavers realised that their high standard of living was threatened by the power loom and banded together to resist its introduction. Cartwright's attempt at partnership with a Manchester firm (1791) failed when their factory was deliberately burned to the ground. Threatening letters from weavers left no doubt as to the culprits. One of them said: 'We have sworn together to destroy your factory . . . and to have your lives for ruining our trade.' But the weavers were fighting a losing battle. In the early years of the nineteenth century, an improved, all-metal power loom was produced. The competition was too severe for the hand-weavers and they were gradually reduced to starvation wages. In 1830 handlooms still outnumbered power looms by three to one, but by the 1840s the power loom was supreme in the cotton industry.

The inventions which made possible the 'revolution' in the cotton industry were not all the work of Englishmen. The American plantations could not have kept up with the rapidly increasing demand for raw cotton without the aid of **Elias Whitney's 'gin'** (engin') invented in 1793. This greatly speeded up the tedious process of 'cleaning' the cotton (separating the little black seeds from the fibre). One horse-worked gin could clean as much cotton as fifty Negro slaves working by hand. The need for such an invention can be seen from the figures for British imports of raw cotton. These alone tell the story of the revolution in cotton manufacture:

British imports of raw cotton

1760	8,000 tons
1800	25,000 tons
1830	100,000 tons

Across the Pennines

Most of the great inventions in cotton-spinning and weaving were later applied to woollen cloth manufacture. But they took an average of thirty years longer. By about 1800 the ancient woollen cloth trade had been surpassed in importance by the cotton industry. Two of the three traditional woollen cloth areas were in decline— East Anglia and the West Country. The third, the **West Riding** of Yorkshire, based on Leeds and Bradford, had already become the centre of the industry.

The supremacy of the West Riding depended on many factors, including the presence of fast-flowing streams for water power and, later on, plentiful supplies of coal to feed the steam-driven machinery. Even so, thousands of small clothiers still worked at home in the villages of the West Riding until well into the nineteenth century. Although machine-spinning of wool began in Yorkshire in the 1780s, it spread slowly. The power loom, which came much later, was not in widespread use until the 1860s.

Businesses were normally smaller east of the Pennines. An exception was **Benjamin Gott**'s large factory in Leeds, which used machines for the spinning and finishing processes from the time it was established in 1793. Britain went to war with France in the same year, and Gott received so many government contracts for army clothing that he ran night shifts to keep his machines at full stretch. He was the first of the great factory-masters in the woollen industry, but he could not rival the wealth and power of the Lancashire 'Cotton Kings'.

Workers in the mills

In their haste to make profits most factory-owners ignored the needs of their workers, with the result that conditions in the early mills were exceedingly harsh. Working hours were very long, especially in the 'brisk time', when trade was good. Twelve to fourteen hours, with brief periods of rest, was a common working day. Occasionally men, women and children worked as long as nineteen hours a day, Monday to Saturday. Many children were employed in spinning-mills, where the work was easily learned and needed little strength. Their delicate touch was an advantage in jobs like 'piecing' (joining broken threads). Some infants began work at four or five years of age, crawling under the machines to collect fluff from the floor. Children were usually paid between a third and a sixth of the adult wage, which was, in turn, only worth about a sixth of a present day labourer's wage. Payment was often made partly or wholly in 'truck' tickets, which had to be exchanged in the employer's own shop for goods like flour, sugar and clothing, frequently at inflated prices.

At first, most of the factory workers were **orphan children,** obtained by employers from parish Poor Law authorities who were glad to be rid of the responsibility of caring for them. They were supposed to be apprentices but, instead of learning a trade, they were given monotonous and unskilled tasks. Long hours in a hot, stuffy

Children at work winding cotton (about 1820)

mill and too little sleep soon ruined their health and deformed their bodies. They were often underfed. In one mill, apprentices struggled with pigs in the yard to get some of the food in their troughs! As machinery became more complicated and steam-engines were used for power, more adults were needed. But child labour continued, for fathers and mothers could rarely support their families on their wages alone.

Surprising as it may seem, most workers enjoyed a higher standard of living in the new factory towns than they had been used to previously. Many of them—men, women and children alike—had worked equally long hours at home or in a small workshop, probably for lower wages. Certainly the earnings of agricultural labourers were well below those of factory hands. Before long **hand-workers** like cottage spinners and weavers were either forced out of work by the competition of the new machines, or toiled night and day to make a bare living, in conditions that would have shocked a factory inspector. Their only real advantage was independence. They were free to start and stop when they chose. It was the *discipline* in the factories that the town workers hated most of all; the regular hours and strict rules and regulations laid down by the employers. Heavy fines were imposed for the most trivial offences, such as whistling or 'leaving an oil can out of place'.

Not all the early **factory-masters** grew rich through ill-treatment of the poor. Some of them, like Robert Peel (senior) and Robert Owen (see Chapters 11 and 12) showed that it was possible to make good profits while, at the same time, considering the welfare of their workers. Benjamin Gott even set up his own scheme of social insurance. Old employees were retained as pensioners and part- or full-time wages were paid to workers absent through sickness or injury. Gott encouraged the regular attendance of children at Sunday school and even prohibited the use of the cane or whip. But humane employers like Peel, Owen and Gott were few and far between. In most cases there was an urgent need for new laws to control factory conditions and hours of work. The Factory Acts, by which Parliament gradually took on these responsibilities, are described in Chapter 11.

Timeline

1721	John and Thomas Lombe's silk-throwing mill.
1733	John Kay's 'flying shuttle'.
1738	Lewis Paul's roller-spinning machine.
1765	James Hargreaves' 'spinning-jenny'.
1768	Richard Arkwright's 'water frame'.
1771	Arkwright's factory at Cromford.
1779	Samuel Crompton's 'mule'.
1785	Steam power first used in spinning.
1785–9	Reverend Edmund Cartwright's 'power loom'.
1793	Elias Whitney's 'gin'.
1793	Benjamin Gott's factory in Leeds.

See *Further Study of the Industrial Revolution* at the end of Chapter 8, p. 92.

7 The New Iron Age
Industrial Revolution 2

Iron was the key to the whole Industrial Revolution. Without great advances in both the quality and quantity of iron, mechanisation in other industries would have been severely restricted. At the beginning of our period the British iron industry was relatively backward, well behind countries like Sweden and Germany. Yet, as a result of a series of technical improvements, Britain soon led the world in the *mass production* of iron and iron goods.

The stages in production and the problem of fuel

There were two main branches of the industry. The first consisted of **mining** and **smelting** (melting, to separate the metal from the ore). These were usually carried out close together, to avoid transport difficulties. The ore was smelted in an open-topped blast-furnace, built of brick or stone. Charcoal was used for fuel, mixed with lime-stone or clay to help remove the impurities. The molten iron was then run off into sandy moulds called 'pigs' (their shape resembled a sow feeding her piglets).

The main areas of mining and smelting were where the necessary raw materials could all be found fairly close together—iron ore, timber (for converting into charcoal fuel), and swift-flowing streams (water power was often used to drive the bellows which stirred up the flames in the furnace). Around 1700 the main iron-smelting areas were Sussex, the Forest of Dean (Gloucestershire and Herefordshire) the West Midlands, South Wales and the district round Sheffield.

Some goods were made of **cast iron,** a process which was really a continuation of smelting and therefore carried on in foundries next to the blast-furnaces. The pigs were simply re-melted and ladled into moulds of the required shape. But cast iron contained a lot of carbon and other impurities which made it very brittle. It could only be used for a limited range of manufactures, such as cannon, cooking-pots, stoves and grates. Most of the pigs went through further stages of refining, during which impurities were removed and 'wrought' or 'bar iron' was produced.

The second branch of the industry was the working of the metal. This was done by the **smith** at his forge. By continued hammering and re-heating he produced **wrought iron,** which was less hard than cast iron but much more supple and workable. It was then made into tools, weapons and a whole range of hardware, including nails, millions of which were made annually at a time when ships, many houses, and even machines were almost entirely made of wood. Water power was often employed for lifting hammers in the larger forges, and coal was used for heating the metal, as well as charcoal. Therefore the smithing trades were already becoming located near fast-flowing rivers and coal-mines at the beginning of our period.

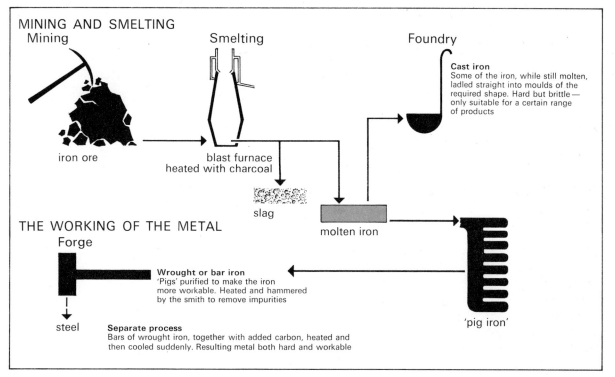

MINING AND SMELTING

Mining   Smelting   Foundry

iron ore

blast furnace
heated with charcoal

slag

molten iron

Cast iron
Some of the iron, while still molten,
ladled straight into moulds of the
required shape. Hard but brittle —
only suitable for a certain range
of products

THE WORKING OF THE METAL

Forge

steel

'pig iron'

Wrought or bar iron
'Pigs' purified to make the iron
more workable. Heated and hammered
by the smith to remove impurities

Separate process
Bars of wrought iron, together with added carbon, heated and
then cooled suddenly. Resulting metal both hard and workable

The two main metal-working centres were the districts round Birmingham and Sheffield. **Birmingham** was already well known for its ironmongery. Great quantities of locks, bolts, pins, buttons, nails and the like were produced in backyard workshops by skilled craftsmen with the aid of a few simple tools. Frequently the whole family worked together. Children of five or six were not too young to help in the family trade, even if they mostly ran errands. **Sheffield** had gained a reputation for fine **steel** cutlery, scissors, hammers, files and other tools. Steel was made from bar iron by heating it with charcoal to add a little carbon. (It was a separate process, and is therefore left to the last section of the chapter.)

By 1700 Britain's iron industry faced a serious difficulty. The production of pig iron was diminishing every year. The reason was a grave **shortage of charcoal,** which was at that time the only fuel used in the blast-furnace. Timber was scarce and was used for many other things besides making charcoal, including shipbuilding, on which the nation's safety and prosperity depended. Parliament had passed laws to restrict the felling of trees for charcoal-burning ever since the end of the sixteenth century. Thus by 1720 there were only about sixty blast-furnaces still working in England, where before there had been hundreds. Their total output was much less than that of *one* modern furnace, and barely supplied half the country's requirements.

Thus Britain's great natural deposits of iron ore were almost entirely unworked. Many had been abandoned because the woodlands

The stages in Iron
Production

Abraham Darby's iron-works at Coalbrookdale

around them had been felled. With the demand for iron goods increasing rapidly, the smiths had no alternative but to import large quantities of pig and bar iron from Sweden and Russia. Unless a new fuel for smelting could be found, Britain's hardware industry might have to rely entirely on imported pig iron. The obvious answer to the problem seemed to lie in the use of 'pit coal' instead of charcoal. After all, Britain was rich in deposits of coal and it was already widely used by smiths, as well as by glass-makers, brewers, brick-makers and others. Unfortunately, countless attempts to smelt with coal had failed. Its sulphur compounds made the pig iron brittle and unworkable.

The Darby family and coke-smelting

In 1708 **Abraham Darby** (1677–1717), a Quaker ironmaster, moved to Coalbrookdale in Shropshire and took over an old iron-works there. In the following year, he tried, like many others before him, to find a new fuel for smelting. His efforts were described, many years later, in a letter written by his daughter-in-law: 'He first try'd with raw coal as it came out of the mines, but it did not answer. He not discouraged, had the coal coak'd into cynder, as is done for drying malt, and it then succeeded to his satisfaction.' **Coke,** which finally solved the problem, is almost pure carbon, like charcoal. But,

*un*like charcoal, it could be produced cheaply and in great quantities. It became the basis for a new Iron Age, but not for another half a century.

The pigs produced in Darby's coke furnace were only suitable for casting. This made his discovery less useful because the most urgent need was for pig iron of a kind which could easily be converted into wrought iron. It was really the work of his son, another **Abraham Darby** (1711–63), that opened the way for a great expansion of iron-smelting in the second half of the eighteenth century. Abraham Darby II was not satisfied with his father's method of coking the coal in heaps (like charcoal-burning). He used coking-*ovens,* which produced a superior form of coke. He also strengthened the bellows, to give a stronger blast during smelting. The quality of the resulting pig iron was improved to the extent that it was now suitable for refining into bar iron at the forge.

From about 1760 onwards, mining and smelting became centralised in areas where good supplies of both coal and iron ore were available—South Wales, the West Midlands, South Yorkshire, the North-East of England and Central Scotland. With the exception of the Midlands, all of these areas had the advantage of being near the sea, which made transportation easier. The Darby family's business continued to flourish under **the third Abraham Darby** (1750–91). He built the world's first iron bridge (1779) across the river Severn, south of

The world's first iron bridge (1779). It still stands across the River Severn at Ironbridge, Shropshire

Coalbrookdale. It was eight yards wide and a hundred yards long, made entirely of cast iron. A small town grew up close by it and was appropriately named Ironbridge.

The importance of coke-smelting to the British iron industry can be seen in the following figures:

British output of pig iron

1750	below	30,000 tons
1788	approx.	68,000 tons
1804	approx.	250,000 tons

'Puddling' and 'rolling'

No sooner had the advances in coke-smelting made possible the mass production of pig iron than a new problem arose. The next stage in the process—the conversion of the pigs into bar iron—was now slow by comparison. In other words, the 'bottleneck' which had previously existed in the smelting stage was now transferred to the process of forging wrought iron. A way of removing this bottleneck was found by **Henry Cort** (1740–1800) who had set up a forge near Portsmouth and was under contract to the Admiralty to supply wrought iron goods to the Royal Navy. In 1783 and 1784 he took out patents for two inventions which together could turn large quantities of pig iron into good quality bar iron, without the need for heating and hammering at the forge.

Puddling, the first of Cort's processes, required a 'reverberatory' furnace, with two main sections, separated by a bridge. On one side was a fireplace and on the other a sandy hearth where the pigs were placed. By keeping the fire and the metal separate, Cort found he could use raw coal without any risk of spoiling the iron. The flames swept over the bridge on their way to the outlet (flue) and melted the pigs by striking down (reverberating) from the roof of the chamber. To help drive off the remaining impurities, workmen stirred ('puddled') the molten iron with long bars (rabbles) through an opening in the front of the furnace.

When it was purified, the iron became spongy and was formed into balls (loops) by the puddler. These were taken out with tongs and,

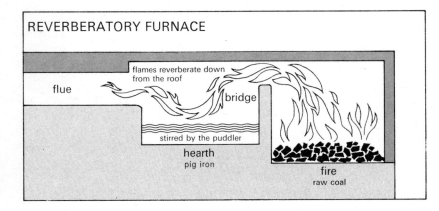

REVERBERATORY FURNACE

flue

flames reverberate down
from the roof

bridge

stirred by the puddler

hearth
pig iron

fire
raw coal

Henry Cort's puddling process

Puddlers at work. Notice the hot rabbles cooling in trays of water

after the slag had been separated, the loops went to the **rolling-mill** — the second of Cort's processes. Here the iron, still hot, was passed between grooved rollers. The rollers were shaped in such a way that the iron took the shape of the space left between them, for example that of a rail. Therefore, by a single operation, an iron bar or sheet, according to what was required, could be produced quickly and cheaply from a mass of iron. It had previously taken about twelve hours to forge one ton of bar iron by heating and hammering. Now the same amount was rolled in three-quarters of an hour.

Cort's mass-production methods were quickly taken up by other forge-masters, and, before long, the output of bar iron kept pace with pig iron production. Puddling and rolling enabled the iron industry to cope with the increasing demands being put upon it by the end of the eighteenth century. There was hardly an industry, from farming to shipbuilding, that did not benefit from cheap mass-produced wrought iron. For example, the early machines in textiles had been made almost entirely of wood, but the later iron ones were much longer wearing and far more accurate. Forge-masters could now manage entirely without charcoal fuel, so the production of finished iron goods became completely centralised in the coalfield areas, alongside the blast-furnaces. More large-scale businesses developed, with one company often controlling all the stages of manufacture and situating them next to each other.

The great ironmasters

Just as the textile inventions produced great mill-owners, so the new techniques in iron-making saw the rise of rich and powerful iron-masters—men like **John Wilkinson** (1728–1805). He was not an inventor, but, just like Richard Arkwright, he was quick to take note of new ideas and use them for profit. Wilkinson was the first to exploit Abraham Darby II's improved coke-smelting process on a large scale. He was also one of the first to employ a Watt steam-engine, instead of a water-wheel, for working the bellows of the blast-furnace (1775). He and his brother William controlled three large ironworks at **Bersham,** near Chester; **Broseley** in Shropshire, and **Bradley** in South Staffordshire. The last two were established during the Seven Years War (1756–63) largely as a result of government contracts for weapons, especially cannon.

Throughout his remarkable career, Wilkinson's industrial 'empire' went on growing. Apart from his own ironworks, he controlled coal-mines and had financial interests in Welsh foundries and Cornish tin-mines. He even owned two farms, on which he introduced the first steam threshing-machines. Like some other important businessmen of the period, he issued his own coinage in those areas where he was an employer. Copper and silver 'tokens' and guinea notes, stamped with his profile and inscribed 'JOHN WILKINSON, IRONMASTER', were in use in several Midland and Western counties between 1787 and 1808. It was the great business skill and tireless energy of men like Wilkinson that put Britain far ahead of her industrial rivals by the early nineteenth century.

'Iron-mad' Wilkinson believed that iron would eventually replace most of the materials then in use. He personally did much to extend its range of uses. He helped Abraham Darby III to build the first iron bridge (1779) and, eight years later, he successfully launched a boat made of bolted iron plates. Most people had thought this impossible but, as Wilkinson later wrote: 'It answers all my expectations, and has convinced the unbelievers, who were nine hundred and ninety-nine in a thousand.' He followed this up by making forty miles of cast iron pipes for the water supply of Paris (1788). Even then he had not exhausted his ideas for new uses of iron. He built a cast iron chapel for the Methodists at Bradley and, when he died, he was buried in an iron coffin.

Each of the main centres of iron production could boast of at least one great ironmaster, although none of them could rival the wealth of John Wilkinson of the West Midlands. In South Yorkshire there was **Samuel Walker** of **Rotherham,** famous as a manufacturer of 'cast steel'. He began with a small forge 'in an old nail-shop' in 1741, yet by persistent hard work, left a small fortune to his sons some forty years later. He greatly helped the progress of agriculture in the Midlands with his 'Rotherham plough', which had a cast iron coulter (cutting-piece).

Meanwhile, South Wales was becoming one of the great iron

John Wilkinson's own
coinage (front and back)

centres, with plentiful resources of coal and iron ore and easy access to the sea. Its greatest ironmaster was **Richard Crawshay,** often called 'the Iron King'. At his **Cyfarthfa** works in Merthyr Tydfil, he was one of the first to use Cort's puddling process in the 1780s. Less than twenty years later he was employing 2000 workers at Cyfarthfa, and Merthyr Tydfil had grown from a village to an industrial town. In 1840 the Crawshays' business was described as 'the largest in the kingdom'.

Scotland's modern iron industry was founded in 1760 at **Carron,** near Falkirk, by **Dr John Roebuck.** Like Wilkinson, Roebuck saw the opportunity to profit from the demand for munitions during the Seven Years War. The site for the Carron works was well chosen. There were great quantities of coal and iron ore on the spot and the Firth of Forth was nearby. Roebuck went bankrupt in 1773, having taken on too many projects at once, but the works continued to prosper under the Carron Company. It soon became famous all over Europe for its manufacture of weapons; especially naval guns called 'carronades'. A French visitor to Carron (1784) was greatly impressed by 'huge cranes, every kind of windlass, lever and tackle for moving heavy loads . . . darting flames leaping from the blast-furnaces . . . heavy hammers striking the echoing anvils and the shrill whistling of the air pumps', and likened it to 'a volcano in eruption'.

Hot blast and steam hammer

By the end of the eighteenth century, Britain's iron industry was second to none. The mass-production methods of Abraham Darby and Henry Cort were the basis for the 'revolution in iron'. But there was still plenty of room for further improvements; two of which deserve special mention.

The first concerned the smelting process. As blast-furnaces got bigger, the strength of the air blast from the bellows was often insufficient. Water-powered bellows were replaced by steam-driven blowing engines from the 1770s onwards, yet this was not a complete answer to the problem. It was not until 1828 that **James Neilson,** Manager of Glasgow Gas Works, hit upon the idea of heating the air *before* it entered the furnace. It had always been believed that a very cool blast was essential for making good quality iron. Neilson, on the other hand, pre-heated the air to several hundred degrees centigrade—with the result that it expanded and greatly increased the force of the blast. The **Hot Blast** had the extra advantage of saving fuel. *Cold* air from the bellows lowered the temperature inside the furnace, but Neilson's blast, which was so hot it could melt lead, made it possible to use far less coke. Moreover, raw coal of the cheapest quality could be used for heating the air because it did not come into contact with the iron. Seven or eight tons of coal had been used previously to produce a ton of pig iron; now only five tons of coal were needed.

Meanwhile, the forging branch of the industry could not afford to stand still. By the 1830s, developments like iron bridges and the building of the first ocean-going steamships (see Chapter 13) meant there was a demand for iron bars of increasing size and weight. In response to this need, a Manchester engineer, **James Nasmyth,** invented a great **steam hammer** (1839) which could make forgings of greater size than ever before. A heavy iron hammer-head was driven downwards by steam which, added to the force of gravity, enabled blows of great force to be delivered. The gap between the raised hammer-head and the anvil was large enough to take a paddle-wheel shaft for a steamship.

Cast steel

Steel is bar iron blended with a little carbon to make it harder yet still flexible. Nowadays it has replaced iron in the manufacture of a wide range of articles, but before the 1850s it was too costly to be in general use. At the beginning of the eighteenth century the average steel furnace, where bar iron and charcoal were heated together in clay pots, took nearly three weeks to produce ten tons of 'blister steel'. This was uneven in quality, being harder on its blistered surface than it was nearer the centre.

Benjamin Huntsman, a Yorkshire clock-maker, was not satisfied with the quality of most of the steel he had to use. He decided to look

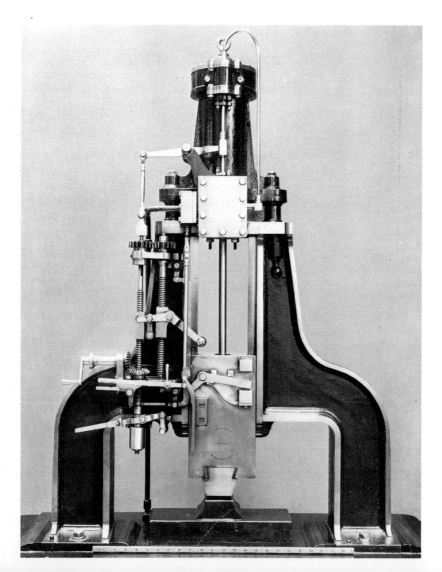

Model of James Nasmyth's steam hammer

Preparing crucibles for casting steel

for a better way of making it, and, after many experiments, he succeeded some time in the 1740s. He put pieces of blister steel and a little charcoal in closed fireclay pots or *crucibles*. He then burned away all the impurities at a very high temperature in a coke-fired furnace. The resulting **cast steel** was of exceptionally high quality, suitable for articles like clock springs and razor blades as well as cutlery and edge tools.

The early British advances in factory engineering, which followed some years later, owed much to Huntsman's discovery. The quality of cast steel has never been bettered since, and a few Sheffield firms still make it today. But, because it could only be produced in small quantities and was therefore costly, the steel trade continued on a small scale in comparison with iron. It was not until the 1850s, a century after Huntsman's process was perfected, that further invention led to the mass production of cheap steel (see Chapter 15).

Timeline

1709   Abraham Darby I's coke-smelting process.
1740s   Benjamin Huntsman's 'crucible casting process'.
1779   The first iron bridge (Abraham Darby III).
1783–4 Henry Cort's puddling and rolling.
1787   The first iron boat (John Wilkinson).
1828   James Neilson's hot blast.
1839   James Nasmyth's steam hammer.

Further study

See *Further Study of the Industrial Revolution* at the end of Chapter 8, p. 92.

8 The Triumph of Steam
Industrial Revolution 3

Water-wheels provided the main form of motive power in the early stages of the Industrial Revolution. They had been in use for centuries, first to grind corn in flour-mills, later to drive the mallets of fulling-mills (where cloth was beaten to thicken and cleanse it), and then to work the bellows and hammers of furnaces and forges. By the second half of the eighteenth century, wheelwrights were making huge water-wheels for cotton-mills and ironworks. The one that worked the forge-bellows at the Cyfarthfa works was fifty-two feet in diameter. Wheels of this size could power large factories, *but* only in areas where there were good streams of swiftly flowing water. Manufacturers needed a new kind of motive power if they were to have greater freedom in choosing sites for their factories. Steam was the answer. The introduction of steam-driven machinery was, without question, the greatest single achievement of the whole Industrial Revolution.

Raising water by fire

The possibility of using the expanding force of steam had been realised nearly 2000 years earlier by the Greeks. But not until the seventeenth century did experiments with steam begin to lead to a practical invention. In 1690, a Frenchman named Denis Papin produced a 'steam-atmospheric engine'. It was the first to have a cylinder (combined with a boiler) and a piston which was driven up by steam pressure and down by the force of the atmosphere after the steam in the cylinder was condensed. Eight years later, an Englishman, **Thomas Savery,** used the same principles to construct the first 'fire'- or steam-engine to be used for industrial purposes. Savery came from Cornwall, where flooding in the tin- and copper-mines was a serious problem, and his invention was a simple pump designed to overcome this difficulty. However, in practice, his 'Engine to raise Water by Fire' was not powerful enough to drain the deeper mines.

It was left to **Thomas Newcomen,** a locksmith and blacksmith from nearby Dartmouth, to improve on Savery's pump in 1705–6. His **steam-atmospheric engine** was the first to be widely used in industry. Steam from the boiler was fed into an open-topped cylinder through a valve. Meanwhile, the piston rose, under the weight of the pump-rods, until a jet of cold water from the cistern caused the steam in the cylinder to condense. A vacuum, or absence of air, was thus created underneath the piston which caused the atmospheric pressure above to force it back to the bottom of the cylinder. As it sank it pulled its end of the beam down and the pump-handle at the opposite end up. The repetition of this see-saw motion sucked the water from the mine-shaft. In the original design, the steam was condensed by the application of cold water *outside* the cylinder, but, in later models, condensation was speeded up by injecting the water *inside* so that

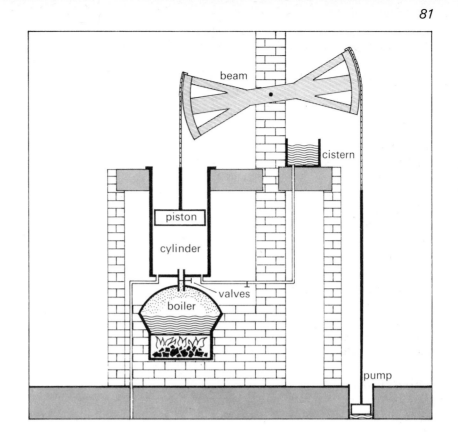

Thomas Newcomen's
steam-atmospheric engine

it came into direct contact with the steam.

Newcomen's first models were clumsy and inefficient. It was not yet possible to manufacture the parts with precision, so much power was lost through inaccurately bored cylinders and ill-fitting valves. Nevertheless, soon after 1711, when a company was formed to build and sell the engines, their most serious faults were overcome and they came into fairly general use. They were most popular in the coal-mines of the Midlands and the North-East, but some sold as far afield as the Continent. They could pump water from a considerable depth, and thus made possible the working of deeper mines. By the 1770s, about 100 Newcomen engines were at work in the Northumberland and Durham coalfield alone. They were also used for supplying water to London and other large towns, and, indirectly, for blowing blast-furnaces by raising water to drive a wheel. Abraham Darby II installed one for this purpose at Coalbrookdale.

The career of James Watt

It is often said that **James Watt** (1736–1819) invented the steam-engine. This is partly true, since he was the first to design an engine driven entirely by steam, without the aid of atmospheric pressure. But such a statement is misleading, because Watt took Newcomen's pump as his starting-point and built upon the foundations of a century of research. Much more misleading, however, is Watt's own story that his first invention resulted from a sudden flash of inspiration.

He knew very well that all his ideas depended firstly upon long study and careful experiment. He could have achieved nothing without a thorough grounding in mechanics and scientific theory. Born in 1736 at Greenock, near Glasgow, he was the grandson of a mathematics teacher. His father, an architect and shipbuilder, made sure James had a sound education, which enabled him to set up in business at the age of twenty-one as a scientific instrument maker. His workshop was in the grounds of Glasgow University, from which he kept in touch with the main scientific developments of the time.

Among the apparatus belonging to the University was a demonstration model of a Newcomen engine. In 1763 Watt was asked to repair it. While doing so he was struck by its inefficiency. Each time water was injected into the cylinder, much of the next intake of steam was wasted in re-heating the cylinder to the necessary 100 degrees centigrade. Watt's solution was a **separate condenser** (1765) into which steam could be drawn from the cylinder after each upward thrust of the piston. He explained his reasoning as follows: 'To avoid useless condensation, *the vessel in which the steam acted upon the piston ought always to be as hot as the steam itself* . . . (therefore) the steam must be condensed in a *separate* vessel, which might be cooled (with water) to as low a degree as was necessary without affecting the cylinder.' The result was a great saving of steam, so that much less fuel was needed.

James Watt

This first improvement led to an even more important one. Watt thought of fixing an airtight cover on the cylinder and using steam 'to act upon the piston in place of the atmosphere'. He therefore began to experiment with a **valve-box,** which could inject steam into the cylinder on *both* sides of the piston alternately.

Watt required financial support in order to manufacture his improved steam pump and continue with his experiments. In 1768 he had the good fortune to be taken into partnership by **John Roebuck,** founder of the Carron ironworks. Watt's first engine, called 'Beelzebub', was patented and set up near Edinburgh in 1769. Its production raised many problems. The engineers at Carron were unable to make sufficiently accurate cylinders and closely fitting pistons. It would take time to develop the necessary skills. Meanwhile, 'Beelzebub' never worked properly and had to be given up. To make matters worse, Roebuck was soon in great financial difficulties and went bankrupt in 1773.

Watt's invention, still far from complete, was rescued by the foresight of **Matthew Boulton** (1728–1809) a successful hardware manufacturer from Birmingham. He was a friend of both Watt and Roebuck, and had taken a special interest in Watt's work. Roebuck owed Boulton £1200. When he went bankrupt, Boulton offered to let him off the debt in exchange for his two-thirds share in the partnership with Watt. Therefore, in 1774, Watt came down from Scotland to settle near Boulton's **Soho** factory, north of Birmingham. The Soho works had already won a European reputation for quality, using only the best materials and the most skilled workmen. It was this accuracy of workmanship, combined with Watt's inventive genius, which soon made the firm of Boulton and Watt one of the most famous in the history of engineering. Able assistance was given by John Wilkinson, who had just patented a new method of boring cannon (1774). This he used to manufacture precision-bored cylinders for Watt's engines.

The trial engine was rebuilt, with more accurate parts. Soon afterwards, Watt wrote to his father, in a hopeful mood: 'The fire engine I have invented is now going and answers much better than any other that has yet been made.' In 1775 his patent was renewed for twenty-five years, and the first Soho engines were delivered to customers, one of them to Wilkinson's Broseley works. Forty engines were erected in the next five years, most of them in the Cornish tin- and copper-mines. Owners of coal-mines had less to gain from changing to Watt's engine, because the saving of fuel was not so important when there was plenty of it on the spot.

Matthew Boulton's Soho works

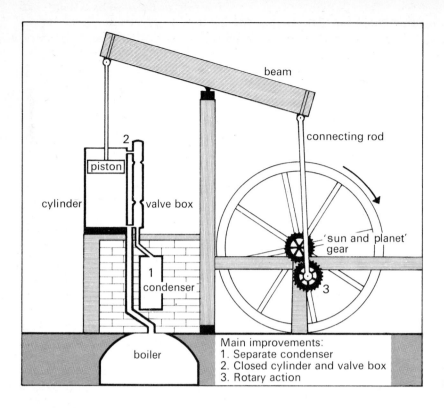

beam

connecting rod

2

piston

cylinder

valve box

'sun and planet' gear

1
condenser

3

boiler

Main improvements:
1. Separate condenser
2. Closed cylinder and valve box
3. Rotary action

James Watt's rotative steam engine.

At this stage Watt's engine was still only a pump. If it had not been developed further its influence on British industry would have been relatively small. It was the invention of **rotary motion** (1781) which really began the Age of Steam. This was based on the simple principle of fixing the beam to a connecting rod which turned a flywheel. By attaching a belt to the wheel, steam power could be used to work all kinds of machinery. In the early models, the connecting rod had a cogwheel at the end. This was geared to another cogwheel, which was attached to the flywheel itself and rotated with it. This part of the invention—the 'sun and planet gear'—was suggested by **William Murdock,** foreman at Soho. Murdock, a self-taught engineer from Scotland, played a major part in the success of the firm and made some important discoveries of his own. He was the first Briton to build a steam locomotive (1784) and the first to use coal-gas for lighting. (The Soho works was lit by gas as early as 1798.)

The 'rotative engine' greatly extended the range of uses of steam. It was first employed to drive bellows, rollers and hammers in the making of iron. Shortly afterwards, the first steam spinning-mill was set up in Nottinghamshire (1785). By 1800 Boulton and Watt had also erected engines in sugar-refineries, waterworks, flour-mills and breweries— in fact, almost anywhere where coal could be got at a reasonable price. Their patent allowed them a monopoly in the years 1775–1800, and they took full advantage of it, erecting more than 300 engines all over Britain, most of them of the rotary type. When the patent expired, they handed over the business to their sons and spent their last years in ease and comfort. It was just a matter of time before rotative engines replaced water-wheels in most industries. Although water power was still supreme in 1800, by the 1830s the Steam Age was in full swing. Large-scale industry, freed from its dependence on rivers, was becoming concentrated in coalfield towns.

Changes in the coal industry

The development of the steam-engine, together with the new mass production methods in the iron industry, meant the output of coal had to be greatly increased. The central importance of coal in the Industrial Revolution can be seen geographically. Almost without exception, the new manufacturing towns grew up in areas where large deposits of coal lay under the surface.

In 1700 small quantities of coal were already being mined in most of the present day coalfields. Large deposits could still be found on the surface in many areas. Because of transport difficulties, most of the output was used in or near the mining districts for domestic fires, but coal fuel was also used in brewing, soap- and brick-making, forging and sugar-refining.

The **North-East** of England, around the valleys of the rivers Tyne and Wear, was the chief coal-mining area. Since the sixteenth century, most of its output had been shipped to London, where it was known as 'sea coal'. By 1705 the north-eastern coal trade employed over 1200 ships of various kinds and was looked upon as 'the nursery of the English navy'. This same coalfield saw the first 'rail-ways' in Britain. They were wooden wagon-ways, along which horses pulled trucks of coal to the loading quays (staiths) on the rivers. At the staiths, the coal was loaded into riverboats (keels) and carried to the main ports, like Newcastle and Sunderland, where it was transferred into coastal vessels called 'colliers'.

A Boulton and Watt rotative engine, built in 1788. On view in London's Science Museum

Very few mine-shafts went down beyond 200 or 300 feet in the early eighteenth century, and it was rare for more than forty or fifty miners to be employed in one pit. However, as time went by, shafts had to be sunk deeper to keep pace with the rising demand for coal. This, in turn, increased the **hazards of mining**—floods, fire and poisonous air. Attempts to reduce these dangers and difficulties in the eighteenth and early nineteenth centuries met with varying degrees of success.

Drainage was the first problem to be tackled seriously. In 1700 the usual method was to use a chain of buckets, often worked by a horse. But this was too slow, and only suitable for shallow workings. It was Newcomen's steam-atmospheric engine which made possible the drainage of deep mines, not only for coal, but also tin and copper.

Most mines contain harmful **gases,** like 'fire damp' (methane). These are liable to explode if they are not dispersed by currents of fresh air. In the eighteenth century, explosions were so frequent and the loss of life so great that it was not usual for inquests to be held on the victims of pit disasters. At Chester-le-Street, County Durham, in 1708, a particularly violent explosion killed a hundred miners and did '. . . great damage to many houses and persons for several miles around. One man was blown quite out of the mouth of the shaft, which is fifty fathom [300 feet] and found at a prodigious [great] distance from the place'. No wonder mining had a reputation for being the most dangerous way to earn a living!

The traditional method of **ventilation** was to sink two shafts at different levels and draw fresh air down one while foul air was

The pithead of a Staffordshire coal mine

forced up the other. The draught was often drawn through the mine by a series of trapdoors, operated by small children crouching in the darkness. Alternatively, a brazier full of burning coals could be hung in the 'up' shaft to create rising convection currents. But such methods were not satisfactory in deep mines. At the end of the eighteenth century **John Buddle,** a mining engineer from Wallsend, near Newcastle, invented an 'exhaust fan' to ventilate larger pits. It drew the bad air out of the 'up' shaft by suction, and this, in turn, caused a current of fresh air to descend down the other shaft.

A great threat to miners was the open candles they took underground. A naked flame could explode 'fire damp' without any warning. Early in the nineteenth century several 'safety lamps' were invented which greatly reduced this hazard. The most famous was that of **Sir Humphrey Davy** (1815) which won a prize from the Royal Society. It shielded the flame with a fine metal gauze, which allowed enough air to get in yet so reduced the heat of the flame that it could not explode any gas outside. If gas was present the flame merely turned blue, which provided a useful warning. The miners' safety lamp helped to increase the output of coal because it made possible the working of pits which had previously been thought too dangerous. Davy could have made a fortune if he had taken out a patent, but he refused, saying: 'I am only too happy to have been able to help our miners. That is my reward.'

Several other improvements helped to increase output, even though the actual cutting of the coal was still done by pick and shovel. Instead of leaving pillars of coal uncut in order to support the ceilings of the galleries, wooden **pit-props** began to be used in the late eighteenth century. By this time pit ponies hauled trucks on some of the main underground passages, although in the smaller galleries women and children still had to get down on all fours and harness trucks to their waists. Watt's rotative engine was ideal for hauling coal to the surface and was a great improvement on the traditional method whereby women and girls carried baskets up a series of ladders. In one case they had to climb a distance equal to the height of St Paul's Cathedral! **Steam haulage** was not, however, in general use until the introduction of wire cables in the 1840s— after which shafts of up to 1000 feet could be worked.

The steady increase in the size and number of pits, together with the technical improvements, enabled the coal industry to keep up with the new demands put upon it. Coal output increased by 400 per cent in the eighteenth century, and by a further 250 per cent in the next thirty years.

British coal production (approximate figures)

1700	2,500,000 tons
1800	10,000,000 tons
1830	25,000,000 tons

Josiah Wedgwood and 'The Potteries'
In general, it was the major industries—especially iron and textiles— which were the first to be revolutionised. But an outstanding

Two original Davy safety lamps (on view in London's Science Museum)

A Wedgwood tea service

exception was the pottery industry of North Staffordshire, which established a worldwide reputation well before 1800.

The making of earthenware pots and jars had been a cottage industry for centuries in **The Potteries** – the district round Stoke-on-Trent – where turf ovens were fed with local clay mixed with charcoal fuel. In the mid eighteenth century, however, the pottery industry began to undergo a series of rapid changes. There were three main reasons for this. First, there was a new demand for fine quality earthenware, due to the growing popularity of tea and coffee drinking. By 1765 nine families out of ten drank tea at least twice a day. Second, it was discovered in the 1760s that white Cornish clay (kaolin) could be mixed with china stone to produce porcelain – a highly valued, fine earthenware. Third, the industry was transformed by the inventiveness and business skill of **Josiah Wedgwood** (1730–95) the most famous potter in British history.

The modern pottery industry really dates from 1769, the year in which Wedgwood opened his new **Etruria** works, near Burslem. (It was named after the ancient Etruscans, whose vases and urns inspired many of his own designs.) At Etruria, Wedgwood greatly increased the output per man by means of a 'division of labour'. In other words, he subdivided all the traditional skills of the potter – mixing, shaping, firing and glazing – and allocated each to specialist workers, who concentrated on the one operation. Although he later introduced steam-engines for mixing clay and grinding flints, most of the processes in his factory continued to be done by hand. His superior production methods, together with his new designs, colours and glazes, enabled him to improve the quality not only of fine, ornamental china, but also the ordinary earthenware in everyday use. Even the simplest articles were attractive and well finished – like his famous 'willow pattern', which was soon being used in hundreds of thousands of British homes.

Few industries have owed so much to one man. Wedgwood was one of the keenest supporters of the Grand Trunk Canal (see Chapter

9) which linked the river Trent with the west coast via the Mersey (1777). He put a great deal of his own money into the scheme, for he realised how much it would benefit the pottery trade.

Survival of the old handicrafts

By the early nineteenth century, Britain held a long lead over the rest of the world as an industrial nation. But the speed of change should not be exaggerated. As a writer of the time, William Eden, said in 1797: 'With regard to mechanical knowledge, it is probable that we are still in our infancy . . . fifty years hence some new contrivance may be thought of in comparison with which the steam-engine and spinning-jennies . . . will be considered as slight and insignificant discoveries.' Although we could not regard the steam-engine as an 'insignificant' discovery, Eden was correct in thinking that the industrial advances of his lifetime were only a beginning. Even in 1830, when the use of steam power was well established, machines had replaced skilled hands in only a few industries. Half the population still lived in the countryside, where life was often much the same as it had been a century or more before.

Handicrafts continued to flourish. (Even today, in an important industry like building, masons, bricklayers, carpenters and plasterers still use many traditional tools and old-fashioned methods.)

Shipbuilding was one of the most vital industries in the early nineteenth century, yet it was only just beginning to be affected by the Industrial Revolution. Shipwrights and sail-makers still worked in small yards, and most boats were made of wood before 1850. Even in the regions round Birmingham, Manchester and Glasgow, where the most advanced industries were centralised, **small workshops** predominated until well into the nineteenth century. While handloom-weavers resisted the introduction of the power loom until the 1840s, thousands of blacksmiths, nail-makers, cutlers and other metalworkers

A traditional nail forge

earned a living at the forge, using anvil, hammer, chisel and file like their grandfathers.

The Industrial Revolution set the pattern for the future, but in the early nineteenth century factory workers and machine-minders were only a small proportion of Britain's total working population.

The industrial towns

In areas where the growth of factory industry was most rapid, villages and hamlets became manufacturing towns almost overnight. The earliest and most dramatic changes came in Lancashire. Bolton, which in the 1750s consisted of 'a single rough and ill-paved street, with thatched cottages', had a population of 17,000 by the end of

Nineteenth century slums

the century. In the same period Oldham grew from a village of about 300 inhabitants to a town of 12,000. At the other end of the scale, **Manchester** became one of the world's greatest industrial and commercial centres. Although there had been a settlement on its site since Roman times, Manchester's population in 1700 was below 10,000. Yet in the first census (1801) it was the largest British town outside London, with 95,000 inhabitants. The introduction of steam-powered machinery was the chief factor in this remarkable growth. In 1786 only one chimney rose above the town—that of Arkwright's mill—yet, just fifteen years later, there were fifty mills in Manchester. In the next twenty years, while Manchester's population exceeded 150,000, Glasgow, Liverpool and Birmingham rose above the 100,000 mark. None of these had been of any great size or importance a century before.

In the rush to put up factories and rows of workers' dwellings, many important services were neglected. There were no proper building regulations and no sanitary inspectors, with the result that houses were often damp; streets were unpaved and full of holes; proper sewers were almost unheard of; there was no collection of refuse, and drinking-water was so scarce that if often had to be bought from street traders. Not surprisingly, epidemic diseases like cholera and typhoid frequently swept through these towns. As soon as new houses were built, the overflowing population reduced them to crowded, disease-ridden **slums.** Seeing the chance to make quick profits, builders put up as many houses as space would permit, using materials of the cheapest quality. Rows of dwellings were often built 'back-to-back', which meant that through ventilation was impossible and parts of the houses received no direct light. In the older towns, like Manchester and Liverpool, larger tenement houses were each crammed with several families, and even waterlogged cellars were let as separate dwellings.

Much of the reforming activity of Parliament in the years to come was concerned with the social problems created by the new industrial towns. The first attempts to control public health and housing are dealt with in Chapter 16.

Timeline
1698   Thomas Savery's 'fire engine'.
1705–6 Thomas Newcomen's steam-atmospheric engine.
1765   James Watt invents the separate condenser.
1769   Josiah Wedgwood's Etruria works opened.
1774   Watt begins his partnership with Matthew Boulton.
1781   Watt invents the rotative engine.
1815   Humphrey Davy's miners' safety lamp.

Further study of the Industrial Revolution
This section treats the last three chapters as a single unit. The story of industrial change continues in Chapter 15, where particular attention is given to advances in steel production and engineering and the development of electric power in the nineteenth and early twentieth centuries.

Visits

The Science Museum at South Kensington (Exhibition Road, London SW7) has a world-famous collection of scientific, engineering and industrial exhibits, both historical and modern.

Lower ground floor: Coal-mining; collection of miners' safety lamps (including Davy's); reconstruction of a wheelwright's shop.

Ground floor: The Motive Power section contains numerous examples of steam-engines, from Savery onwards. A Boulton and Watt rotative engine can often be seen working.

First floor: Iron—including pig iron production and the making of wrought iron from pig iron; textiles—including a replica of a spinning-jenny, the original wooden model of the water frame, and models of Crompton's mule and an early power loom.

Many other museums, all over the country, contain exhibits from the Industrial Revolution period. For example, the Museum of Science and Industry in Birmingham, or, for textiles only, Samuel Crompton's home—Hall-in-the-Wood, near Bolton.

General accounts

Stella Davies, *Living Through the Industrial Revolution* (Routledge) Chapters 1, 2, 4, 5 and 6.

M. E. Beggs Humphreys, *The Industrial Revolution, 1760–1860* (Allen & Unwin). Pages 1–24

P. Lane, *The Industrial Revolution* (Batsford, Visual Sources)

G. Middleton, *The Factory Age* (Longman, Focus on History series)

Special topics

L. T. C. Rolt, *Thomas Newcomen* (David and Charles Books)

James Watt and Steam Power (Cape, Jackdaw series no. 13)

R. Hennessey, *Factories* (Batsford, Past-into-Present series)

R. R. Sellman, *Newcomen and Smeaton* (Methuen, Brief Lives)

R. L. Hills, *Richard Arkwright and Cotton Spinning* (Priory Press)

The First Industrial Revolution (Longman, Secondary History Packs)

D. Birt and J. Nichol, *Ironmaster* (Longman, History Games)

J. G. Crowther, *Josiah Wedgwood* (Methuen, Brief Lives)

Longman's Then and There series has the following:

E. G. Power, *A Textile Community in the Industrial Revolution*

John Addy, *A Coal and Iron Community in the Industrial Revolution*

K. McKechnie, *A Border Woollen Town in the Industrial Revolution*

S. M. Archer, *Josiah Wedgwood and the Potteries*

J. Addy and E. G. Power (Eds.), *The Industrial Revolution* (Sourcebook)

Methuen's Outlines series includes the following:

S. E. Ellacott, *Forge and Foundry* and *Spinning and Weaving*

M. Tomalin, *Coal Mines and Miners* and *The Growth of Mechanical Power*

Filmstrips

The Revolution in Textiles, and *Coal, Metal and Steam*, two parts of 'Introduction to the Industrial Revolution' (Common Ground)

The Industrial Revolution (Longman, Then and There Filmstrips)

Iron and Coal, 1770–1870 (Nicholas Hunter Filmstrips)

Factories and their Towns, 1770–1870 (Nicholas Hunter Filmstrips)

9 Turnpikes and Canals
Transport and Communications 1

There were no mechanical forms of transport in the eighteenth century. The fastest method of travel was on horseback and the quickest way of moving bulky goods was by sailing ship. Similarly, news could not out-speed the swiftest horseman (unless the message was prearranged and fires lighted on hilltops) for there was no wireless or telephone. It was a far cry from our Space Age of satellites and rockets. Nevertheless, the eighteenth century was a time of rapid change in transport. The great increase in traffic resulting from a rising population and the developments in industry and agriculture made improved roads and waterways essential. In fact, without them there could have been no Industrial Revolution. The increasing output from the factory and the farm was only made possible by quicker and cheaper transportation to and from the ports and the main centres of population.

Roads, rivers and coastal traffic
In the early eighteenth century, Britain's **roads** were, for the most part, little more than paths or rough tracks across the countryside. They were usually impassable in winter, when they were flooded or churned into thick mud by herds of cattle and horse-drawn vehicles. In some places the highway was full of holes so deep that travellers had been known to drown in times of heavy rain. Even in dry weather, coaches and wagons were frequently overturned in the ruts left by previous traffic. Some of the roads connecting the main towns of

A gentleman's carriage jolted to pieces by the rough road

A 'traffic jam' of sedan chairs in a fashionable quarter of London

southern England were in a reasonable state of repair, but, these apart, there had been little attempt to build proper roads with hard surfaces and solid foundations since the Romans left Britain 1300 years before. The original Roman paving was still used in some places; for example on parts of the Great North Road and on Watling Street, which remained the best overland route from London to Chester.

Horses and farm-carts were used for most local journeys. Longer distances were sometimes travelled by **stage-coaches,** but these ran infrequently and were uncomfortable and very expensive. In addition, they were the favourite prey of highwaymen. 'Outsiders', who travelled at a reduced rate on the roof of the coach or on the luggage at the rear, were called upon to keep a lookout, and also to get down occasionally and push up hills. There were few carriages in the streets of most towns for, although the surfaces were usually cobbled, they were likely to be as uneven and dangerous as country roads. Sedan-chairs became the fashion for town ladies attending balls and dinner-parties and for town doctors on their rounds. Goods and luggage were carried on the better roads in huge **wagons,** drawn by teams of six or eight horses. But **packhorses** were more common. Merchants sometimes employed trains of thirty or forty of them.

The backward state of road transport in the early eighteenth century was reflected in the busy life on the rivers and the heavy volume of coastal traffic. Britain's natural waterways provided the best means of transporting bulky goods like coal, iron, clay and timber. **The sea** had been an important highway for centuries, because, added to the advantage of being an island, Britain has a coastline indented with long estuaries which bring many inland areas within easy reach of open water. Ocean-going vessels were very small by modern standards, but they were capable of carrying much greater loads than wagons or packhorse trains. It was cheaper and often quicker to make long detours by sea rather than carry goods overland. London not only received its coal by sea; corn from Sussex and Hampshire and cheese from Cheshire were also brought round the coast in preference to the overland routes.

Most of Britain's industries and almost all the major towns were located on the six main river systems—the Thames, Severn, Trent, Mersey, Humber and Great Ouse. The improvement and extension of these **river navigations** was the most important development in inland transport up to the mid eighteenth century. 'Cuts' (artificial river-beds) were made to straighten bends, and rivers were deepened and supplied with locks to make them navigable in their shallower reaches. The rivers of the West Riding were improved in this way, as were the Trent and Derwent, to assist the industrial development of Nottingham and Derby. In South Lancashire, the improved navigation of the Mersey and its tributaries greatly helped the growth of the port of Liverpool.

Nevertheless, in spite of improvement schemes, few of Britain's rivers could be navigated far inland without becoming too shallow or being obstructed by low bridges and other hindrances. Even the sea had drawbacks, for fragile cargoes were easily broken or spoilt by salt water, and enemy 'privateers' were a serious threat in war-time. If Britain's industries were to develop and expand into new areas, a lot would depend on the roads. Something had to be done to improve them.

'Turnpike fever'

Since the sixteenth century, the people of each parish had been required by law to devote six days a year to repairing the roads. But, in practice, parish responsibility was an obstacle to progress. Villagers, who were not paid for their labour, worked only on the local roads. They neglected the *main* roads passing through the parish because these were mostly used by strangers. Much-needed improvements in Britain's trunk roads were unlikely to be carried out until the costs of building and maintenance were put upon the people who used them.

It was for this reason that **turnpike trusts** came into being in the eighteenth century. These were groups of landowners and business-men, who got Parliament to pass private Acts authorising them to take over and rebuild stretches of road. To recover the money they invested and to pay for repairs, the trustees were permitted to erect barriers at both ends of the road and make travellers stop and pay a

fee or **toll** for using it. Most of the early toll-bars had pikes (spikes) on them, and it was from these that the roads got their name. Tolls ranged from a penny to as much as two shillings (worth well over £1 today) depending on the length of the road and the nature of the traffic. Different rates were charged for horse and rider, wagon, coach, livestock and so on.

Toll gates at Hyde Park, London

The earliest Turnpike Acts, dating back to 1663, concerned road improvements carried out by county magistrates. It was not until 1706 that Parliament first made a group of local gentry trustees of a turnpike road. From then on rapid progress was made. In the next fifty years, over 400 Acts dealing with the construction and upkeep of roads were passed by Parliament. In some areas the erection of turnpikes was bitterly opposed by the local inhabitants. They protested against having to pay for what they regarded as their own. Riots broke out, and severe penalties were imposed on 'disorderly persons' who 'cut down, pulled down, burnt and otherwise destroyed . . . turnpike gates and houses'. But, as time went on, opposition declined. In the period 1750–91, no fewer than 1600 Turnpike Acts were passed and a kind of *turnpike fever* took hold of the business community.

Better road surfaces made passenger transport swifter and safer and reduced the cost of carrying goods. Horses could draw heavier loads at higher speeds and cattle could be driven to market quicker yet arrive in better condition. But turnpikes had their shortcomings too. There was no overall authority to see that equal attention was given to the whole road. Most turnpike trusts controlled only short stretches of about a dozen miles and these were frequently followed by long sections where no attempt had been made to improve the surface. Thus travellers might pay several tolls yet still find their route impassable at some point. Only a truly national system could overcome such difficulties, but this did not arise until the Age of the Motor Car. Meanwhile, perhaps the greatest problem was the shortage of skilled engineers. Roadmaking was a lost art in Britain and it took time for it to be rediscovered.

The great roadbuilders

The first of Britain's great road engineers was **General George Wade** (1673–1748) who built 250 miles of roads and forty bridges in Scotland in the 1720s and 1730s. Like the Romans, he considered firm foundations to be the first essential of roadbuilding, and he curved (cambered) the surface so that water drained off into ditches on each side. Wade's work was financed by the Government, which wanted roads good enough to carry an army into the Highlands in case the Jacobites rose again after the 1715 Rebellion (see Chapter 2).

One of the most remarkable surveyors and roadbuilders was **John Metcalfe** (1717–1810) from Knaresborough in Yorkshire. Although totally blind from the age of six, following an attack of smallpox, he led a long and active life. 'Blind Jack', as he was called, was nearly fifty years old when he built his first turnpike road (1765) but in the next twenty-seven years he supervised the construction of 180 miles of turnpikes, mostly in Yorkshire and Lancashire. He paid special attention to the bed of the road, and where the soil was soft he laid great quantities of heather as a foundation for layers of stone and gravel. He realised that smooth, hard-wearing surfaces could not be made with rounded stones, for these were pushed aside by the traffic. He used jagged broken stones which, in time, bound together under the pressure of wheeled vehicles.

Road construction was only one of the activities of **Thomas Telford** (1757–1834) a Scottish shepherd's son who rose from being a humble stonemason to one of the greatest civil engineers in British history. In addition to surveying and building roads, he designed and constructed bridges, canals, lighthouses, harbours and docks. Much of his early experience was gained as Surveyor of Roads in Shropshire in the 1780s and 1790s. He first came into prominence when he was put in charge of a government scheme of road-, bridge- and canal-building in Scotland (1803). In the next eighteen years he built nearly 1000 miles of road, over 1000 bridges and the great Caledonian Canal, which made a continuous waterway cutting across northern Scotland from coast to coast. The overall effect of his work was to revolutionise trade and travel north of the Border and quicken communications between England and Scotland.

The work for which Telford is most famous was the **London–Holyhead road,** which took over ten years to build, starting in 1815. The old road had become increasingly unsatisfactory after the Act of Union with Ireland in 1801 (see Chapter 10) for it was one of the main overland routes from London to the Irish Sea. Telford was instructed by Parliament to make it as near perfect for coach traffic as he could. Therefore he set out to achieve gentle gradients and moderate curves, which often meant leaving the line of the old road and building entirely new sections. Bangor, on the mainland, was

Thomas Telford

linked with the Isle of Anglesey and Holyhead by a completely new stretch of twenty-two miles. It crossed the Menai Straits by means of a magnificent 570-yard suspension bridge, designed and built by Telford and opened in 1826.

Like the Romans, Telford believed that the surest way of keeping a road hard and smooth was to have solid foundations of hand-laid stone blocks, and proper drainage, so that the heaviest rain could not wash away the surface. These techniques were successful but very expensive. Turnpike trusts, with limited money to spend, normally preferred quicker and cheaper methods—like those of another Scotsman, **John Macadam** (1756–1836). He showed that if the subsoil was well drained and the surface of the road slightly raised, it would carry heavy traffic all the year round without the need for costly foundations. Like Metcalf, Macadam covered the road's surface with a carpet of fine, chipped stones which packed tightly together under the weight of traffic. 'Every piece of stone put into a road which exceeds one inch in any of its dimensions is mischievous,' he said. His methods are still used, but nowadays Macadamised roads are sprayed with tar to give a waterproof 'tarmac' surface.

In common with other great roadbuilders of the period, Macadam had no special training. Roads were merely his hobby for many years. It was not until 1815, when he was made Surveyor of the Bristol Turnpike Trust, that he began to build up a nationwide reputation.

Part of Thomas Telford's Menai Suspension Bridge. Built in 1826, it is still in use today.

His methods were popular with the turnpike trusts because they were ideal for carrying out low-cost improvements to old roads, rather than building new ones. Although he assisted dozens of separate trusts all over the country, he believed no lasting progress would be made until groups of them amalgamated to produce long, *continuous* sections of good road. He eventually persuaded Parliament to consolidate all the turnpikes in the London area under one **Metropolitan Turnpike Trust** (1825) to which he was appointed Surveyor-General. This was a great step forward and the nation's debt to him was recognised by a special parliamentary grant of £10,000.

The Coaching Age

Between 1790 and 1830 the network of turnpike roads spread all over the kingdom. In that time Parliament passed 2450 Turnpike Acts, compared with 1600 in the previous forty years. There were parallel improvements in road vehicles. Wagons and carts gradually replaced packhorses for the carriage of goods; in the towns, sedan-chairs gave way to private horse-drawn carriages and hired cabs, and there were great advances in stage-coach travel. **Coaches** in the mid eighteenth century were heavily built and without proper springs, which made them slow and uncomfortable. But by the turn of the century they had improved to such an extent that it was faster to send mail by coach than by postboy on horseback.

John Loudon Macadam

London—Exeter mail coach

BOLT-IN-TUN

ROYAL MAIL & COACH ESTABLISHMENT,

Sussex Tavern and Family Hotel,

FLEET STREET, LONDON.

Royal Mails.

PORTSMOUTH & ISLE of WIGHT, With a Branch to Chichester, Bognor, & Petworth. | HASTINGS & TUNBRIDGE WELLS, With a Branch to Rye and Hawkhurst.

Every Evening ············ at Half-past Seven o'Clock.

Fast Coaches.

	Morning	Afternoon
ABERYSTWITH, Kington, Penybont, and Rhayader	7	½ past 5
ALRESFORD, Alton, and Farnham	½ past 8	······
BATH, Melksham, Devizes, Marlborough, and Hungerford	7	¼ to 7
BIRMINGHAM and Stratford-on-Avon,	7	······
BLACKWATER, Sandhurst (Royal Military College,) Egham, and Staines	······	3
BRISTOL, Clifton, Bath, Devizes, and Newbury	7	¼ to 7
BRIGHTON, Reigate, and Crawley	½ past 8 ½ past 10	······
CHELTENHAM, Witney, and Oxford	7 & ¼ to 8	¼ to 6
CHICHESTER, Midhurst, Hazlemere, Petworth, and Godalming	9	½ past 7
CHIPPING NORTON, Enstone, Woodstock	10	······
CHERTSEY, Shepperton, Halliford, Sunbury, and Hampton	······	½ past 3
CAERMARTHEN, Llandilo, Llandovery, Brecon, and Crickowell	7	½ past 5
DOVER, Deal, Canterbury, Sittingbourne, and Rochester	9	½ past 6
ESHER, Claremont, Ditton, and Kingston	8 & 9	½ past 3
EXETER, Cullumpton, Wellington, Bridgewater, Taunton, and Wells	7	¼ to 7
FROME, Trowbridge, and Devizes	7	······
GLOUCESTER, Cheltenham, Northleach, Burford, Witney, and Oxford *(In direct communication with Coaches for all parts of South Wales.)*	7 & ¼ to 8	¼ to 6
GODALMING, Guildford, Ripley, Cobham, and Esher	8 & 9	½ past 3
HAMPTON COURT, Hampton, Twickenham, and Richmond	8 & ½ p. 10	½ past 3 ½ past 6

	Morning	Afternoon
HEREFORD, Ross, Gloucester, Cheltenham, and Oxford	¼ to 7	¼ to 6
HASTINGS, Battle, Robertsbridge, Flimwell, and Tunbridge	10	½ past 7
MARGATE and Ramsgate	9	½ past 6
MONMOUTH, Whitchurch, and Ross	7	½ past 5
OXFORD	7, 8 & 10	¼ to 6
PORTSMOUTH, Horndean, Petersfield, Liphook, and Godalming	½ past 11	½ past 7
READING, Wokingham, Bracknell, and Virginia Water	½ past 11	4
RYE, Northiam, Sandhurst, Hawkhurst, and Lamberhurst	11	½ past 7
SHREWSBURY, Bridgenorth, and Kidderminster	7	½ past 5
SOUTHAMPTON, Winchester, Alton, Farnham, and Guildford	½ past 8	······
St. LEONARDS and Hastings	10	½ past 7
SEVEN OAKS and Riverhead	10 & 11	½ past 3 ½ past 7
SWANSEA, Neath, Cowbridge, Cardiff, Newport, and Chepstow	7	½ past 5
TUNBRIDGE WELLS, Tunbridge, and Seven Oaks	10	½ past 2 ½ past 7
TROWBRIDGE and Devizes	7	¼ to 7
WEYBRIDGE, Oatlands, Walton, Moulsey, and Hampton Court	······	4
WINCHESTER and Farnham	½ past 8	······
WINDSOR, Eton, and Slough (Patronized by Her Majesty.)	½ past 9	½ past 2 4
WORCESTER and Tewkesbury	7	¼ to 6
WANTAGE, Wallingford, and Henley	8	······

ROBERT GRAY & CO. Proprietors.

Every information relative to the different STEAM PACKETS from
BRISTOL ··········· to Cork, Waterford, Swansea, Ilfracomb, Haverfordwest, and Tenby.
PORTSMOUTH ··········· to the Isle of Wight, Torquay, Plymouth, and Falmouth.
SOUTHAMPTON ··········· to the Isle of Wight, Guernsey, Jersey, St. Maloes, Havre de Grace, France, and Italy.

☞ NOTICE—No Parcel, or Passenger's Luggage, will be accounted for above the Value of Ten Pounds unless entered as such, and Insurance paid accordingly.

Timetable of mail coach departures from London (1839)

The growth of a regular **postal service** was one of the chief results of better transport in this period. There was no really national system before 1720, when **Ralph Allen** of Bath was granted a monopoly of all postal deliveries outside London. Although his postboys were easy prey for highwaymen, he managed to run a regular service roughly three times a week between all the main towns. By the 1780s, stage-coaches on the new roads could out-speed the horse post. As a result **John Palmer,** also from Bath, was given a Post Office contract to carry the mails between London and Bristol by coach, beginning in 1784. Palmer's coaches did the journey in sixteen hours and were such a success that within a few years fast mail-coaches served London and all the main towns. They carried passengers as well as the mail, and each coach had a guard armed with a blunderbuss as a protection against highwaymen. Like the postboys before them, mail-coaches were exempt from turnpike tolls. The guard sounded his post-horn on approaching the toll-gates to avoid unnecessary delay. This privilege helped mail-coaches gain a reputation for speed and punctuality.

Mail-coaches also delivered **newspapers.** Most large towns had their own daily papers by this time, and London had several. They were a fairly recent development, for, although periodicals appeared well before 1700, the first *daily* newspaper—*The Daily Courant*—began in 1702. It was printed on one side of a sheet of paper measuring eight inches by fourteen. During the course of the century, papers of several pages began to appear. More than half of their news space was normally devoted to parliamentary debates, and the remainder to articles, gossip, letters and columns of small advertisements. Since the great majority of the population could not read, 2000 copies was considered a good daily sale for a leading London newspaper, even in the Coaching Age.

The mail-coaches were built for speed, with lighter, more stream-lined bodies, steel springs and thinner wheels. These advances in design were taken up by private coach companies, which competed with each other to provide the fastest, most comfortable services. By the 1820s and 1830s, a good stage-coach, changing horses frequently at coaching inns, could average up to ten miles an hour on a long run. The 'Independent Tally-Ho' averaged fourteen miles an hour from London to Birmingham. By the 1830s, when competition from railways became a serious threat (see Chapter 13) improved roads, thoroughbred horses and better-designed coaches had together brought about a remarkable reduction in travelling times in comparison with the mid eighteenth century.

Average travel times under favourable conditions

	1750s	1830 approx.
London–Newcastle	6 days	Just over 1 day
London–Edinburgh	10 days	2 days
London–Brighton	1 day	$5\frac{1}{2}$ hours

'Canal mania'

Even after road improvements it was still very costly to send freight by stage-wagon. Manufacturers continued to prefer water transport. For example, a Shropshire company, in 1775, sent pig iron more than 400 miles by sea and river to avoid a sixty-mile journey overland. But navigable rivers were few, and many of them were too short or too shallow. By the second half of the eighteenth century growing industrial areas like South Lancashire and the West Midlands urgently needed more waterways. The answer was to follow the example of countries like Holland and France and cut artificial canals for carrying goods in bulk.

The beginning of the canal-building period in Britain is closely bound up with the lives of two men from very different social backgrounds. Francis Egerton, **Duke of Bridgewater** (1736–1803) was rich and educated. **James Brindley** (1716–72) his chief engineer, began life as a humble millwright and never learned to read and write properly. Their association began in 1759, when the Duke obtained an Act of Parliament allowing him to build a canal to Manchester from his estate at Worsley, seven miles away. He had large deposits of coal on his land and wanted a better method of transporting it to Manchester than on the backs of packhorses. It was not the first 'deadwater navigation'. Liverpool was already receiving coal via the Sankey Brook Canal (1757) which linked the St Helens coalfield with the river Mersey at Warrington. But the **Bridgewater Canal** became the starting-point of a systematic network of waterways linking Britain's main industrial areas.

The construction of the Bridgewater Canal presented many problems. Brindley's method of tackling them was not to do complicated calculations but to retire to bed to think and stay there until he found a solution. In this way he hit upon the idea of carrying the canal forty feet above the river Irwell with an aqueduct, or bridge, at Barton. People came from all over Europe to stare at it in wonder. By 1764 the canal was carrying coal into the heart of Manchester. One horse pulled more on water than sixty packhorses could carry, with the result that the price of coal in Manchester was halved and the demand for it greatly increased. By 1762 Brindley was already working on a thirty-five-mile extension of the canal, to meet the Mersey estuary at Runcorn. When it was completed (1776) the cost of carrying cotton and cotton goods between Liverpool and Manchester was reduced to less than a sixth.

Meanwhile, in 1766, Brindley began his most ambitious scheme—

James Brindley's Barton aqueduct, on the Bridgewater Canal

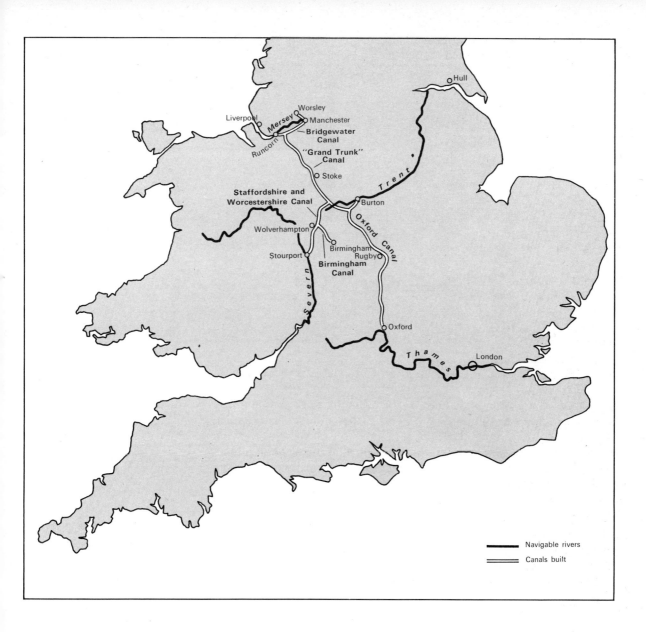

Navigable rivers
Canals built

'Grand Trunk' Canal
System

the **Trent and Mersey Canal**—to provide a continuous waterway across England from coast to coast. It ran a distance of ninety-three miles, from the Bridgewater Canal, near Runcorn, via the salt and pottery districts of Cheshire and Staffordshire, to a point on the river Trent where it was navigable all the way to the Humber estuary. One of its main financiers was **Josiah Wedgwood,** the potter. He had much to gain. Cornish clay, brought by sea to Chester or Liverpool, could be carried along the canal to his Etruria works, which was sited on its banks. The fragile finished goods could travel by barge to Liverpool or Hull instead of being jolted along the roads by packhorses.

Brindley called the Trent and Mersey Canal the **Grand Trunk;** for he made it the basis of a whole system of waterways linking England's greatest rivers. The Staffordshire and Worcestershire Canal

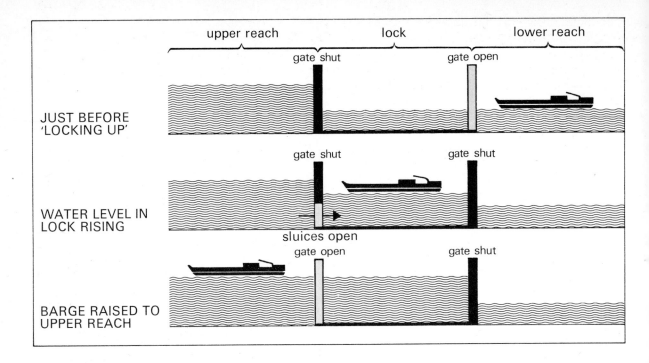

upper reach | lock | lower reach

JUST BEFORE 'LOCKING UP'
gate shut — gate open

WATER LEVEL IN LOCK RISING
gate shut — gate shut
sluices open

BARGE RAISED TO UPPER REACH
gate open — gate shut

joined the river Severn at Stourport, and a branch to Wolverhampton and Birmingham ran through the heart of the industrial Midlands. Brindley also surveyed another canal to link the Grand Trunk with the Thames at Oxford. But he did not live to see his schemes completed, dying from overwork in 1772. His friends were not surprised. Five years earlier Wedgwood had written: 'I am afraid he will do too much, and leave us before his vast designs are executed.'

In the thirteen years they were together, Brindley and the Duke of Bridgewater built 365 miles of canals. While the Duke provided the money, obtained the necessary Acts of Parliament and negotiated with the landowners, Brindley took charge of all the planning and construction. He even recruited and trained his own gangs of 'navigators' ('navvies')—to do the digging—many of them Irish immigrants.

The Canal Age was in full swing by the time of Brindley's death. He had provided much of the framework for the great system of navigable waterways which served all the main industrial areas by the early nineteenth century. South Lancashire and the West Midlands remained the chief areas of canal development, while Birmingham became the largest single centre—'the canal metropolis'. With most canal companies making handsome profits and paying large dividends, there was no shortage of willing investors. However, in the years 1791–6, this enthusiasm got out of hand. The urge for quick profits led to a *canal mania,* when scores of impossible schemes were eagerly supported, bringing ruin to those who put money into them.

When Brindley surveyed his canals he usually followed a winding course in order to avoid obstacles like hills and valleys. But later engineers, including Thomas Telford, tried to keep the line of the canal

The workings of a lock

straight, by building high embankments over valleys and driving deep cuttings through hillsides. Every engineer aimed to keep the canal as level as possible, but, in crossing hilly country, **locks** had to be built. These were like stone-walled basins, with gates at each end. By means of sluices (inlet and outlet channels) in the gates, the water level could be changed within the lock to raise or lower barges, depending on the direction in which they were travelling. Long stairways of locks had to be built on the northern canals crossing the Pennines, where the hills were especially steep. The Rochdale Canal, for example, which was the first satisfactory water connection between Yorkshire and Lancashire (1804) had ninety-two locks in only thirty-three miles.

By 1830 Britain had over 4000 miles of canals. So long as roads

A coal barge 'locking down' on the Staffordshire and Worcestershire Canal

provided the only alternative, canals enjoyed a clear superiority as carriers of freight. But the coming of railways (see Chapter 13) suddenly exposed their limitations. Although barges could carry anything from thirty to a hundred tons, they were very slow — particularly in hilly country, where there were many delays in getting through locks. With the development of a railway network after 1830, the Golden Age of canals came to an abrupt end.

Timeline
1663   First Turnpike Act.
1702   *The Daily Courant* — the first daily newspaper.
1759–64 Bridgewater Canal (Worsley to Manchester).
1766–77 Trent and Mersey Canal ('Grand Trunk').
1772   Death of James Brindley.
1784   John Palmer's mail-coaches.
1791–6   'Canal mania'
1825   Metropolitan Turnpike Trust (Macadam Surveyor-General).
1826   Thomas Telford's Menai Straits Suspension Bridge.

Further study

Project
Find out as much as you can about the old turnpikes, coaching inns, canals and river navigations in your locality. What happened to them after the coming of railways in the 1830s? (Consult the books on local history in the reference section of the public library.)

General accounts
R. Aickman, *The Story of Our Inland Waterways* (Pitman)
Stella Davies, *Living Through the Industrial Revolution* (Routledge) Chapter 3
M. Greenwood, *Roads and Canals in the Eighteenth Century* (Longman's Then and There series)
Roads and Waterways (Ginn's History Bookshelves, Orange Shelf)

Special topics
L. Meynell, *James Brindley — Pioneer of Canals* and *Thomas Telford* (Bodley Head)
H. Malet, *The Canal Duke* (David and Charles Books)
B. Barker and R. Boden, *Canals* (Longman, History Games)
Transport (Longman, Secondary History Packs) Pack 16
R. R. Sellman, *Brindley and Telford* (Methuen, Brief Lives)
Shire Publications' Lifelines series includes the following:
Rhoda M. Pearce, *Thomas Telford*
Harold Bode, *James Brindley*

Filmstrips
Roads, Rivers and Canals, Part 8 of G. D. H. Cole's 'Introduction to the Industrial Revolution' (Common Ground)
Thomas Telford, Pictorial Biographies (Hulton)
Roads, Bridges and Canals, 1770–1870 (Nicholas Hunter Filmstrips)

10 Storm Clouds over Europe

The French Wars, 1793-1815

The American Revolution (1776–83) which gave the Thirteen Colonies their independence (see Chapter 3) also had important results for Britain and France. The failure of British forces discredited the King's ministers and thereby assisted the rise to power of **William Pitt 'the Younger'** (1759–1806) so called to distinguish him from his famous father. Pitt was only twenty-four when he became First Lord of the Treasury (1783) but Britain's youngest Prime Minister proved to be one of the greatest. Remaining in power almost without a break until his death in 1806, he guided Britain through one of the most difficult and dangerous periods in its history.

In contrast, France, who had joined the colonists in the American War to settle old scores with Britain, paid a great price for victory. The French *National Debt* (money borrowed by the Government on long-term loan) was no greater than Britain's, but, in the absence of wise and firm leadership, France failed to recover from the cost of the war. In the 1780s, while Pitt was putting Britain's finances on a firm footing, France went bankrupt.

The French Revolution

The French Government had long been in financial difficulties, mainly because the wealthiest citizens—the nobles and the higher clergy—were like drones in a bee-hive. Unlike their British counterparts, most of them paid no taxes and did little to serve their country in return for the privileges they enjoyed. Very few even troubled to farm their land efficiently. At the other extreme, the peasants, who were much worse off than the labouring classes in Britain, were severely taxed. The poor peasants, together with the middle-class merchants and manufacturers, had to bear almost the entire cost of the eighteenth-century wars and of maintaining the extravagant royal court at the Palace of Versailles, near Paris. King **Louis XVI**'s advisers had pointed out the need for drastic reforms in taxation and royal expenditure. But Louis was too weak to risk the displeasure of the nobles by making them pay their share of taxes and too stupid to realise the danger if he did not do so.

In May 1789 the French **States General** (similar to the early English Parliament) was called together, for the first time since 1614, to deal with the financial crisis and discuss possible reforms in government. Many members of the Third Estate (Commons) had been influenced by the views of the American rebels. They openly accused the aristocracy and the monarchy of extravagance and misrule, and demanded a full share in governing the country and justice and freedom for all. When they were outvoted by the nobles and clergy, the commoners broke away to form their own National Assembly.

The storming of the Bastille,
14 July 1789

Meanwhile, the Paris 'mob', including thousands of starving peasants from the surrounding countryside, grew impatient. On 14 July they captured the **Bastille** (the state prison) and the Revolution began. In the 'bloodbath' of the next few years, the Royal Government of France was swept away and thousands of nobles were executed.

At first, British public opinion strongly supported the ordinary citizens of France in their fight for 'liberty' and 'equality'. Leading Members of Parliament spoke in favour of the Revolution—Charles Fox called it 'the greatest event that has happened in the world'. All over Britain, working men formed societies to keep up regular correspondence with the French revolutionaries and to promote the views of reformers at home. The greatest influence on these **Corresponding Societies** was a political pamphleteer called **Tom Paine** (1737–1809). He believed that the people as a whole had a right to choose their rulers. His pamphlet *Common Sense* (1776) had greatly influenced the American Declaration of Independence. Now his book *The Rights of Man* (1791–2) applauded the French revolutionaries; attacked monarchy and aristocracy everywhere; and urged sweeping reform of the British system of government. Paine's

influence can be seen in hundreds of 'reform clubs' like the London Corresponding Society (1792) whose main aim was the extension of the vote to all adult males.

Meanwhile violence in France was increasing. By the winter of 1792–3, when Louis XVI and his Queen, Marie-Antoinette, were executed, Pitt's Government and large sections of the British public took a different view of the Revolution. There was now strong support for the views of **Edmund Burke** (1729–97) the only outstanding Parliamentarian who had completely opposed the Revolution right from the beginning. In his book *Reflections on the Revolution in France* (1790) he claimed that revolution could never be justified, for it 'can only lead to bloodshed and disorder'. While events in France took the course forecasted by Burke, the British Government began to fear the spread of revolutionary ideas at home. Even demands for peaceful reform were regarded with suspicion; political societies were closed down and many of their leaders arrested. In 1794 Parliament went so far as to suspend the Habeas Corpus Act, thus making it possible for suspected persons to be imprisoned without a trial.

Britain goes to war

The leaders of the Revolution realised that the main threat to them came from outside France. Thousands of aristocrats had fled across the borders for safety, and these *émigrés* (emigrants) were urging the monarchs of Europe to help them put down the Revolution. In self-defence, the Revolutionary Government declared war on Austria and Prussia, two of the strongest military powers in Europe (April 1792).

Pitt did all he could to keep out of the war. He wanted the British

The execution of Louis XVI (January 1793)

JOHN BULL Happy.

JOHN BULL going to the WARS.

JOHN BULL'S Property in danger.

J.Gy des. et fecit.

JOHN BULL'S glorious Return.

to remain 'spectators of the strange scenes in France' so that he could continue his policy of financial reform without interruption. But events on the Continent soon left him no option. France's intention of carrying the Revolution outside her own frontiers was made clear in November 1792, when she offered 'assistance to all people who wish to recover their liberty'. Two months later, following the execution of the King and Queen, French troops occupied Belgium. Pitt could not stand by much longer. Had the French not declared war (1 February 1793) he would have done so himself.

Britain's wealth and advanced industries should have enabled her to crush France single-handed. But the **British army** was small and badly organised. The people would not allow a large army to be kept in peace-time, in case control of it got into the wrong hands, so whenever war broke out whole new regiments had to be raised. This was very difficult, for conditions of service were so harsh that a man had to be desperate or stupid to enlist as a volunteer. Pay was low and almost always in arrears, and discipline was maintained by

Cartoon showing the perils of soldiering

means of the most barbaric punishments. Thus the ranks had to be filled mostly with men from the gaols and poorhouses—'the scum of the earth', as the Duke of Wellington called them. In contrast, the officers came from wealthy, aristocratic families and lived in luxury, even during campaigns. Most of them had little or no knowledge of military matters and simply purchased their rank for social reasons.

A British force of about 50,000, together with some hired German troops, was sent to the Netherlands in 1793 under the Duke of York. It was soon clear that such an army stood little chance against France, which was, by this time, 'a nation in arms'. The population of France was nearly three times greater than that of Britain, and French forces were fighting for the cause of the Revolution. The British were soon forced to return home (1794) and, one by one, their allies were defeated or dropped out of the struggle. In 1793 France had faced a great coalition of practically all the major countries of Europe, including Britain, Austria, Prussia, Holland and Spain. By 1797, 'the year of peril', Britain faced France alone.

Naval mutiny and Irish Rebellion

Britain's last line of defence was the English Channel, which throughout history has been her greatest ally in war-time. Provided the navy did not lose its command of the seas, Britain would be safe. Before the war Pitt had built and repaired many ships and improved the dockyards. His policy now paid off, as the navy blockaded French ports, kept trade routes open and won several major sea battles. It is thus not difficult to imagine the seriousness of the situation when, in the 'year of peril', mutiny broke out in the fleet—at Spithead, near Portsmouth, and in the Nore anchorage, at the mouth of the Thames. While enemy ships prepared for invasion, Britain's main source of strength was suddenly paralysed.

Less than five per cent of all British sailors in this period were volunteers. The navy was no more attractive than the army. More than half of the average crew was obtained by 'press-gangs'. These were groups of sailors (usually volunteers) who swooped on coastal

A press gang at work

towns and villages, and even merchant vessels, in order to 'press' civilians into service. They were supposed to capture only seafaring men, but, when the need for sailors was urgent, as it was during the French Wars, they were less choosy and sometimes searched many miles inland. In addition to captives of the press-gang, large numbers of orphans were put in the navy when they reached fourteen or fifteen; and, after 1795, each county had to supply a yearly quota of men for the fleet. The size of the quota depended on the population; thus Yorkshire supplied 300 while Rutland only had to find thirty. Needless to say, captains refused shore leave when ships were in home waters, otherwise almost their entire crew would desert the moment they set foot on land.

Refusal of shore leave was one of the grievances of the mutineers; but their chief complaint concerned the rates of pay, which had not been increased since 1652, even though the cost of living had doubled since then. Pay was often years in arrears, for it was withheld until the home port was reached. To make matters worse, the crew's rations frequently went bad, and the discipline was so severe that a hundred strokes of the 'cat o' nine tails' was a common punishment, even though the legal maximum was thirty-six.

When petitions to the Admiralty had no effect, carefully laid plans to mutiny were put into effect at **Spithead** on Easter Sunday 1797. The leaders wisely turned down vague promises of better pay and conditions, and refused to return to work until an Act of Parliament dealt with their complaints and an official pardon was given by the King. The mutiny at **the Nore,** which began in May, was less well organised and many of the men's demands were unreasonable. The Admiralty managed to put it down and hang thirty of the ringleaders.

No sooner were the mutinies settled than, in the following spring, the government faced an **Irish Rebellion.** Trouble had long been brewing in Ireland, where the great majority of the people, because of their Catholic religion, were treated as second-class citizens. The Irish Parliament could only pass laws approved by the United Kingdom Parliament, and the entire population—Protestant and Catholic— suffered from severe trade restrictions, particularly on the export of wool and cattle.

Not surprisingly, the Irish took advantage of every British difficulty to press for fairer treatment. During the American Revolution, they had gained freer trade and wider powers for the Irish Parliament. Now, influenced by the French Revolution, a **Society of United Irishmen** was formed (1791) which sought French aid in expelling altogether English landlords and English influence from Ireland. Only bad weather prevented a French fleet from landing in Ireland in 1796 and again in 1797. However, when the long-awaited Rebellion came (1798) many leaders of the United Irishmen had already been arrested. Without French support, the rebels were heavily defeated at the Battle of **Vinegar Hill.**

Pitt realised he had been lucky. If the French had established a base in Ireland they might have altered the course of the war. In the interests of security Pitt proposed a full political union with Ireland, similar to the one with Scotland in 1707. After some difficulty, the

The Plumb-pudding in danger; — or State Epicures taking un Petit Souper — the great Globe itself and all which it inherit, is too small to satisfy such insatiable appetites

Pitt (left) and Napoleon
as shown in a cartoon of
1805

Act of Union was passed in 1801. The separate Irish Parliament was abolished. Henceforward the two countries shared the same king, Parliament and army; and all trade restrictions on Ireland came to an end. One hundred Irish M.P.s sat in the Commons and twenty-eight Irish peers and four bishops in the Lords. Unfortunately, the crucial part of Pitt's plan—**Catholic emancipation** (freedom for Catholics to hold any public office)—was blocked by George III, who feared it as a threat to the Church of England. Pitt resigned, realising the Union was a fraud if Irish Catholics could only be represented by Protestant M.P.s. The Irish continued to press for Catholic emancipation until it was finally granted in the reign of George IV (1829).

The struggle against Napoleon

In 1790 Edmund Burke prophesied that in France 'bloodshed and disorder . . . will give place to a military tyrant'. Nine years later, **Napoleon Bonaparte** (1769–1821) overthrew the Republican Government and became dictator of France (November 1799). He was, without question, a military genius. Born in the island of Corsica, he began his career as an artillery officer in the Revolutionary army. By the time he was twenty-six he had risen to the rank of general, and four years later he controlled the destiny of France. Time and again

Death of Lord Nelson at
the Battle of Trafalgar

in the next fifteen years he destroyed the mightiest armies on the
Continent, only to see his ambition of becoming master of Europe
checked by British sea power.

After crushing a second European coalition (1800–1) and
reorganising the French government and legal system during a brief
period of peace (1802–3) Napoleon prepared for his **Grand
Design**—the invasion of Britain. Thousands of flat-bottomed boats
and 150,000 of his finest troops were assembled at Boulogne, while
the British built coastal defences. But the climax never came. The
French fleet failed to gain control of the Channel and make it safe for
the troop-carriers. In disgust Napoleon broke up his invasion camp
(1805) and moved eastwards to smash yet another hostile coalition.

Having helped to postpone the Grand Design, the British Mediterranean Fleet, commanded by **Lord Nelson,** now made it impossible.
On 21 October 1805 Nelson destroyed the French and Spanish fleets
at the Battle of **Trafalgar,** near Gibraltar. 'Our dear Admiral Nelson',
as an ordinary seamen described him, was fatally wounded; but he
died knowing that he had removed all danger from the French at sea.
The last great battle between sailing ships was one of the most
decisive in history.

The war now entered a new phase. Napoleon decided his best
chance of defeating Britain was to destroy its rich foreign trade.
Therefore, in 1806, he issued the **Berlin Decree,** forbidding any
country under his control from trading with Britain or accepting any
ship that had called at a British port. Napoleon hoped this 'Continental System' of blockades would make the 'nation of shopkeepers'
bankrupt, for over half of Britain's trade was with Europe. The British

reply was a series of **Orders in Council (1807)** claiming the right to seize neutral shipping bound for French-controlled ports. This policy caused much bitterness abroad, and even led to a brief war with the U.S.A. (1812–14) but it helped Britain to survive.

Clearly, if either side was to win, the deadlock between French land power and British sea power had to be broken. Britain's chance to end the deadlock came in the **Peninsular War,** beginning in 1808. While the Spanish were in revolt against French rule, a small British expeditionary force landed in Portugal, which was also refusing to co-operate with Napoleon. Under the command of the **Duke of Wellington** (1769–1852) the British built a series of fortifications, called the Torres Vedras Lines, near Lisbon (1809). Wellington now showed his tactical skill; wearing down the French army in Spain with short campaigns followed by orderly retreat behind his defences. By 1813 he was able to advance right across Spain and over the Pyrenees into France. On arriving at Toulouse (April 1814) he heard that the French had already surrendered.

Napoleon suffered his first land defeat when shortage of supplies forced him to retreat from **Moscow** (1812). The bitter winter and Russian flank attacks reduced his Grand Army of 600,000 to a quarter of its former size. Total defeat for France was now almost certain, and the Allies finally entered Paris early in 1814. Napoleon was banished to the island of Elba *but,* in March 1815, while the peace conference was still sitting at Vienna, he escaped, landed on the French mainland and rallied support.

For a hundred days the outcome was again in the balance, until 18 June, when the Allied forces under Wellington and the Prussian

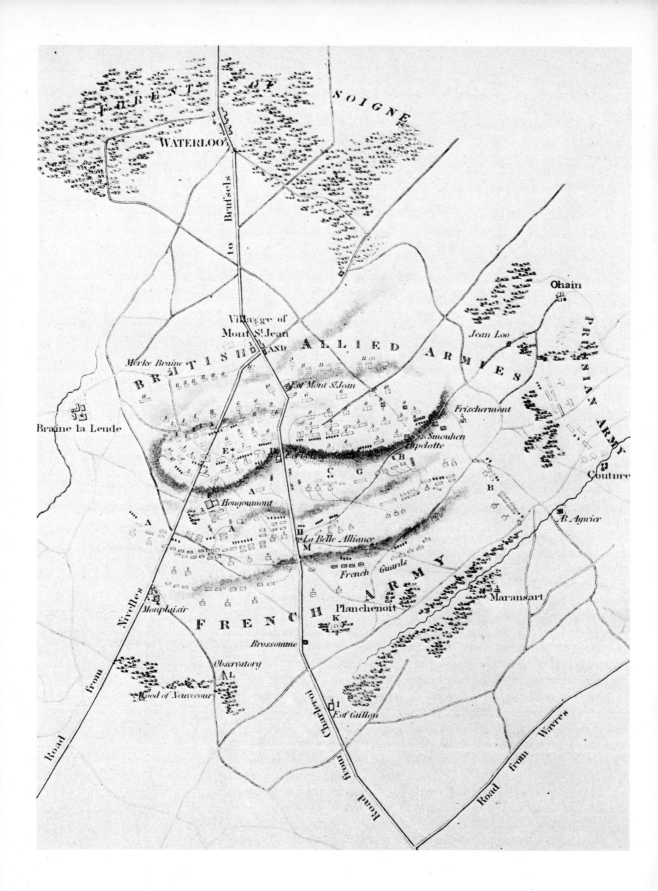

Plan of the battle of
Waterloo

General Blücher defeated Napoleon at **Waterloo,** near Brussels. The battle was, in Wellington's words, 'the nearest run thing you ever saw in your life'. Napoleon was again banished, this time to St Helena, where he died in 1821. The Allies, influenced by Britain's Foreign Secretary, Castlereagh, treated the French leniently, thus giving them no cause to reopen the war. France was restored to its old frontiers, and Britain kept only Malta, Ceylon, the Cape of Good Hope and a few West Indian islands.

Life and work in war-time

During previous wars, life at home had hardly been affected. Britain's empire in Canada and India had been secured by a few thousand soldiers and sailors. But the French Revolutionary and Napoleonic Wars were different. In the latter stages of the struggle, over ten per cent of the male population of military age was in arms—a total of almost half a million men. The remainder of the population had to put up with invasion scares, food shortages, high prices, periodic unemployment and increased taxation.

For wealthy families in remote country mansions it was a time of increasing prosperity and comfort. But even they were firmly reminded of the war when Pitt introduced **income tax** in 1798. It ranged from twopence to two shillings in the pound, according to size of income. Since those earning less than £60 a year were exempt, it did not affect the labouring class. In contrast, higher taxes on food-stuffs, manufactures and raw materials were a great burden on the poor, for these were paid at the same rate by all citizens, regardless of income.

In the countryside, the war years were marked by a great accelera-tion in the progress of **enclosure** (see Chapter 5). In a normal year, British farmers still produced just about enough to feed the rising population, but in years of poor harvests grain was usually imported from Europe. The war on the Continent made this increasingly difficult, especially during the Napoleonic blockade, with the result that there were frequent shortages. In years of scarcity, the price of grain rose to double or almost treble its pre-war level and landlords and farmers made large profits. Therefore, where open fields were still in existence, there was a great rush to enclose them so as to make them better suited to the large-scale production of corn. For the same reason, thousands of acres of wasteland were enclosed and ploughed up for grain crops.

Parliamentary Enclosure Acts

1760–93 (33 years)	1355 Acts
1793–1815 (22 years)	1934 Acts

High prices benefited farmers and landlords, but only at the expense of the rest of the community, who had to pay more for bread. Serious distress appeared in the countryside quite early in the war, with thousands of **agricultural labourers** existing on starvation wages. In Berkshire the county magistrates met at Speen, near Newbury (1795), with the intention of fixing a minimum wage which all employers in the county would have to pay. Unfortunately, after

A group of Luddites
shooting Mr Horsfall, a
factory master

strong objections from the landowning interest, they decided on an
alternative scheme which proved to be disastrous. Labourers who
earned less than a certain basic minimum (calculated according to
the size of their family and the price of bread) would have their wages
made up out of the parish rates.

Ever since the first Poor Law (1598) in the reign of Elizabeth I,
every parish had been obliged to collect rates in order to provide for
its poor, handicapped and destitute people. The Poor Law authorities
usually discouraged the 'able bodied' from applying for relief, in the
hope that they would find regular work. But the **'Speenhamland'**
or **'Allowance System',** which was soon taken up all over southern
England, paid relief to men who were not only 'able bodied' but *in
regular work* as well. It was humiliating for fully employed labourers
to receive part of their income in the form of parish charity. Farmers
took advantage of the Allowance System to refuse deserved increases
in wages; for they knew their workers could always fall back on
parish relief. Needless to say, rates went up alarmingly, and in 1834

the whole system was swept away by Parliament (see Chapter 11).

The Allowance System did not spread to the industrial areas of the Midlands and the North—mainly because wages in industry were normally higher. Even farmers in these areas had to pay better wages than their counterparts in the South, to prevent their labourers from moving to the towns. Nevertheless, **industrial workers** had hardships of their own as a result of the war. Napoleon's Continental System was designed to prevent British manufacturers from selling their goods in Europe. Although it was partly overcome by smuggling and by increased trade with the rest of the world (especially the Americas) many industries were seriously affected. When trade was lost, periods of severe unemployment occurred.

Workers in industries directly concerned with the war effort enjoyed the greatest regularity of employment and a fair measure of prosperity. This was particularly true of the metal industries, where the demand for cannon, firearms and shot accelerated the introduction of steam power and new techniques like puddling and rolling. Similarly, the Yorkshire woollen industry, which specialised in the making of coarse cloth, was kept very busy with government contracts for army uniforms. Elsewhere, the textile industry was not so fortunate. The cotton industry, for example, suffered from the difficulties and uncertainties of trading in war-time. All its raw material came from overseas and three-quarters of its output was exported. During the war with the U.S.A. (1812–14) supplies of raw cotton were seriously upset and thousands of workers suffered periodic unemployment.

The most desperate period for the poor was 1811–12, following a serious failure of the harvest in 1810. As the price of bread soared, the Napoleonic blockade resulted in ships laying idle and men being thrown out of work. There were serious outbreaks of machine-breaking and factory-burning in the textile districts, especially Nottinghamshire, where a thousand stocking frames were smashed in this period alone. These machine-breakers were said to have been organised by one Ned Ludd—from whom they got the name **Luddites**—but it is doubtful if such a person existed. The Government, wrongly thinking that Luddite activities were part of an organised political conspiracy, put them down with great severity. Machine-breaking was made punishable by death, and roughly twenty persons were hanged as a result. But this was only a foretaste of even more severe distress and disorder when the war ended.

Timeline

1783	Pitt 'the Younger' Prime Minister, aged twenty-four.
1789	French Revolution begins.
1793	Britain at war with France.
1794	Habeas Corpus Act suspended.
1795	'Speenhamland' or 'Allowance System'.
1797	Naval mutinies at Spithead and the Nore.
1798	Irish Rebellion—Battle of Vinegar Hill.
1799	Napoleon Bonaparte dictator of France.
1801	Act of Union with Ireland.

1805	Battle of Trafalgar.
1806	Napoleon's Berlin Decree—start of 'Continental System'.
1807	Orders in Council.
1808–14	Peninsular War.
1811–12	Machine-breaking—the 'Luddites'.
1812	Napoleon's Russian campaign.
1812–14	Britain at war with the U.S.A.
1815	'Hundred Days'; Battle of Waterloo; Napoleon banished to St Helena.

Further study

Lack of space makes it impossible to do justice to the many great and colourful personalities of the period. But it is an age much written about elsewhere, and the references below are a very small selection from the wealth of detailed and interesting material available.

Visit

Nelson's flagship at the Battle of Trafalgar, H.M.S. *Victory,* preserved in dry dock at Portsmouth.

General accounts

D. Lindsay and E. S. Washington, *A Portrait of Britain, 1688–1851* (O.U.P.) pp. 187–234

Denis Richards and Anthony Quick, *Britain, 1714–1851* (Longmans) Chapters 12–14

Special topics

M. Hutt, *Napoleon* (O.U.P., Clarendon Biographies)

I. Ribbons, *Monday 21 October, 1805* (O.U.P.)

P. Richardson, *Nelson's Navy* (Longman's Then and There series)

P. F. Speed, *Wellington's Army* (Longman's Then and There series)

M. Rosenthal, *The French Revolution* (Longman's Then and There series) is detailed but not too long.

N. Wymer, *Soldiers and Sailors* (O.U.P., Lives of Great Men and Women, vol. 5) includes Nelson and Wellington.

The Jackdaw series (Cape) provides source material on:

The French Revolution, Parts 1 and 2, nos, 57, 58

The Peninsular War, no. 72

The Battle of Trafalgar, no. 1 and *The Battle of Waterloo*, no. 18

Sailors and Ships (Ginn's History Bookshelves, Orange Shelf) has a short piece on H.M.S. *Victory* and useful information on trade.

Nelson and the Age of Fighting Sail and *The Battle of Waterloo* (Cassell, Caravel Books)

Filmstrips

The French Revolution, Parts 1 and 2 (Hulton)

Nelson, Pitt the Younger, Wellington (Common Ground, Lives of Famous Men and Women)

Napoleon (Common Ground, Lives of Great Rulers)

Napoleon Bonaparte (Hulton, Pictorial Biographies)

The Victory (Visual Publications, Famous Ships)

11 The Darkest Hour and the Dawn
Social distress and the beginnings of reform

The Allied victory at Waterloo (1815) ended the threat from Napoleon but brought no immediate end to the hardships of the war years. A severe depression in trade and industry caused widespread unemployment and distress among the labouring class. Mass meetings, protest marches and reform societies voiced the discontents of the poor, but the Government, still haunted by the ghost of the French Revolution, continued its policy of repression and opposition to reform. There is a saying that 'the darkest hour comes before the dawn'. This is true of the post-war years in Britain, for conditions got worse before they got better. It was only after 1820 that an improvement in trade led to relative calm, and Parliament gradually became less opposed to the demands of reformers.

'The post-war discontents'

After the collapse of Napoleon's blockade in 1813 European countries were again free to export corn to Britain. This should have brought down the price of bread, for the imported corn was cheaper than the home product. But landlords and farmers, many of them threatened with bankruptcy, used their great influence in Parliament to protect themselves against foreign competition. A **Corn Law (1815)** prohibited the import of corn unless the home price rose to eighty shillings a quarter.* This gave home growers a virtual monopoly, for prices remained well below eighty shillings. As a result, the price of bread was kept artificially high after 1815, and the poor suffered great hardship.

The ending of government contracts for armaments, ships and clothing meant industries which had prospered during the war now experienced severe **unemployment.** The rapid demobilisation of over a quarter of a million soldiers and sailors only increased the numbers of unemployed. To make matters worse for the labouring population, they now had to pay a greater share of **taxation.** The National Debt rose from £228 million in 1793 to £876 million in 1816. Yet the Government kept an earlier promise to abolish Pitt's income tax when the war ended. Consequently the only way of paying off the yearly interest on the debt was to increase taxes on ordinary goods. These were a great burden on the poor; unlike income tax, which did not apply to those with low incomes.

Expensive bread, high unemployment and rising taxation led to widespread discontent among the poorer classes. They began to put their faith in political reform, believing that if they could get a share in the government of the country their hardships would receive attention. Political clubs again flourished; so did newspapers

* A measure of capacity, equal to 64 gallons or 8 bushels.

William Cobbett (1763–1835)

representing the views of the working classes. There were strong demands for reform of Parliament and the granting of the right to vote to all adult males, whether they owned property or not. **William Cobbett,** a political journalist, was the chief inspiration behind the Reform movement—through his weekly *Political Register.* It is said that when the coach carrying it arrived in the industrial towns, eager crowds tore open the parcels and read aloud in the streets.

But the Tory Government had other ideas. **Lord Liverpool,** Prime Minister 1812–27, had been in Paris at the start of the French Revolution and never forgot it. He and his Cabinet did not trust the masses and had no intention of giving them any political power. Like Pitt after 1793, Liverpool concentrated on keeping law and order, believing that weakness would lead to disaster. This fear of revolution was exaggerated, but the Government's anxiety when faced with any kind of mass movement is understandable. After all, there was no proper police force and weapons and communications were not as efficient as they are today. Governments of this period were not only poorly equipped to deal with serious disorder, they were also *incapable of preventing its causes.* They could not have controlled variations in wages, prices and unemployment, even if they has been prepared to interfere with the rights of employers.

Discontent soon came to the surface. Before the end of 1815 there were riots against the Corn Law in several northern towns. In the following year, when unemployment was at its worst, reform meetings were held in many areas. After one such gathering, at **Spa Fields** in London, a mob marched through the streets, breaking into shops. As in 1794, the Government was so alarmed that it suspended the Habeas Corpus Act for a year, thus again allowing suspects to be imprisoned without trial. Soldiers even broke up a peaceful 'hunger march' of unemployed workers from Manchester (1817). The **Blanketeers,** as they were called (they carried blankets for bedding), intended to walk to London and present petitions about their grievances to the Prince Regent. But soon after setting out they were dispersed and their leaders were arrested.

The post-war Reform movement reached a climax in the summer of 1819, with a great open-air demonstration in St Peter's Fields, Manchester. On Monday, 16 August, roughly 80,000 people from all parts of south-east Lancashire assembled to hear several well-known speakers—notably **Henry Hunt,** who first came into prominence at the Spa Fields meeting. Although the crowd was in good order the magistrates lost their nerve and demanded the arrest of Hunt while he was on the platform. The soldiers sent to carry out the order were unaccustomed to such a large gathering. They panicked and began to cut their way through with swords. In the resulting stampede, eleven people were killed and hundreds injured. Public opinion was shocked, and the episode was called **Peterloo**—in mocking memory of the Battle of Waterloo. Nevertheless, the Government congratulated the magistrates, and strengthened the powers of law and order with **Six Acts,** which severely restricted the right to hold public meetings and prevented the publication of newspapers and pamphlets likely to stir up unrest.

The 'Peterloo Massacre'. Soldiers cut their way through the crowd

Peel at the Home Office; Mrs Fry at Newgate

The Six Acts made it much more difficult for the working classes to express their grievances. Thus it was fortunate for them that they had less cause to protest in the years following Peterloo. A general improvement in trade from about 1820 brought fuller employment and therefore less hardship. By 1822 Lord Liverpool's Cabinet reflected these changing conditions. Several younger, more open-minded men were brought in, including **Robert Peel** (1788–1850), who became Home Secretary (the minister responsible for law and order). Peel now made the first serious attempt to reform the prisons and make punishments less severe. Previously the efforts of humanitarians like John Howard (see Chapter 4) had brought little state action on these issues, but now reformers began to have a real

influence on government policy. A good example can be seen in the persons of Robert Peel and **Elizabeth Fry** (1780–1845).

Even before her marriage at the age of twenty to Joseph Fry, a London banker, Elizabeth Gurney, daughter of a wealthy Norwich merchant, had opened a free school for poor children. She was a Quaker, and her strong religious beliefs made her eager to serve people less fortunate than herself. Her interest in prison reform dates from 1813, when a visiting American Quaker told her about the wretched conditions in **Newgate.** There were no proper beds, only filthy straw; no doctors or medicine for the sick, and great over-crowding. Mrs Fry and her friends first took bundles of clothing for the children and clean straw for the women to lie on. Eventually she went into the prison yard to speak directly with the women. The gaolers tried to stop her, fearing she would be attacked, but, to their astonishment, the entry of the dignified figure of Mrs Fry, in the dress of a 'plain Quaker', made the prisoners stop in their tracks. After listening quietly to her words of comfort they begged her to come again.

For thirty years Mrs Fry worked tirelessly to make prisons and convict ships more humane. 'Punishment', she said, 'is not for revenge, but to lessen crime and reform the criminal.' Her visits to Newgate became regular events and she arranged a rota of visitors

Elizabeth Fry

The condemned cell in Newgate prison

and readers, set up a prison school and began women's sewing classes. It was some time before she had any success in official quarters. Lord Sidmouth, Home Secretary 1812–22, resisted her suggestions, believing that nothing was gained by 'soft' methods. Peel, on the other hand, was influenced by her. While he was Home Secretary (1822–30) prisons began to be regularly inspected; gaolers were paid, instead of taking 'fees' from the inmates, and women prisoners were supervised only by women warders.

Many reforms suggested by Mrs Fry were not carried out until after her death; the abolition of transportation (1853) is one example. But her influence resulted in women no longer being put in irons on the convict ships. Elizabeth Fry—'the Angel of the Prisons'—ranks with Florence Nightingale (see Chapter 16) as one of the greatest women in English history, at a time when it was thought improper for women to be active in public affairs.

A London policeman, photographed in 1856

For Peel prisons were only one aspect of the legal system that needed reforming. He considered the **Penal Code** (the range of punishments imposed on law-breakers) to be both savage and stupid. Over 200 separate offences carried the death penalty, including horse and sheep stealing, forgery, and absurd crimes like cutting down a tree in Downing Street. Offenders were thus encouraged to commit murder in order to escape arrest—for, as the saying goes, 'you might as well be hanged for a sheep as a lamb'. Even when they were convinced of a prisoner's guilt, juries often refused to convict if they thought the penalty was too severe. This made a mockery of the law. Therefore Peel got Parliament to abolish the death penalty for about half the crimes to which it then applied. Rapid progress followed. After 1861 no one was hanged in Britain for any crime other than murder or treason.

Peel was more concerned with preventing crime than punishing it. For this reason, he established the first regular **police force** (1829). The lack of any effective means of keeping order was one of the main reasons why governments were so easily alarmed by mass meetings or riots. Large towns were particularly lawless, and authorities often used troops to keep the peace—a much-hated practice, especially after Peterloo. In London, the 'runners' from Bow Street Magistrates' Court performed a useful service, but there were too few of them to deal with any serious disorder. Peel established a regular police force in London and the suburbs (1829). At first, there were 3000 'Bobbies' (nicknamed after their founder) recruited and controlled by the Home Office. They wore top-hats and blue frock-coats and were armed only with wooden truncheons, but their presence soon forced many criminals to move out of the capital. Consequently, other towns began to employ 'Peelers' until finally, in 1856, every county and borough was obliged to maintain a police force.

The great Reform Act

Peterloo and the Six Acts were a setback to the working class Reform movement. But nothing could stop the growing *middle* class of factory-owners, merchants and professional people from demanding changes in the outdated system of parliamentary representation. They

The burning of Nottingham castle in a 'Reform riot'

complained that corrupt elections and an unfair distribution of seats (both described in Chapter 2) produced a Parliament which was dominated by the landowning gentry. The Corn Law (1815) was a striking example of the way landowners could use their majority in Parliament to protect their own interests, while ignoring the protests of the bulk of the population. The middle classes in the towns rightly demanded a greater say in the running of the country—to be achieved by Parliamentary Reform.

Changes in the old system were debated in Parliament on several occasions in the eighteenth century, but nothing was done. Pitt himself introduced a Bill in 1785, aiming to abolish thirty-six 'rotten boroughs' and transfer their seats to the more populated areas. But M.P.s rejected even this mild proposal. Soon afterwards, the French Revolution (1789) turned Parliament even more strongly against the idea of reforming itself. Nevertheless, during and after the French Wars the repressive policy of the Government could not conceal the fact that the people as a whole were dissatisfied with their political system. Demands for reform varied considerably. While members of the working class wanted nothing less than 'one man, one vote', the industrial and commercial middle classes urged that seats should be taken away from the rotten boroughs and redistributed among the new industrial towns.

In November 1830 the main obstacle to Parliamentary Reform was removed. The Tory Party, which had consistently opposed any change in the constitution, lost its majority in the Commons for the first time in half a century. Soon afterwards (March 1831) a **Reform Bill** was introduced by Lord Grey's Whig Government. The Tories still had a majority in the Lords, and it was only after a long and bitter struggle that the Bill was finally passed in June 1832. Meanwhile 'political unions' of workmen organised marches and demonstrations to protest at the delay, and there were Reform riots in some towns. Nottingham Castle was burned, and so were several public buildings in Bristol, where a mob broke into the prisons.

The changes made by the Act did not justify all the fuss it caused. They can be briefly summarised under two headings:

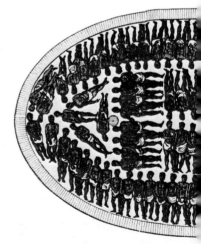

1. *Distribution of seats.* Most of the rotten boroughs were abolished, leaving 143 seats for re-allocation. The counties and large towns got 65 each, and the remaining 13 went to Scotland and Ireland.
2. *Voting rights.* In the boroughs, owners or tenants of houses worth at least £10 a year could vote. In the counties, ownership of land worth £10 or more a year was the main qualification. The existing rights of freeholders were maintained.

To qualify for the vote on these terms, a man probably needed an annual income of at least £150. Since ordinary workmen seldom earned more than £50 a year, it is safe to say that *the Act did nothing for the working classes,* in spite of their enthusiastic demands. It was the factory *owners* rather than the factory *workers* who benefited. Only about 300,000 new voters were added to the existing electorate of under half a million. In other words, the landed gentry had merely shared a little of its political power with the new industrial and commercial middle class.

The abolition of slavery

The membership of the 'reformed' House of Commons was much the same as before. Yet, although there were very few new faces, somehow the *spirit* of Parliament was changed by the 1832 Act. The Whig Government, having gained a reputation for reform, now seemed to feel obliged to live up to it. Consequently a number of major reforms were passed in the next few years.

In 1833 the campaign to abolish slavery achieved its final triumph, after half a century of activity in and out of Parliament. (For details of the eighteenth century slave trade, see Chapter 3.) The outstanding leader of the movement was **William Wilberforce** (1759–1833), a wealthy businessman from Hull, who first entered the Commons in 1780. After leading a gay and reckless life, he suddenly underwent a religious conversion and, in 1787, he was won over to the growing anti-slavery movement by the arguments of the Reverend Thomas Clarkson. As a boy of fourteen, Wilberforce had written a letter to a

Plan showing the terrible crowding on board a slaving ship. Part of the evidence brought before Parliament by Wilberforce and his friends

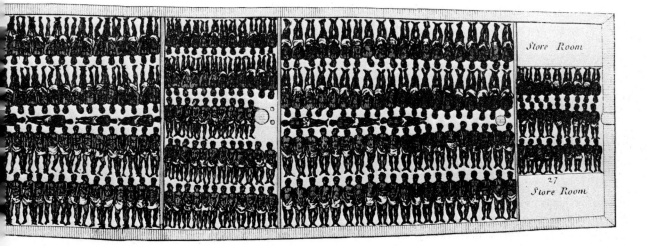

newspaper condemning the 'odious [hateful] traffic in human flesh', and now he decided to devote his wealth and talents to fighting it. A **Society for the Abolition of the Slave Trade** was formed (1787) and received powerful support from notable public figures like John Wesley and Josiah Wedgwood.

The immediate aim of the Society—the end of the *trade* in slaves— was finally achieved in 1807, when Parliament made it an offence for British subjects to take part in the capture and transport of slaves. The next step was to *set free* all the existing slaves in the British Empire; they numbered at least 800,000 as late as 1830. To this end the **Anti-Slavery Society** was founded in 1823, under the leadership of Wilberforce and Clarkson. They had little difficulty in winning over the general public, but met stiff resistance from the merchants and plantation-owners in Parliament, who claimed they would be ruined and the valuable West Indian sugar trade destroyed if the slaves were freed. Ill-health compelled Wilberforce to retire from Parliament (1825) but he remained a great inspiration to the movement and lived just long enough to hear that the cause was won. By an **Act of 1833,** slavery was abolished throughout the British Empire. To compensate the planters, the Government paid them a total of £20 million—an average of about £37 per slave.

Lord Ashley and factory reform

Within months of the abolition of slavery, an important landmark was reached in the movement to improve the working conditions of factory children. It was well over fifty years since child labour was first introduced into the textile mills (see Chapter 6). Dragged from their beds in the early hours of the morning and set to work all day in foul, stuffy conditions, they often became so exhausted that they had to be beaten to be kept awake. Many slave children were better treated on the plantations. As a West Indian planter put it: 'I have always thought myself disgraced by being the owner of slaves, but . . . never thought it possible to be so cruel as to require a child of nine years old to work twelve and a half hours a day.' Most factory-owners saw nothing wrong in this. When it was suggested that Parliament should pass laws to protect factory children they were quick to defend their 'rights', as employers, to run their businesses as they pleased.

But a small group of enlightened factory-owners had long been in favour of parliamentary action to control hours and conditions of work, not only for children but for all workers in the mills. **Robert Owen** (see Chapter 12) showed in his New Lanark Mills that shorter hours and excellent conditions could still produce good profits. **John Fielden** owned one of Britain's largest textile businesses, at Todmorden in Yorkshire. His employees had a maximum working day of ten hours, yet handsome profits were made. **Robert Peel (senior)** was another who tried to set a good example, but he soon realised that this was not enough. It was he who got the first Factory Acts passed, in 1802 and 1819—both attempts to protect children from excessive hours of labour. But they had little effect, for Justices of the Peace, often mill-owners themselves, failed to enforce them.

Anthony Ashley Cooper, seventh Earl of Shaftesbury

By 1830 textile factories employed a quarter of a million workers, most of them under the age of eighteen. At the same time a nationwide reform movement began to press for an effective Factory Act to limit the working day to ten hours. Leadership of the 'Ten Hours Movement' in Parliament soon fell upon **Lord Ashley** (Anthony Ashley Cooper, 1801–85, later Lord Shaftesbury). For Lord Ashley it was only the start of a long and noble career as a social reformer. He was concerned with many aspects of the welfare and education of working children—including apprentices in the coal-mines and 'climbing boys' (sweeps) who were sent up chimneys (until Parliament banned the practice in 1875). In later life, Shaftesbury was President of the Ragged Schools Union (see Chapter 18).

It was some years before the Ten Hours Movement achieved its aim; but Parliament took an important step towards it with the **Factory Act of 1833.** Children under nine were barred from all textile factories, and the hours of older children were limited to a maximum of forty-eight a week for those under thirteen, and sixty-nine for 'young persons' of thirteen to eighteen. Four full-time inspectors were appointed to see that the regulations were carried out, and employers who broke the law could be fined. In addition, it was laid down that every factory child should receive two hours' schooling a day. But this part of the Act was difficult to enforce and thus often ignored. The reformers had hoped for more, and renewed their fight to get a ten-hour day for *all* textile workers. Nevertheless, the 1833 Act firmly established the *principle* of state intervention between employers and workers to control factory hours.

Encouraged by Ashley and others, the Government appointed a Royal Commission on Children's Employment in 1840. Two years later, it issued a report on the condition of underground workers in the mines. The public was horrified to learn that women and girls carried baskets of coal weighing up to three hundredweight on their shoulders, or dragged loaded trucks, on all fours, along narrow underground passages. This work, said the Commission, 'makes them old women at forty'. Peel's Government took immediate action, despite

A chimney sweep's 'climbing boy'

Right: Children hauling coal underground

the opposition of the coal-owners. The **Mines Act of 1842** prohibited the employment of women and girls underground, and a minimum age of ten was fixed for the employment of boys.

The Commission reported on other industries in the following year, and its findings led to another important **Factory Act, 1844.** This controlled women's hours for the first time, by including them under the same regulations as 'young persons' of thirteen to eighteen, whose hours were now reduced to twelve. The working day for children under thirteen was cut to six and a half hours, and all dangerous machinery had to be fenced.

Ashley's great aim, a **ten-hour day,** was achieved for women and young persons in the mills in 1847; although it was increased to ten and a half in 1850. Because the work could not be carried on by men alone, this had the effect of reducing *men's* hours as well. Ashley and his friends now worked to extend the principles of the Acts beyond textiles to other trades, and to workshops as well as factories. Hours were further reduced in 1874, to a maximum of fifty-six a week (ten hours Monday to Friday and six on Saturday). Meanwhile, more inspectors were appointed, with greater powers, and safety regulations were tightened.

In opposing the Factory Acts many employers had claimed that they would be ruined, because their profit was made 'in the last hour of the day'. Yet, within a few years, they had to admit that the Factory Acts actually helped to increase output, for their workers were much more efficient when they were not exhausted by long hours.

The new Poor Law

The Poor Law was perhaps the most urgent of all the problems tackled by Lord Grey's Whig Government after 1832. The existing 'Speenhamland' or 'Allowance System' (described in Chapter 10) was unsatisfactory in almost every respect. The giving of Poor Relief to labourers with regular jobs encouraged farmers to pay less than a 'living wage'. It was also an enormous drain on the parish rates. In one parish in southern England the annual cost of Poor Relief rose from £18 to £367 in the space of thirty years.

A **Poor Law Amendment Act** was therefore passed in 1834. It discouraged the 'able-bodied' poor from applying for relief by making it necessary for them to enter a workhouse to get it. To deter idlers from trying to get free board and lodging, life in a workhouse was deliberately made less comfortable than that of the lowest-paid labourer. It was intended to be nothing more than a *last resort for the totally destitute.* The inmates were set to work, in return for which they received the bare minimum of food and some kind of bed. Discipline was strict—families were separated, visitors prohibited and smoking and drinking not allowed.

Workhouses were paid for out of the parish rates, and the ratepayers elected local Boards of Guardians to run them. The Guardians were ratepayers themselves, so they had a personal interest in keeping down the running costs of the workhouse. Thus the food provided was usually just enough to keep body and soul together. In a work-

GOD IS GOOD

GOD IS HOLY

GOD IS JUST

Marylebone workhouse in London. A new ward for the homeless poor, 1867

house near Leeds, inmates were fed in a trough like pigs, six at a time! By the terms of the Act, the sick and aged on Poor Relief were allowed to stay in their homes. In practice, it was cheaper for the Guardians to herd everyone together under one roof. In some places the sick were looked after by the insane in filthy workhouse infirmaries. Children mixed with hardened criminals, and destitute mothers with prostitutes; while those who had lived respectable lives but were forced to enter the workhouse in old age were mixed with those whose poverty was due to drunkenness and vice.

These places were so hated and feared by the poor that· many preferred to face starvation rather than enter a workhouse. Thus the aim of the authorities was achieved, for they intended the workhouses to be a deterrent. They were delighted to see the numbers applying for Poor Relief dropping sharply after 1834.

It was in the industrial areas of the North that the new Poor Law met most opposition. It swept away the money relief on which workers had relied during periods of unemployment. During a severe industrial depression in the years 1837–42, Guardians often had no option but to pay money relief to the unemployed and overlook the workhouse altogether. In the agricultural districts of the South, however, the Act was largely successful. It forced farmers to pay their labourers better wages, otherwise they would have lost their services altogether. For all its faults, the new system was more efficient than the old. As time went by conditions were gradually improved. Workhouse schools were introduced to prepare children for an independent life, and care of the sick was made more humane.

Timeline

1807   British slave trade abolished.
1813   Elizabeth Fry's first visit to Newgate.
1815   Corn Law.
1816   Spa Fields meeting.
1817   March of the 'Blanketeers'.
1819   'Peterloo' and the 'Six Acts'.
1829   Metropolitan Police established (Peel).
1832   Parliamentary Reform Act.
1833   Abolition of slavery and first effective Factory Act.
1834   Poor Law Amendment Act.
1842   Mines Act.
1850   Factory Act—ten-and-a-half-hour day.

Further study

Later Parliamentary reforms are dealt with in Chapters 17 and 20.

Visit
William Wilberforce's house in Hull has been preserved. It contains pictures and documents relating to the abolition of slavery.

Special topics
Longman's Then and There series includes:
J. Addy, *Parliamentary Elections and Reform*
P. F. Speed, *Police and Prisons*
Roger Watson, *Edwin Chadwick—Poor Law and Public Health*
J. J. and A. J. Bagley, *The English Poor Law* (Macmillan)
Stella Davies, *Living through the Industrial Revolution* (Routledge) includes an interesting account of 'Peterloo'.
K. Dawson & P. Wall, *Factory Reform* (O.U.P., Society and Industry in Nineteenth Century Britain). Documentary approach.
Towards Democracy (Longman, Secondary History Packs) Packs 21, 23
M. St J. Fancourt, *The People's Earl* (Longmans). Shaftesbury
G. R. Kesteven, *Peterloo, 1819*, and *The Triumph of Reform, 1832* (Chatto & Windus, Studies in English History)
E. White, *Elizabeth Fry* (Cassell, Women of Devotion and Courage)
J. Gibson, *John Howard and Elizabeth Fry* and *Chadwick and Shaftesbury* (Methuen, Brief Lives)
The Jackdaw series (Cape) includes:
Shaftesbury and the Working Children, no. 7, *The Slave Trade and its Abolition*, no. 12, *Elizabeth Fry and Prison Reform*, no. 63, *London's Peelers and the British Police*, no. 88

Filmstrips
Shaftesbury (Common Ground, Lives of Famous Men)
Wilberforce (Common Ground, Lives of Famous Men)
Elizabeth Fry (Visual Publications, Famous Women)
Unrest, Reform and Organised Labour, 1770–1870 (Nicholas Hunter Filmstrips)

12 Combination, Chartism and Co-operation
Working-class movements 1

Workmen were used to toiling long hours for low wages before the Industrial Revolution. Most of them accepted their fate as part of the natural order of things. But the beginnings of factory industry brought numbers of them together in one place. They now began to develop a sense of unity and common purpose, for they were more aware of the weakness and inferiority of their position than their fathers and grandfathers had been. As the new 'working class' became established in the industrial towns, its members began to realise the power they could possess if they acted *together* instead of separately. Thus they organised themselves in various ways to bring about improvements in their standard of living.

Early combinations and the law

Before the Industrial Revolution there were no trade unions in the modern sense. However, during the eighteenth century, **trade clubs** had become established in many towns. These contained workmen in a particular trade or occupation and usually met regularly at a local public house, many of which still bear their names today, like 'the Bricklayers' Arms'. Good company and strong ale were the first priority, but they also attended to more serious matters—such as accepting new apprentices, and putting aside a penny or twopence a week to help those out of work. These taverns also became 'places of call', where employers could recruit extra workmen. Occasionally, when their employers threatened to reduce rates of pay or refused them increases when the cost of living rose, members banded together to defend their interests. As early as 1720 thousands of London tailors joined together in this way against their masters.

It was a short step from the activities of trade clubs to full-scale **trade unions**. These began when a number of clubs 'combined' to fight for a common aim. In the eighteenth century, trade unions usually arose to deal with a particular problem and then broke up when it was settled. Their most powerful weapon was a threatened stoppage of work, or **strike**. Workmen realised that if they all asked for the same thing, and refused to go on with their jobs unless they got it, they would be in a good bargaining position with their employers. Faced with loss of business and possible ruin, employers were usually forced to reach some sort of agreement with the union. Strikes were quite common in the late eighteenth century. Among the most successful were those of the London tailors, who managed to raise their wages by a quarter (from 18s 9d to 25s) as a result of strike action between 1775 and 1800. The naval mutinies of 1797 (see Chapter 10) were really strikes against low pay and unsatisfactory working conditions.

Needless to say, employers strongly opposed the formation of trade

An early trade union
membership card

UNITED · TO · PROTECT

The Bearer

Ellen Reilly

Has been admitted a Member of the
WEST OF SCOTLAND
Power Loom Female Weavers Society

Glasgow 22 March 1833   No. 5701

unions. **The law** was on their side, for workmen who planned joint action against their masters could be prosecuted for 'conspiracy in restraint of trade'. In addition, Parliament passed a number of Acts throughout the eighteenth century forbidding combinations in particular trades. After the outbreak of the French Wars (1793–1815) the ruling class in Parliament suspected the intentions of *all* working-class organisations. Fearing the spread of revolutionary ideas from France, they first outlawed political societies (see Chapter 10). But trade unions did not escape for long. In an atmosphere of alarm and suspicion, it was feared that they might provide a 'cover' for political activities, including plots to overthrow the State. In April 1799 the Commons received a petition from a group of master-millwrights complaining of 'a combination of . . . millwrights within the Metropolis and twenty-five miles round'. Parliament took the opportunity to pass a general law prohibiting *all* such combinations.

The **Combination Acts** of 1799 and 1800 forbade workmen from meeting to plan joint action to raise wages or shorten working hours by bargaining with their employers or threatening them. The penalty was up to three months' imprisonment, with hard labour. Although a number of unions were driven out of existence, most of them continued their activities in secret. The Society of Ironfounders met at night on the moors and buried all books and records in the ground. Some workmen combined quite openly, and there were even strikes, for example those organised by the Cotton Spinners' General Union in Lancashire and Cheshire (1810). There were few prosecutions under the Combination Acts, although nineteen printers on the staff of *The Times* were imprisoned in 1810 for what the judge called 'a most wicked conspiracy' to injure 'the very employers who gave you bread'.

Around 1820, when conditions began to improve after the difficult post-war years of 1815–19, a campaign was started to achieve the **repeal** (abolition) **of the Combination Acts.** It was led by **Francis Place,** a tailor, whose shop in London's Charing Cross Road was a meeting-place for reformers of all kinds. With the help of **Joseph Hume,** M.P., a Parliamentary Committee of Inquiry was set up, and its report led Parliament to repeal the Combination Acts in 1824. Immediately, there was an outbreak of strikes, as secret unions came into the open and pressed for wage increases. Employers blamed the 1824 Act and soon got Parliament to change it. By an Act of 1825, which no longer satisfied Place and Hume, workmen could still form trade unions, *but* they were not allowed to 'molest' or 'obstruct' either employers or fellow workers. This meant, in practice, that it was difficult to strike without falling foul of the law, for courts could interpret the wording of the Act almost as they pleased. Nevertheless, after 1825 at least the trade unionist was no longer an outlaw.

Robert Owen

Robert Owen, the 'Grand National' and Tolpuddle

Most early trade unions were small, local organisations. It was not until after 1825 that large *national* unions began to combine workers in different parts of the country. An important figure in these developments was **John Doherty,** an Irishman and leader of the Lancashire cotton-spinners. In 1829 he formed a Grand General Union of Spinners, the first really national trade union. In the following year he went further and set up the **National Association for the Protection of Labour,** which aimed to unite *all* the trades in Britain. Such an ambitious scheme had little chance of success, but in the two years it lasted it claimed over 100,000 members and had its own newspaper, *The Voice of the People.* More national unions followed— among builders, potters, textile workers and others. But overshadowing them all was the **Grand National Consolidated Trades Union** (G.N.C.T.U.) established in October 1833. Within months it had over half a million members from every sort of trade.

The inspiration behind the G.N.C.T.U. was **Robert Owen** (1771—

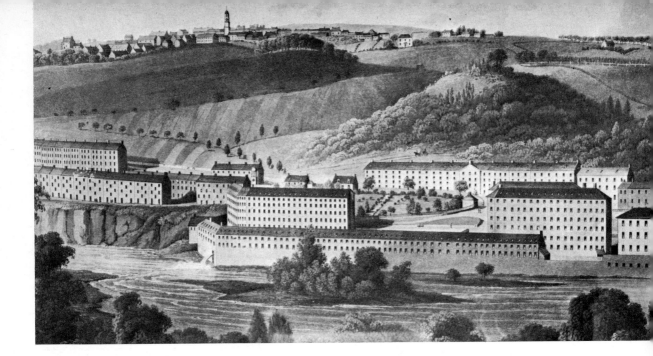

New Lanark cotton-mills

1858), a remarkable Welshman from Newtown, Montgomeryshire. He rose from being a draper's apprentice to a great cotton manufacturer before he was thirty. In 1800 he became managing partner of the New Lanark cotton-mills, on the banks of the Clyde near Glasgow. He immediately made himself personally responsible for the welfare of the 2000 workers—providing recreational facilities, replacing slums with decent houses and opening shops which sold essential goods at cost prices. He abolished child labour below the age of ten; giving these children free full-time schooling instead. No adults could work more than ten and a half hours a day; yet they were paid good wages which continued during sickness and temporary unemployment.

Other mill-owners were amazed to see that Owen made good profits, in spite of his lavish expenditure on workers' welfare. Owen explained that if factory hands were contented they would work harder and more efficiently. Nevertheless, few factory-masters followed his example and Owen soon took an active part in the Factory Reform movement, realising that new laws were needed to give workpeople proper protection.

Owen was not satisfied with being just a 'model employer'. In his book *New View of Society* (1814) he put forward ideas for changing the whole basis of living by replacing the existing system of *competition*—'between manufacturers for markets and between workers for jobs'—with *co-operation,* which he believed could bring peace and plenty for all. Owen suggested the setting up of **Villages of Co-operation,** where people could exchange their products with each other on equal terms and no one would live on profits from another man's work. He proposed this as a remedy for the distress after 1815, but the ruling classes would have nothing to do with it. Formerly, they had admired him as a successful businessman, but

now they distrusted him, realising that he was opposed to the whole idea of profit-making, on which their wealth and status depended.

After unsuccessful attempts to establish his own Co-operative Communities, both in the U.S.A. and in Britain, Owen attempted to put his ideas into practice in the Trade Union movement. The result was the 'Grand National' of 1833, which aimed to unite all the trades, after which industry would be organised under National Companies according to the principle of co-operation. Employers were naturally alarmed by Owen's revolutionary scheme, and in self-defence set out to crush the G.N.C.T.U. Workers had to sign a statement, which became known as **The Document,** declaring that they were *not* members of the Grand National. All those who refused were sacked.

Meanwhile, an even more damaging attack on trade unions in general, and the G.N.C.T.U. in particular, occurred in the Dorset village of **Tolpuddle.** In October 1833 some forty villagers formed a branch or 'lodge' of the Friendly Society of Agricultural Labourers, intending to join up with the Grand National. The authorities in the neighbourhood, most of them employers of the men, immediately set out to crush the lodge—with the agreement of the Home Secretary and a number of M.P.s. The villagers had taken the usual secret oath of loyalty to the Union, and this gave the magistrates their excuse. Six members of the lodge were arrested and charged with taking secret and unlawful oaths; under an Act of 1797, which had been passed to deal with naval mutinies. In March 1834, at nearby Dorchester, they were sentenced to be transported to Australia for seven years.

The six men of Dorset and the causes they stood for

William Lovett, Secretary of the London Working Men's Association

Members of the G.N.C.T.U., preparing for an all-out attack upon employers, now hesitated. They saw the Tolpuddle case as a threat to their right of combination, and feared that their rulers would stop at nothing to crush the Union. Within months the G.N.C.T.U. fell apart in a series of bitter local disputes. In the end it proved too big and scattered to be manageable, at a time when most workers could neither read nor write and there was no rapid communication by letter, telegraph and rail.

The offensive of the employers and the Government in 1834 succeeded in crippling the Trade Union movement for the time being. But the workers had the last word. While the six men of Dorset endured the brutality of the convict settlements, a great movement of protest swept across England. There were countless petitions and public meetings, and a great procession of trade unionists in London's Copenhagen Fields. In 1836 the Government finally gave way and a free pardon and passage home was granted to the 'Tolpuddle Martyrs'. Even then, it was a further three years before the last of the six returned.

The People's Charter

As the events of the 'black year' of 1834 showed, successful trade union action still depended upon the goodwill of Parliament. But Parliament was unlikely to be sympathetic with working-class organisations so long as it was dominated by the upper and middle classes. Thus the fight for Parliamentary Reform was soon renewed.

In 1836, a group of skilled tradesmen and small shopkeepers founded the **London Working Men's Association** (L.W.M.A.) which aimed to 'seek by every legal means to place all classes of society in possession of equal political and social rights'. The inspiration behind the L.W.M.A. was its Secretary, **William Lovett** (1800–77) a cabinet-maker by trade. Under his influence, the L.W.M.A. drew up a **Charter** of political demands (1838) with the intention of presenting it to Parliament. It ran to many pages, but the real core of it was the following six points:

1. The vote for all adult males.
2. Election by secret ballot.
3. Equal electoral districts.
4. Abolition of the property qualification for M.P.s.
5. M.P.s to be paid a salary.
6. Annual Parliaments, with a general election every June.

Other societies of working men eagerly supported the Charter, and before long mass meetings and torchlight processions were held all over the country, particularly in industrial areas. Meanwhile at a great meeting in Birmingham (1838) the 'Chartist movement' was officially launched, with the aim of getting Parliament to accept the six points.

Right from the start, the movement lacked unity. Different sections had widely differing aims and tactics. In the Midlands, members of the Birmingham Political Union, led by **Thomas Attwood,** a banker and M.P., wanted, of all things, a change in the monetary system—to be achieved by a reformed Parliament. Like the L.W.M.A., the men from

The Newport Rising,
November 1839

Birmingham believed in using 'moral force' (non-violent methods), through petitions, public meetings and the like. On the other hand, the largest group, from northern England and South Wales, represented the most depressed ranks of society, like the unemployed industrial workers and the wretched handloom weavers. In their desperation, they were unlikely to stop short of violence and bloodshed. The 'physical force' Chartists, as they were called, wanted, above all, the repeal of the new Poor Law of 1834 (see Chapter 11) which made it necessary for the unemployed to enter a workhouse in order to get Poor Relief.

The leader of the 'physical force' Chartists, **Feargus O'Connor** (1794–1855) was 'a hot-headed Irishman', capable of driving audiences into a frenzy with his violent attacks on the middle and upper classes. His Leeds newspaper, *The Northern Star,* soon achieved a circulation of 50,000 copies, giving him enormous influence over the movement. Although London and Birmingham supported Lovett, the industrial workers of northern England and South Wales were under the spell of O'Connor, and it was these that provided the most active support for Chartism. O'Connor was unreliable and had little self-control, but he had powers of leadership that Lovett lacked. By 1839 he had virtually taken over the movement.

The **first National Petition,** containing 1,250,000 signatures, was presented to Parliament by Thomas Attwood in July 1839. Not surprisingly, the Commons rejected it by a large majority—235 votes to 46. A general strike or 'Sacred Month' had been threatened if the Petition was refused, but this fell through due to lack of organisation. However, Chartists from the Welsh valleys, led by **John Frost,** an ex-mayor and magistrate, were not prepared to accept defeat so easily. On the night of 3–4 November, over 1000 of them—mostly miners, armed with old muskets and clubs—gathered on the hills above **Newport.** Soon after dawn, they marched into the town in columns, but were surprised by a small military garrison which dispersed them with gunfire. Frost and two other leaders were transported to Australia for life.

The most serious phase of Chartism was over, but the movement was far from dead. In 1842, a **second National Petition,** six miles long, containing more than 3 million signatures, was rejected by a Commons vote of 287 to 49. Mass strikes and riots in the industrial areas followed, but the ringleaders were soon arrested and the authorities regained control. By now, Lovett and most of the 'moral force' Chartists had abandoned the movement. 'Muskets are not what are wanted, but education and schooling of the working people,' said Lovett. 'Violent words do not slay the enemies but the friends of our movement.'

O'Connor now began a scheme to establish co-operative communities of working people. The **Chartist Co-operative Land Society** (1845) quickly raised £80,000 in subscriptions and bought an estate in Hertfordshire. Members were allocated cottages and allotments of land, to enable them to be self-supporting. But success was short-lived. The Society was financially unsound and collapsed four years later.

Meanwhile, the return of distress and unemployment (1847–8) again resulted in the masses taking up the Chartist banner. A **third National Petition** was organised and, in April 1848, a demonstration was held on London's Kennington Common. The Queen was sent to the Isle of Wight for safety, and the aged Duke of Wellington, in charge of the defence of London, packed it with troops and special police. The huge Petition was carried in three cabs to Parliament, where many of the signatures were found to be forgeries—like 'Queen Victoria' and 'Mr Punch'. The name of the Duke of Wellington appeared sixteen times! When the Commons threw out the petition, by 222 votes to 17, Chartism was as good as dead. Later attempts to revive the movement failed, while O'Connor went out of his mind and died in an asylum (1855).

Chartism failed chiefly because its support came from the poorest and most powerless section of the population. Most of the better-paid workers deserted the movement when it fell under the control of the reckless O'Connor. The People's Charter was little more than a banner, behind which flocked a vast assortment of discontented working men with different aims and tactics. It gained most of its support in periods of distress. The years of the three petitions were also years of severe unemployment and high corn prices. Increasing prosperity, in which the working classes shared to some extent, finally killed Chartism. Nevertheless it was the first nation-wide movement of working-class protest, and it drew the attention of the ruling classes to the sufferings of the poor.

Between 1858 and 1918 five of the six points of the Charter were partly or wholly accepted into the British constitution.

Friendly Societies and Co-operatives

Today, we live in a so-called Welfare State; but in the nineteenth century there were no state schemes of social security for people

Chartist demonstration on Kennington Common, April 1848

who suffered hardship. Every man was expected to provide for himself and his family entirely by his own efforts. It was not considered the duty of the Government to interfere in these matters, with the exception of the Poor Law, which provided a 'last resort' for the destitute. This attitude was summed up by **Samuel Smiles,** an Edinburgh doctor, in his book *Self-Help* (1859). He said hard work was the *only* answer to poverty, for 'they who work in the truest spirit will invariably [always] be the most successful'. But, in practice, this was just wishful thinking as far as unskilled workers were concerned. They rarely earned enough to make ends meet in a normal week, let alone when their income was suddenly reduced by sickness, unemployment or death.

WORKING CLASS MOVEMENTS NB Each overlapped the others

TRADE UNIONS	REFORM MOVEMENTS, SOCIETIES AND PARTIES	FRIENDLY SOCIETIES AND CO-OPERATIVES
'Industrial Action' To get a better standard of living.	*'Political Action'* To get a share in government.	*'Self-help'* Schemes of security and welfare.
AIMS Higher wages. Shorter hours. Better working conditions.	AIMS The right to vote. General reform of Parliament to make the vote effective.	AIMS Insurance against sickness, unemployment, etc. Production and/or distribution of goods on non-profit making basis. Encouragement to save.
METHODS Negotiation with employers. Strikes.	METHODS Meetings and demonstrations. Newspapers and pamphlets. Petitions.	METHODS Collection of weekly subscriptions. Joint ownership of non-profit making shops, factories, etc.

On the other hand, the better-paid, more highly skilled workers *could* help themselves. They could afford weekly subscriptions to a **Friendly Society,** in return for which they got cash benefits in time of need—usually an allowance during sickness, a pension in old age, and a sum of money at death to help with funeral expenses. Friendly Societies of various kinds had been a feature of working-class life since the late seventeenth century. They were mostly small, local organisations (like trade clubs) providing members with social life and comradeship. Some of them, like the Oddfellows and the Foresters (the two largest) were run on a national basis, with branches all over the country.

The Industrial Revolution, by bringing workers together in large numbers, led to a rapid rise in the membership of Friendly Societies, especially in Lancashire. They were the only working-class organisations that were not outlawed in the period of government repression during and after the French Wars. As a result, by the early nineteenth century there were over a million members of Friendly Societies in England and Wales alone, and the numbers were increasing every year.

Lower-paid workers were unable to join Friendly Societies because they could not afford the weekly subscriptions, but many of them supported **Co-operative Societies,** which began to be established in the 1820s under the influence of Robert Owen. Some Co-operatives were simply small grocery stores which tried to cut out shopkeepers' profits by buying goods in bulk and selling them to members at reduced prices. Others concentrated on spreading the gospel of Robert Owen, or attempted co-operative production of goods. By 1832 there were altogether nearly 500 Co-operative Societies in Britain, but scarcely any were successful, largely because of insufficient funds to finance their schemes.

The real history of the Co-operative movement began in 1844, when twenty-eight weavers each invested £1 towards setting up a grocery store in **Toad Lane, Rochdale.** Goods such as flour, oatmeal, sugar, butter and candles were sold at normal prices. Then, after running costs had been deducted, the 'dividend' (profit) was shared out among the customers in proportion to the amount of goods they had bought. Dividends could be left in the business to

The original store of the Rochdale Pioneers

accumulate as shares on which interest was paid. This encouraged members to build up savings, and also provided a steady growth of funds which helped the store to expand. After a year the original membership had risen to seventy-four and profits of £22 were made. By 1875 it had no less than 8,415 members, with annual dividends totalling nearly £50,000.

The example of the 'Rochdale Pioneers' was soon followed throughout Lancashire and the North. As early as 1851 there were 130 similar societies; some of them in the industrial towns of Scotland. An important reason for their popularity was that they sold *pure* food. A co-operative store had no reason to swindle its members by watering down milk and butter or putting sand in the sugar, as many shopkeepers did in this period.

In 1863 a **Co-operative Wholesale Society** (C.W.S.) was established in Manchester to buy from producers in large quantities (wholesale) and supply individual stores. At first, it confined its activities to the North, but within ten years it became a nationwide organization. In 1875 the C.W.S. began manufacturing its own products. Beginning with flour-mills and factories making biscuits, shoes, soap and clothing, it soon offered a wide range of household goods.

Some of the Rochdale Pioneers, photographed in 1860

Total Membership of the Co-operative Movement

1851	*1881*	*1914*
15,000	546,000	over 3,000,000

By the end of the century, some of the profits of co-operation were being used to provide adult education and other services for members.

Timeline

1799–1800	Combination Acts—trade unions illegal.
1824–5	Repeal of Combination Acts.
1830	John Doherty's National Association for the Protection of Labour.
1833	Robert Owen's Grand National Consolidated Trades Union.
1834	The 'Tolpuddle Martyrs' and the collapse of the G.N.C.T.U.
1838	Appearance of The People's Charter.
1844	The 'Rochdale Pioneers'.
1848	Collapse of the Chartist movement.
1863	Co-operative Wholesale Society (C.W.S.).

Further study

The account of working-class movements continues in Chapter 17.

Project

Try to find out when and how five of the six points of The People's Charter became law in the seventy years following the collapse of Chartism. Make a list of reasons why the sixth—annual Parliaments—would *not* be a wise step.

General account

Andrew Robertson, *The Trade Unions* (Hamish Hamilton) pp. 9–40
P. Lane, *Trade Unions* (Batsford, Past-into-Present series)

Special topics

J. J. Bowles, *Dramatic Decisions* (Macmillan). Chapter 3 gives a dramatised account of the trial of the Tolpuddle Martyrs.
K. Dawson and P. Wall, *Trade Unions* (O.U.P.). For documents.
Peter Searby, *The Chartists* (Longman's Then and There series)
C. Thorne, *Chartism* (Macmillan, Sources of History series)
N. Wymer, *Social Reformers* (O.U.P., Lives of Great Men and Women, vol. 1) for Robert Owen.
D. B. O'Callaghan, *The Chartists* (Longman, Making the Modern World series)
The Early Trade Unions (Cape, Jackdaw series no. 35)
Towards Democracy (Longman, Secondary History Packs) Pack 22

Filmstrips

Trade Unionism—Historical, Part 1, by G. D. H. Cole (Common Ground)
Life of Robert Owen, Parts 1 and 2, by G. D. H. Cole (Common Ground)

13 The Railway Age
Transport and Communications 2

'Canals will last my lifetime, but what I fear is those damned tramways.' So said the Duke of Bridgewater, 'the father of inland navigation', shortly before his death. The **tramways** he referred to had been in use in mining areas for about 200 years. Their purpose was to ease the passage of horse-drawn wagons carrying coal from the pithead to the nearest navigable waterway. At first they were made of wood; later, iron plates were fixed to the rails to reduce wear, until about 1790, when rails made entirely of iron came into general use. But they were still confined almost entirely to mines and quarries. Not until 1804 was the first *public* railway built—from Croydon in Surrey to the Thames at Wandsworth.

It seemed unlikely that tramways would put either the canal companies or the turnpike trusts out of business. Both were enjoying great prosperity; together carrying vast quantities of freight and thousands of passengers every year. The Duke's forecast was only proved correct by an entirely new development which even he did not foresee—the combination of iron rails *and* steam-powered locomotives.

Richard Trevithick and 'strong steam'

The application of Watt's engine to driving a wheel (1781) aroused widespread interest in the possibility of steam-powered transport. But Watt himself was opposed to the idea, on the grounds that it was unsafe. When his foreman, William Murdock, built a working model of a high-pressure steam locomotive (1784) he discouraged him from proceeding any further. Watt preferred to keep the steam at atmospheric pressure, or very little above it, so that the creation of a vacuum was the most important part of the working process (see Chapter 8). His refusal to use high-pressure steam removed the risk of explosion, but it also made his engine unsuitable for any kind of wheeled transport.

Richard Trevithick (1771–1833) a young Cornish engineer, did not share Watt's fears. In 1802 he patented a **high-pressure steam-engine,** without all the clumsy mechanism of condenser and beam. The piston was driven directly by 'strong steam' (super-heated steam at higher than atmospheric pressure). Critics said the boiler would burst, but Trevithick safely let in steam at a pressure of 50 lb per square inch (atmospheric pressure at sea-level is less than 15 lb) and, before long, he was using pressures of over 100 lb. His compact little engine not only required less fuel to do the work of pumping (his original aim) but was light enough to be carried on a cart. Trevithick immediately realised the possibility of making the engine drive the cart. After experiments with steam road-carriages in Cornwall and London, he hit on the idea of building a railway locomotive.

Poster advertising the Surrey Iron Railway

Trevithick's 'Catch-me-who-can'

On a cold February morning in 1804 a historic journey was made along ten miles of tramway in South Wales. Trevithick's locomotive drew five wagons, a coach and about seventy passengers from **Penydaren** Ironworks (near Merthyr Tydfil) to the Glamorganshire canal. After frequent stoppages, mostly caused by the five-ton locomotive cracking the tramway, it completed the journey in four hours, to become the first steam-engine to run on rails and haul a train behind it.

Four years later Trevithick displayed his latest locomotive on a special circular track near Euston Square in London. He called it the 'Catch-me-who-can' and gave shilling rides to the public at

speeds of up to twelve m.p.h. But lack of money forced him to dismantle it a few weeks later. After more unsuccessful ventures, including an attempt to introduce his engine into the silver-mines of Peru, the forgotten Cornishman died in poverty, leaving others to benefit from his work.

William Hedley's 'Puffing Billy' (1813)

George Stephenson and the 'Rocket'

Although London businessmen failed to give Trevithick's invention the necessary financial support, it aroused great interest in the coal-mining areas of the North. Fodder for horses was in short supply during the Napoleonic Wars, so mine-owners were willing to consider any alternative means of moving coal. In 1805 Trevithick had built a locomotive for a colliery near Newcastle. It proved too heavy for the track and was never used, but it impressed many northern engineers. Before long, they were building locomotives of their own. In 1812, 'Prince Regent', designed by **John Blenkinsop**, a colliery engineer, began to operate a regular steam railway on the outskirts of Leeds. A year later, in the North-East, **William Hedley** produced 'Puffing Billy', which could draw nine laden wagons at four or five m.p.h.

These developments greatly interested a young engine-wright at

Killingworth Colliery in Northumberland. His name was **George Stephenson** (1781–1848). He is often credited with the invention of the locomotive, but, like James Watt, he was a great improver rather than a pioneer. The main features of an efficient steam piston-driven locomotive were already present in Trevithick's engines.

From the age of fourteen, when he became an assistant colliery fireman, Stephenson devoted his life to engineering. He was skilfully repairing all kinds of machines, including steam-engines, before he learned properly how to read and write. His employer, Lord Ravensworth, had heard of Blenkinsop's and Hedley's locomotives, and when Stephenson suggested building one he provided the money. The result was 'Blücher' (named after a Prussian general) which pulled eight laden wagons at four m.p.h. on its first run in 1814. In the next seven years, Stephenson built sixteen locomotives and many miles of track; gaining a high reputation as an engineer.

The turning-point in his life came in 1821. Edward Pease, a wealthy landowner, appointed him engineer in charge of a new public railway to join the coal-mines of South Durham with the river-port of Stockton. Stephenson surveyed and constructed a route of twenty-seven miles, running from Witton Park Colliery, via Darlington. He laid the rails 4 feet $8\frac{1}{2}$ inches apart (the gauge still used today) after measuring the wheelbase of over 100 country carts and taking an average. Pease had assumed that all the traffic on the railway would be horse-drawn, but Stephenson convinced him of the advantages of steam. Thus, at the ceremonial opening of the **Stockton–Darlington line** (September 1825) twelve loaded wagons, a coach and twenty-one passenger-cars were hauled by Stephenson's 'Locomotion', one of four engines specially built for the new railway. The triumphant journey to Stockton Quay was witnessed by thousands of cheering spectators.

The Stockton–Darlington railway aroused great interest among the merchants of **Liverpool** and **Manchester**. They had long been dissatisfied with their canals, which were not only slow but likely to run short of water in the summer or freeze in the winter. In 1826 they got parliamentary permission to build a railway and appointed Stephenson Chief Engineer at the princely salary of £1000 a year. But in spite of generous offers of compensation this pleased neither the canal-owners nor those who owned land between the two towns. They raised all kinds of objections to the proposed use of locomotives, saying these would pollute the countryside and terrify livestock. They claimed passengers would be blinded and deafened by the appalling speed of the trains and suffocate in the tunnels. When words failed to have an effect, they resorted to spoiling tactics. Surveyors were forced to work at night with lanterns to avoid pitched battles with farmers and their hired thugs.

The hostility of man was matched by that of nature. Stephenson, now working with his son **Robert**—an engineer as capable as himself—had enormous obstacles to overcome in laying the track. The greatest of these was Chat Moss, a huge spongy bog, which threatened to swallow up the track until a solid foundation of earth was sunk right to the bottom. In 1829, with the line nearing

1829.

GRAND COMPETITION

OF

LOCOMOTIVES

ON THE

LIVERPOOL & MANCHESTER RAILWAY.

STIPULATIONS & CONDITIONS

On WHICH THE DIRECTORS OF THE LIVERPOOL AND MANCHESTER RAILWAY OFFER A PREMIUM OF £500 FOR THE MOST IMPROVED LOCOMOTIVE ENGINE.

I.

The said Engine must "effectually consume its own smoke," according to the provisions of the Railway Act, 7th Geo. IV.

II.

The Engine, if it weighs Six Tons, must be capable of drawing after it, day by day, on a well-constructed Railway, on a level plane, a Train of Carriages of the gross weight of Twenty Tons, including the Tender and Water Tank, at the rate of Ten Miles per Hour, with a pressure of steam in the boiler not exceeding Fifty Pounds on the square inch.

III.

There must be Two Safety Valves, one of which must be completely out of the reach or control of the Engine-man, and neither of which must be fastened down while the Engine is working.

IV.

The Engine and Boiler must be supported on Springs, and rest on Six Wheels; and the height from the ground to the top of the Chimney must not exceed Fifteen Feet.

V.

The weight of the Machine, WITH ITS COMPLEMENT OF WATER in the Boiler, must, at most, not exceed Six Tons, and a Machine of less weight will be preferred if it draw AFTER it a PROPORTIONATE weight; and if the weight of the Engine, &c., do not exceed FIVE TONS, then the gross weight to be drawn need not exceed Fifteen Tons; and in that proportion for Machines of still smaller weight—provided that the Engine, &c., shall still be on six wheels, unless the weight (as above) be reduced to Four Tons and a Half, or under, in which case the Boiler, &c., may be placed on four wheels. And the Company shall be at liberty to put the Boiler, Fire Tube, Cylinders, &c., to the test of a pressure of water not exceeding 150 Pounds per square inch, without being answerable for any damage the Machine may receive in consequence.

VI.

There must be a Mercurial Gauge affixed to the Machine, with Index Rod, showing the Steam Pressure above 45 Pounds per square inch; and constructed to blow out a Pressure of 60 Pounds per inch.

VII.

The Engine to be delivered complete for trial, at the Liverpool end of the Railway, not later than the 1st of October next.

VIII.

The price of the Engine which may be accepted, not to exceed £550, delivered on the Railway; and any Engine not approved to be taken back by the Owner.

N.B.—The Railway Company will provide the ENGINE TENDER with a supply of Water and Fuel, for the experiment. The distance within the Rails is four feet eight inches and a half.

THE LOCOMOTIVE STEAM ENGINES,

WHICH COMPETED FOR THE PRIZE OF £500 OFFERED BY THE DIRECTORS OF THE LIVERPOOL AND MANCHESTER RAILWAY COMPANY.

DRAWN TO A SCALE ¼ INCH TO A FOOT.

THE "ROCKET" OF Mr. ROBt. STEPHENSON OF NEWCASTLE,

WHICH DRAWING A LOAD EQUIVALENT TO THREE TIMES ITS WEIGHT TRAVELLED AT THE RATE OF 12½ MILES AN HOUR, AND WITH A CARRIAGE & PASSENGERS AT THE RATE OF 24 MILES. COST PER MILE FOR FUEL ABOUT THREE HALFPENCE.

THE "NOVELTY" OF MESSrs. BRAITHWAITE & ERRICSSON OF LONDON,

WHICH DRAWING A LOAD EQUIVALENT TO THREE TIMES ITS WEIGHT TRAVELLED AT THE RATE OF 20½ MILES AN HOUR, AND WITH A CARRIAGE & PASSENGERS AT THE RATE OF 32 MILES. COST PER MILE FOR FUEL ABOUT ONE HALFPENNY.

THE "SANSPAREIL" OF Mr. HACKWORTH OF DARLINGTON,

WHICH DRAWING A LOAD EQUIVALENT TO THREE TIMES ITS WEIGHT TRAVELLED AT THE RATE OF 12½ MILES AN HOUR, COST FOR FUEL PER MILE ABOUT TWO PENCE.

The competitors at Rainhill

completion, the Directors of the company offered a £500 prize for the best steam-engine to work it. The contest, held on part of the new track at **Rainhill,** was a triumph for the Stephensons. Their entry, the **'Rocket',** was the undisputed winner, reaching a speed of twenty-nine m.p.h. From now on, there could be no doubt that people were going to travel faster than horses could carry them. When the two-way track was opened in 1830, worked by eight engines from the Stephensons' Newcastle factory, it was the first to be devoted entirely to steam locomotives. The real 'Railway Age' had begun.

The Railway Revolution

The Liverpool to Manchester line connected two great cities whose combined population totalled 350,000. With over 1000 passengers a day and a large volume of freight, profits reached £80,000 in 1831 alone. Businessmen all over the country, seeing these rich rewards, rushed to promote railway companies by private Act of Parliament. Canal 'navvies' provided a ready-made labour force to carry out the work of railway construction. This tough new breed of unskilled labourers, working almost entirely without machinery in all weathers, became the backbone of the Railway Age. Meanwhile canal-building came to an abrupt halt. Hundreds of canal companies and turnpike trusts were ruined as the growing railway network claimed an increasing share of long-distance traffic. Short-haul road traffic in and around the towns actually increased, but country roads and their coaching inns became almost deserted. If ever there was a 'revolution' in inland transport this was it.

There was no attempt to plan a proper railway system. Parliament allowed a general 'free for all', which resulted in a haphazard network with frequent duplication (more than one line to the same place). Nevertheless, progress was remarkably rapid. By 1843 London was linked with Dover, Brighton, Southampton, Bristol, Birmingham, Lancaster and York. In the next three years (1844–6) Parliament gave permission for a further 438 lines to be built. A *railway mania* had gripped the nation and the urge for quick and easy money led to great speculation in railway shares on the Stock Exchange. Small companies amalgamated or were swallowed up by larger ones, and a handful of financiers gained great power. The most famous of these was **George Hudson,** 'the Railway King', who bought control of most of the Midland and northern companies. But his success was short-lived. When some of his schemes collapsed, he continued to pay dividends to shareholders with money he had raised to form new companies. By 1848 his double-dealing was exposed and he was ruined, along with thousands of others.

The railway mania had constructive results as well. By 1852, when most of the railways resulting from it were completed, almost all the *main* lines of the present day network had been laid.

Total track mileage in Britain

1840	1,857 miles
1855	8,000 miles approx
1870	15,557 miles

The scheduled time for fast trains between important business centres was already above forty m.p.h. in 1850. As the following table shows, there has been little progress since:

Box tunnel—built by Isambard Brunel

London to Southampton by 'fast train' (79 miles)

1848 1 hour 47 min average speed 44 m.p.h.
1909 1 hour 38 min average speed 48 m.p.h.
1967 1 hour 33 min* average speed 51 m.p.h.

Passengers travelled in first-, second- or third-class **coaches.** The first-class compartments were like stage-coaches inside, usually with eight cushioned seats. But there was no lighting or heating in the early years and no lavatories before the 1870s. Second-class coaches provided shelter, but little else; while the earliest third-class passengers travelled in open trucks with perhaps a few planks for seating. Third-class travel was rare before an **Act of 1844** compelled all future companies to provide it; this was one of the rare examples of parliamentary action. At least one train a day in each direction had to stop at all stations and give third-class passengers a seated and covered ride at no more than a penny per mile.

George and Robert Stephenson continued to play a leading part in railway development after 1830. They engineered the London to

* During 1967 electrification of the line helped to reduce the time to 1 hour 12 minutes.

Birmingham line (1833–8) and made further progress in locomotive design. Other great engine-builders included **Sir Daniel Gooch** of the Great Western Railway (G.W.R.). By the late 1840s, his expresses like 'Great Western' could exceed sixty m.p.h. and pull from London to Bristol in two and a half hours.

The London to Bristol line was a fine piece of engineering. It was built (1835–41) under the direction of **Isambard Kingdom Brunel** (1806–59) Chief Engineer of the G.W.R. With slight gradients and few bends, it still provides the fastest regular run in Britain. Brunel's remarkable skill was displayed to great effect in the course of driving the line through the Cotswolds. A two-mile tunnel was built at Box Hill—the longest and most difficult so far attempted. Brunel showed his complete mastery of the situation by setting the incline so that the rising sun shone through from end to end on his birthday (9 April)!

Brunel's colourful personality was in complete contrast to the careful and reserved Stephensons. He delighted in breaking with tradition. For example, he laid his rails seven feet apart, to help trains hold the track more firmly on the bends, especially at high speed. He hoped other companies would follow suit, but he was fighting a losing battle. By the mid 1840s, well over eighty per cent of Britain's railways had been built on Stephenson's 4 feet 8½ inches gauge. Parliament, seeking to establish a standard gauge for the whole country (1848), had little alternative but to forbid any extension of the broad gauge outside G.W.R. territory. By 1892 the G.W.R. had converted the last of its broad tracks to the standard gauge, and what might have been Brunel's greatest monument was gone for ever. Today the chief remains of his work are his fine bridges— notably the 1000-feet **Royal Albert Bridge** across the river Tamar at Saltash. It was completed in 1859, just before his death.

Brunel's magnificent Royal Albert Bridge

By this time railways had begun to affect almost every aspect of national life. Country areas, previously isolated, were brought into direct contact with towns and cities. All branches of industry benefited—especially iron and steel, mechanical engineering, coal and agriculture. Railways themselves became a new major industry, with valuable export markets in four continents, and 'railway towns' sprang up in places like Swindon, Eastleigh and Crewe. The last had a population of 203 in 1841; thirty years later it was nearly 18,000.

Meanwhile social habits were changing as a result of railways. Quick daily travel enabled many people to live away from their work. Suburbs grew up on the outskirts of large towns. Railways also made it possible for increasing numbers to take annual holidays by the seaside, at expanding resorts like Brighton and Blackpool. Only the middle classes could afford this luxury at first, but by the end of the century, the 'holiday habit' was spreading among better-off working-class families.

Electric telegraph and Penny Post

To ensure safe and efficient operation of the railways, various methods of signalling were introduced. At first, signalmen stood by the track holding coloured flags—or lanterns after dark. They were soon replaced by mechanical 'arms' attached to posts and connected by rods to a shed (signal-box). But by far the most important development was that of *telegraphy* or distance communication.

The discovery that electric signals could be sent along wires dates back to the eighteenth century. In the earliest experiments with 'electric telegraph' a separate wire was used to represent each letter of the alphabet. But this method was very troublesome, particularly if numbers were used as well. In 1837 two British scientists, **Charles Wheatstone** and **William Cooke,** invented a 'needle telegraph', with an appropriate signalling code. Five magnetic needles were deflected by electricity to point to letters of the alphabet arranged on a board. The first telegraph wires were set up between Euston and Camden Town railway stations in London. Paddington was then connected with Slough on the G.W.R. In 1845 the success of the new device was assured when a suspected murderer was arrested at Paddington due to a telegraph message sent ahead of his train!

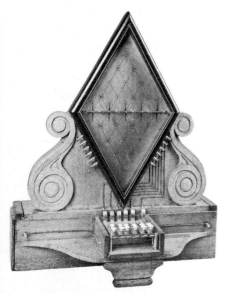

Cooke and Wheatstone's five-needle telegraph

The electric telegraph was confined almost entirely to use on the railway before 1850, by which time the inventors had perfected a single-needle model. In 1851 a cable was laid across the Channel to establish contact between London and Paris. From then on telegraphy progressed rapidly. A transatlantic cable was laid in 1866. Three years later, Parliament granted a monopoly of all inland telegraph business to the Post Office, paying £11 million in compensation to the private companies. Meanwhile the needle device had been given up in favour of the system invented in America by **Samuel Morse,** which employed a code of dots and dashes.

Another great advance in communications during the Railway Age was the introduction of a nationwide **penny post.** Reform of the postal service was long overdue even before the coming of railways. Letters were charged according to weight and distance, and payment

The famous 'penny black' (1840)

was made by the receiver—a complicated and expensive procedure. Parliament's decision to tax letters (1801) only made matters worse, and encouraged the public to find ways of sending mail privately. By the 1830s, when a single sheet from London to Edinburgh cost no less than 1s 3½d, a Parliamentary Committee discovered that over three-quarters of the mail on some long-distance routes was not carried by the Post Office at all!

At this point, an ex-schoolmaster named **Rowland Hill** (1795–1879) published a plan for Post Office reform (1837) based on cheapness and simplicity. He calculated that the main cost of the postal service resulted from the need to tax each individual letter and collect the postage on delivery. Hill argued that if a prepaid standard rate of a penny was charged for every letter, regardless of distance, the volume of mail would so increase that the Government's total revenue would rise. His plan was accepted and he was asked to supervise its introduction early in 1840. All letters up to half an ounce paid a penny, after which additional charges were made for extra weight. To enable payment to be made quickly and in advance, the world's first **postage stamps** were produced—the famous Victorian 'penny blacks'. They had to be cut out with scissors until 1854, when sheets were perforated. Meanwhile, Hill's idea spread rapidly throughout the civilised world.

'Smokeboats'

Steamships were invented *before* railway locomotives—for it was possible to use a low-pressure 'condensing engine' on the water. But whereas railways quickly established superiority over other forms of land transport, steamships met stiff opposition from sailing vessels and did not replace them on the main ocean routes until the second half of the nineteenth century.

Following experiments with steam-powered boats in France and North America, the first British steamer went noisily afloat on a Scottish loch in 1788. It was a double-hulled paddleboat, designed by **William Symington** (1763–1831) a Scottish millwright. His second effort, the *Charlotte Dundas* (1802) pulled two heavily-laden

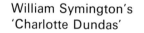

William Symington's 'Charlotte Dundas'

barges for twenty miles on its maiden voyage along the Forth-Clyde Canal. Symington was asked to build eight steam-tugs for the Bridgewater Canal, but the Duke's death (1803) resulted in his contract being cancelled. This was the nearest he got to business success. Like Trevithick, he eventually died in poverty while others profited from his invention.

Robert Fulton, an American, had inspected the *Charlotte Dundas* during a visit to Britain. In 1807, he launched *The Clermont,* powered by a Boulton and Watt engine, which proved the merits of steam navigation beyond question in a series of voyages on the Hudson river. Within ten years, 'smokeboats', as the Red Indians called them, were running regularly on the Mississippi. Meanwhile, paddle-steamers were becoming equally familiar on the river Clyde. Europe's first commercially successful steamship service was started in 1812 by **Henry Bell's** *Comet,* which he advertised 'to ply upon the River Clyde, from Glasgow; to sail by the power of wind and steam'. In addition to her three horse-power engine, *Comet* had a sail, to catch any favourable wind. Most steamships carried sails for another fifty years or more, to economise on fuel and as a safeguard in case of engine failure.

Regular cross-Channel steamers between Dover and Calais started in 1818. The next step was for steamships to meet the challenge of the oceans. This was no easy task, for their high coal consumption greatly reduced their range. When the American steamship *Savannah* crossed the Atlantic to Liverpool (1819) her engine could only be used for eighty-five hours of the twenty-seven-day voyage. Neverthe-less she was the first steam vessel to cross *any* ocean—a clear pointer to the future. In 1838 at least three English ships crossed the Atlantic using steam all the way. The first was *Sirius* from London, followed, only a day later, by the faster *Great Western* from Bristol, designed by **I. K. Brunel.** He aimed to link it up with the London to Bristol railway (then under construction) to provide a combined land and sea route from London to New York. The age of long-distance steam naviga-tion had begun. Two years later, the first regular line of ocean-going steamships was started by **Samuel Cunard,** a shipowner from Halifax, Nova Scotia.

All the early steamships were driven by paddle-wheels, but these were very exposed and hence easily damaged. The Admiralty in particular had misgivings about using ships which could be crippled by a single shot. The answer was to replace paddles with a propeller under the stern. The first successful 'screw-steamer', the S.S. *Archimedes* (1838) was designed by an Englishman, **Francis Pettit-Smith.** Seven years later, Brunel's *Great Britain* made the first screw-propelled Atlantic crossing. More important still, she was the first ocean-going ship constructed entirely of *iron*. Previous steamers, like *Great Western,* had iron bands round the hull to give additional strength, but they were basically wood.

John Wilkinson, the great ironmaster, successfully launched an iron barge as early as 1787, but it was not until 1822 that an iron ship put to sea. This was the *Aaron Manby,* a steamer, which crossed the Channel after being built in sections in the Midlands and assembled

Isambard Kingdom Brunel, photographed in front of *The Great Eastern*

on the banks of the Thames. Most shipbuilders still preferred to work with wood, but the growing shortage of timber gradually forced them to use iron, and thus to discover its great advantages. It was so much stronger than wood that half-inch iron plates could be used in place of timbers a foot thick. As a result, an iron ship was actually lighter than a wooden one of the same size.

The added strength of iron made it possible to build much larger ships, a fact which did not escape the inventive genius of Isambard Brunel. The last years of his life were devoted to his most ambitious project, the **Great Eastern**. She was 700 feet long, with five funnels and six masts, a double hull and both screw-propeller and paddle-wheels (the only ship to combine the two). Built at Millwall (East London) she was eventually floated on the Thames in January 1858, after defying all attempts at launching for three months previously! With accommodation for 4000 passengers and a top speed of fourteen knots (about sixteen m.p.h.) she was a triumph of engineering. The *Great Eastern* remained the world's biggest ship for over forty years— yet she was a commercial failure, like many of Brunel's daring schemes. She was intended for the Eastern trade, but the only profitable use to which her vast storage space could be put was laying telegraph cables in the Atlantic.

The Great Eastern

The challenge of the clipper

Steamships were faster and more punctual than sailing vessels. They did not have to wait for favourable winds, so their time of arrival could be advertised with reasonable accuracy. Nevertheless, the need to carry great loads of coal severely reduced their cargo space, making them uneconomical on a long voyage. Right up to the 1870s, sail held its own on the longest trade routes—in the shape of the **clipper,** the swiftest and most graceful of all wind-driven ships. Originating in the U.S.A. in the 1840s, they were long and narrow, with sharp bows, almost straight sides and an enormous spread of sail. Their great cargo space and relatively small crew made possible a large reduction in long-distance freight charges. In favourable conditions they were capable of remarkably high speeds. In 1854, the American *James Baines* crossed the Atlantic to Liverpool in twelve days—three days faster than the *Great Western* on her maiden voyage.

British shipbuilders went one better than their American rivals, making clippers with hulls of iron instead of timber. These were not only cheaper to construct but held even more cargo. Famous British clippers included the *Cutty Sark, Thermopylae* and *Sir Lancelot,* whose sails would have covered fifteen tennis courts. They were mostly employed in bringing tea from China and wool from Australia.

But, even in the heyday of the clipper, the scales were tipping in favour of steam. In 1854, **John Elder,** a Scotsman, invented a **compound engine,** with two cylinders. The steam exhaust from the first was used again, at reduced pressure, to drive the piston in the second, resulting in a reduction of nearly sixty per cent in fuel consumption. Steamships gained a further advantage when the **Suez Canal** was opened (1869). Their passage to the East was shortened by 3000 miles, yet sailing ships continued to go round the Cape of Good Hope because of unfavourable winds in the Mediterranean and the expense of hiring canal tugs. Meanwhile **coaling stations** on the principal sea routes, at places like Gibraltar, Suez, Aden and Singapore, further assisted steamships by allowing them to devote more space to cargo.

The Cutty Sark

Timeline

1802	Richard Trevithick's high-pressure steam-engine.
	William Symington's *Charlotte Dundas.*
1804	Trevithick's Penydaren locomotive.
	Surrey Iron Railway.
1808	Trevithick's 'Catch-me-who-can'.
1825	Stockton to Darlington railway.
1829	Stephenson's 'Rocket' wins the Rainhill trials.
1830	Liverpool to Manchester railway.
1837	Wheatstone and Cooke's electric 'needle telegraph'.
1838	*Sirius* and *Great Western* cross Atlantic under steam.
1840	Rowland Hill's Penny Post.
1844–6	'Railway mania'.
1854	John Elder's compound steam-engine.
1858	Isambard Kingdom Brunel's *Great Eastern.*
1869	Suez Canal opened.

Further study

Visits

Collections of railway locomotives and rolling stock can be seen in the National Railway Museum, York; the GWR Museum, Swindon; Steamtown Railway Museum, Carnforth; Glasgow Museum of Transport; Dinting Railway Centre, Glossop; Somerset Railway Museum, Weston Super Mare; Scottish Railway Preservation Society, Falkirk; Quainton Railway Society, nr Aylesbury, and many other centres.

London's Science Museum has small sections on rail transport (ground floor); telegraphic apparatus (first floor); and many exhibits on navigation and shipping (second floor) including models of *Savannah, Sirius, Great Eastern* and other early steamships.

The clipper *Cutty Sark* can be seen in dry dock at Greenwich.

General accounts

G. C. Allen, *Railways* (Blackwell)

G. Hamilton Ellis, *A Picture History of Railways* and *A Picture History of Ships* (Vista Books). Both are packed with photographs, sketches and newspaper illustrations.

L. E. Snellgrove, *From Rocket to Railcar* Chapters 1–7, and *From Coracles to Cunarders* (Longmans) pp. 78–107

R. Watson, *The Transport Revolution* (Longman, Focus on History series)

Special topics

B. Barker and R. Boden, *Railway Mania* (Longman, History Games)

M. Robbins, *George and Robert Stephenson* (O.U.P.)

L. T. C. Rolt, *Brunel* (Methuen's Story Biographies)

R. R. Sellman, *Watt and Trevithick, George and Robert Stephenson,* and *Isambard Kingdom Brunel* (Methuen, Brief Lives)

J. A. Williamson, *George and Robert Stephenson* (A. and C. Black)

Clipper Ships and the Cutty Sark (Cape, Jackdaw series no. 97)

Transport (Longman, Secondary History Packs) Packs 17, 18

Shire Publications' Lifelines series includes the following:

James Hodge, *Richard Trevithick*

D. J. Smith, *Robert Stephenson*

Richard Tames, *Isambard Kingdom Brunel*

Longman's Then and There series includes:

A. Grant, *Sailing Ships and Emigrants in Victorian Times*

M. O. Greenwood, *The Railway Revolution*

A. James, *Sir Rowland Hill and the Post Office*

Filmstrips

Story of a Railway (Hulton: in colour) deals with the development of the London and North-Western Railway.

Railway Carriage Development (British Transport)

The Railways, 1770–1870 (Nicholas Hunter Filmstrips)

Development of the Ship, *Part 3,* The Nineteenth and Twentieth Centuries (Rank)

Clipper Ships (Visual Publications)

14 'Free Trade'
Foreign Trade, the Corn Laws and Agriculture

Much government revenue (income) had long been obtained from taxes on overseas trade. Of these, the most important were *tariffs* (customs duties on imported goods). But tariffs often had an additional purpose. Like the Navigation Acts or 'Laws of Trade' (see Chapter 3) they were one of the ways by which Parliament *controlled* the nation's trade. For example, the French and Italians could produce high quality silk goods at prices below those of British manufacturers. Therefore, to protect the home industry from foreign competition, Parliament raised the price of imported silk by putting a tariff on it. In addition, duties were put on certain *ex*ports which Parliament considered 'undesirable', like the sale of scarce raw materials to foreign rivals.

By the early nineteenth century, however, most of these trading restrictions were no longer necessary. Britain was the world's greatest industrial nation, mass producing large quantities of cheap goods, and thus had little to fear from open competition with other countries. In fact, many tariffs had become more of a hindrance than a help. They increased the cost of imported raw materials and so put up the prices of finished articles. Consequently, the period up to about 1860 saw a gradual withdrawal of trading restrictions, giving the British greater freedom to buy and sell where they pleased.

Followers of Adam Smith

The real starting-point of the movement towards 'free trade' was a book published in 1776 by **Adam Smith** (1725–90) a Professor at Glasgow University. It was called ***An Inquiry into the Causes of the Wealth of Nations*** and it concluded that all attempts to restrict foreign trade by tariffs, which made cheap goods from abroad artificially dearer, were entirely wrong. Smith considered it natural for each country to export goods it could produce most cheaply and import goods that were more cheaply produced elsewhere. As he put it: 'The tailor does not attempt to make his own shoes, but buys them of the shoemaker. The shoemaker does not attempt to make his own clothes, but employs a tailor. . . . What is prudence [common sense] in the conduct of every private family can scarce be folly in that of a great kingdom.'

The purpose of many tariffs was not to control trade but simply to raise revenue for the Government. Duties on imported tobacco and tea, for instance, were straightforward taxes, because in neither case was there a home industry to 'protect' from foreign competition. Adam Smith did not regard these 'revenue duties' as a hindrance to free trade. On the contrary, he had them in mind when he suggested that enough revenue for the Government 'might be drawn from duties upon the importation of only a few sorts of goods

Adam Smith

Smugglers bringing their
goods ashore

of the most general use and consumption'.

Pitt the Younger was one of the first to be influenced by *The Wealth of Nations.* In 1784, soon after becoming Prime Minister, he began to reduce some of the heaviest duties on imports. He did this in the hope of stopping the activities of smugglers, which Adam Smith had condemned. For example, he cut the duty on imported tea from 119 per cent to $12\frac{1}{2}$ per cent of its value, which made the profits of smuggling no longer worth the risk. He took up another of Adam Smith's suggestions in 1786, when he made a trade treaty with France. This lowered tariffs on imported French wines, spirits and silks in return for reduced French duties on British hardware and textile goods. But a change of policy was forced on Pitt by the outbreak of war with revolutionary France (1793), which brought the trade treaty to an end. The Government needed every penny it could get to pay for the war. Therefore duties were *increased* and a number of new trading restrictions were introduced.

Not until the 1820s was the policy of free trade resumed—by **William Huskisson** (1770–1830) President of the Board of Trade from 1823 to 1827. To help British manufacturers, he lowered tariffs on many imported raw materials, especially those used in textiles and the metal trades. Realising that British industry need no longer fear foreign competition, he reduced the maximum duty on imported manufactures from fifty to thirty per cent. He hoped this would set an example to other countries and perhaps encourage them to lower *their* tariffs against British goods. For similar reasons, Huskisson removed many of the restrictions in the old Navigation Acts, which had been strongly attacked by Adam Smith. British shipping, like British industry, no longer needed parliamentary protection. In addition, Huskisson continued Pitt's policy of offering trade treaties to other countries, in order to achieve reduced tariffs on both sides.

Although Huskisson did a great deal in a short time, the main steps towards free trade were taken in the middle years of the century, by Robert Peel and W. E. Gladstone. As Prime Minister (1841–6) **Peel** set out to encourage British industry and trade through a massive reduction of tariffs. By 1845 he had abolished all remaining export duties and practically all tariffs on imported raw materials. The maximum duty on foreign manufactures was also reduced, to ten per cent. Altogether, in the space of five years, Peel

The chief steps to Free Trade

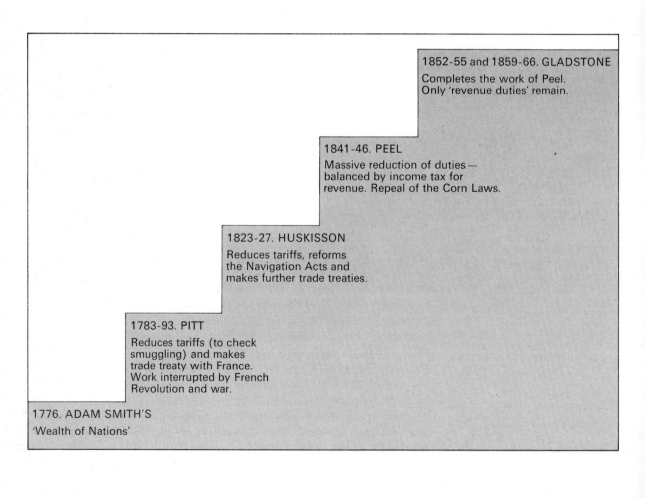

1852-55 and 1859-66. GLADSTONE
Completes the work of Peel.
Only 'revenue duties' remain.

1841-46. PEEL
Massive reduction of duties —
balanced by income tax for
revenue. Repeal of the Corn Laws.

1823-27. HUSKISSON
Reduces tariffs, reforms
the Navigation Acts and
makes further trade treaties.

1783-93. PITT
Reduces tariffs (to check
smuggling) and makes
trade treaty with France.
Work interrupted by French
Revolution and war.

1776. ADAM SMITH'S
'Wealth of Nations'

Sir Robert Peel

entirely abolished the duties on over 600 articles (more than half the existing total when he took office) and greatly reduced the remainder.

Partly as a result of Peel's policy, the volume of trade increased rapidly. The value of British exports rose from £47 million in 1842 to £57 million four years later. Although this brought increased revenue from the duties which remained, the Government still had to find another source of income to balance its tariff losses. Peel therefore reintroduced **income tax** (1842) at the rate of sevenpence in the pound on incomes over £150 a year. It was intended to last for a trial period of three years, but has remained ever since. Nevertheless, income tax has great advantages over other forms of taxation. It does not hinder trade, and, unlike most customs duties, it can be confined entirely to the well-to-do classes.

Thus the effects of Peel's free trade policy were felt not only by manufacturers and merchants but by the poor. While the burden of taxation on them was lightened, the reduction of duties on everyday essentials like meat, sugar, tea and soap brought down the cost of living. Above all, prosperous export industries resulted in regular employment and often higher wages too.

The repeal of the Corn Laws

British manufactured goods were normally cheaper than those of other countries; but, in contrast, home-grown food was often *dearer* than that produced overseas. Therefore landlords and farmers, unlike the rest of the community, *feared* the movement towards free trade. They claimed they would be ruined if cheap foreign food, especially corn, was allowed into the country free of duty. It was for this reason that the Corn Law of 1815 had been passed at the end of the French Wars (see Chapter 11). It had the effect of preventing foreign corn from entering Britain. But, because it artificially raised the price of bread, it was really a tax on the bulk of the population for the benefit of landlords and farmers alone. From the start, it was hotly opposed by manufacturers, town workers and, not least of all, agricultural labourers. No matter how prosperous farmers became, the wages they paid their labourers remained the lowest in the land.

In 1828 a new Corn Law replaced the prohibition on foreign corn by a 'sliding scale' of duties. These went down as the home price rose, until when the price of home-grown corn was 73 shillings or more a quarter, the duty on imported corn was only a shilling a quarter. But this had little effect on bread prices. By the late 1830s, when a series of bad harvests coincided with a depression in industry, a small 2-lb loaf could cost as much as a shilling—almost the entire daily wage of many labourers. In these circumstances, there was a greatly increased demand for the repeal (abolition) of all laws restricting the import of foreign corn. To achieve this aim, an **Anti-Corn Law League** was formed in Manchester, early in 1839, by 'representatives from all the great sections of our manufacturing and commercial population'.

There now followed a bitter struggle for supremacy between the rising industrial middle classes in the towns and the old land-owning gentry in the countryside. Supporters of the League claimed

that the future prosperity of Britain depended on the needs of manufacturers being given priority over the interests of landowners. They said that because Britain was the leading industrial nation, it was sensible to *concentrate* on manufacturing goods for export. If the Corn Laws were repealed, foreign countries would sell more food to Britain and, as a consequence, they would be able to afford to buy more British manufactures in return. The result would be a more rapid increase in the volume of both imports and exports.

With financial backing from rich manufacturers, the League ran a nationwide publicity campaign. Cheap postage after 1840 enabled millions of pamphlets and newspapers to be distributed, and full use was made of the new railways to send speakers on tours round the country. Almost everywhere, they received enthusiastic support. In the space of three months, early in the campaign, 150 meetings were held in London alone. Two of the League's main spokesmen, **Richard Cobden** (1804–65) and **John Bright** (1811–89) carried the campaign into Parliament after being elected to the Commons in 1841 and 1844 respectively. For them, repeal of the Corn Laws meant even more than an expansion of trade and cheaper bread. They considered free trade among nations the best means of securing international peace and friendship. Cobden and Bright were both fine speakers. Before long, they gained the support of a powerful group of 'free traders' in the Whig Opposition Party.

Cobden addressing the Anti-Corn Law League Council.

Cobden taking 'Master Robert' (Peel) on a Free Trade Walk

TO FREE TRADE

As Prime Minister, Peel was in a very difficult position. Having set out to achieve free trade in manufactured goods, it seemed reasonable for him to do the same in the case of foodstuffs. But the Conservative Party, which he headed, was dominated by landowners. They would regard any attempt by their leader to repeal the Corn Laws as down-right treachery. Nevertheless, Peel found the arguments of the League so convincing that they eventually converted him. On one occasion, early in 1845, while Cobden was speaking in the Commons, he screwed up his notes and whispered to one of his colleagues: 'You must answer this, I can't.'

The Conservatives had been elected to maintain the Corn Laws. Therefore Peel's best plan was to wait until the next general election (1847 at the latest) before making his views public and trying to win over both his party and the voters to free trade in corn. But time ran out for him in the summer of 1845. Exceptionally heavy rain spoilt the English harvest and, worse still, led to the destruction of three-quarters of the Irish potato crop. The peasants of Ireland lived almost entirely on potatoes. Therefore food had to be provided for them immediately, for they were already dying of starvation by the thousand. There was no alternative but to import large quantities of foreign corn. In such a situation, it seemed senseless to stand by the Corn Laws, but it was realised that if they were suspended now they would probably not be brought back.

By October 1845 Peel had made up his mind. The Corn Laws must be repealed at once. But his Cabinet was divided, so he resigned (December). However, the Whigs failed to form a Government and Peel returned to office. Although a majority of Conservatives opposed repeal, they were outnumbered in the Commons, largely because almost all the Whigs supported Peel's decision. After a long struggle, Peel convinced most of his Cabinet and got the necessary approval of Parliament in June 1846. The Corn Laws were repealed at last; although a small duty of four shillings a quarter remained until 1849, when it was reduced to one shilling. One of the greatest political struggles of the century thus ended in defeat for the landowners. Having lost their control of Parliament, they could never again force their will on the rest of the nation.

'Rotten potatoes have done it all,' said the Duke of Wellington, 'they put Peel in his damned fright.' But this was not strictly true. Peel's views had already changed before the crisis came. In the end, it proved to be the ruin of his political career. On the very day that Repeal was accepted by Parliament, Peel was defeated in the Commons on a different issue, many Conservatives voting against him. He was forced to resign. Nevertheless, although many of his supporters felt he had 'betrayed' them, the people as a whole admired him for his great services to the nation. When he died, four years later, after a riding accident, *The Times* described him as 'the greatest statesman of his time'. He put country before party when he realised that only he could command enough support on both sides of the House to repeal the Corn Laws. Above all, his great ministry of 1841–6 provided the basis for thirty years of unequalled prosperity, founded on a policy of free trade.

The Irish potato famine: starving peasants at the gate of a workhouse

The Irish were not so fortunate. At least a million of them died during the great famine. In the previous thirty years, the population of Ireland had increased from 6 to $8\frac{1}{2}$ million. Yet, because there had been no equivalent increase in food production, the country was unable to withstand a setback like that of 1845. The only immediate solution to the problem was mass emigration—to north-western England and particularly to the U.S.A., where 2 million Irishmen settled in the next fifteen years. By 1871 the population had fallen to $5\frac{1}{2}$ million. Meanwhile, the rest of Britain continued to support a *rising* population by producing an ever-growing surplus of manufactures which could be exchanged for foodstuffs. The root cause of Ireland's difficulties was the backwardness of *both* her agriculture and her industry.

A task completed

Repeal of the Corn Laws removed the last major obstacle to free trade. Shortly after Peel's death his work was rounded off by one of his greatest admirers—**W. E. Gladstone** (1809–98). As Chancellor of the Exchequer (1852–5 and 1859–66) Gladstone's aim was to remove all tariffs except those necessary to provide revenue for the Government. Like Adam Smith, he came to the conclusion that sufficient revenue could be obtained from duties on a small range of articles in widespread use—for instance, wines and spirits, tobacco, tea, coffee and sugar. By 1860, when only forty-eight such articles continued to be taxed, Britain had become virtually a free trade country.

The move to free trade was achieved without any serious injury to British industry because, at the time, there was little effective competition from overseas. Between 1842 and 1870 the annual value of British exports rose from £47 million to almost £200 million. Most of this trade (along with that of many other countries) continued to be carried in British ships, even though the old Navigation Acts were finally abolished in 1849. These had long ceased to be necessary, for British merchant shipping dominated most of the world's major trade routes.

Although Britain remained a free trade country until the 1930s (see Chapter 22) few other nations followed suit. France, for example, was prepared to enter into a trade treaty with Britain (1860) but had no intention of allowing completely free trade. Countries like the U.S.A. and Germany, keen to build up their *own* industries, preferred to keep high tariffs, in order to reduce competition from cheap British manufactures.

The rise and decline of British agriculture

In its *immediate* effects upon British farming, repeal of the Corn Laws justified neither the hopes of the free traders nor the fears of land-owners. Supporters of the Anti-Corn Law League had argued that large quantities of cheap grain were being kept out of the country, but this was shown to be an exaggeration. Nowhere was there a great surplus of corn freely available to Britain—at least, not before the 1870s. For over twenty years after repeal, wheat prices remained steady at about fifty-two shillings a quarter, which had been the average in the five years *before* 1846. Nevertheless, since bread was almost the only thing that did not rise in price during the 1850s and 1860s, it is fair to say that repeal *did* keep down the cost of food—even if its results were less spectacular than the free traders had promised.

The campaign against the Corn Laws had coincided with a period of growing prosperity for British agriculture. Helped by quicker transport, more machinery and the steadily rising demand for food in the towns, many of the larger farms had become, in the words of William Cobbett, 'factories for making corn and meat'. To the delight of the farmers, repeal did not turn back the tide of prosperity. In fact, the threat of foreign competition simply led to greater efficiency, so that the period from around 1840 to 1875 is often referred to as the **'Golden Age' of British agriculture,** a time of great technical advance and steady profits for farmers. The rising standard of living among all classes meant a greater demand not only for corn but for meat and dairy produce. Thus the output of meat, butter and cheese was increased—with the spread of enclosed dairy farms along the lines laid down by Robert Bakewell (see Chapter 5).

Meanwhile arable farming was also improved. Underground drains made of tile pipes replaced the old methods of surface drainage, especially on heavy soil. The seed-drill at last came into general use, and steam power was more widely applied, for threshing, ploughing and reaping. There was also a greater application of science to agriculture. Here the chief British pioneer was **Sir John Lawes** (1814–1900). Following important German research into soil chemistry, he tried to discover which chemicals plants took from

William Ewart Gladstone

Rothamsted Experimental
Station

the soil and tested the nourishing effects of various kinds of manures. In 1843 he established an experimental farm on his family estate at **Rothamsted,** near Harpenden in Hertfordshire. It was like an open-air laboratory, made up of scores of separate plots. At the same time, he opened a factory in London for the manufacture of artificial fertilizers, including 'superphosphate of lime', which he patented. Use of fertilizers became normal farming practice during the 'Golden Age'.

However, the threat to British agriculture that had been expected in 1846 was not avoided, it was merely delayed. The prosperous years came to an abrupt end in the mid 1870s. Five unusually bad summers in a row (1873–7) marked the turning-point, but there were more serious factors than the weather. Up to this time there had been little foreign competition; but countries like the U.S.A., Canada, Argentina, Australia and New Zealand now entered upon a period of great agricultural expansion. One by one, from the 1870s onwards, they began to flood European markets with enormous quantities of cheap food.

The first of the 'new lands' to begin exporting on a large scale were the **prairies** of the American Mid-West—taking advantage of mechanisation, particularly the use of combine harvesters, and cheaper long-distance transport. Between 1860 and 1880, the total railway mileage of the U.S.A. trebled, as trans-continental lines opened up the Mid-West. Meanwhile, improved steam navigation brought great reductions in shipping freight charges; making it possible to sell American corn across the Atlantic at well below European prices.

Cost of carrying corn from Chicago to Liverpool

1868	*1882*
65 shillings a ton	24 shillings a ton

By the 1880s, with the construction of the Canadian Pacific Railway, large quantities of Canadian wheat increased the competition from North America.

With British wheat prices falling rapidly, farmers pleaded for the reintroduction of a tariff on foreign corn. This was the policy of other European countries, including France and Germany; but in Britain, where the landed gentry had lost much of their political influence, it was not given serious consideration. Both major political parties had become firmly committed to free trade. Food was part of the currency in which foreign nations paid for their imports of British manufactures. Besides, the majority of voters were now town-dwellers. They were more interested in cheap food than in the prosperity of farmers. The Government knew that if it protected agriculture it would suffer almost certain defeat at election time.

Falling profits and rents forced many farmers to convert arable land to pasture and take up livestock- and dairy-farming. As a result, the total area under wheat fell by nearly a million acres in the years 1875–85. But this was no answer to foreign competition. Before long, 'new lands' in the southern hemisphere, taking advantage of the invention of refrigeration, began mass exports of meat and dairy

Transporting grain near Winnipeg, Canada

produce. In the early 1880s, the first cargoes of frozen meat (mostly mutton) from **Australia** and **New Zealand** arrived in London. They were soon followed by chilled beef from **Argentina,** and butter, cheese, poultry and fruit from all parts of the British Empire. Foods that were not frozen were usually canned.

Livestock- and dairy-farming was saved from total collapse by the rising demand for milk and the willingness of the wealthier classes to pay more for *fresh* meat. Some specialised branches of agriculture actually expanded in these years—notably market-gardening, in areas like Cheshire, the Vale of Evesham and Greater London; near the main centres of population. In the end it was arable farming that suffered most from foreign competition. With unemployment rising and wages falling, labourers drifted off the land to find work in the towns or to emigrate overseas. From 1870 to 1914 the number of workers on the land fell from $1\frac{1}{4}$ million to well below a million, even though the total population rose by about forty per cent in the same period. The result was a rapid decline in the traditional life of the countryside, made worse by the tendency for go-ahead young people to leave the villages in order to 'better themselves' in the towns.

Timeline

1776	Adam Smith's *Wealth of Nations.*
1786	Anglo-French Trade Treaty (Pitt).
1815	Corn Law.
1828	New Corn Law—'sliding scale' of duties.
1839	Anti-Corn Law League founded.
1842	Peel's Income Tax.
1843	Rothamsted Experimental Station (Sir John Lawes).
1845–7	Irish Potato Famine.
1846	Repeal of the Corn Laws.
1860	Anglo-French Trade Treaty (Gladstone).
c. 1840–75	'Golden Age' of British Farming.
c. 1875–1914	Agricultural Depression.

Further study

For later developments in agriculture see Chapters 22 and 25. The ending of free trade in the 1930s is dealt with in Chapter 22.

Special topics

Longman's Then and There series includes:

E. G. Power, *Robert Peel, Free Trade and the Corn Laws*

P. Speed, *The Irish Potato Famine and Irish Emigrants*

The Oxford Junior Encyclopaedia vols. 6 (*Industry and Commerce*) and 7 (*Farming and Fisheries*) on trade and agriculture.

On agriculture see:

M. and C. H. B. Quennell, *A History of Everyday Things in England* (Batsford) Part IV, Chapter 2

G. Winter, *A Country Camera, 1844–1914* (Penguin). Collection of photographs depicting life in the English countryside.

F. E. Huggett, *A Day in the Life of a Victorian Farm Worker* (Allen & Unwin)

15 Prosperity and Progress
Industry in the 'Victorian Age'

Queen Victoria and Prince Albert, photographed in 1854

Queen Victoria came to the throne in June 1837, at the age of eighteen. For the greater part of her sixty-four-year reign—the longest in British history—her people were the richest and most powerful on earth; with the greatest empire, the strongest navy and, above all, the most advanced industries. Of course, these things were not achieved by the Queen herself. She had little say in the government of the country which was, by now, firmly in the hands of Parliament. Yet Victoria was the *symbol* of British greatness. Whenever we speak of this period we speak of the 'Victorian Age'; a time of peace, security and seemingly unlimited prosperity.

The Great Exhibition
In 1840, the year in which her image appeared on the world's first postage stamps, Victoria married **Prince Albert** of Saxe-Coburg-Gotha in Germany. At the outset, many people were reluctant to accept a foreigner as the first man of the kingdom, but Albert gradually won their trust and affection. His keen interest in both science and the arts soon left its mark on his new country. Today he is best

remembered as the chief inspiration behind the Great Exhibition of 1851.

The Society of Arts, of which Albert was President, put on several trade fairs in London in the 1840s. Their success led to the suggestion that a really spectacular trade show should be held; to display the latest industrial, scientific and artistic achievements from all over the world. A Royal Commission was appointed to plan it, under the leadership of Prince Albert. He firmly believed that such an exhibition would not only assist overseas trade (by displaying the fruits of Britain's advanced industrial production) but would also help peace and understanding between nations. That the Victorians should want to display their achievements alongside the pick of those from abroad was an indication of their great confidence in the superiority of British skill and workmanship. It was the same attitude that had brought about free trade—the belief that Britain need fear no competition. In fact, some of the strongest support for the Great Exhibition in government circles came from 'free traders' like Gladstone and Cobden.

Throughout 1850 and the early months of 1851, preparations went ahead for what was officially entitled **The Great Exhibition of the Works of Industry of All Nations.** A sixteen-acre site was chosen by Prince Albert on the south side of Hyde Park and a competition held to choose a design for the buildings. However, none of the 245 entries proved acceptable. It was only at the last minute that **Joseph Paxton,** the Duke of Devonshire's head gardener, came to the rescue of the organisers with a revolutionary design in glass and

The Crystal Palace

iron. **The Crystal Palace,** as it was called, was like a huge green-
house, almost a third of a mile long and high enough to house
several tall elm trees beneath its roof. Two thousand workmen
laboured through the winter of 1850–51 to finish it on time.

There were 7381 exhibitors from the British Isles and 6556 from
other countries. Needless to say, the machinery and manufacturing
sections were dominated by Britain. Railway locomotives capable
of travelling at a mile a minute, boats, bridges, textiles and machine
tools showed the progress of steam power and the supremacy of
iron. Other manufactures included telescopes, cameras, barometers,
an electric telegraph and surgical instruments. The Exhibition also
showed the taste and fashion of the age; furniture that was well made
but lacking in simplicity, hardware, china, glass, gold- and silverware
which was also excellent in craftsmanship but over-ornamental
in design.

'God bless my dear country which has shown itself so great today.'
Thus wrote Queen Victoria in her diary on 1 May 1851, the day of
the offical opening of the Exhibition. In the next five and a half
months, before it closed on 11 October, over 6 million visitors came
to the Crystal Palace—an average daily attendance of more than
43,000. In the end, a clear profit of £186,437 was made—a great
fortune in those days. The money was well used. An eighty-seven-
acre site was purchased in South Kensington, where today the
Victoria and Albert Museum, the Science Museum, The Royal
Colleges of Art and Music, the Royal Albert Hall and many other fine
buildings stand—a monument to the success of the Exhibition and the

The Royal Albert Hall:
built out of profits from the
Great Exhibition

foresight of Prince Albert. The Crystal Palace was re-erected at Sydenham in South London, where it was destroyed by fire in November 1936.

The new steel

The Great Exhibition marked the height of the Iron Age. The structure of the Crystal Palace was made of iron, as were many of the outstanding exhibits in it. But within a few years the domination of iron was ended by the discovery of cheap methods of mass producing steel.

Henry Bessemer (1813–98), the pioneer in the making of cheap steel, was a professional inventor. Among his earlier achievements were a perforated stamp which could not be re-used and a new method of making plate glass. During the Crimean War against Russia (1854–6) he was employed in trying to find a way of making better cannon; for cast iron, being brittle, was liable to shatter under the force of an explosion. Steel, which is hard yet not brittle, provided the obvious answer, but methods of making it were too slow and expensive. There was still no satisfactory alternative to Benjamin Huntsman's century-old 'crucible casting process' (see Chapter 7). After many difficult and costly experiments, however, Bessemer found a quick and simple method of converting large quantities of pig iron *directly* into steel (1856).

Molten pig iron, straight from the blast-furnace, was poured into a special **converter**—a large vessel like a concrete-mixer, which could be tilted for filling and emptying. A blast of air was then blown through holes in the base of the converter. After only twenty minutes, the impurities in the liquid iron had either been expelled in the form of burning gases or turned into slag. Finally, small quantities of carbon and manganese were added, to produce *mild steel.* 'While it is much harder and is not worn or indented so easily as soft iron,' wrote Bessemer, 'at the same time it is not so brittle or hard to work as ordinary cast steel.' Moreover, the liquid steel could be cast immediately into girders, rails or whatever shape was required, without having to be forged like bar iron.

After further experiments, Bessemer set up his own works in Sheffield (1859) and was soon producing steel at around £5 a ton (compared with normal prices in the region of £50). Orders flooded in for steel rails and girders, tools, steel wire ropes and many other articles. In the early 1870s he was able to sell his works for twenty times its original value. By then he had also received over £1 million from other firms in patent rights.

Meanwhile an alternative method of making cheap mild steel had been developed. A serious disadvantage of the open-topped converter was that it wasted a lot of heat and some of the iron was carried away with the blast. To remedy this **William Siemens,** a German who settled in England, introduced the **open-hearth process** (1866) which owed much to the work of two Frenchmen, the brothers Pierre and Emile Martin. His converting vessel was a large, shallow bath or 'open hearth', which held up to 300 tons of pig iron and scrap metal. A mixture of coal-gas and air was burned over it to melt the iron and expel the impurities. The key to its success was the very high temperature of the hearth (about 1650 °C). This was partly achieved by using the hot exhaust gases to pre-heat the incoming coal-gas and air.

The open-hearth process took longer than the Bessemer converter, but it was easier to control the quality of the steel. Its greatest advantage was that its high temperature enabled large quantities of *scrap iron* to be converted directly into mild steel. In 1867 Siemens set up his own works at Landore, near Swansea. The business grew steadily in importance, and many other companies took up his process, until, by the end of the century, the quantity of steel produced by open-hearth methods exceeded that from the Bessemer converter. Today most of our steel is made in this way; but more modern methods, using oxygen, are gradually being introduced. The Bessemer converter has now almost disappeared.

At first both new processes had a serious drawback. They could only be used with iron containing very little phosphorus, because neither of them could get rid of it. Since many types of British iron ore were phosphoric, additional supplies had to be imported from Spain and Sweden. But this defect was overcome by **Sidney Gilchrist Thomas** (1850–85) clerk in a London magistrates' court;

Two Bessemer Converters in a South Wales steel plant (about 1860)

The Forth railway bridge, made of steel

assisted by his cousin, Percy Gilchrist, who was a chemist. Working in a tiny laboratory in his backyard, Gilchrist Thomas had the idea of lining a Bessemer converter with limestone. This absorbed the phosphorus from the pig iron and deposited it in the slag as calcium phosphate (which proved a valuable fertiliser). The same principle could be applied to the open-hearth process.

Gilchrist Thomas announced his discovery in 1878, but little notice was taken of it. In the following year, he gave a successful demonstration in Middlesbrough, using highly phosphoric ore from the nearby Cleveland iron ore field. He was at once internationally famous. Countries like Germany and the U.S.A. had enormous fields of phosphoric ore which could now be exploited. They gained much more than Britain did from the new process. Unhappily, Gilchrist Thomas did not live to fully enjoy his success. His health was ruined by overwork and he died in 1885 at the age of thirty-four.

Mild steel was now so cheap and plentiful that it rapidly replaced iron in structural engineering. Railway companies were the first to buy it in large quantities, for steel rails could safely carry heavier locomotives. Bridges could be made stronger and therefore larger, like the great Forth Bridge (1886). Steel plates, lighter yet stronger than wrought iron ones, made possible the construction of larger ships. Even in building, steel girders were used for reinforcing concrete. The list does not stop there; cheap steel also led to immediate improvements in guns, boilers and all kinds of machinery.

'The Workshop of the World'

The Great Exhibition demonstrated to the world the long lead held by British manufacturers over all rivals. Yet it came only at the *beginning* of a period of even greater prosperity for the country's industries, in the third quarter of the nineteenth century. From 1850 to 1872, the annual value of Britain's exports increased by more than three and a half times, from £71 million to £256 million. It was with good reason that Britain became known as 'the Workshop of the World' in these years.

The most important development since the Industrial Revolution was the growth of **mechanical engineering** as a separate, highly-skilled industry. *Machine tools* (machines which are themselves tools) were replacing the old hand-tool methods of engineering, which depended upon the accuracy of the human eye. Thus, for the first time, standardised parts could be made and large numbers of identical articles could be mass produced.

At the end of the eighteenth century, while Boulton and Watt were still dependent upon hand tools, two of the earliest 'master engineers', **Joseph Bramah** and **Henry Maudslay,** were laying the foundations for the mechanical engineering industry. Bramah (1748–1814) made machine tools for the manufacture of his 'unpickable locks', and his former pupil Maudslay (1771–1831) perfected a screw-cutting lathe in 1800. Screws had previously been made with a crude hand tool called a burr, which often broke the metal and rarely produced two screws that were alike. Maudslay's lathe could cut any number of screw-threads of fixed proportions. He also invented a machine which measured up to a thousandth of an inch, making possible finer work on the lathe. These and many other machine tools were coming into common use at the beginning of the Victorian Age, resulting in far greater accuracy throughout British industry.

Around 1840, when Henry Bessemer was ordering machinery for one of his early inventions, he gave out the work, 'some in Manchester, some in Glasgow, some in Liverpool and some in London'. When he assembled the parts they fitted and worked. This would have been impossible at the beginning of the century. It was a clear illustration of the progress of mechanical engineering; progress which was reflected in many of the exhibits at the Crystal Palace (1851).

Two of the leading firms in the growth of precision engineering were those of James Nasmyth and Joseph Whitworth. Both were ex-pupils of Maudslay, and both established their workshops in Manchester in the 1830s. **James Nasmyth** we have already met as the inventor of the steam hammer (see Chapter 7). He was also well known for his power-driven tools, including planing machines. **Joseph Whitworth** (1803–87) had no fewer than twenty-three exhibits in the Great Exhibition, which together earned him a world-wide reputation. They included lathes, accurate measuring devices and self-acting machines for planing, drilling, slotting and shaping.

He is most famous today for his **classification of screw-threads** (1843). After examining sample screws from many other workshops, he proposed that the angle between the sides of the threads should be 55 degrees and the number of threads to the inch should be standardised for various diameters. By the 1860s, these 'Whitworth gauges' were in general use.

Whitworth's tools mostly originated in the Iron Age, but it was in the new Steel Age, following Bessemer's discovery, that they came into general use. By the 1870s, British engineers were capable of dealing with almost any problem industry could set them.

Meanwhile, the basic industries were still coal, iron and textiles —each of which roughly doubled its total production in the period 1850–75. **Coal** continued to be the foundation of all industrial development, providing the power to drive the machines.

British coal production (in millions of tons)

1846	1870	1891
44	110	185

Yet, despite the enormous increase in output, it remained almost entirely a hand industry. The bulk of the work was done by pick and shovel, and pit ponies and manual labour were still generally used for moving the coal. As late as 1900, well under five per cent of British coal was cut by machinery. But more powerful steam-engines were introduced for draining mines and for operating the winding gear, and pits were sunk to greater depths than ever before.

When all the needs of industry had been satisfied, Britain still managed to export considerable quantities of coal, to north-western Europe and the Mediterranean countries.

Unlike the coal industry, **textiles** were completely mechanised by the second half of the nineteenth century. Most technical developments consisted of improvements to existing machines rather than wholly new inventions. For example, the spinning-mule was now fully automatic. Cotton goods were still Britain's major export. Almost nine-tenths of the total output was sold overseas. In 1880 this amounted to a third of *all* exports. Thus Britain was even more the world's clothing shop than its workshop. But, as the output of finished goods increased, so did imports of raw cotton. This dependence on foreign raw materials proved a serious handicap in the early 1860s, when the American Civil War interrupted supplies and caused widespread unemployment in Lancashire. At one time, almost half the population of Preston was receiving Poor Relief.

The **heavy industries**—mainly iron, steel and hardware—were expanding even faster than textiles. For instance, pig iron output increased threefold in the period 1850–75. An increasing proportion of it was converted into steel after the introduction of the new processes of Bessemer, Siemens and Gilchrist Thomas.

British output of steel (tons)

1850	*1870*	*1880*
40,000	240,000	1,250,000

Joseph Whitworth's patent screwing apparatus

The West Midlands, especially South Staffordshire, continued to be the chief iron manufacturing area. However, in the year of the Great Exhibition (1851) the greatest English iron ore field was discovered, in the Cleveland district of North Yorkshire. As a result, Middlesbrough grew from a village to a town of 40,000 people within twenty years.

The chill wind of competition

In 1870 the total volume of British foreign trade was greater than that of France, Germany and Italy combined. But this unchallenged supremacy could not last for long once countries like the U.S.A. and Germany began to exploit their greater resources more fully. In the last quarter of the nineteenth century, British manufactured goods began to be seriously rivalled in the markets of the world, for the first time since the Industrial Revolution.

'The superiority of the United States to England is ultimately as certain as the next eclipse.' So said *The Economist* newspaper in 1851. It was a warning that few people took seriously in the triumphant year of the Great Exhibition, but it was soon proved correct. After the American Civil War (1861–5) the **United States** entered upon a period of remarkably rapid industrial growth. While railways opened up the interior and linked the expanding manufacturing towns in the eastern states, vast numbers of settlers from Europe came to swell the labour force. Similarly, the new **German Empire,** established in 1871 out of many smaller states, increased its industrial

A coal mine in South Staffordshire. Notice the pillars of uncut coal which support the ceiling

CAUGHT NAPPING!

Punch cartoon of 1896

production at an astonishing rate. While Britain maintained a policy of free trade (see Chapter 14), the U.S.A., Germany and other European rivals protected their own developing industries from foreign competition by means of high tariffs.

A reliable guide to a country's industrial capacity in this period was its production figures for coal and steel and the size of its population. Both Germany and the U.S.A. exceeded the British output of steel by the 1890s. At about the same time the U.S.A. overhauled Britain in coal production too—Germany somewhat later. There was little that Britain could do about it, since both its main rivals had far greater supplies of coal and iron ore. In addition, their populations were larger and growing at a faster rate:

Growth of population (in millions)

	United Kingdom	*Germany*	*United States*
1871	32	41	38
1911	45	66	93

Britain's loss of industrial supremacy should not be exaggerated. The basic industries were still expanding and the overall standard of living was rising. Despite tariffs, large quantities of British goods continued to sell in the U.S.A. and Europe; and there was a massive increase in sales to the dominions and colonies. Britain still dominated the world's trade routes long after its industrial production had been surpassed. In 1885 no less than a third of all sea-going ships were registered in Britain. Meanwhile the country's shipyards had no serious rival. In the early years of the twentieth century the British were building almost two-thirds of the world's shipping tonnage!

Electric power

For a hundred years there was no real alternative to the steam piston-engine in providing power to drive machines. However, by the 1880s, electric power stations began to appear. At about the same time the internal combustion engine was introduced from Germany; providing for the first time a relatively cheap power unit for the use of craftsmen in small workshops. (The internal combustion engine is dealt with in Chapter 21, since its greatest impact was on transport.)

These new forms of power, together with new materials like rubber, petroleum, aluminium and celluloid, gradually changed the whole basis of industry. In fact the period from about 1880 to the 1930s is often referred to as the 'Second Industrial Revolution'. However, great as these changes were, they were not really 'revolutionary', and were thus unlike those of the late eighteenth and early nineteenth centuries, which led to a new kind of society. The industrial advances of the last hundred years have resulted in the *fuller* development of a way of life already well established.

Scientists of many nations contributed to man's understanding and use of electricity. But it was an Englishman, **Michael Faraday** (1791–1867) who first found a mechanical method of producing a continuous flow of electric current. In 1831 he showed that an electric current was produced when a coil was rotated between the poles of a horseshoe magnet. His principle of *electro-magnetic induction* was the starting-point for both the dynamo and the electric motor. A dynamo turns 'mechanical power' (needed to rotate the coil) into electric current. An electric motor (based on the same principle in reverse) converts the current back into mechanical energy, which can be used to drive a machine.

Many problems had to be overcome before the first dynamos were manufactured and sold (1867). There was a further timelag before electric power stations were built. The earliest ones (in the 1880s) began by providing current for **electric lighting**—another new invention, made by **Joseph Swan** in England (1878) and **Thomas Edison** in America (1879). They later joined forces to produce 'Ediswan' bulbs. Meanwhile electricity gradually replaced gas in the lighting of streets, public buildings and, finally, private houses.

Ordinary steam piston-engines drove the dynamos in the first power stations. But they were unable to achieve a sufficiently high speed of rotation to be really efficient generators of electricity. The need for a faster-running steam-engine led to the invention of

Michael Faraday

the **steam turbine** (1884) by **Charles Parsons** (1854–1931), an engineer from Newcastle. It worked on the same principle as a windmill. A continuous blast of high-pressure steam was forced along a tube containing a *rotor,* made up of vanes (blades) mounted on a central shaft. This turned at great speed. By replacing the back and forward motion of a piston with the *spinning* motion of the turbine, Parsons made it possible to drive a dynamo much faster.

Electric-powered factories were cleaner and simpler. No shafts or belts were needed for driving the machines, which could be switched on or off individually. Yet British manufacturers were much slower in changing to electric power than most of their foreign rivals. By the outbreak of the First World War (1914) only a few areas like Tyneside and Manchester had sufficiently large generating stations to supply power as cheaply as in Germany or the U.S.A. The newer industries made most use of electricity. Since it was carried by means of wires, it was possible for new factories to be built in areas where there was no coal supply. It was not even necessary for the power station itself to be on the coalfield if **hydro-electric power** (h.e.p.) was generated. This was done by using falling water instead of steam-engines to drive the dynamos. After 1900, h.e.p. stations began to appear in areas like the Scottish Highlands, where coal was difficult to obtain yet there was no shortage of fast-flowing streams.

As the demand for electricity increased, in both industry and the home, Parliament decided to create a **National Grid** or network (1926) to carry the current all over Britain. In the towns, cables were buried below the streets, but tall steel pylons carried wires across the countryside, to avoid unnecessary interference with agriculture. The output from the power stations now went into a common pool; making it possible for an area with a specially heavy demand to draw immediately on electricity produced in other areas.

Sir Charles Parsons's steam turbine, with part of the casing removed to show the *rotor*

Timeline

1800	Henry Maudslay's screw-cutting lathe.
1831	Faraday demonstrates *electro-magnetic induction*.
1837–1901	Reign of Queen Victoria.
1843	Joseph Whitworth's standard system of screw-threads.
1851	The Great Exhibition.
1856	Henry Bessemer's Converter.
1866	William Siemens's Open-Hearth Process.
1878	The Gilchrist Thomas Process.
1878–9	Electric light bulb (Joseph Swan and Thomas Edison).
1884	Sir Charles Parsons's steam turbine.
1926	The National Grid.

Further study

More recent developments in British industry are dealt with in Chapters 22 and 25.

Visit

The Science Museum at South Kensington (Exhibition Road, London SW7). On the ground floor: the Motive Power section contains steam turbines—including the original Parsons turbine and dynamo; the Electric Power section has models of power stations. On the first floor: Machine tools—including the original machines of Bramah, Maudslay, Nasmyth and Whitworth; steel—including the Bessemer Converter and the Open-Hearth Process.

Special topics

J. G. Crowther, *Six Great Engineers* (Hamish Hamilton) includes Sir Charles Parsons.

N. Wymer, *Great Inventors* (O.U.P., Lives of Great Men and Women, vol. 3) includes Sir Henry Bessemer.

On the Great Exhibition of 1851:

Josephine Kamn, *Joseph Paxton and the Crystal Palace* (Methuen)

G. R. Kesteven, *1851: Britain Shows the World* (Chatto & Windus)

J. R. C. Yglesias, *London Life and the Great Exhibition of 1851* (Longman's Then and There series)

The Great Exhibition (Cape, Jackdaw series no. 43)

The Great Exhibition—A Commemorative Album (H.M.S.O.)

On the development of electric power:

J. Gordon Cook, *Michael Faraday*, and Henry Thomas, *Thomas Alva Edison* (both in A. and C. Black's Lives to Remember series)

Faraday and Electricity (Cape, Jackdaw series no. 86)

I. Tenen, *This England, 1714–1960* (Macmillan) pp. 257–64

For reference:

The Oxford Junior Encyclopaedia, vol. 8 (Engineering) has information on machinery, tools, instruments, etc.

Filmstrip

The Great Exhibition, 1851 (Hulton: in colour)

16 The Fight Against Disease
Public Health and Medical Science

In Britain in recent years, the death of a child or of an adult in the prime of life has become a sufficiently rare occurrence to be considered a tragic misfortune. This could not be said of any earlier period in the country's history. In the early eighteenth century, it is likely that almost half the children born died before reaching the age of five. A family of eight could expect a death in the house once every five years. More than a hundred years later, despite advances in medicine, people still lived in the shadow of the graveyard. In some of the industrial towns in the Early Victorian Age, the death-rate was actually higher than it had been anywhere a century before.

Most of the major improvements in the health of the nation thus belong to the last hundred years or so. In that time, infectious diseases like typhoid and typhus fever, smallpox, cholera and diphtheria—which together claimed hundreds of thousands of victims every year—have been almost eliminated as a cause of death. The hazards of childbirth and the dangers of infancy have also been largely conquered, so that many parents now regard the motor car as the greatest threat to the safety of their children. Broadly speaking, progress has been made in two directions—the practice of medicine and the organisation of public health facilities.

The world of Edward Jenner
In the eighteenth century most medical practice was a combination of guesswork and superstition. *Physicians* (qualified doctors with university training) numbered only a few hundred in the whole kingdom. They practised almost entirely among the wealthy classes, who alone could afford their fees. The poor man's doctor was usually the *apothecary* (pharmacist) who dressed wounds, set broken bones and performed many other medical duties in addition

to his main work of providing drugs. Routine operations were carried out by the *barber-surgeon,* who pulled teeth and let blood (a popular remedy in those days) as well as cutting hair, shaving chins and trimming wigs. Hospitals were few in number and most of them were lacking in sanitation. Nevertheless, more than 150 hospitals and dispensaries were founded between 1700 and 1825, largely through private charity, to provide the poor with free medical attention. Many of them had their own medical schools, which helped to raise both the quality and quantity of trained doctors and surgeons.

At this time many poor people suffered from malnutrition (not enough of the right kind of food). Knowledge of vitamins and the part they play in a healthy diet belongs to the twentieth century, but many earlier discoveries were made simply by careful observation. In the eighteenth century two of the commonest 'deficiency' diseases were *rickets* and *scurvy.* Rickets is found in young children. Because of a shortage of what we now call 'vitamin D' their bones fail to harden, with the result that they suffer deformities of the spine or limbs—for example, 'bow legs'. The Agricultural Revolution made sources of vitamin D—milk, butter, eggs and cheese—more plentiful, and thus helped to reduce the danger of rickets. Even so, it was still very common in the nineteenth century.

Meanwhile, scurvy—a horrible disease in which blood escapes from the veins and causes swellings all over the body—was almost eliminated by 1800. It results from a lack of 'vitamin C', found in fresh fruit and vegetables, which explains why it was particularly fatal to seamen on long voyages. In the mid eighteenth century it was suggested that the seaman's restricted diet of salted meat and biscuits might be the vital clue to the cause of scurvy, and Captain James Cook provided clear proof of this on his long voyage of 1772–5. He took every opportunity to land and collect fresh fruit and vegetables, and consequently lost only one of his crew of 118. In 1791 the Admiralty began to issue lemon or lime juice to all warships.

But by far the most important medical advance of the eighteenth century was achieved by **Edward Jenner** (1749–1823) the son of a Gloucestershire vicar. It was he who introduced the first satisfactory method of preventing **smallpox**—a highly infectious and often

Interior of a ward in Guy's Hospital for incurables, London

deadly disease which leaves hundreds of pits or 'pock marks' on the surface of the skin. In the eighteenth century it was at least as common as chickenpox is today. Roughly one person in ten died of it, more than half of them in childhood, and many of the survivors were disfigured and made lame, deaf or blind. Eastern countries had long practised *inoculation* – an injection of a mild form of the disease in the hope of making the patient immune to further infection. This was introduced into Britain in the early eighteenth century, with some success, although a small proportion of patients died from it. But inoculation also helped the disease to spread, for the patient could pass on smallpox in its full strength.

As a youth, Jenner overheard a milkmaid saying she would not get smallpox because she had suffered from **cowpox**, a mild disease common among dairy-maids. This was a widely held belief among country folk, but it was dismissed by doctors when they found cases of smallpox among those who had previously caught cowpox. Nevertheless, after finishing his studies in London and becoming a doctor in his home county, Jenner decided to investigate the effects of cowpox. He found that those who had suffered from it *rarely* got smallpox, and even if they did, they only had a *mild* attack. After many years of careful observation, he put his theory to the test. His most celebrated experiment, although it was only one of many, was in 1796, when he transferred matter from a cowpox sore on a dairy-maid's hand to the arm of an eight-year-old boy, James Phipps. Six weeks later, when young James was injected with discharge from a smallpox sore, there was a negative reaction.

In 1798 Jenner finally published details of his experiments, together with his conclusion that a *vaccine** of cowpox provided immunity against smallpox. Within two years Jenner's writings had been translated into several languages and circulated round the world. But although the practice of vaccination was soon established, Jenner had to fight much ignorance and jealousy among other physicians. One of them even suggested that the human body would gradually take on the features of a cow if vaccination became general practice. Nevertheless, Jenner's great service to mankind was widely recognised. Parliament granted him a total of £30,000 in public gratitude for his work. Soon after his death inoculation was made illegal (1840) after which free vaccination was made available to all who could not afford it. By about 1880 smallpox had been practically wiped out in Britain and Jenner's methods were being used to prevent other diseases.

Portrait medals of Edward Jenner, in honour of his discovery of vaccination

Cholera and Edwin Chadwick

In 1831 an epidemic of **cholera** broke out in Britain for the first time. Spreading from Asia, it began in the port of Sunderland and killed many thousands of people all over the country. Cholera is swift and deadly in its effect. Violent pains in the stomach are usually followed by diarrhoea, sickness and death. People were panic-stricken; not only because of the terrible nature of the disease

Opposite: An example of the state of medical knowledge in the mid nineteenth century

---

* The word comes from the Latin *vacca,* a cow.

ONE HUNDREDTH THOUSAND.]   [Price 1d. each, or 8d. per dozen, 4s. 6d. per 100.

HOW TO AVOID THE CHOLERA:

BEING

PLAIN DIRECTIONS FOR POOR PEOPLE.

By DR. CHALLICE, of Bermondsey,

AUTHOR OF "MEDICAL ADVICE TO MOTHERS ON THE MANAGEMENT OF CHILDREN."

☞ *Whatever may be the cause of Cholera, thus much is certain, that hitherto, almost without exception, this pestilence has been the portion of the poor, and we know that those who are in want of food and clothing most readily fall the victims of this disease. Let therefore the working man, the head of a family, reflect, that by idleness or drunkenness he not only exposes himself, but in all probability his wife and his children, to the attacks of Cholera, by depriving them of the comforts and the necessaries of life.*

1. Good health, good spirits, and industry, are the best preservatives. If you are ill, send for a doctor.

2. Keep the whole of the body clean; do not spare soap and water; rub the skin well dry after washing Cholera is fond of *filth*. Parents, apply this rule to your children.

3. Live plainly, and avoid all excesses. Go early to bed; the hard-working man requires rest, not excitement, after his day's work. Drunkenness and late hours are great friends of the Cholera.

4. Sleep as few in the same room, or in the same bed, as possible; make every shift, rather than be crowded at night.

5. Early in the morning, remove all dirty or offensive matters, open your windows and doors, turn down the bed-clothes, to let the fresh air pass over them.

6. Do not take your meals in the bed-room; if you cannot help yourselves in this respect, there is still greater necessity for cleanliness and fresh air.

7. Washing or drying clothes in the bed-room is always bad, and, in times of sickness, very dangerous.

8. EAT ONLY OF GOOD FOOD. Half a pound of good meat is better than one pound of bad. One good loaf is better than two bad ones. Cyder and sour or hard beer are injurious. Let not your children stuff themselves with apples, plums, pears, or sweet stuff. Rice, tapioca, barley, and oatmeal, are cheap, nourishing, and wholesome.

9. Cleanse out, and thoroughly scour, your water-butts or cisterns; boil the water before you drink it or give it to your children. Impure water is the cause of many diseases.

10. If there be offensive smells in your house, from sewers or cesspools, complain to your landlord; if he take no steps for removing the nuisance, complain to the parish authorities; if they don't assist you, apply to the magistrates. The *law* now protects from *poison* as well as starvation.

11. If you get wet, change your clothes as soon as you can; warm and dry clothing, however homely or coarse, will do much to keep off Cholera. Flannel should be worn next the skin round the body, and the feet be kept dry and warm with worsted stockings.

12. Go out, and take your children, into the fresh air as often as you can; pure air and wholesome exercise may keep off Cholera, as well as Fever.

13. Take no *strong physic*, as Epsom salts, senna, &c. If opening medicine is wanted, a small tea-spoonful of powdered rhubarb, with a little ginger and carbonate of soda, or a small wine-glassful of the compound tincture of rhubarb, or the compound *rhubarb* pill, (which may be bought for 4d. or 6d. per dozen,) may either be taken with advantage. For children, nothing is better than rhubarb with magnesia, in *small doses*, repeated every four hours till the proper effect is produced.

14. If you have bowel complaint, leave off work. Rest and lying in bed are most necessary; many a working man has lost his life by neglect of this rule. Get this mixture, for preparing which a druggist ought not to charge a poor man more than sixpence:—

1 drachm of Aromatic confection.		
1	„	Prepared chalk.
1	„	Sal Volatile.
½	„	Laudanum.
2	„	Tincture of ginger
2	„	Tincture of kino.
3 ounces of Cinnamon water.		

A table-spoonful to be taken every two hours till the relaxation is stopped. A child under ten years, half the dose; and from three to five years old, a fourth part only. For infants it is not suitable. Broths and hot tea are injurious, and increase the relaxation of the bowels. Arrowroot, or rice boiled in milk, or gruel, with some grated ginger or cinnamon powder, should be taken, and these not *hot*, but nearly cold.

15. Should the Cholera, however, attack you, or any in your house, don't be alarmed—it is not catching—the disease is now better understood than heretofore; mild cases are easily cured, and the worst cases are not always fatal.

16. Neighbours and friends have a bad custom of crowding a sick room. Where there is *Cholera*, it makes the disease more dangerous; therefore, don't do it.

17. As a measure of precaution, every family should, if possible, have a pound of the best mustard, one quart of vinegar, half a pint of brandy, (which must be close corked and sealed,) and two pounds of salt, in the house; also, the fire laid ready for lighting at a moment's notice, with a large kettle full of water on the hob. Then, in case of sudden attack before a doctor can be fetched, apply a vinegar-and-mustard poultice over the whole belly, as long as it can be borne, or at least for twenty minutes, and let the arms, feet, and legs be constantly rubbed with flannels dipped in hot vinegar. Constant friction in this manner may save many a life. The body of the sufferer becomes in the same state as one nearly dead from drowning or suffocation, and every one knows how often life is restored in such cases by persevering exertion for *hours*. Two of these pills should be taken at *once*, with a table-spoonful of brandy, and one pill with a table-spoonful of brandy-and-water, cold, every half hour. But don't delay getting a doctor.

Cayenne pepper	12 grains.
Camphor	12 „
Calomel	12 „

Aromatic confection sufficient to make into twelve pills.

Brandy is certainly most valuable in Cholera to those who have not been in the habit of spirit-drinking: those who have constantly taken it, derive little or no good from it.

Lastly. It cannot be too often repeated, that bad bread or bad vegetables, unsound meat or stale fish, tend most powerfully to derange the stomach and bowels, and to bring on Cholera. Let the *dealers* in these staple commodities of life reflect on their very serious responsibility at the present moment, and on the public indignation which will most justly fall upon them should *human life* be sacrificed by the sale of unwholesome food—a too common practice, and a wicked imposition upon the poorer classes.

LONDON: HENRY RENSHAW, MEDICAL PUBLISHER, 356, STRAND.

Savill & Edwards, Printers, 4, Chandos-street, Covent-garden.

Sir Edwin Chadwick

but because doctors could find no answer to it. However, one thing was clear. It struck hardest in poor, overcrowded and insanitary areas, particularly the working-class slums of the towns. It was in these districts that other epidemic diseases like typhoid and typhus fever claimed most victims. Yet, despite the obvious connection between dirt and disease, little had been done to provide pure water supplies and effective sewage and drainage facilities, which experience showed were the best safeguards against infection.

This neglect resulted partly from lack of scientific knowledge and ignorance of town planning. But a more important reason was simply that public health was no one's special responsibility. Local authorities had little power, and Parliament was reluctant to interfere with the freedom of property-owners. Nevertheless the sensational nature of cholera at last began to scare the Government into action. Following a further outbreak in 1837, detailed investigations were made into public health facilities and living conditions. Outstanding among them was a nationwide survey compiled by **Edwin Chadwick** (1800–90), Secretary of the Poor Law Commission.

Chadwick's **Report on the Sanitary Condition of the Labouring Population** (1842) revealed a grim state of affairs— hundreds of thousands of families living in waterlogged cellars; terrible overcrowding in damp, unventilated houses; unpaved streets full of refuse, and an almost total lack of proper drainage and sewage disposal. Fresh running water—the first essential for hygienic living— was found only in the houses of the wealthy. The poor had to fetch it from pumps, and a regular flow could not be relied on. In many towns the water was only turned on for a few minutes a day. Under these conditions, it is not surprising that Chadwick found 'the minor comforts of cleanliness . . . foregone, to avoid the greater discomforts of having to fetch the water.' In London, the Thames was used for both drinking-water *and* sewage disposal. So great was the stench from the river that the windows of the House of Commons had to be closed during debates.

'Disease', said Chadwick, 'is always found in connection with damp and filth, and close and overcrowded dwellings.' Thus the death-rate (which rose in the period 1810–50) was higher among the working class than the middle class, and higher in the town than in the country—as Chadwick's figures showed:

Average age at death (1840)

	labourers	gentry
Rutland (an agricultural county)	38	52
Manchester (an industrial town)	17	38

Differences like these had existed for centuries—although in a much less exaggerated form. But they were especially alarming in this period because the extent of Britain's disease-ridden slums was increasing with each passing year. The total population (excluding Ireland) roughly doubled between 1780 and 1830, and was to double again before the end of the nineteenth century. Almost all of this increase was concentrated in the towns. When Victoria came to the throne (1837) about half of her people were town-dwellers, but the proportion had increased to three-quarters by the time of her death (1901).

No matter how great the advance in the knowledge and skill of doctors, there could be no real improvement in the health of the nation until attention was paid to the *environment* (surroundings) in which people lived.

Public health and housing reform

Absence of effective local government was an important reason for the lack of public health facilities. It was not until 1835 that a **Municipal Corporations Act** provided for the creation of town councils, elected every three years by all male ratepayers. At this time, places like Manchester, Birmingham and Sheffield still depended on J.P.s for any kind of local government, for most of the 250 'chartered boroughs' in England and Wales had gained their status long before the Industrial Revolution. As the newer towns established elected corporations under the 1835 Act, some of them began to construct proper sewage and water systems and to pave and cleanse the streets. But in most towns progress was hindered by the powerful opposition of property-owners. They feared that sanitary regulations would involve them in heavy expenses, and objected to the necessary increases in the rates.

Chadwick and his fellow reformers wanted *Parliament* to take responsibility for improving public health. But this was easier said than done. The idea that the state should intervene to safeguard the welfare of its citizens was not generally accepted until the twentieth century. Nevertheless Chadwick argued that parliamentary action was in the national interest. 'The annual loss of life from filth', he said, 'is greater than the loss from death or wounds in any wars in which the country has been engaged in modern times.'

The first **Public Health Act (1848)** set up a Board of Health in London, with Chadwick and Lord Ashley among its members. It had the power to create *local* boards of health around the country, to control necessary services like cleansing, paving and draining the streets. But nothing was compulsory. A district need not have a health board unless its death-rate was exceptionally high. When the national Board was disbanded, six years later, only a sixth of the population was served by local boards. In many other areas there had been strong opposition to parliamentary interference; an attitude summed up by *The Times,* which called the 1848 Act 'a reckless invasion of property and liberty'.

However the Act created opportunities for local action, and where this was taken epidemic disease was reduced. In London, **John Simon,** a young surgeon, was made the first Medical Officer of Health (1848). He set out to provide a pure, filtered water supply and an efficient sewage system, and began medical inspection of the houses of the poorest people. Meanwhile Chadwick took a hand himself, experimenting with glazed earthenware pipes for making sewers. He found them a great improvement on the brick-lined tunnels then in use. Pipes prevented blockages, and they were soon regarded as essential for all sanitary engineering.

Not until the Conservative ministry of **Benjamin Disraeli** (1874–80) did the state finally make itself responsible for really large-scale improvements. 'Health is the first essential' was Disraeli's motto, and, in 1875, his Home Secretary, Richard Cross, got a very important Public Health Act through Parliament. It set up a nationwide system of sanitary authorities, with responsibility for sewage, drainage, street cleansing and water supply. Minimum standards of sanitation were to be observed in building new houses, and medical officers of health and sanitary inspectors were to be appointed in every locality.

By the end of the century British towns were much healthier, although still far below present day standards. The average expectation of life increased by ten years in the period 1850–1900; by which time the public health problem had become largely a housing problem. Overcrowding was the root of the trouble. Mainly as a result of the enormous increase in population, the demand for houses was greater than the supply—as, indeed, it has been ever since. Whenever things are scarce they become more expensive and people with the lowest incomes have to go without. Housing is no exception. Even the cheapest houses were let at rents which lower-paid workers could not afford. Millions of families rented single rooms or were forced to *share* a room with others. In the mid nineteenth century, it was common to find four or five families living in one room. Yet, as late as 1904, a case was discovered in East London where one bed was let out three times in every twenty-four hours to six people at a time!

Benjamin Disraeli, Earl of Beaconsfield

Not until 1868 was any attempt made to give town councils power to deal with housing. Even then very little was achieved, for the authorities were, as always, reluctant to interfere with private property. However, in 1875 Disraeli's Government passed an **Artisans' Dwellings Act** which permitted councils to take over and clear whole slum districts. Although it was not compulsory, prompt action was taken in some areas. In London nearly 30,000 people were rehoused in the next thirty years. In Birmingham, under its great Mayor, **Joseph Chamberlain** (1836–1914), over forty acres of slum land were cleared to make way for new houses and a shopping centre (Corporation Street). Between 1873 and 1876 Birmingham was, in Chamberlain's words: 'parked, paved, assized, marketed, gas and watered and *improved*'.

Unfortunately, many councils that were willing to pull down slums were not prepared to provide low-cost houses to replace them. Private builders redeveloped the cleared sites and let their houses to higher-paid workers; the rents the former slum-dwellers could afford were insufficient to meet even the costs of building. Local authorities were not urged to build houses themselves until 1890. But little was done until after the 1914–18 War, when the Treasury began to give grants for council housing schemes (see Chapter 23). It was easy to remove slums but it was quite another matter to replace them with better homes at rents within the reach of everyone.

In step with these developments it was necessary to reshape the system of local government. No reform could be effective without proper local authorities to carry out the day-to-day administration.

Opposite: Street scene in a Newcastle slum (about 1880)

Borough councils had been established in many industrial towns since the 1835 Act, and Birmingham under Joseph Chamberlain showed how effective the best of them could be. But progress was much slower in the countryside. As late as the 1880s most country-dwellers had no say in the running of their locality. A Local Government Act (1888) remedied this by setting up elected **County Councils.** At the same time, some sixty large towns were made separate County Boroughs, with their own local self-government. London became a separate county. A further Act of 1894 established nearly 7000 Parish Councils and also the system of Urban and Rural District Councils, all based on direct election by the inhabitants.

The foundations of modern surgery

In the early nineteenth century, surgical operations were performed without proper anaesthetics. Drugs were used — including Indian hemp and opium, rum and other kinds of 'hard liquor' — but they failed to produce complete unconsciousness. In 1800 Humphrey Davy found he could make himself unconscious by inhaling *laughing gas* (nitrous oxide vapour). Some twenty years later, his pupil, Michael Faraday, showed that *ether* produced a similar effect. But neither of these was

Artist's impression of James Simpson and his friends experimenting with chloroform

Joseph Lister's carbolic spray

suitable for long operations. The effects of laughing gas quickly wore off, so that its use was restricted almost entirely to dentistry. Ether lasted longer, but made the patient feel very sick and ill. In 1847 **James Simpson** (1811–70) Professor of Midwifery at Edinburgh University, demonstrated anaesthesia by means of **chloroform.** He invited two students to his home and together they inhaled the sweet-smelling vapour. A few minutes later, Mrs Simpson heard a crash and came running in to find all three unconscious on the floor! But they suffered no ill-effects and were delighted with the results.

Chloroform remained the chief method of anaesthesia until well into the twentieth century. No longer hindered by the cries and struggles of the patient, surgeons could perform long and delicate operations, *but* only after a greater problem had been overcome—the danger of *infection* of the operation wound. When the great **Joseph Lister** (1827–1912) was appointed Surgeon to Glasgow Royal Infirmary (1861) internal operations were hardly ever attempted because of the risk of infection. Even after amputations, or in cases of compound fracture, about a third of the patients died from *sepsis* (poisoning) of the wound. The cause was not understood, so the importance of cleanliness was not realised. Surgeons wore their old clothes, spattered with blood, and rarely washed their hands or their instruments. Lister, who found the stench of the surgical wards revolting, insisted on cleanliness at operations and ventilation and less overcrowding of the wards. This brought some improvement, although sepsis remained an everyday occurrence.

Then, one day in 1865, Lister read accounts of the work of **Louis Pasteur,** a great French scientist. Pasteur's recent researches showed that it was tiny living organisms (microbes) that caused wine to ferment. Lister wondered whether a similar explanation could be applied to the infection of wounds. If sepsis resulted from different kinds of living organisms (bacteria) present in the air then it only remained to find a way of killing the bacteria. As events showed, Lister's assumption was correct. He had, in fact, anticipated part of Pasteur's later **Germ Theory of Disease**—the most important medical discovery of all time.

When Lister heard that a thick black fluid called **carbolic acid** was being used in Carlisle for purifying sewage, he decided to experiment with it. A dilute solution of up to five per cent carbolic acid was used to clean the wound and to disinfect the hands and instruments of the surgeon and his helpers. In addition, a fine spray of the solution was blown over the patient during the operation. The immediate effect of Lister's *antiseptic* method was a great reduction in the death-rate from sepsis. Internal operations previously considered too dangerous could now be done in safety.

Further researches showed that the germs existing in the air were of little importance and that sepsis was normally caused by *direct* infection from the surgeon's hands or instruments, towels, sponges and the like. Thus Lister's spray (a great hindrance to the surgeon) was eventually discarded, and there arose the *aseptic* method, based on the principle that simple cleanliness was sufficient. The healing

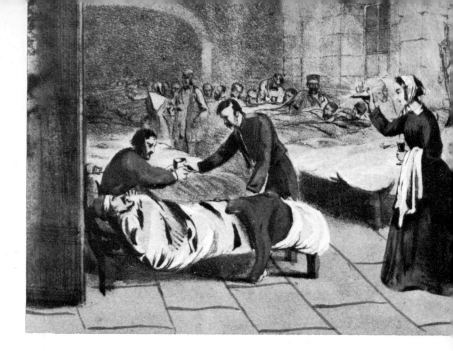

of the wound was left to nature, and everything brought into contact with it was carefully sterilised. Today the risk of death through infection of an operation wound is practically non-existent.

'The Lady with the Lamp'

Simpson made operations painless; Lister made them safe. But this revolution in surgery could only be really effective if hospitals were clean and nurses were efficient. In both these respects conditions in the first half of the nineteenth century were unsatisfactory. Hospitals in the towns became so overcrowded that most of them were breeding grounds for disease. Many patients who did not have fatal diseases when they were admitted acquired them in the normal course of treatment. It was much safer to stay at home. As late as 1869 James Simpson found that two-thirds of the operations carried out in hospitals of London, Edinburgh and Glasgow proved fatal, compared with only one in nine performed in private houses. But positive remedies were already on the way, in the shape of antiseptic surgery and the long overdue development of a trained nursing profession.

In 1854 Britain, supported by France, went to war in the Near East, with the aim of protecting Turkey against Russian aggression. The Allies landed in the **Crimea,** a peninsula on the northern shores of the Black Sea, and began to attack the Russian naval base at Sebastopol. Before long cholera and dysentery swept through the British ranks. The emergency British hospital, established in a Turkish barracks at Scutari, was quickly overwhelmed. The filth and overcrowding were almost indescribable. Men from the battlefield in blood-soaked bandages shared the floor with rats; the lavatories were blocked and stinking, and, to make matters worse, there was a serious shortage of basic stores like bandages, soap, blankets and even beds.

Florence Nightingale in the military hospital at Scutari

At this point **Florence Nightingale** (1820–1910) entered the scene. She was the daughter of a rich family, brought up to a life of luxury and idleness; but, to the astonishment of her friends and relations, she chose to go to Germany in 1851 to train as a nurse. By the autumn of 1854 she was in the Crimea, leading a party of thirty-eight nurses. She immediately set about the mammoth task of cleaning up the wards, corridors and lavatories of the hospital at Scutari. Next, the kitchens and the laundry were reorganised and a proper nursing service introduced. After six months of efficient administration and almost superhuman effort, the death-rate per 1000 patients had been reduced from 420 to 22! Her remarkable achievement won her the love and devotion of thousands of sick and dying soldiers. They called her 'the lady with the lamp', on account of her daily practice of touring the wards last thing at night to make sure all her instructions had been carried out.

The war finally ended in 1856, with the prohibition of Russian fortifications in the Black Sea. Florence Nightingale was a national heroine. But her life's work had only just begun, despite the ruin of her health in the Crimea, which made her an invalid at forty. After assisting in a thorough reform of army medical services, she turned to her greatest ambition, the establishment of nursing as a trained profession for women. It had previously been regarded as an unskilled job, fit for the lowest class of domestic worker. In 1860 Miss Nightingale founded a **nurses' training school** at St Thomas's Hospital in London. It set the pattern of training for the future and inspired similar establishments in most of the country's major hospitals. Entrants had to be of good character and have some educational background. After a course ranging from two to four years, a certificate was awarded on the result of a final examination.

By 1900 there were 64,000 trained nurses in Britain, bringing much higher standards of hygiene and discipline to hospital wards. Parliament began the first State Register of qualified nurses in 1919.

The march of medical science

In the last hundred years the rapid advance of medical knowledge has been greatly assisted by international co-operation. Thus, while some British doctors have made important contributions to tropical medicine (like **Ronald Ross,** who, in 1898, traced the cause of malaria to a species of mosquito) millions of British lives have been saved by new forms of treatment discovered abroad. For example, in *bacteriology* (identifying the particular germs responsible for each disease) and the accompanying search for prevention and treatment, very few of the major discoveries have been British. Foremost in this field was a German doctor, **Robert Koch,** who identified the microbes that cause tuberculosis and cholera (1882–3). About the same time typhoid and diphtheria were similarly traced.

It was another German, **Wilhelm Röntgen,** who discovered *X-rays* (1895). For the purposes of diagnosis, this was the most valuable gift ever given to medicine. Now that hidden parts of the body could be observed easily, all kinds of surgery were improved (especially the setting of broken bones), and the treatment of tuberculosis and other diseases was greatly advanced. Röntgen's work, together with experiments on uranium carried out in France, inspired a further great achievement. In 1898, at the Sorbonne University of Paris, **Marie Curie** and her husband Pierre discovered *radium*. Like X-rays, it could be made to act *selectively* on diseased cells, destroying them without harming healthy ones. It was soon applied to the treatment of cancers and other deadly growths beyond the reach of surgeons.

The chief medical achievements of the twentieth century have been discoveries of new drugs; for vaccinations and inoculations are of little use in treating patients already suffering from a disease. Roughly four-fifths of all drugs prescribed by present day doctors have originated in the last thirty-five years. The outstanding example is *penicillin,* found accidentally by **Sir Alexander Fleming** (1881–1955) a Scotsman, working at St Mary's Hospital, Paddington. One day in 1928 Fleming noticed that on one of the dishes where he was growing bacteria a mould had formed which killed all the cultures of bacteria around it. The mould turned out to be penicillium, from which he developed the famous drug, or 'antibiotic', which revolutionised the treatment of pneumonia, meningitis and septic conditions. More than ten years of further research was necessary before penicillin could be processed by chemical firms and given by injection (1939–40). Soon afterwards Fleming received the Nobel Prize, as did two other doctors who worked with him.

Sir Alexander Fleming being presented with the Albert Medal—one of many honours he received

Timeline

1798   Edward Jenner's smallpox vaccine.
1842   Edwin Chadwick's *Report on the Sanitary Condition of the Labouring Population.*

1847	James Simpson's chloroform anaesthetic.
1848	First Public Health Act.
1854–6	Florence Nightingale in the Crimea.
1865	Joseph Lister's antiseptic surgery.
1875	Public Health Act (Disraeli).
1875	Artisans' Dwellings Act.
1878	Louis Pasteur's *Germ Theory of Disease* published.
1895	Wilhelm Röntgen's X-rays.
1898	Marie Curie discovers radium.
1928	Alexander Fleming's discovery of penicillin.

Further study

Housing conditions following the two world wars are referred to in Chapters 23 and 24.

General accounts
The Fight for Health (Ginn's History Bookshelves, Grey Shelf)
R. K. Allday, *The Story of Medicine* (Ginn)
R. W. Johnson, *Disease and Medicine* (Batsford)
T. McCulley, *Man Against Disease* (Pergamon)
J. Robottom, *The Health of the People* (Longman, Making the Modern World series)
A. Swinson, *The History of Public Health* (Pergamon)

Special topics
Social Problems Arising from the Industrial Revolution (Longman, Secondary History Packs) Packs 8, 9
J. H. Bowles, *Dramatic Decisions* (Macmillan) has a chapter on 'Edwin Chadwick, the Most Hated Man in England'.
K. Dawson and P. Wall, *Public Health and Housing* (O.U.P.)
M. N. Duffy, *Medicine* (Blackwell, Twentieth Century Topic Books)
The Crimean War (Cape, Jackdaw series no. 11)
Pasteur and Germ Theory (Cape, Jackdaw series no. 84)
Cecil Woodham Smith, *Lady-in-Chief* (Methuen's Story Biographies) tells the story of Florence Nightingale.
I. Eberle, *Edward Jenner and Smallpox Vaccination* (Chatto & Windus, Immortals of Science)
W. H. Hughes, *Alexander Fleming and Penicillin* (Priory Press)
J. Rowland, *The Chloroform Man* (James Simpson); *The Mosquito Man* (Ronald Ross); and *The Penicillin Man* (Alexander Fleming) (Lutterworth Press)
The Then and There series (Longman) includes:
A. Delgado, *A Hundred Years of Medical Care*
Roger Watson, *Edwin Chadwick—Poor Law and Public Health*

Filmstrips
Lister and Antisepsis, Pasteur and Microbes (Common Ground, Lives of Famous Men and Women)
Florence Nightingale (Common Ground; Hulton Pictorial Biographies; and Visual Publications, Famous Women)

17 Trade Unions Take Root
Working-class movements 2

An important reason for the failure of many trade unions in the 1830s was that they attempted to do too much too quickly (see Chapter 12). Influenced by Robert Owen's schemes for workers' control of industry, they set out to displace their masters. But the employers, backed by the Government, were much too powerful to be defeated by un-educated and badly organised trade unionists. By the middle years of the century, the new generation of working men had learned from the mistakes of the past. They aimed to establish trade unions that were well organised, financially sound and capable of improving their position *gradually* by more peaceful means.

The 'new model unions'

In January 1851 a new kind of trade union was born. Well over a hundred local trade societies of millwrights, machinists, engineers and toolmakers came together to form the **Amalgamated Society of Engineers** (A.S.E.). The members of this union were well paid, highly-skilled technicians, men on whom the future prosperity of Britain depended. They could afford the high weekly subscription of a shilling (at a time when most working men still earned less than £1 a week). Many of the benefits they received in return were similar to those of a Friendly Society. For example, the rules of the union stated that one of its tasks was 'to promote the welfare of its members; to assist them when out of work or in distressed circum-stances, to support them in case of sickness, accident or super-annuation [old age] and loss of tools by fire, to provide for their burial and the burial of their wives'. Within nine months the A.S.E. had 11,000 members and a permanent headquarters, with a full-time, paid Secretary.

The A.S.E. became the 'model' for several national **craft unions** formed in the 1850s and 1860s, among boilermakers, carpenters and joiners, bricklayers, plasterers and others. An important feature of their tactics was an attempt to restrict the number of new entrants into their trade, for, according to the 'law of supply and demand', people will pay more for things that are scarce. If these unions could succeed in keeping down the number of apprentices that a master could employ, they would increase the value of the skilled worker and make it easy for him to obtain good wages, without the need for strikes. In fact, head-on collisions with employers were avoided as far as possible. But if they were considered really necessary these unions had ample funds for strike pay. The A.S.E., for instance, astonished everyone in 1859 when it presented the London Builders with £3000 in three weeks, thus helping them to defeat their employers in a dispute.

The strength of their financial position enabled the 'model unions'

Opposite: A.S.E. member-ship card

PROPOSED CONGRESS OF TRADES COUNCILS

AND OTHER

Federations of Trades Societies.

⸺◦◦⊱⊰◦◦⸺

MANCHESTER, FEBRUARY 21st, 1868.

FELLOW-UNIONISTS,

The Manchester and Salford Trades Council having recently taken into their serious consideration the present aspect of Trades Unions, and the profound ignorance which prevails in the public mind with reference to their operations and principles, together with the probability of an attempt being made by the Legislature, during the present session of Parliament, to introduce a measure detrimental to the interests of such Societies, beg most respectfully to suggest the propriety of holding in Manchester, as the main centre of industry in the provinces, a Congress of the Representatives of Trades Councils and other similar Federations of Trades Societies. By confining the Congress to such bodies it is conceived that a deal of expense will be saved, as Trades will thus be represented collectively; whilst there will be a better opportunity afforded of selecting the most intelligent and efficient exponents of our principles.

It is proposed that the Congress shall assume the character of the annual meetings of the British Association for the Advancement of Science and the Social Science Association, in the transactions of which Societies the artizan class are almost entirely excluded; and that papers, previously carefully prepared, shall be laid before the Congress on the various subjects which at the present time affect Trades Societies, each paper to be followed by discussion upon the points advanced, with a view of the merits and demerits of each question being thoroughly ventilated through the medium of the public press. It is further suggested that the subjects treated upon shall include the following :—

1.—Trades Unions an absolute necessity.
2.—Trades Unions and Political Economy.
3.—The Effect of Trades Unions on Foreign Competition.
4.—Regulation of the Hours of Labour.
5.—Limitation of Apprentices.
6.—Technical Education.
7.—Arbitration and Courts of Conciliation.
8.—Co-operation.
9.—The present Inequality of the Law in regard to Conspiracy, Intimidation, Picketing, Coercion, &c.
10.—Factory Acts Extension Bill, 1867: the necessity of Compulsory Inspection, and its application to all places where Women and Children are employed.
11.—The present Royal Commission on Trades Unions: how far worthy of the confidence of the Trades Union interest.
12.—The necessity of an Annual Congress of Trade Representatives from the various centres of industry.

All Trades Councils and other Federations of Trades are respectfully solicited to intimate their adhesion to this project on or before the 6th of April next, together with a notification of the subject of the paper that each body will undertake to prepare; after which date all information as to place of meeting, &c., will be supplied.

It is also proposed that the Congress be held on the 4th of May next, and that all liabilities in connection therewith shall not extend beyond its sittings.

Communications to be addressed to MR. W. H. WOOD, Typographical Institute, 29, Water Street, Manchester.

By order of the Manchester and Salford Trades Council,

S. C. NICHOLSON, PRESIDENT.
W. H. WOOD, SECRETARY.

to become firmly established; so did their willingness to accept the existing organisation of industry and to work *with* their employers rather than against them. Because the emphasis was on negotiation (discussion) rather than strike action as a means of settling disputes, each union had to have strong central control over its 'lodges' or local branches. Thus *executive committees,* normally based on London, tried to handle local grievances on behalf of the men. Employers came to respect the patient and responsible attitude of experienced union secretaries like **Robert Applegarth** of the Carpenters and Joiners and **William Allen** of the A.S.E.

The new type of trade unionism was not favoured by all workers. The lower-paid could not afford to establish such elaborate societies and remained largely unorganised. Even among the skilled trades, members of some smaller unions had no wish to submit to such control and discipline. Unionists in the Sheffield cutlery trades even resorted to violent and murderous attacks upon 'blacklegs' (fellow workers who refused to join them). Middle-class opinion was shocked in 1866 when a tin of gunpowder was exploded in the house of a non-unionist. These **Sheffield Outrages** undid some of the good work of the amalgamated societies in gaining a more respectable reputation for trade unions. But a Royal Commission of Inquiry (1867) decided that the incidents in Sheffield were exceptional and that most unions were peaceful and constructive.

By the 1860s, union representatives from many parts of Britain began to meet together from time to time to discuss matters of common interest, such as the regulation of working hours, technical education and conditions of apprenticeship. In 1868, at one such gathering in Manchester, it was proposed that regular meetings should be held every year in future. The **Trades Union Congress** (T.U.C.) was born. At Birmingham in the following year there were forty-eight delegates, representing the interests of nearly a quarter of a million unionists. Within a few years well over a million members were represented and the T.U.C. rapidly became an important unifying force in the trade union movement.

The struggle for legal protection

One of the chief concerns of the T.U.C. was the question of legal rights. Trade union activities had always been hampered by a lack of legal protection (see Chapter 12). Long before they were outlawed in the Combination Acts (1799–1800) unions had run the risk of prosecution under the law of conspiracy. Even after the Combination Acts were repealed (1824–5) they frequently fell foul of the law, as in the unfortunate case of the 'Tolpuddle Martyrs' (1834). They were, in fact, fighting two powerful opponents at once—their employers and the state.

Influenced by the Royal Commission of 1867, Gladstone's Liberal Government passed two important new laws in 1871. The first, the **Trade Union Act,** enabled unions to register themselves in the same way as Friendly Societies. There was no longer any difference between collecting money for benefit purposes and collecting it to support strike action; therefore trade unions could in future claim

Robert Applegarth, Secretary of the Amalgamated Society of Carpenters and Joiners

Opposite: The birth of the T.U.C.: a broadsheet issued by the Manchester and Salford Trades Council

legal assistance in recovering stolen funds. This Act was favourable
to them, but a **Criminal Law Amendment Act** which followed it
seriously restricted union activities. With the Sheffield Outrages in
mind, the Government repeated the old warnings against 'molesting'
or 'obstructing' fellow workers, and then went on to outlaw even
peaceful forms of *picketing* (attempting to prevent non-unionists, or
blacklegs, from working during a strike). This was a serious handicap
because in those days union members were nearly always a minority
in any group of workers. To carry out a successful strike picketing was
almost essential.

A number of working men had recently been granted the right to
vote—in the Reform Act of 1867 (see the last section of this chapter).
Angry with Gladstone's Government, trade unionists voted against
the Liberals in the 1874 election and helped to return a Conservative
Government under Disraeli. The Conservatives, grateful for this
temporary support, repaid the unions by passing the **Conspiracy and
Protection of Property Act** (1875). It permitted picketing during a
strike, so long as no violence was used, and made the law of conspiracy no longer applicable to trade disputes. Union members now
had the same rights as any other citizens, even though they might be
acting together. In future they could only be prosecuted under the
ordinary criminal law of the land.

'The dockers' tanner' and the rise of 'unskilled unions'

The 'new model unions' covered only a small section of the working
class—probably not above ten per cent, even in the 1870s. Meanwhile
the great mass of unskilled and semi-skilled labourers remained
largely unorganised. There were some exceptions, like the Miners'
National Union and the Agricultural Labourers' Union (1872) started
by **Joseph Arch,** a Warwickshire labourer. But it was not until the
late 1880s that large numbers of poorer workers began to organise
themselves. Their opportunity was provided by an improvement in
overseas trade, which resulted in almost full employment for a time.
The 'bargaining position' of unions is always strengthened in such
conditions because employers find it almost impossible to break
strikes by bringing in new workers.

The turning-point was marked by a number of successful strikes
among unskilled and semi-skilled workers in the years 1888–9.
London was the main centre of the revival. It was there that the
match girls of Bryant and May's organised a stoppage in 1888. They
gained great public sympathy and financial assistance when it
became known that they earned about a penny an hour for the
dangerous work of dipping matches in phosphorus. Within three
weeks they gained considerably better pay and conditions. In the
following year 20,000 **London gas-workers** struck, to achieve a
reduction in their twelve-hour day. Led by **Will Thorne,** a young
Birmingham-born Irishman who could barely read and write, they
quickly forced the South Metropolitan Gas Company to cut the
working day to eight hours. Immediately after this triumph, a strike
began among the London dockers which captured the attention of
the whole nation.

Ben Tillett (1860–1943)
the dockers' leader

Most dockers were casual labourers who were taken on, as and
when required, to unload cargoes and carry goods in and out of
warehouses. During slack periods, when few ships were in port,
thousands of men were idle; waiting at the dock gates or standing
about the streets of the East End. A small Society of Tea Warehouse-
men had recently been formed. But it was a remarkable achievement
of discipline and organisation when its Secretary, **Ben Tillett,**
brought 10,000 poverty-stricken dockers out on strike in the hot
summer of 1889. They demanded at least four hours continuous work
at a time, with a minimum rate of sixpence an hour—**the 'dockers'
tanner'**—and eightpence for overtime. While the Port of London was
closed and the Thames crowded with shipping, the strikers paraded
through the City carrying fish-heads and rotten vegetables on sticks,
to show what they had to live on.

At first the dock directors refused all the demands of the strikers,
believing it was just a matter of time before their funds ran out and
they were forced to surrender. But just as the dockers were on the
verge of defeat they were saved by a flood of public sympathy and
support. Subscriptions to their strike fund began to pour in from all
over Britain and even from abroad. Every other union made a
donation, so did the Salvation Army. Some football clubs even sent

their gate money. Above all, Australian sympathisers contributed no less than £30,000! After five weeks, with the tide of public opinion running strongly against them, the employers realised they were beaten and granted all the dockers' main demands. The triumphant union was now established on a permanent basis, with Tillett as its full-time Secretary. Only three months after the end of the dispute it claimed a total of 30,000 members.

The dockers had won a victory not only for themselves but for *all* lower-paid workers. Their strike immediately inspired the formation of several powerful national unions among unskilled and semi-skilled workers. For instance, a **General Railway Workers' Union** was formed (1889) to cater for those who could not afford the subscriptions of the 'craft' union—the Amalgamated Society of Railway Servants. At the same time the **Miners' Federation of Great Britain** was created, to represent most miners in England, Scotland and Wales. This great union was at the centre of some of the bitterest struggles of the next forty years. All these developments in the trade union movement were reflected in steadily rising membership figures:

Total membership of trade unions (approx. figures)

1888	*1900*	*1914*
750,000	2,000,000	4,000,000

These new unions differed from the older 'model unions' in several ways. They were usually organised on an 'industrial' rather than a 'craft' basis—in other words, they set out to enrol *all* workers in a particular industry, no matter what their jobs were. They rarely collected money for benefit schemes, preferring to keep subscriptions to a minimum. Above all, they were less prepared to co-operate with employers. They wanted higher wages and better conditions almost immediately and would not listen to excuses.

There were many strikes in the years ahead. Great successes mingled with bitter defeats. Yet the worst setback of all occurred not on the 'industrial battlefront' but in the law courts. In 1901, following a strike by members of the Amalgamated Society of Railway Servants, the **Taff Vale Railway Company** in South Wales sued the union for damages. They were granted £23,000 in compensation; a decision which was confirmed on appeal to the House of Lords. This new ruling virtually eliminated the unions' major weapon, for every strike automatically causes the employers to lose money. Eventually, in 1906, the newly elected Liberal Government passed a **Trade Disputes Act** which protected unions against similar claims for damages in the future.

Rising prices in the early years of the twentieth century caused frequent strikes for higher wages, reaching a climax in the years 1910–14. A railway stoppage in 1911 paralysed most of the country. It also led to an amalgamation of railwaymen's unions. Three of the four existing societies joined together in 1913 to form the **N.U.R.** (National Union of Railwaymen). In 1912 the Miners' Federation organised the largest single strike that had ever taken place in Britain up to that time. Over a million miners came out in support of a claim for a minimum wage of five shillings a day for men and

Cheque paid to the Taff Vale Railway Company, following the court case of 1901

two shillings for boys. After six weeks, Parliament intervened and set up a Minimum Wage Board which settled the dispute to the satisfaction of the strikers.

Just as the railway strike brought many other industries to a standstill, so the coal stoppage forced factories to close and railways to restrict services. With this in mind, representatives of the 'big three' —the Miners' Federation, the N.U.R. and the National Transport Workers' Federation (formed in 1910 out of various dockers' and transport workers' unions)—met in April 1914 to discuss ways of co-operating in future strike action. The outcome was the **Triple Industrial Alliance,** representing almost $1\frac{1}{2}$ million trade unionists. It was intended that each section of the alliance should be prepared to strike 'in sympathy' with other members. The outbreak of the First World War (August 1914) meant the scheme had to be shelved, for an 'industrial truce' was agreed between unions and employers, in the national interest. But it was clear that this powerful alliance could provide the basis for a future general strike. As the President of the Miners' Federation said: 'it may well be found advisable later on to extend the scope of the alliance in the general interests of labour as a whole'.

Parliamentary reform and the origins of the Labour Party
The right to vote in parliamentary elections continued to be based on wealth and ownership of property after the 1832 Reform Act (see Chapter 11). It was the resulting lack of working-class political rights that inspired the Chartist movement (see Chapter 12) but it failed to achieve its aims and collapsed in 1848. By about 1860, when the right to vote was still a privilege held by just under a tenth of the adult male population, a new campaign for working-class franchise (voting rights) began. A **National Reform League** was

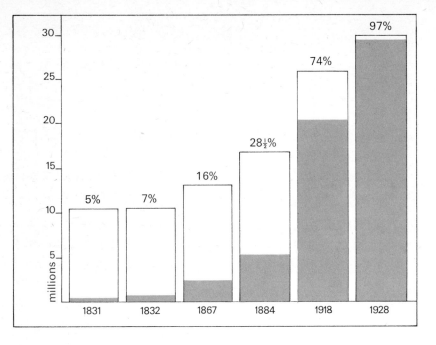

Percentage of the adult population entitled to vote, 1831–1928

established, with the support of trade union leaders, a few ex-Chartists and many middle-class Liberals. Meetings were held all over the country, reaching a climax in 1866 with a great demonstration in Hyde Park.

The 'new model unions' had greatly increased the respectability and influence of skilled workers; but it was the support of middle-class M.P.s like John Bright, the 'free trader', that proved decisive. A second **Parliamentary Reform Act (1867)** almost doubled the number of voters by granting the franchise to all male householders in the boroughs, and to holders of leases to the value of £12 or more in the counties. In addition, some seats were taken from small boroughs and given to expanding towns. Five years later, open voting was replaced by **secret ballot (1872).** It was now unnecessary for a man to declare his political views in public and risk offending those in authority over him. But the number of working-class voters remained small, until a further **Reform Act (1884)** gave the franchise to all householders in the counties, thus putting agricultural labourers on the same footing as town workers.

After 1884 most adult males had the franchise, and working-class voters were in a majority for the first time. But many of them were dissatisfied with having only Conservatives and Liberals to chose from. They felt it was time they had a political party of their own. The first really working-class M.P.s (two miners) had been elected in 1874. They sat with the Liberals in Parliament but were often known as 'Labour' or **'Lib-Lab'** members. Their numbers slowly increased until there were eleven 'Lib-Labs' in 1885. But it was soon clear that the Liberal Party offered little prospect of carrying out the kind of far-reaching social reforms that most working men wanted. The creation of a separate workers' political party was just a matter of time.

In 1892 **Keir Hardie** (1856–1915) a Scottish miner, was elected for West Ham and created a sensation by sitting among top-hatted M.P.s dressed in cloth cap and working clothes. He immediately took the lead in forming an **Independent Labour Party** (I.L.P.) in 1893.

James Keir Hardie, addressing a meeting in Trafalgar Square (1913)

James Ramsay MacDonald (1866–1937) Secretary of the Labour Representation Committee. Later Britain's first Labour Prime Minister

Its programme was based on *Socialism*—the belief that the state should control the main sources of the country's wealth, including key industries, railways and the banking system, for the benefit of the whole community rather than a few wealthy owners. Small socialist societies already existed, like the **Fabians** (1884) which included several well-known writers like George Bernard Shaw and H. G. Wells. But the Fabian Society consisted mainly of middle-class intellectuals. It had no direct working-class support, unlike the I.L.P., which had followers in the industrial North and the Scottish Lowlands. Nevertheless, in the 1895 election all twenty-eight I.L.P. candidates were defeated, including Hardie himself.

There seemed little chance of success without *official* support from the trade unions, the only workers' organisations really large enough to launch a new political party. Growing support for Socialism among younger trade unionists finally led to the formation of a **Labour Representation Committee** (L.R.C.) in 1900, backed by the Trades Union Congress. A fund was started to pay the expenses of Labour candidates and the salaries of those that were successful, for M.P.s were not yet paid. The election of 1900 came too soon for the L.R.C. to get to work. Only two of its candidates were elected, including Keir Hardie. In the next few years, however, under its busy Secretary, **James Ramsay MacDonald,** a Scottish journalist, the L.R.C. built up a nationwide following. The Taff Vale decision (1901) had finally convinced trade unionists of the need for an independent party to defend their interests in Parliament.

In the general election of 1906, no fewer than twenty-nine L.R.C. candidates were successful—plus twenty-four miners and 'Lib-Labs'. The Labour Party, as it was now called, was at last capable of having some influence, although it was not large enough to form a Labour Government for many years to come. Its main task at this stage was to gain wider support beyond the areas of mining and heavy industry, where most Labour voters were concentrated. This was difficult, for many people who were sympathetic towards Labour policies were frightened away by the revolutionary ideas of a few extremists who preached 'class war' against the rich.

Money subscribed by trade unionists made these early successes possible. But not all union members voted Labour. **W. V. Osborne,** an official in the Amalgamated Society of Railway Servants, was a Liberal, and he took his union to court for allocating part of members' subscriptions to Labour Party funds. He won his case, and the House of Lords confirmed the decision in 1909. This was a great setback for Labour, since the 'political levy' from the unions was its main source of income. However in 1911 the old Chartist demand for **payment of M.P.s** was granted, at the rate of £400 a year (allowing for tax, this was worth more than the present salary). Working men could at last support themselves as M.P.s. Nevertheless Labour continued to demand a reversal of the Osborne judgment. They finally succeeded when a **Trade Union Act (1913)** allowed union funds to be used for any lawful purpose, provided a majority of members showed approval in a ballot. Individuals could 'contract out' (be exempted) from the political levy if they wished.

Timeline

1851   Amalgamated Society of Engineers.

1854–66 'Sheffield Outrages'.

1867   Second Parliamentary Reform Act.

1868   Trades Union Congress.

1871   Trade Union Act (Gladstone).

           Criminal Law Amendment Act.

1872   Secret ballot in parliamentary elections.

1875   Conspiracy and Protection of Property Act (Disraeli).

1884   Third Parliamentary Reform Act.

1889   The 'dockers' tanner'.

1900   Labour Representation Committee; became Labour Party, 1905.

1901   Taff Vale Case.

1906   Trade Disputes Act (reversing Taff Vale decision).

1909   Osborne Judgment.

1911   Payment of M.P.s.

1913   Trade Union Act (reversing Osborne Judgment).

1914   'Triple Industrial Alliance'.

Further study

The next—and most dramatic—stage in the history of trade unions and the Labour Party is dealt with in Chapter 23.

General accounts

W. G. Hall, *The Labour Party* (Collins)

Andrew Robertson, *The Trade Unions* (Hamish Hamilton, Men and Movements) pp. 40–80

Special topics

K. Dawson and P. Wall, *Trade Unions* and *Parliamentary Representation* (O.U.P., Society and Industry in Nineteenth Century Britain)

J. W. Derry, *Parliamentary Reform* (Macmillan, Sources of History)

K. O. Morgan, *Keir Hardie* (O.U.P., Clarendon Biographies)

M. and C. H. B. Quennell, *A History of Everyday Things in England*, Part IV, pp. 155–7, is useful on co-operatives.

J. Robottom: *Keir Hardie and the Labour Party* (Longman, Making the Modern World series)

The Vote, 1832–1928 (Cape, Jackdaw series no. 16) contains several documents relating to the period covered in this chapter.

Towards Democracy (Longman, Secondary History Packs) Packs 22, 23

Longman's Then and There series includes:

D. Wasp and A. Davis, *The Great Dock Strike, 1889*

H. Shapiro, *Keir Hardie and the Labour Party*

Filmstrips

Trade Unionism—Historical, Part 2, by G. D. H. Cole (Common Ground)

The Development of the Electoral System, Part 2: Chartism to Universal Suffrage (Common Ground)

18 Schools for Everyone
The Beginnings of a National System of Education

Nowadays we are all required by law to devote roughly a seventh of our lives to full-time education. But the growth of 'state schools', financed out of rates and taxes, has only taken place in the last hundred years. Before then, 'schooling' was a private matter; left for parents to decide.

In the days before compulsory schools, there were great differences in education north and south of the Border. Most villages in Scotland had their own schools, maintained by local rates, as early as 1700. These took children from the poorest families as well as those of the lairds (landowners). 'You find very few [Scottish] gentry either ignorant or unlearned', said Daniel Defoe, writing in the early eighteenth century. 'Nay, you cannot ordinarily find a *servant* in Scotland but he can read or write.' But in England and Wales (our chief concern in this chapter) the situation was quite different. Full-time education was a privilege, enjoyed by only a minority of the population. The well-to-do could afford the necessary school fees; but many working-class children were totally deprived of education because their parents were unable to pay for it. Even when free elementary schools were provided by private charity, many parents felt it was more important to keep their children at work in order to make up the family income.

The education of the well-to-do

In the eighteenth century, sons of the 'landed gentry' received private tuition in basic skills, including reading and writing, and were then sent as boarders to expensive **public schools** like Eton, Winchester, Harrow and Rugby. Life in many of these schools was harsh and sometimes even violent. The boys fought and bullied each other, and the teachers usually maintained discipline by means of savage floggings. Since most public schools had insufficient staff, the senior boys virtually ruled the younger ones, using them as 'fags' (servants). Occasionally the pupils rose in open rebellion against their teachers. Two companies of troops, with fixed bayonets, were needed to put down a revolt at Winchester in 1818. The public school curriculum consisted almost entirely of Latin and Greek (together known as 'Classics') and teaching methods were dull and mechanical. Needless to say, few pupils acquired any real knowledge and fewer still showed a genuine interest.

The same was true of the Universities of **Oxford** and **Cambridge,** where the sons of the upper classes normally finished their education. Most of the staff and students neglected their studies, preferring hunting, gambling and drinking. University teaching, like most schoolmastering, was in the hands of clergymen, and many of them had no qualifications in the subjects they taught. In the 1760s, it was

Right: Pupils at Rugby School

Below: 'Young ladies' learning geography with the help of their tutor

said that the Professor of Chemistry at Cambridge had never read a book on the subject! Examinations for degrees were a formality; presenting no difficulty to the most idle and stupid.

The daughters of the upper classes rarely went to school. They were thought to be less in need of 'mental cultivation' than their brothers. But they were expected to have certain 'accomplishments', which would help them to enter fashionable social circles and find desirable husbands. Therefore most well-to-do parents engaged **governesses** to teach their daughters reading and writing, music, painting and dancing, and a little 'general knowledge', like the dates of kings and queens. Mothers often assisted governesses, particularly in the teaching of sewing, cookery and the management of household accounts.

Sons of the lesser gentry usually attended a **grammar school** in the nearest town. Many of these schools had been *endowed* (provided with a regular income by their founders) in the sixteenth century, and were intended for able boys of any social class. But, as prices rose, fixed endowments became increasingly insufficient for the upkeep of free schools. A good schoolmaster earned about £10 a year in the sixteenth century, but, by the early nineteenth century, some headmasters were paid up to 100 times as much. Therefore fees were charged. This was how public boarding-schools first developed. They grew out of a few local grammar schools which managed to attract paying pupils from a wide area. Meanwhile most of the remaining grammar schools declined rapidly. As the number of free places diminished and fees increased, smallholders and tradesmen no longer sent their sons. In any case, the curriculum, based on Classics, was particularly unsuitable for the education of working men.

In general, the best schools of the eighteenth and early nineteenth centuries were the **Dissenters' academies,** run by Nonconformists (especially Quakers) who were excluded from most other schools because of their religion. These gave a general education which was more suited to the world of business, where many of the pupils were highly successful. Book-keeping, science and natural history were normally provided, as well as English and Classics.

By the beginning of the nineteenth century rapidly growing numbers of wealthy manufacturers and merchants were sending their sons to public boarding-schools in order to get them accepted in the highest ranks of society. Amid this rising popularity, public schools at last began to reform themselves, under the inspiration of a few exceptional headmasters. **Samuel Butler,** Head of Shrewsbury, 1798–1836, set an example by introducing subjects like mathematics and history. So did **Thomas Arnold,** the famous Headmaster of **Rugby** (1828–42). He added modern history, geography and French. Dr Arnold wanted, above all, to make his pupils 'Christian gentlemen'. The chapel became the centre of school life, and he chose only outstanding boys in the sixth form to be prefects, for he expected the highest standards of conduct from them. 'What we must look for', he said, 'is, first, religious and moral principles; secondly, gentlemanly conduct; thirdly, intellectual ability.'

Dr Thomas Arnold (1795–1842)

Rugby became the model for other public schools, both old and new. Altogether, fifty-four were founded during the nineteenth century, to meet the growing demand for a 'gentleman's education'. Some taught a variety of subjects, including science and handicrafts, and team games became increasingly popular. In the 1860s it was estimated that a typical pupil at Harrow might devote fifteen hours a week to cricket. A number of new ideas were put into practice by **Edward Thring,** Head of Uppingham, 1853–87. He introduced a gymnasium and a swimming-bath, music rooms and workshops for carpentry. But, despite improvements, most public schools failed to provide satisfactory courses in technical and scientific subjects. Thus even though many of the pupils were sons of manufacturers, they mostly became politicians, civil servants, teachers and clergymen, and rarely took up the kind of work on which the country depended for its livelihood.

Meanwhile many of the old grammar schools were reformed along similar lines (particularly after 1869, when Parliament made extra charitable funds available to them), and the higher education of girls at last began to receive attention. In 1850 **Frances Buss** founded the North London Collegiate School, and, eight years later, **Dorothea Beale** became Principal of Cheltenham Ladies' College. Both set out to prepare young women for a serious career, and several new girls' public schools soon followed their example. In the past, girls' schools had concentrated on accomplishments like music and dancing. But the work of Miss Beale and Miss Buss, like that of Florence Nightingale, made people realise that daughters of wealthy families could play a fuller part in national life if they had a broader education.

Finally, there were important developments in university education. The monopoly of Oxford and Cambridge was ended in 1828, when **University College, London,** was founded. It was open to men of all religious views, in contrast to the older universities where Nonconformists could not take degrees before the 1850s and were barred from joining the teaching staff until 1871. The first women's colleges at Oxford and Cambridge were established in the 1870s, by which time many new subjects were being introduced, including sciences and modern languages. Meanwhile, new **civic universities** began to appear in the major towns. Durham (1832) was the first, but by 1914 Manchester, Liverpool, Birmingham, Leeds, Sheffield and Bristol had followed suit, and the University of Wales was founded in 1893. They all took students of either sex and any religion, most of them day scholars who lived in the area. The civic universities were soon well known for their degrees in engineering, science and medicine. They gave higher education to many young people who would not otherwise have had the chance. Oxford and Cambridge continued to be dominated by ex-public school pupils from rich families until well into the twentieth century.

University College, London

School run on the moni-
torial system

Voluntary schools for the poor

Despite the work of parish charity schools and the newer Sunday
schools (see Chapter 4) most children of the poor in England received no education of any kind at the beginning of the nineteenth
century. Many charity schools had, in any case, run short of money
and fallen into decay by this time—throwing a greater burden on
the Sunday schools and various new foundations run by Church
societies.

Sunday schools were particularly important in manufacturing
towns, where they provided almost the only education for the working
classes during the first fifty years of the Industrial Revolution.
Robert Raikes, who founded the first Sunday school, in Gloucester
(1783), did so *not* for the benefit of the poor but simply to prevent the
hooliganism which broke out in the streets when a nearby factory
was closed. Although elementary instruction in reading and writing
was normally given, Raikes and his imitators aimed above all to
teach the children 'a sense of subordination and of due respect to
their superiors', as well as some knowledge of the Bible.

The desire to give the poor free instruction in the Christian
religion led Andrew Bell, an ex-army chaplain, and Joseph
Lancaster, a Quaker, to set up rival elementary schools in London
(1798). Both were short of money and teachers, so they operated a
monitorial system. By this method (which Bell and Lancaster
each claimed to have invented) one master could supervise the

teaching of hundreds of children. He simply gave each lesson to a group of older pupils—the 'monitors'—and these, in turn, passed it on to the juniors. 'Give me twenty-four pupils today,' said Bell, 'and I will give you twenty-four teachers tomorrow.' Two **Church societies** were founded to run schools on the same pattern. Bell established the Church of England National Society for the Education of the Poor (1811) and Lancaster's Nonconformist supporters organised the British and Foreign Schools Society (1814). But the 'teaching' in these voluntary schools was almost worthless. Pupils were drilled to reply to set questions in chorus. On one occasion, an inspector decided to rearrange the questions, only to receive the replies in the original order!

Although the Church societies provided many schools (the National Society alone founded 3000 in twenty years) they only catered for a small fraction of England's children. In many areas the only education available to the working classes was that provided in small private **dame schools**—so called because they were usually run by women. In the absence of government regulations, there was nothing to stop people from opening schools in their own homes and charging a few coppers a week, even though they might be totally ignorant. Many 'dames' were little more than child-minders. They often attended to a shop or did washing and sewing while the children were in their care. 'If I can keep them quiet,' said one, 'it's as much as I can do and all I'm paid for.'

Such was the sorry state of education for the poor at the beginning of the Victorian Age. The first sign of parliamentary interest was in 1833, when £20,000 was granted to the Church societies for school-building. But, considering that more was spent that year on the royal stables, education remained very low on the Government's list of priorities! In 1839 the grant was slightly increased and a special Education Committee was set up. Its secretary, **James Kay-Shuttleworth,** was not satisfied with the monitorial system, so he made great efforts to increase the supply of teachers. He started a Teachers' Training College at Battersea (1840) which soon led to the development of voluntary colleges in other areas. Meanwhile, to get over the immediate shortage, he encouraged a 'pupil teacher system'. Starting about the age of thirteen, **pupil teachers,** who were like apprentices, helped the older teachers during the day and studied in their spare time. After five years they took exams to become assistant teachers or qualify for entry to a training college. Meanwhile, to help raise standards, Kay-Shuttleworth appointed more inspectors (there were only two in 1839).

By the middle of the century, the annual parliamentary grant had risen to £500,000. But there was still nothing like a proper state system of education. Voluntary societies continued to depend largely on private subscriptions. Several new societies had been founded, including the **Ragged Schools Union.** By about 1850, when it had established roughly 100 schools for poor children (many of them orphans) it received welcome support from **Lord Ashley,** the factory reformer. He became President, and set about building new schools and improving old ones. Lack of money was always a

A 'Ragged School'

problem, especially as food and clothing had to be provided for many of the pupils before they were in a fit state to learn anything. Ashley contributed every penny he could lay hands on. He even resorted to begging money from M.P.s as they entered Parliament.

'Payment by results'

A Royal Commission on elementary education (1858–61) found that less than half of the $3\frac{1}{2}$ million children in England and Wales went regularly to school, and of these only a tenth learned reading, writing and arithmetic successfully. In an attempt to raise existing standards, the Commission suggested a system of **payment by results.** In other words, the amount of money granted by the Government to each school would depend on 'the attainment of a certain degree of knowledge by the children . . . during the year preceding the payment'. **Robert Lowe,** Vice-President of the Department of Education, liked the idea. It promised something definite in return for money spent. 'If it is not cheap, it shall be efficient,' he said; and 'if it is not efficient, it shall be cheap.'

'Payment by results' was started almost immediately (1862). Her Majesty's Inspectors visited grant-aided schools once a year to test pupils in the '3 Rs' (reading, 'riting and 'rithmetic) and up to twelve shillings per child was paid on the result of the examination. Teachers, whose salaries normally depended on the size of the grant, sometimes resorted to underhand methods—for example, signalling the answers to pupils from behind the Inspector's back. The new system helped to even out standards from one district to another, and it spurred many teachers to make a greater effort; but in other ways it was a backward step. It encouraged 'parrot learning' of facts, regardless of whether they were understood. Bright children were neglected while the teacher concentrated on bringing the slower ones up to the required standard; and many schools taught nothing else but the elementary work necessary for the exam.

This method of paying grants to schools continued until 1897. But long before then it was realised that voluntary schools *alone* could not satisfy the urgent need for more elementary education. The state would have to take direct responsibility. In industry, there was an increasing demand for people who could read and write. Great strides were being made to meet this demand in countries like Germany and the U.S.A., Britain's main trading rivals. To many observers it seemed certain that British industrial supremacy would be lost if half the nation's children remained uneducated. In addition, many of the middle and upper classes now believed that crime, unrest and drunkenness were the result of ignorance, and that uneducated workers might be a danger to the peace and security of the country.

Reformers had long been suggesting that elementary schools should be provided in *all* areas out of local rates. But Parliament was reluctant to make such a scheme compulsory because of the great difficulties involved. Many of the well-to-do were opposed to paying extra rates for the education of their social inferiors. Moreover, the Churches had been squabbling among themselves for thirty years about how the available money should be spent. Ratepayers who belonged to the Church of England objected to paying for the upkeep of schools which did not teach their religion. Nonconformists took a similar view when they were asked to give aid to Church of England schools. Feelings were so strong, on both sides, that many churchgoers preferred children to have no education at all rather than attend schools run by their rivals.

The event which finally forced the Government to take decisive action was the 1867 Parliamentary Reform Act (see Chapter 17). It gave the vote to working-class householders in the boroughs, but they could hardly be expected to understand political affairs and use their vote wisely if they were unable to read or write. Most M.P.s agreed with Robert Lowe when, referring to the new voters, he said: 'We must educate our future masters.'

'Board school brats'

The outcome was the **Education Act of 1870,** introduced by W. E. Forster on behalf of Gladstone's Liberal ministry. 'Our object', he said, 'is to complete the present voluntary system; to fill up the gaps.' Therefore the existing Church schools, which now numbered 20,000, carried on as before, assisted by larger government grants. In all other areas, where proper schools were not provided, Parliament ordered that local **School Boards** were to be elected by the rate-payers. The Boards would provide elementary schools for the five to ten age group, paid for partly out of local rates and partly by direct government grants. Parents were charged a small weekly fee, unless they were very poor, in which case they were excused. Attendance was not yet compulsory, since it would take time for enough schools to be built. But individual Boards were given the right to make schooling compulsory in their own districts.

To get over the religious problem, the Forster Act stated that Christian teaching should be restricted to reading and explaining the Bible. In other words, there was to be no attempt to teach religion according to the views of any one Church or denomination. Parents were given the right to withdraw their children from Scripture lessons if they wished. These arrangements did not satisfy a number of religious leaders, but it was clearly better to force them to accept a compromise than to allow their disagreements to hold up reform any longer.

By modern standards, Board schools were drab and poorly equipped. Classes of eighty or ninety were common. All the different

Left: An infants' school in London before the First World War. Rather different from modern 'activity methods'!

Below: Playground drill in a London girls' school (1908)

ages and different subjects often had to be taught together in one large hall. There were not enough trained teachers, so school managers had to recruit many unqualified assistants and pupil teachers. The children themselves were mostly dirty and ragged, with skin diseases and running noses. More fortunate middle-class children, from expensive private schools, called them 'board school brats'. Before the 'brats' could be educated they had to be civilised, and often fed and clothed as well. In 1889 over 50,000 pupils in London alone were reported to be 'attending in want of food'. The curriculum still consisted of little more than the bare essentials of reading, writing, arithmetic and Scripture. Elementary education in this period was designed to teach the poor to 'know their duty and keep their place', *not* to help them rise above their station.

Nevertheless it was from these beginnings that Britain's 'state system' of education developed. This alone makes the 1870 Act the most important milestone in the country's educational history. By 1880 there were enough schools for attendance to be made compulsory up to the age of ten. (It was raised to twelve in 1899 and fourteen in 1918.) **Compulsory attendance** brought to light hordes of children who were starving, suffering from infectious diseases, and without shoes or proper clothes. Many School Boards had to arrange for cheap meals, free medical attention and the distribution of charity clothing for the most ragged ones. Fees were low, yet many families had great difficulty in paying them. Even a penny or twopence a week was a lot of money when the difference between weekly earnings and the rent was only a few shillings. Therefore elementary education was made free to all in 1891.

One immediate result of the spread of elementary education was the rise of the 'popular press'. Its chief creator was Alfred Harmsworth, later **Lord Northcliffe** (1865–1922) who realised that most of the new reading public found existing **newspapers,** with their stress on parliamentary news, too dull and difficult. After a successful start with a weekly paper called *Answers* (1888) he founded the *Daily Mail* in 1896. It sold for a halfpenny (half the price of most dailies). Its eye-catching headlines and photographs and its 'chatty' style quickly attracted a mass readership. Within three years, its daily circulation was over half a million, twice that of any other newspaper. The *Daily Mail* set the standard for the 'popular' newspapers of the twentieth century, including the *Daily Mirror* and the *Daily Express.*

The 1902 Act and the 'educational ladder'

Full-time education *beyond* the elementary stage was still only available to those who could afford the fees of private, grammar or public schools. The rest mostly had to make do with Mechanics' and Working Men's Institutes, which provided evening lectures, reading-rooms and lending libraries in return for a small subscription. By the 1890s, some local Boards provided 'higher grade schools', and County Councils began to run evening classes—mostly in technical and commercial subjects. But these opportunities were only available in a few areas. Most children from Board schools had little chance of continuing their education, even if they were very able.

No industrial country could afford such wastage of ability. There-fore, in the 1890s, a Royal Commission was set up 'to consider what are the best methods of establishing a well-organised system of secondary education in England'. Some of its proposals became law in the **1902 Education Act,** which made secondary schools for the first time a concern of the state. The 2568 School Boards were abolished and their duties handed over to County and County Borough Councils. The Boards had done well, providing nearly $2\frac{1}{2}$ million school places, but they were too small to be really efficient. On the other hand, the newly created **Local Education Authorities** (328 in all) were large enough to build and maintain elementary *and* secondary schools.

It was intended that all secondary schools, both old and new, should charge fees. But in 1907 an important change was made. Secondary schools receiving public grants were instructed to make a quarter of their places available free of charge to the cleverest children from the elementary schools. These **free places,** later called scholarships, at last made it possible for a child from a poor family to get a full secondary education, continuing beyond the normal leaving age. In the early years, up to the First World War (1914–18) places were scarce, and less than one child in twenty from the elementary schools won a 'scholarship'. Nevertheless, it was an important departure from the traditional view that education should teach children to 'know their station in life'. An 'educational ladder' had been built which could be climbed by able and hard-working children from any social background.

Meanwhile rapid strides were made in organising social services for schoolchildren. Parliament in 1906 encouraged the provision of

Schoolchildren receiving dental attention (1911)

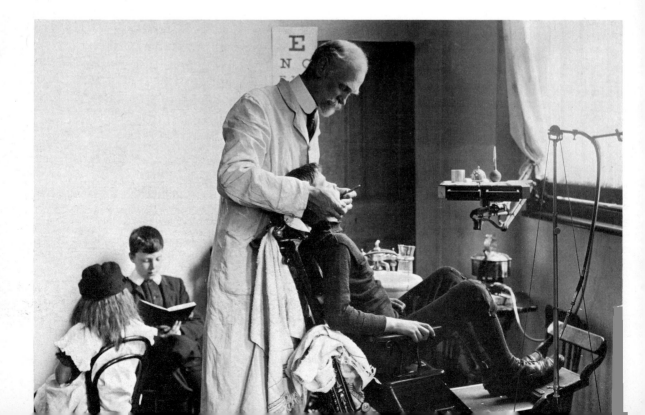

school meals, and in the following year medical examinations were made compulsory in elementary schools (see Chapter 20). Medical attention was extended to secondary schools in the **Education Act of 1918.** The same Act (largely the work of **H. A. L. Fisher,** President of the Board of Education) fixed the school leaving age at fourteen and restricted the employment of schoolchildren to little more than a paper round. Fisher also encouraged part-time education up to the age of sixteen, but lack of money almost ruled this out from the start.

The ultimate aim of reformers was 'secondary education for all'. But that was a thing of the future (see Chapter 24).

Timeline

1783	Robert Raikes founds the first Sunday school.
1798	Introduction of the 'monitorial system'.
1828	University College, London founded.
1828–42	Thomas Arnold Headmaster of Rugby.
1833	First Parliamentary grant for education (£20,000).
1862	'Payment by results' introduced.
1870	Elementary Education Act (W. E. Forster).
1880	Elementary education made compulsory.
1891	Elementary education made free.
1902	Education Act.
1907	'Free places' in grant-aided secondary schools.
1918	Education Act (H. A. L. Fisher).

Further study

For state education since the 1920s see Chapter 24.

General accounts

M. Hutchinson, *Education in Britain* (Hamish Hamilton) pp. 9–44

J. Robottom, *Education for the People* (Longman, Making the Modern World series)

Special topics

K. Dawson and P. Wall, *Education* (O.U.P., Society and Industry in Nineteenth Century Britain). For documents.

P. F. Speed, *Learning and Teaching in Victorian Times* (Longman's Then and There series)

L. W. Cowie, *Bell and Lancaster*, and *Miss Buss and Miss Beale* (Methuen, Brief Lives)

Education is well represented in Victorian novels. Rugby in the days of Dr Arnold is the scene of the most famous of English school stories, *Tom Brown's Schooldays* by Thomas Hughes (1857). For a somewhat exaggerated account of the sufferings of pupils in an early nineteenth century private school see *Nicholas Nickleby* by Charles Dickens.

Filmstrip

Education (Educational Productions) begins with a survey of conditions in the nineteenth and early twentieth centuries.

19 The British Overseas

The Empire (1783-1914) and the Irish Problem

Life in Britain in the Victorian Age would have been very different if the country had not been the centre of a vast empire. The attitudes and habits of Englishmen had been influenced by contacts across the oceans since the reign of Elizabeth I (1558–1603). But it was not until the nineteenth century that the British built 'an empire on which the sun never sets'—stretching into every corner of the world.

To those living at the time of the American Revolution (1775–83) this would have seemed an unlikely prospect. The loss of the thirteen American colonies (see Chapter 3) which were then the most important of Britain's foreign possessions, came as a great shock. People had second thoughts about the value of overseas settlements. If colonists were likely to revolt against the mother country as soon as they were strong enough to stand on their own feet, then it was felt that all the trouble and expense of establishing them would not be worthwhile. Thus, for many years, the British tried to increase their trading connections while *avoiding,* as far as possible, the responsibility of founding settlements.

Interest in *imperialism* (the founding of colonies) revived only slowly in the early nineteenth century. It was encouraged by Britain's control of the seas, the discoveries of men like Captain Cook (1728–79), and, above all, by the desire of growing numbers to emigrate and start a new life elsewhere. The tide of **emigration** began to flow strongly in the 1830s and early 1840s (a time of great distress among the poor) but it became a flood after gold discoveries in

Emigrants leaving for Australia (1848)

California (1849) and Australia (1851). Altogether in the period 1815–1914, about 19 million Britons, many of them Irish, left for foreign lands. After 1865 the yearly total of emigrants never fell below 100,000.

The growth of the Dominions

In the second half of the eighteenth century Britain obtained, almost by accident, vast, underpopulated territories—Canada, Australia and New Zealand—which were suited to European settlement. But their future prospects were not realised at the time.

Canada, gained at the Treaty of Paris (1763), was thought by many observers to be less valuable than the small West Indian sugar islands of Martinique and Guadeloupe, which were returned to France. Pitt's Canada Act (1791) divided its inhabited area into two provinces, 'Upper Canada' **(Ontario)** where British settlers lived, and 'Lower Canada' **(Quebec)** which was populated by the earlier French colonists. Each was granted an elected assembly to control local affairs, but in most other ways the two provinces were very different. French Quebec consisted mainly of isolated farmers and fur traders, scattered along the banks of the St Lawrence river. Ontario had busy, thriving towns, inhabited largely by 'Empire Loyalists' who had left the Thirteen Colonies after they became independent.

The two races did not get on well together. French-speaking

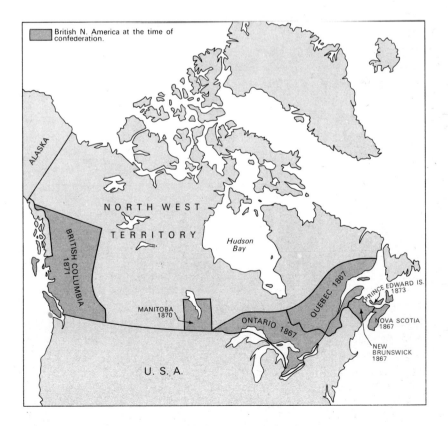

Canada at the time of Confederation

Canadians feared that the British wanted to impose their own customs and traditions upon them, while British settlers complained that their trade was hampered by the French along the St Lawrence. In 1837 there were riots in both provinces. They were easily put down, but the British Government sent Lord Durham to investigate the causes of unrest. He stayed only a few months in Canada, but the report he wrote on his return became the basis of all future relations with the 'white colonies'. The **Durham Report (1839)** suggested, first, that the separate provinces should be reunited, and, second, that Canadians should be given responsibility for managing their own affairs. Then they would have no cause to rebel against the British connection, as the Thirteen Colonies had done. The first proposal was accepted almost immediately. The second eventually became law in the **British North America Act of 1867.** Quebec, Ontario and the coastal provinces of New Brunswick and Nova Scotia were formed into a self-governing colony, or *Dominion,* with a central government at Ottawa.

Dominion status gave Canadians control over the destiny of their country, yet maintained close and co-operative relations with Britain. It coincided with a period of expansion into the vast territories of the interior. Beyond the Rocky Mountains, parts of the western coastal region of **British Columbia** had already been populated by a 'gold rush', beginning in 1857. British Columbia agreed to join the Dominion (1871) provided a railway was built to link it with the east. The result was the great **Canadian Pacific Railway,** which ran for 3000 miles through lonely prairies and mountains, many of them unknown even to the Indians. Its completion (1885) united Canada more securely than any Act of Parliament could do. Settlers followed the engineers, and soon the prairies of **Manitoba** (which joined the Dominion in 1870) **Alberta** and **Saskatchewan** (1905) were transformed into vast wheatlands. The total wheat crop multiplied twenty times in the period 1870–1914, while the population doubled.

Driving the last spike in the Canadian Pacific Railway, 7 November 1885

Population of Canada (now over 20 million)

1815	1870	1911
Half million	nearly 4 million	over 7 million

The first landings in **Australia** were made in 1788, when 700 convicts were transported there. But the government had little interest in the new continent, so that a further forty years went by before it was officially declared a British territory. Meanwhile it continued to be a dumping ground for convicts, who outnumbered free settlers until the 1830s. The long voyage and the presence of thousands of criminals discouraged large-scale emigration from Britain; even though the crossing of the Blue Mountains (1817) opened up fine grazing land suitable for sheep-farming. The colony of **Victoria** was founded in the same year, as an alternative to the original convict settlements in **New South Wales** and Van Diemen's Land **(Tasmania).**

The next stage in the development of Australia resulted from the efforts of **Edward Gibbon Wakefield** (1796–1862). He wanted the new colonies to become 'real British nations', not just places of refuge for the poor and unfortunate. He therefore worked out a method of *systematic colonisation,* whereby the Government took possession of the land and sold it to wealthy settlers. The money could then be used to pay for the passages of new immigrants who would farm the land for wages. In this way a colony could contain people of all social classes—a true cross-section of Britain—and would be capable of governing itself. Wakefield established a company which successfully applied his principles to the settlement of **South Australia** (founded in 1836). Land was sold to 16,000 settlers at a minimum of £1 an acre, and the proceeds were used to bring labourers out from Britain. It soon became a prosperous wheat-growing area.

However, not until the **discovery of gold** in New South Wales and Victoria (1851) did free settlers come in large numbers. The population rose from about 400,000 in 1850 to over a million ten years later. Meanwhile, by 1855, most of the colonies had been granted 'responsible government', with their own Parliaments. **Queensland** obtained the same rights in 1859 and **Western Australia** in 1890. All the states depended largely on sheep- and cattle-farming. At first, livestock were bred mainly for hides and fat. Much meat was wasted because the small population could consume only a small fraction of it. But the introduction of refrigeration in the 1880s led to mounting exports of beef and mutton carcasses to Britain and Europe. In 1914 Australia had about a sixth of the world's sheep. They far outnumbered the small human population of 5 million.

The harbour at Melbourne, Victoria (1883)

Throughout the nineteenth century, Australia's isolated settlements went their own separate ways. But by the 1890s they began to seek closer unity, because of the colonial ambitions of other countries. Germany controlled nearby Papua. The French were in Tahiti. Japan was growing powerful and eager to expand overseas. A single Australian Government was needed to organise the defence of the whole continent. Therefore by the **Commonwealth of Australia Act (1900)** Parliament joined the separate states in a self-governing dominion. Soon afterwards a 'white Australia' policy was declared. It was feared that if immigrants from the overcrowded countries of South-East Asia were admitted, they would quickly outnumber white Australians and swamp their Western way of life.

The settlement of **New Zealand** followed a similar pattern. In 1839 Gibbon Wakefield formed the New Zealand Company, which followed his principle of selling land and using the money to bring out more emigrants from Britain. It was a successful start, although there were many disputes with the Maoris over land ownership. In the 1870s a central government was established at Wellington, and New Zealand became the third self-governing dominion in 1907. Its prosperity depended on exports of chilled lamb and mutton, and by 1914, when its population was less than 1 million, it had begun to rival Denmark as a dairy-farming nation. Meanwhile rapid social progress was made. All men were given the vote in 1889, and all women in 1893. New Zealand had old age pensions, state-aided hospitals, labour exchanges and many other social services well before they were introduced into Britain.

The British in India

English merchants founded the East India Company (1600) in order to trade with the East *not* to conquer India. But in the eighteenth century, the Company was forced to wage war and take control of certain territories in order to secure its isolated trading stations against attack, especially from the French (see Chapter 3). As a result the British Government became directly involved in Indian affairs. **Pitt's India Act, 1784,** set up a Board of Control in London which supervised many of the Company's activities. It was hoped that further conquests would be unnecessary, but dangers from native rulers and continued French interference led to more wars and more British gains. By 1819 the conquest of India was almost complete and Britain was responsible for law and order throughout the whole subcontinent.

The British soon began to influence the Indian way of life. For example, they tried to stamp out cruel customs like 'suttee' (the burning alive of a widow on her husband's funeral pyre). During **Lord Dalhousie**'s term as Governor-General (1848–56) a cheap postal service and electric telegraph were introduced, and 4000 miles of good roads and the first railways were built. Dalhousie also began a system of elementary education in village schools. But the pace of reform was too rapid. The British took it for granted that Indians wanted to be Westernised, and ignored many Eastern customs and religious practices. As a result, there was mounting opposition to

Sikh officers in the Indian army (1858)

'British interference', especially among landowners, who objected to Dalhousie's policy of deposing native rulers who were weak or incompetent. Even education in Western knowledge was suspected of being the first step in a drive to convert Indians to Christianity.

Amid the general unrest brought about by Dalhousie's reforms, a serious revolt, known as the **Indian Mutiny,** broke out among the 'sepoys' (native troops) in the Bengal army of the East India Company. Discipline had been bad for some time when, in May 1857, sepoys from three regiments murdered British officers and their families in order to release from gaol eighty-five of their comrades who had disobeyed orders. Fortunately for the British, the rising that followed did not spread over the whole country. Only about a quarter of the sepoys in the Bengal army took part. Nevertheless the British were outnumbered and in great danger. The mutineers struck quickly and occupied Delhi, but then they hesitated, allowing the Company's troops time to organise and counter-attack. Within a few months the British were back in control, but order was not fully restored for two years.

Neither side emerged from the Mutiny with credit. Indians massacred British families that had surrendered, and the British, in turn, took merciless revenge before peace was officially declared. The resulting hatred and distrust between the races was never quite forgotten. However, at least the British learned not to push their Westernising policy too far in the future. There were no more conquests of Indian territory after 1858, when the East India Company was abolished and its army transferred to the Crown. As an extra precaution, the proportion of British troops in each regiment was raised to at least a third.

At last India settled into a period of calm, during which new irrigation schemes and railways improved the cultivation and distribution of crops. But, with a population of more than 200 million, terrible famines were still unavoidable if the rains failed—as they did

Indian peasants with their primitive corn mill (1880s)

in 1877, when at least 5 million people died of starvation. By the end of the century, Indians had been granted a small share in government. This was increased in 1909, but the educated ones were not satisfied. They were still members of a conquered race, and, as such, were treated as second-class citizens. As late as 1914, only about five per cent of the senior posts in the Civil Service were filled by Indians, and all important government decisions were made by the British.

South Africa – the Boer War

The first British foothold in South Africa was the **Cape of Good Hope,** taken from the Dutch during the Napoleonic Wars and purchased for £14 million in 1815. It was a valuable naval base on the sea route to India and the Far East, particularly before the opening of the Suez Canal (1869).

From the start, British settlers found the Africans easier to handle than the Dutch farmers **(Boers)** who had founded the colony. Boers were tough, religious folk who disliked all government and hated paying taxes to the British. They used Africans as slaves, but in 1833 slavery was abolished throughout the British Empire. Disgusted with

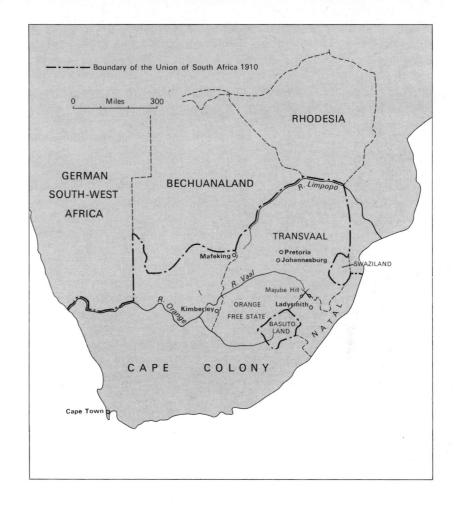

South Africa in the early
twentieth century

the 'soft' attitude of the British, and eager to have greater freedom and
more land, they clambered into their ox-wagons and started the
Great Trek inland. From 1835 onwards Boers left Cape Colony in
their thousands, to found new homes in Natal and in the territories
later known as Orange Free State and Transvaal.

The trekkers wanted complete independence. But when fighting
broke out with the African tribes of the interior, British troops arrived
to help restore order. This happened in **Natal,** which Britain took
over in 1843 (causing the Boers to move out again). **Transvaal** and
Orange Free State were granted self-government in the 1850s.
Britain occupied Transvaal for a brief period after 1877, to defend it
against the warlike Zulus on its frontiers. But after the Zulu danger had
been removed, the Boers demanded that their independence should
be restored. While Gladstone's Government hesitated, the Boers
routed a small British force at **Majuba Hill (1881).** Britain now gave
in to their demands, in preference to fighting a difficult and costly war.

Lasting peace between the two Boer republics and the two British
territories of Cape Colony and Natal seemed unlikely. Any chance of
it was ruined when rich seams of **gold** were discovered in Transvaal

(1886). The Boers were farmers and took no part in exploiting the gold for themselves. But thousands of settlers, mostly British, poured into the republic and created a thriving town—Johannesburg—around the diggings. The Boers strongly disliked these **Uitlanders** (outsiders) who were upsetting their simple, independent way of life. **Paul Kruger** (1825–1904), the President of Transvaal, was a bitter opponent of Britain. Although he did not want to expel the foreigners, for they were making his country rich, he refused to give them the vote and squeezed every available penny out of them through taxation.

Kruger's policy, though unfair, was understandable. 'Those who do not like my laws can leave my country,' he said. This attitude infuriated **Cecil Rhodes** (1853–1902) the Prime Minister of Cape Colony. Having made a fortune in diamonds and gold, Rhodes had set out to use his wealth to make the British masters of Africa. His greatest ambition was to establish a wide belt of British territory running the length of the continent, from the Cape to Cairo. He therefore encouraged settlement in the area north of Transvaal (later Rhodesia). This, together with British control of Bechuanaland, prevented the Boers from extending their lands. A clash between Rhodes and Kruger was unavoidable, for the Boer republics stood in the way of Rhodes's ambitions.

Rhodes planned to crush Transvaal by encouraging a Uitlander rebellion in Johannesburg and supporting it with his own British South Africa Company police. But the scheme collapsed disastrously. The Uitlanders failed to revolt, and Dr L. S. Jameson, in command of the British force, grew tired of waiting. In December 1895 he crossed the Transvaal border with only 470 men, and was easily captured. The **Jameson Raid** discredited Rhodes, who was forced to resign, and blackened Britain's reputation in the eyes of the world. The German Emperor, Wilhelm II, even sent a telegram to congratulate Kruger. This encouraged the Boers in the mistaken belief that they could expect German support in the event of a decisive contest with Britain. Transvaal's expenditure on armaments—most of them German—rose 400 per cent in the next two years, and an alliance was made with Orange Free State (1897). Britain sent troop reinforcements to Natal, but Kruger demanded their withdrawal from his frontiers. When the British refused (October 1899) the **Boer War** began.

The Boers took the offensive immediately, besieging the British in **Ladysmith** (Natal) **Kimberley** (Cape Colony) and **Mafeking** (Bechuanaland). But early in 1900 reinforcements arrived and a series of British successes followed, under the leadership of Lord Roberts. The three garrisons were relieved, and by 5 June Roberts was in **Pretoria,** the Transvaal capital. But, even though the last of the Boer armies was defeated in August, they refused to surrender. For another eighteen months they raided and ambushed the British, forcing **Lord Kitchener,** now in command, to conquer every inch of the countryside. Farms were destroyed and Boer families crowded into **concentration camps,** where insanitary conditions caused 20,000 deaths in fourteen months. There were storms of protest from all over the world. Foreigners accused Britain of bullying the Boers in

Above top: President Paul Kruger

Above: Cecil Rhodes

The British army enters
Ladysmith (1900)

order to steal their gold. Even at home, the Leader of the Liberal
Party denounced Kitchener's 'methods of barbarism'.

The war was finally ended by the **Peace of Vereeniging (May
1902)**. The two republics lost their independence and Britain paid
£3 million towards restocking the devastated farms. It had taken
450,000 British troops nearly three years to defeat 50,000 Boers—at
the cost of 22,000 lives and £220 million of the taxpayers' money.
Never again were the people so enthusiastic about their Empire. In
1906–7 the newly elected Liberal Government tried to wipe out some
of the bitterness by again granting independence to Transvaal and
Orange Free State. Soon afterwards the four independent South
African states came together in a self-governing dominion, the
Union of South Africa (1910). Louis Botha, one of the Boer
generals, was its first Prime Minister.

'The scramble for Africa'

At the beginning of the nineteenth century, British possessions in
Africa were confined to forts and slave-trading stations along the
west coast. The interior of the continent was still largely unknown to
Europeans. However, as the century progressed, explorers revealed
the courses of the great rivers and mapped the lakes, forests and

Following rumours that Livingstone was dead, the *New York Herald* sent another explorer, H. M. Stanley, to find him. The famous meeting of Stanley and Livingstone took place at Ujiji, on the shores of lake Tanganyika (1871)

mountains. None stirred the public imagination more than **David Livingstone** (1813–73), a self-educated Scotsman who started work in a cotton-mill at the age of ten. After taking a degree in medicine when he was twenty-seven, Livingstone spent the rest of his life journeying in 'darkest Africa'. Risking death from disease and hostile tribes, he became the first white man to discover the Victoria Falls, Lake Nyasa, the upper waters of the Congo and many other great landmarks.

To the man in the street, African exploration was an exciting adventure; but to businessmen and politicians it uncovered great new sources of wealth and power. By this time European factories were mass producing goods in such large quantities that manufacturers were constantly searching for new regions of the world where they could sell their products and invest their wealth. Africa seemed likely to provide not only markets for manufactured goods but also valuable supplies of raw materials and foodstuffs. Cotton, timber, vegetable oils and mineral ores could be produced there and fed into European industries.

The inhabitants of 'underdeveloped areas' like Africa were powerless to resist this European 'invasion'. White men, with their warships and cannon, their superior discipline and organisation, had little difficulty in mastering spear-throwing tribesmen. They rejected the customs and practices of those they conquered and introduced a European way of life, complete with roads, railways, factories and mines, as well as Christian churches. It is not surprising that the 'imperialists' were hated as much as they were feared.

The real **Age of Imperialism** was the last quarter of the nineteenth century. The Far East had its share of attention; particularly China, where Britain, France and Germany were rivals in establishing trading posts and naval stations. But the main objective was Africa. In 1875 only a tenth of the continent was governed by Europeans, but by 1900 more than nine-tenths had been colonised. Britain led the way in redrawing the map of Africa; taking over a large proportion of the fertile and productive regions. But France, Portugal, Belgium, Germany and Italy all claimed a share. In 1885 they even signed a treaty in Berlin which laid down rules by which the 'scramble' was to be conducted!

Apart from the colonies in the South and West, which continued to expand in this period, the other main area of British activity in Africa was the North-East, **Egypt** and the **Sudan.** In Egypt, the influence of France had been strong ever since French engineers built the Suez Canal (1869). Moreover, half the shares in the Canal Company were French-owned. But British interest in this region grew rapidly after 1875, when Disraeli's Government purchased almost all the remaining Canal shares from the bankrupt Egyptian ruler, Khedive Ismail. Following a rebellion, Britain occupied Egypt (1882) and began to reform its administration and finances. **Lord Cromer** became 'adviser' to the Egyptian Government (1883–1907) and organised the building of dams, reservoirs and canals, to make better use of the precious Nile waters.

Egypt's dependency, the Sudan, was in the hands of a religious

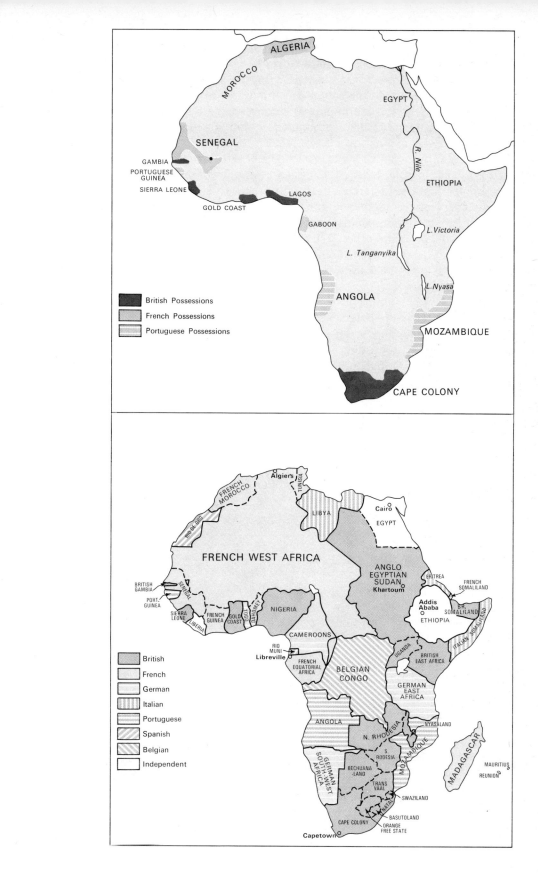

Africa 1875

Africa 1914

fanatic, the Mahdi. The isolated Egyptian garrisons were therefore evacuated, but not before Britain's **General Charles Gordon** had been killed at Khartoum (January 1885) after refusing to retreat. Eleven years later Lord Salisbury's Government sent Lord Kitchener, in command of the Egyptian army, to reconquer the Sudan and gain control of the Upper Nile. Kitchener defeated the Sudanese, but when he arrived at **Fashoda** (July 1898) he found a French flag flying. It was the work of Major Marchand of the French army, who, together with 7 officers and 120 native troops, had travelled nearly 3000 miles from the Atlantic coast with orders to secure the Upper Sudan for France. Kitchener and Marchand wisely referred the matter to their Governments. While British and French newspapers flung insults at each other, Salisbury openly prepared for war. Realising he was serious, the French reluctantly gave way and ordered Marchand to leave. A joint British and Egyptian Government then ruled the Sudan.

Ireland and Home Rule

Ireland never really recovered from the Great Famine of the 1840s (see Chapter 14). The resulting flood of emigration, mostly to the U.S.A., almost halved the population in the next fifty years. Emigrants left with bitter feelings towards Britain. They believed Parliament could have *prevented* famine conditions from arising if it had taken more interest in Irish affairs. In 1858 in New York, discontented Irish-Americans founded the **Fenian Society,** which aimed to achieve an Irish republic, totally independent of the United Kingdom. Fenians believed in using force. They soon began a series of bombings and violent demonstrations in England, which acted as a sharp reminder of Irish grievances.

An Irish peasant, after being evicted from his cottage

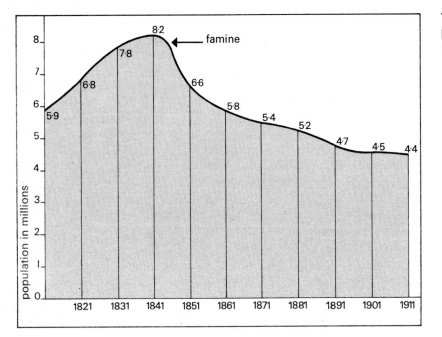

The population of Ireland — before and after the Great Famine

'My mission is to pacify Ireland,' said **W. E. Gladstone,** who first became Prime Minister in 1868. During the next twenty-five years he led the country on four separate occasions, and tried desperately to find a lasting solution to the Irish problem. First, he dealt with religious grievances. Only one Irishman in ten belonged to the Church of England; therefore Gladstone **'disestablished' the Anglican Church in Ireland (1869),** taking away its property (worth £15 million) and giving half to charity and education. This pleased the Catholic majority. The other major grievance concerned land, much of which was owned by Englishmen. Every year, hundreds of families were evicted from their smallholdings simply because landlords found new tenants willing to pay more rent. Gladstone's **Land Act (1870)** made landlords pay outgoing tenants compensation for improvements they had made. His second **Land Act (1881)** went much further, stating that tenants could not be evicted as long as they paid their rent, and allowing them to sell their leases without consulting the landlord. Moreover, 'Land Courts' were set up, to fix fair rents in cases where landlord and tenant disagreed.

Rents now dropped by about a quarter. But the Irish Party in the Commons was not satisfied. It demanded nothing less than **Home Rule** by a separate Irish Parliament. Meanwhile there was great unrest in Ireland, with frequent outbreaks of violence against landlords. By 1886 Gladstone gave up hope of 'pacifying Ireland' through a policy of reform and introduced a Home Rule Bill. But his sudden conversion aroused opposition among his own Liberal supporters. Ninety-three of them joined the Conservatives to defeat the Bill. Gladstone tried once more, in 1893, but his Bill was rejected by the Lords, having narrowly passed the Commons. After the Parliament Act of 1911 (see Chapter 20) the Lords could only *delay* Commons' Bills; they could not reject them completely. Thus when Home Rule again passed the Commons but not the Lords, in 1912, it would automatically become law after two years. Ireland would have its own Parliament, although it would still send some M.P.s to Westminster, which retained control over defence, police and taxation.

But Home Rule was strongly opposed by Protestants in the six Northern Counties (together called **Ulster**). They preferred to remain part of the United Kingdom rather than be governed by an Irish Parliament in which Catholics would outnumber them. Moreover, Ulster was the country's main industrial region. Its more prosperous inhabitants anticipated that they would have to pay the largest share of taxation, to support the agricultural South. Determined to resist the wishes of the Catholics, Ulstermen began to arm themselves. In March 1914 Northern Irish officers serving in the British army at the **Curragh** base, near Dublin, resigned rather than march into Ulster to enforce Home Rule. Ireland seemed on the point of civil war when the outbreak of the First World War (August 1914) caused the Home Rule Bill to be postponed for the time being.

Equally serious opposition to the Bill came from a secret organisation called **Sinn Fein** (Ourselves Alone). Like the earlier Fenians, Sinn Feiners wanted *complete* separation from Britain. Yet the terms of the 1912 Bill offered Ireland *less* self-government than a dominion

Ireland

The Easter Rising, 1916:
British soldiers amid the
ruins of the General Post
Office, Dublin

like Canada. On Easter Monday 1916 Patrick Pearse, a poet and
teacher, led a Sinn Fein rebellion in Dublin. About 2000 volunteers
occupied key points in the city, including the General Post Office,
and opened fire on British soldiers. The **Easter Rising** had no
chance of success; but its leaders seemed prepared to give up their
lives as an example to their countrymen. For six days, the streets and
squares of Dublin became a battlefield. When the rebels were finally
captured Dubliners cursed them for causing the ruin of their city.

However the British made a terrible mistake when they tried and
executed Pearse and fourteen others. This turned them into heroes;
and the Sinn Fein cause, which had almost collapsed, received an
unexpected flood of support. In the 1918 election, Sinn Feiners won
76 seats out of 105. Led by their President, **Eamonn de Valera,**
they refused to sit at Westminster and set up their own *Dail* (Parliament) in Dublin, which quickly commanded the support of the
Southern Irish. They had their own armed force, the **I.R.A.** (Irish
Republican Army), which waged war on British soldiers and police.
The British Government replied by sending a special force of ex-
soldiers, nicknamed the **'Black and Tans'** because they wore the
black hat of the Irish police with their khaki uniforms. A deadly
struggle followed. Bloodstained bodies in the streets and wrecked or
burning buildings became familiar sights.

In 1921 **David Lloyd George,** Britain's Prime Minister, met Sinn
Fein leaders and offered them independence similar to that of a
dominion, provided Ulster was free to remain part of the United
Kingdom. For the Southern Irish, the only direct link with Britain
would be a Governor-General, acting as the King's representative.
The **Irish Free State** was thus created (1922). But extreme Sinn
Feiners, led by de Valera, opposed the agreement. They wanted to
remove every trace of English influence in Ireland. When de Valera
gained a majority in the Dail and became Prime Minister (1932) he
gradually reduced the remaining links with Britain. Even the customary oath of loyalty to the King was abolished. The Irish Free State
was renamed **Eire** (1937) and it finally left the Commonwealth in
1949, having stayed neutral in the Second World War.

However the I.R.A. continued to oppose the separation of Ulster, and there were frequent armed clashes along its borders. Even more serious for the future were deep divisions within Ulster itself. The Catholic minority complained of being treated as second class citizens by the ruling Protestant Unionists. In 1969 bitter fighting broke out in the streets of Belfast and other northern towns. British troops were sent in to keep the peace, but long-standing religious differences could not be settled overnight—especially while extremists stirred up hatred on both sides. Ulster came under the direct rule of the U.K. Parliament in London. But gun and bomb attacks by the I.R.A. and militant Protestant groups continued.

Timeline

1788	First landings in Australia.
1815	Cape of Good Hope purchased.
1835	Beginning of the 'Great Trek'.
1839	Durham Report.
1857	Indian Mutiny.
1867	British North America Act (Dominion of Canada).
1882	Occupation of Egypt.
1898	Fashoda incident.
1899–1902	Boer War.
1900	Commonwealth of Australia Act (Dominion of Australia).
1907	Dominion of New Zealand.
1910	Union of South Africa.
1916	'Easter Rising' in Dublin.
1922	Irish Free State (renamed Eire, 1937).

Further study

The story of the British Empire and Commonwealth since the First World War forms the bulk of Chapter 26.

Special topics

B. Barker and R. Boden, *The Scramble for Africa* (Longman, History Games)

T. R. Batten, *Africa Past and Present* (O.U.P.) concentrates on European colonisation.

P. Cardwell, *The Indian Mutiny* (Longman, Then and There series)

A. Dures, *Modern Ireland* (Wayland, Documentary History series)

The Exploration of Africa (A Cassell Caravel Book)

D. Killingray, *A Plague of Europeans* (Penguin, Topics in History)

W. Ritchie, *The British in Egypt* (Longman, Then and There series)

The Jackdaw series (Cape) includes the following:

The Indian Mutiny, no. 22; *The Anglo-Boer War*, no. 68; *The Easter Rising: Dublin 1916*, no. 61

Muller's True Books series includes:

R. Arnold, *David Livingstone*

P. Gibbs, *Cecil Rhodes*

R. Tames, *Cecil Rhodes, Henry Morton Stanley*, and *General Gordon* (Shire Publications, Lifelines series)

Filmstrips

Shipping, Trade and Empire, 1770–1870 (Nicholas Hunter Filmstrips)

Paul Kruger (Hulton) is helpful in understanding the Boer War.

20 'The Two Nations'

Social Life, Attitudes, Reforms – from the Victorian Age to the First World War

As a young man, **Benjamin Disraeli** wrote several novels. In one of them, called *Sybil* (1845) he described the rich and poor as *Two Nations* 'who are as ignorant of each other's habits, thoughts and feelings as if they were dwellers in different zones, or inhabitants of different planets; who are formed by different breeding; are fed by a different food, are ordered by different manners, and are not governed by the same laws.'

Social divisions of this kind had always been part of the traditional life of villages and market towns. But, in the countryside, a few activities and interests, like hunting and farming, were shared to some extent by all classes. In the industrial towns this was not so. The rich, secure in their own neighbourhoods or suburbs, were often completely ignorant of living conditions in the slum areas. It was possible for them to forget that the poor even existed. If Disraeli had been writing fifty or sixty years later, he would have found the situation little changed.

But there were more than *two* 'nations' in the nineteenth century. The Industrial Revolution not only widened the gap between the very rich and the very poor, it also increased the number of *middle* classes in between. Moreover, it raised the standard of living of the skilled workman far above that of the labourer and slum-dweller.

Townsmen and villagers

With industry replacing agriculture as the basis of national life, Britain became, in the mid nineteenth century, the first country in the world to have a majority of its people living in towns. Meanwhile town and country were increasingly separated from each other. Villages became more purely agricultural as, one by one, craftsmen disappeared from the countryside. By about 1900 the blacksmith was the only one remaining in some villages.

Looking at the nation as a whole, those commonly referred to as 'the poor' still made up the largest social group. They mostly consisted of unskilled workers without a regular trade, factory hands, dockers, 'navvies', farm labourers and the like. Much of what was written and said about the extent of **poverty** was guesswork, until, in 1889, **Charles Booth,** a Liverpool shipowner, published the first of seventeen volumes on *The Life and Labour of the People of London* (completed in 1903). He and a team of helpers carried out extensive social surveys, on the basis of which Booth calculated that about a third of London's families lived in poverty, on about £1 a week or less. Many critics said London was exceptional, but, ten years later, **Seebohm Rowntree,** a member of the famous chocolate-making family, conducted a house-to-house survey in York, with similar results. He discovered almost twenty-eight per cent of the total

population in poverty (which he defined in much the same way as Booth).

Slum-dwellers in London (1889)

If these findings were true of the rest of Britain, roughly 10 million people in England and Wales alone were so poor that, in Rowntree's words, they were 'forced to go without some of the necessities of a civilised life'. Those below the 'poverty line' were unable to afford anything better than a damp, dark slum. Their diet may have contained enough bulk to fight off the feeling of hunger, but it almost certainly lacked sufficient nourishment to keep a family in good health. Many wives could not afford butchers' meat, only a little fat bacon. Extras like clothing were often paid for by going short of food. As one woman in York said (1899): 'If there's anything extra to buy, such as a pair of boots for one of the children, me and the children goes without dinner.'

Such conditions were not confined to the towns. **Agricultural labourers** were no better off. Although their wages rose gradually in the second half of the nineteenth century, they were still the lowest-paid of all workers. They mostly lived in cottages of mud, plaster and thatch, with one room up and one down. Few had more than two bedrooms, even though families of ten, twelve or more children

were quite common. They were often damp and draughty as well as overcrowded. More spacious brick-built cottages were normally found only on the larger, more prosperous estates. Cowmen and shepherds got higher wages than ordinary labourers, but less than they could obtain in a factory or workshop. As time went by, emigration overseas and the steady drift to the towns led to serious depopulation of the countryside. Despite reports of the unhealthiness and dissatisfactions of factory life, amid rows of mass produced slums, most villagers regarded the railway line to town as the route to better things. Food, clothing and wages were better, and that counted for a lot.

Charles Booth estimated that 10*s* a week marked the difference between poverty and 'solid working-class comfort'. **Artisans** (skilled tradesmen) normally earned about 25*s* to 30*s* a week. They included mechanics, ironfounders, masons, carpenters and those in newer occupations like railways and the police force. Their clothes were 'respectable' and their houses solidly built. 'In this class', said Booth, 'no one goes short of food. Meat and vegetables are demanded every day.' Entry into the skilled trades was restricted by the 'craft unions' (see Chapter 17). Sometimes the only qualification was to have a relative already in the trade. At the top of the scale, foremen and a few highly-skilled artisans earned up to 70*s* a week. They lived very comfortably indeed, often owning their own houses and investing money in post office savings banks. There was a world of difference, both in attitudes and living standards, between the highly skilled and the labourers. It is thus more accurate to speak not of the 'working class' but of the 'working class*es*'.

Throughout this period, hours of work were gradually reduced. The Saturday half-holiday was general by 1900, and Parliament introduced four Bank Holidays in 1871. As the **leisure time** of working men increased, their interests and activities became more

Farm labourers in the late nineteenth century

civilised. Barbaric spectacles like bull- and bear-baiting (made illegal in 1835) were replaced first by prize-fighting and later by horse-racing and organised games like soccer. The first professional football club, Notts County, dates from 1862. Working-men's clubs grew in number, and music-halls became very popular by the end of the century. But public houses were still the main 'social centres' for working men. They housed the headquarters of Friendly Societies and clubs of various kinds. Pubs also enabled the irresponsible to drink away a large proportion of the weekly wages on a Saturday night.

Most people enjoyed rising living standards in this period, but the greatest gains were made by the **middle classes,** particularly employers and other businessmen. The profits of industry and trade financed the building of large mansions on the outskirts of towns; and paid the wages of butlers, cooks, housemaids and gardeners, as well as public school fees for the sons of the family. Alongside the growing industrial and commercial middle classes were members of the 'professions'—engineers, doctors, lawyers, accountants and higher civil servants. They too were increasing rapidly in numbers and in wealth. Victorians liked to believe that, with hard work, any man of good character could be successful, whatever his origins. But since the owners of most firms kept the best jobs for their relations, it

A public house in the East End of London (1877)

was difficult for a young man to make his way in business without money or family connections. His best chance might be to gain a professional qualification, which would open the door to a secure and well-paid position.

The eventual aim of the average businessman was to buy a country estate and become accepted as a 'gentleman'. Even at the turn of the century, when most people's incomes depended upon factories, mines and international trade, the **landed gentry** retained their great social prestige. Country-house life, with its hunting and shooting parties and its lavish entertaining, was the envy of the town-bred middle classes. By the end of the nineteenth century, it was usually supported by money from industry and commerce, for agriculture had ceased to be profitable. The term 'landed gentry' covered a wide range—from owners of quite small estates up to great aristocratic families, whose vast properties often included mines and quarries and large areas of London or other towns. Among the gentry, it was normal for the eldest son to inherit the family estate. His younger brothers, if any, entered occupations like the army and the Church, where advancement still depended to some extent on family influence.

The gentry owned the land; **farmers** worked it. Some holdings were small enough for a tenant farmer and his family to manage on their own. But the trend was to larger farms, on which labourers were hired. In these circumstances, the farmer and his family might live in some comfort; but they would rarely mix with the gentry—except in activities like the hunt, which involved the whole neighbourhood. The main social barrier between the gentleman and the farmer was educational rather than financial. The former went to public school, while the latter usually considered 'book learning' to be a waste of time.

Faith and doubt – religion and the influence of Darwin

The Victorian Age was a time of strong religious beliefs and strict moral attitudes. Most people went to church or chapel every Sunday, often more than once. In the most 'respectable' households there were daily family prayers, while on Sundays all games and entertainments were forbidden, including card-playing, dancing and theatre-going.

The middle classes were the most religious of all. A large proportion of them attended **Nonconformist chapels**—Congregationalist, Baptist or Wesleyan Methodist. The last, which was the largest of the three, was also strongly supported by the better-off working classes. Members were called upon to be sober, hardworking and self-sacrificing. Their seriousness and their strict moral conduct greatly influenced the 'Evangelical movement', which set out to raise standards in the Church of England (see Chapter 4). **Evangelicals** deplored the slackness of the eighteenth century Church. They encouraged regular Bible reading and believed it was the duty of Christians to preach and work among the poor. Great social reformers like Wilberforce and Shaftesbury came from their ranks (see Chapter 11).

A middle class family

Charles Darwin

The 'Evangelical revival' began to slacken by the mid nineteenth century. But its influence remained strong in the work of men like **Dr Thomas Barnardo** (1845–1905) and **William Booth** (1829–1912). While he was a medical student in London, Barnardo founded the **East End Mission** for destitute children (1867). He gave up his intended career to devote his life to the welfare of London's homeless children. In the next thirty-five years, 60,000 orphans were given a new start in life through Dr Barnardo's Homes. William Booth, an ex-Methodist minister, founded the **Salvation Army** in 1878. Like Dr Barnardo, he considered social work to be part of the Christian mission. Thus Salvation Army relief and training centres were set up to help the poor and unfortunate. Popular methods of 'conversion' were used, including street bands and coloured uniforms, and the whole movement was organised on military lines, with Booth as 'the General'.

Meanwhile, the strict religious attitude of the middle classes in the towns influenced both the landed gentry and the Anglican clergy. Parsons were normally much more conscientious and hardworking than their predecessors in the eighteenth century. Attempts were made to extend the Church of England into working-class districts in the towns. New parishes were created and 'slum parsons' took on the difficult task of bringing the faith to the poor. But organised Christianity continued to be rare among the labouring classes and almost non-existent among the very poor. Apart from the Methodists and growing numbers of Irish Catholics, the masses looked upon church-going as something for the well-to-do, not for the ordinary man. They saw no reason to devote their day of rest and recreation to religion.

In the Early Victorian Age, Christians accepted the exact word of the Bible, believing that its writers had been directly inspired by God. Thus the account of the Creation in the Book of Genesis was taken to be historical fact. But scientists were beginning to cast doubts upon such beliefs. In 1830 **Charles Lyell**'s *Principles of Geology* set out to show that the earth had developed through millions of years of *evolution* (gradual change). If Lyell was right, the universe could not have been created in six days. An even more serious challenge to traditional views was the application of the principle of evolution to plant and animal life—notably by **Charles Darwin** (1809–82). After nearly thirty years of detailed observation and research, he published his world-famous *Origin of Species* in 1859.

Darwin claimed that all species of living creatures had developed over millions of years from one original form of life, which may have been a simple cell. Gradual changes in each species had resulted from the struggle for existence. In other words, the weaker types died out while the stronger ones, which adapted themselves to their surroundings, survived and passed on their superior characteristics. It was a 'survival of the fittest', or, as Darwin called it, *'evolution through natural selection'*.

His conclusion that man had not been separately created but had 'evolved' by pure chance directly challenged long-established religious beliefs. Darwin himself made no attempt to attack Christianity, but many other scientists claimed that his theory made belief in God not only unnecessary but impossible. If Darwin was correct, they said, man could hardly have been made in God's image. At first, most churchmen refused to accept evolutionary theory. The idea of 'man descended from a monkey' horrified them. But Darwin's evidence was strong and the basic principles of his theory were soon generally accepted. In the meantime, religious thinkers came to the conclusion that their beliefs had not been challenged after all. Genesis, they said, was written in such a way as to be understandable to ancient peoples. It answered the question '*who* made the world?' without attempting a scientific explanation of *how* it was done.

Nevertheless, the 'great debate' between scientists and Christians destroyed much of the basic certainty of Victorian religion. By the end of the century the hold of the Church upon the people had begun to slacken, and the growth of scientific doubt was partly responsible. Fewer people attended services, and Sunday observance became less strict. Other activities occupied people's minds – including cycle rides, railway excursions and outdoor sports. However, the change was slow up to 1914. It is only in the last half-century or so that the decline of religion in Britain has been really rapid.

The position of women

At the start of the Victorian Age men and women were even more clearly divided into 'two nations' than the rich and poor. The duties, rights and responsibilities of each were quite different. In any family with sufficient income to be considered 'respectable', the **'ladies'** were not expected to work. If they did, it would be assumed that the husband or father could not afford to support them. Therefore, from the country mansions of the nobility and gentry down to the town-houses of the middle classes, women were encouraged to remain idle and to leave household chores to domestic servants. They were cut off from life and its interests. 'Ladies' were not even encouraged to take exercise, apart from riding and dancing.

Working-class women, on the other hand, had neither comfort nor leisure. Wives had the double burden of raising children and going to work to make up the family income. In the towns, large numbers were employed in factories, laundries or in trades like dressmaking. In the countryside they worked in the fields, especially at harvest-time. But the largest single form of employment for ordinary girls was **domestic service,** which they normally entered between the ages of ten and fifteen. The numbers of household servants rose steadily throughout this period – from about 700,000 in 1840 to a peak of almost $1\frac{1}{2}$ million just before 1914. Life 'in service' could be hard and monotonous, especially in less wealthy families, but at least it provided girls with good food and accommodation and allowed them to see something of the wider world.

Demands for the *emancipation* (setting free) of women from masculine control were rare before the development of **girls' education** in the second half of the nineteenth century. The rise of public schools and university colleges for 'young ladies' and the start of state elementary schools paved the way for changes in female status (see Chapter 18). Women from wealthy families became

increasingly dissatisfied with idleness. Having no money of their own, they were even less independent than factory women. Following the example of Florence Nightingale, they demanded that the professions should be opened to women so that they could play a useful part in society. A start was made when the London School of Medicine for Women opened in 1874. Twenty-five years later, there were over 300 lady doctors.

Lower down the scale, a whole new range of **female occupations** came into being after the introduction of the telephone and the typewriter, from the 1880s onwards. Women and girls who wanted something better than factory work or domestic service now became telephone operators or typists. The idea of employing women in offices had previously been unheard of, yet by 1901 seven per cent of all business and commercial clerks were women. The rapid expansion of elementary schools after 1870 provided yet another career for women in teaching. Meanwhile thousands more became shop assistants. With women becoming more active, there were rapid changes in styles of clothing. Cumbersome Victorian dresses, with long, trailing skirts and thick petticoats, were gradually replaced by simpler and healthier fashions.

As women became more independent, they demanded equal legal and political rights. One of their greatest grievances concerned ownership of property. When a woman married, all her money and possessions—even her children—automatically belonged to the husband. In 1870 Parliament at last took action, allowing married women to keep their own earnings. But not until 1882 were wives granted the right to own property and give it to whom they wished. These **Married Women's Property Acts** gave wives a new legal status, but they were still not entitled to vote in parliamentary elections. Women could vote for County and County Borough Councils after

A group of domestic servants in the 1880s

Mrs Pankhurst being arrested during a demonstration (1914)

1888, and they were allowed to become councillors in 1907, but they continued to play no part in central government. Even Queen Victoria opposed the granting of full political rights to her own sex, believing that politics did not concern women. Many of her subjects thought otherwise, including **Mrs Emmeline Pankhurst** (1858–1928). In 1903 she founded the Women's Social and Political Union (W.S.P.U.) which set out to organise public demonstrations in favour of women's *suffrage* (voting rights). Members were soon known as **suffragettes.**

The Liberal victory in the 1906 election raised the hopes of suffragettes, for many Liberal M.P.s were on their side. But the Cabinet was divided on the issue and no positive action was taken. The W.S.P.U. replied by heckling speakers at political meetings, organising petitions and even chaining themselves to railings outside the houses of Cabinet ministers. By 1912 a campaign of violence was organised, largely by **Miss Christabel Pankhurst.** Members of the W.S.P.U. smashed shop-windows, burned houses and public buildings, cut telephone wires, tore up golf greens and slashed pictures in the National Gallery. **Emily Davison,** a suffragette, threw herself under the King's horse at the Derby (1913) and was fatally injured. It was difficult to punish crimes committed by suffragettes because when they were imprisoned they went on hunger strike. Prison authorities either had to release them or feed them by force and risk a public outcry. To help enforce the law, Parliament passed the so-called **'Cat and Mouse Act' (1913)** which enabled prison governors to release hunger strikers but to rearrest them when they had regained weight.

The use of violent methods did more harm than good to the suffragettes' cause. Their opponents could claim that women had shown themselves to be irresponsible. After the outbreak of the First World War (1914) a truce was agreed, and large numbers of women were employed in essential industries, including armaments factories. This valuable work achieved more than the entire campaign of the W.S.P.U. Immediately after the war (1918) the vote was granted to women over thirty who were householders or wives of householders (and also to all men over twenty-one). Another **Parliamentary Reform Act, 1928,** put women on the same footing as men, when they too were given the suffrage at twenty-one.

Another, less obvious, aspect of female emancipation was the reduction in the size of families resulting from new methods of **birth control,** for nothing restricts a woman's freedom more than continual childbearing. Family planning, in the modern sense, began among the wealthier classes about a hundred years ago. But it was some time before the poor, whose need was the greatest, came to understand and practise it. In the 1890s, working-class wives spent, on average, *fifteen* years either pregnant or with a child under one year old. By the 1950s, the equivalent figure was only *four* years. This represented not only a rapid fall in the birth-rate (largely balanced by the lower death-rate) but also far greater freedom for married women. For example, it was no longer necessary for a 'career woman' to remain a spinster.

Nevertheless, even today, the responsibilities of motherhood put women at a disadvantage in their fight for 'equality'. Most occupations give priority to men at the highest levels and pay women less money for the same work.

The foundations of the Welfare State, 1906–11

The average family was better off at the end of Victoria's reign (1901) than it had been at the beginning (1837). Conditions of labour had improved and working hours were less, yet wages had risen. There had been great progress in medicine; public sanitary services were well established, and a start had been made on the problem of slum clearance. Every child received elementary education, and the vote had been granted to every male householder.

Victorian reformers had achieved a great deal, but they also left many major problems unsolved. In particular, they did little to remove the root causes of **poverty**. Progress in this direction had been hindered by the belief that it was no business of the state to interfere in personal matters. People were simply urged to be thrifty and hard-working and to 'save for a rainy day'. But lower-paid workers could not afford to live decently, even under favourable circumstances. Moreover, among quite highly-paid workers, sickness, old age, unemployment or some other misfortune might at any time force a family below the 'poverty line'.

The wealthy classes mostly took the view that poverty would die out of its own accord as the country got richer. But, by the turn of the

Women war workers in an engineering shop

century, an increasing number of M.P.s in the Liberal Opposition Party thought otherwise. They were determined to attack poverty and other social evils at the first opportunity. Their chance came following the election of 1906, when, with strong working-class support, they gained a massive majority in Parliament. 'The cause of Liberalism is the cause of the left-out millions', said **Winston Churchill,** then a young man of thirty-one. He became President of the Board of Trade in 1908 and played an important part in the reforms of this period.

The welfare of children was the first priority of the **Liberal Governments of 1906–14.** Several local authorities had recently opened clean milk depots and appointed Health Visitors to advise parents on infant care. After 1906, with Government help, **infant welfare clinics** were opened in many areas. Following the introduction of compulsory education (1880) charity organisations in many towns provided meals for children who were too hungry to learn. The Liberals now set out to extend **school meals** to all areas. By an Act of 1906, local authorities could either use existing voluntary schemes or, where these were lacking, provide their own. Meals were only given to children who were 'unable by reason of lack of food to take full advantage of the education provided for them'. Nevertheless it was an important step forward. By 1914 over 150,000 children had school meals; on Saturdays and during holidays as well as in term time. But undernourishment was only part of a general health problem among children. In 1907 the Government compelled local authorities to have children in elementary schools medically examined.

The first truly nationwide social service was **Old Age Pensions,** introduced in 1908. Pensions were paid to citizens over the age of seventy, provided their incomes were not over 12*s* a week. The amount varied between 1*s* and 5*s* weekly, depending on the pensioner's income. Old people were delighted to have this regular money coming in. They were now less dependent on the goodwill of relations or the grudging help of the Poor Law. 'We are lifting the shadow of the workhouse from the homes of the poor,' said **David Lloyd George** (1863–1945), the Chancellor of the Exchequer and the leading social reformer in the Cabinet.

To pay for social welfare schemes (among other things) Lloyd George estimated that an additional £16 million would have to be raised in the Budget of 1909. He aimed to 'make the rich pay'. In addition to increased taxes on drink and tobacco, and a new motor car licence, Lloyd George raised the income tax. It was scaled, so that those with annual incomes above £3000 paid 1*s* 2*d* in the pound, while those with lower incomes paid 9*d*. A further 'supertax' of 6*d* in the pound was imposed on those earning over £5000 a year. Lloyd George also increased death duties on the estates of the rich and placed heavy taxes on profits gained from the ownership and sale of property.

'The People's Budget', as Lloyd George called it, met powerful opposition from the wealthy classes. The Conservatives, many of them landowners who objected violently to property taxes, used their

David Lloyd George in 1910

majority in the House of Lords to reject the Budget. The Government now decided it was time for a showdown with the Upper House, which had obstructed several other Bills. The Budget was forced through (1910) and, after a long struggle, the **Parliament Act, 1911,** drastically cut the powers of the Lords. They were no longer allowed to prevent the passage of 'Money Bills', and they could not hold up other Bills for more than two years (reduced to one year in 1949). The social reformers had won an important victory, for one of the results of the struggles of 1909–11 was a steady growth of state spending on the welfare of the needy.

The Liberals now carried out their most important reform, in the **National Insurance Act, 1911.** Some workmen already insured themselves through Friendly Societies, but lower-paid workers could not afford the necessary subscriptions. Besides, whether they could afford it or not, many preferred to 'take a chance'. The Government therefore introduced compulsory insurance for those who needed it most, keeping contributions down to a minimum. There were two parts to the 1911 Act, providing separate insurance schemes for sickness and unemployment.

Unemployment insurance began on a small scale, applying only to a few trades, like building, shipbuilding and ironfounding, where work was known to be irregular. It was intended to include other trades in the future. Workmen over sixteen, their employers and the state each contributed $2\frac{1}{2}d$ a week—thus spreading the cost over the whole community. In return, 7s a week was payable during unemployment for a maximum of fifteen weeks in any one year. Benefits were paid at **Labour Exchanges.** These were based on a German idea (like several other Liberal reforms). Their main purpose was to

An old age pensioner collecting his money at a post office (1909)

One of the earliest Labour Exchanges (1910)

provide unemployed workers with information of any vacancies which existed. The first eighty-three Labour Exchanges had opened at the beginning of 1910.

The other half of the 1911 Act introduced 'insurance against loss of health and for prevention and cure of sickness'. All wage-earners between sixteen and seventy had to join the scheme if they earned less than £3 a week. Their weekly contribution was 4*d*, to which their employers added 3*d* and the state 2*d*. Payments were recorded by means of stamps stuck on individual cards. In return, free medical attention, with medicine, was given. It did not include hospital or specialist services, however, just 'simple doctoring'. When work was lost through sickness, 10*s* a week was paid, from the fourth day of the illness. This lasted for a maximum of twenty-six weeks, after which 'disablement benefit' of 5*s* could be claimed. An additional 30*s* 'maternity benefit' was paid on the birth of each child.

Churchill described the 1911 Act as 'the most decisive step yet taken upon the path of social organisation. . . . The cruel waste of disease and unemployment, breaking down men and women, breaking up homes and families, will for the first time be encountered by the whole strength of the nation.' Together with Old Age Pensions, National Insurance struck for the first time at some of the deepest roots of poverty. Instead of merely providing workhouses for the destitute, the Liberals tried to *prevent* destitution with specialised services to meet individual needs. It was on these foundations that the Welfare State was later built.

Timeline

1859   Charles Darwin's *Origin of Species*.
1867   Dr Thomas Barnardo's 'East End Mission' founded.
1870–82 Married Women's Property Acts.
1878   Salvation Army founded by William Booth.
1903   Women's Social and Political Union founded.
1906   The Liberals come to power.

1908	Old Age Pensions.
1909	'The People's Budget'.
1910	Labour Exchanges introduced.
1911	National Insurance Act.
1911	Parliament Act.
1918	Representation of the People Act: votes for women over thirty and men over twenty-one.
1928	Representation of the People Act: votes for women over twenty-one.

Further study

The later expansion of National Insurance and other social services is described in Chapters 23 and, more especially, 24.

Special topics

Alan Delgado, *Edwardian England* (Longman's Then and There series) provides a general background to the age.

I. Doncaster, *Changing Society in Victorian England* (Longmans) contains an interesting collection of pictures.

R. J. Cootes, *The Making of the Welfare State* (Longman's Modern Times series), Chapter 5, for the Liberal reforms.

K. Dawson and P. Wall, *The Problem of Poverty* (O.U.P.). Documents.

Edward Bishop, *Blood and Fire* (Longmans) is an account of William Booth and the Salvation Army.

C. L. Mowat, *Lloyd George* (O.U.P., Clarendon Biographies)

D. Ford, *Dr Barnardo* (A. and C. Black, Lives to Remember series)

On Darwin and evolution, see:

Darwin and Evolution (Cape, Jackdaw series no. 85)

D. Laird, *Charles Darwin, Naturalist* (Blackie)

R. C. Olby, *Charles Darwin* (O.U.P., Clarendon Biographies)

J. G. Crowther, *Charles Darwin* (Methuen, Brief Lives)

On the Suffragette movement:

M. N. Duffy, *The Emancipation of Women* (Blackwell)

D. B. O'Callaghan, *The Struggle for Women's Rights* (Longman, Making the Modern World series)

J. G. Quinn, *Mrs Pankhurst and her Daughters* (Methuen, Brief Lives)

L. E. Snellgrove, *Suffragettes and Votes for Women* (Longman's Then and There series) is a balanced general account.

Josephine Kamm, *The Story of Mrs Pankhurst* (Methuen's Story Biographies) is more detailed.

Women in Revolt (Cape, Jackdaw series no. 49)

Jack London, the novelist, described his experiences while living among the poor of the East End of London in *The People of the Abyss* (1902).

Filmstrips

Victorian Social Life (Hulton)

English Social Life, 1902–18 (Hulton)

Charles Darwin (Unesco, distributed by E.F.V.A.)

21 The Shrinking World
Transport and Communications 3

Just as the origin of railway locomotives and powered ships depended upon the steam-engine, so the birth of motor cars and aeroplanes resulted from the *internal combustion engine.* It was not a British invention. France and Germany pioneered the new form of power and, along with the U.S.A., they were the first countries to make effective use of it. Similarly, the British played a minor part in the development of both the telephone and wireless telegraphy, which together revolutionised communications. All these advances, which have done so much to shape the modern world, were made before 1914, although their full effects were not felt until fairly recent times.

The internal combustion engine

Like the steam-engine, the internal combustion engine turns heat into energy; in the form of the up and down movement of a piston in a cylinder. But the heat that makes a steam-engine work is produced by a boiler *outside* the cylinder. It is therefore an *external* combustion engine. To produce a smaller and lighter engine, suitable for road vehicles and aircraft, it was necessary to do away with the boiler-unit altogether and arrange for the combustion (burning) of the fuel to take place *inside* the cylinder.

The steam-engine was first developed for industrial use. Likewise, the internal combustion engine resulted largely from the search for a cheaper and more compact power unit to serve craftsmen in small workshops. These considerations led **Etienne Lenoir,** a French engineer, to produce a **gas engine** in 1859—the forerunner of later developments. A mixture of coal-gas and air was sucked into a cylinder, where it was ignited by an electric spark. The force of 'expansion' following ignition pushed a piston, which, in turn, rotated a wheel. In Lenoir's engine, ignition took place at each stroke, on alternate sides of the piston. This was wasteful. It was left to a German engineer, **Nikolaus Otto,** to produce a *four-stroke compression engine* (1876) the main principles of which are found in most modern cars. Although four movements of the piston are necessary to complete each cycle—suction, compression, combustion and exhaust—the real work is done on the third stroke (see diagram).

Otto's gas engine had several important advantages over steam. It was smaller, its fuel consumption was less and it needed no preliminary heating-up. Above all, it developed more power in relation to its weight (lower 'power-weight ratio'). But it could only be used satisfactorily as a stationary engine for driving machinery, for it depended upon a ready supply of coal-gas. Before it could be used to move a vehicle, a different fuel had to be found which was as portable as the engine itself. The answer was **petrol** (refined petroleum) which had been drilled in the U.S.A. since 1859. At first, petrol

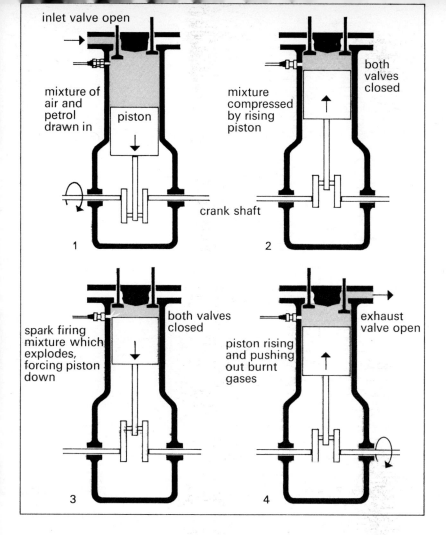

The workings of a four-stroke internal combustion engine

or 'gasolene' was thrown away as a waste product in the production of paraffin. But in 1883, **Gottlieb Daimler,** formerly technical manager at Otto's works, found that petrol was more than just a replacement for coal-gas—it was superior to it, giving a much greater punch to the piston.

In 1885, Daimler fitted his petrol engine to a wooden cycle, thus inventing the motor bike. In the same year, **Karl Benz,** another German, built a motor tricycle which ran at eight m.p.h. Then, in 1887, Daimler made the first petrol-driven, four-wheeled car. It was a genuine 'horseless carriage'—a coach, with the shafts removed and an engine added. Meanwhile, the British had not yet entered the Motor Age, although they shared in other important developments in road transport which prepared the way for the coming of the motor car.

From steam carriages to 'baby cars'

The earliest horseless carriages were powered by steam. Back in 1769 **Nicholas Cugnot,** a Frenchman, drove a **steam carriage**

An early 'safety bicycle'
(1890)

through the streets of Paris. But he was prevented from developing his invention when his second model overturned and terrified pedestrians. **Richard Trevithick** built the first steam cars to travel on English roads (1801–3) before turning his attention to railway locomotives (see Chapter 13). By the 1820s and 1830s, several passenger services employed steam coaches, including London to Bath (1827) and Paddington to the City (1833). The latter route was operated by Walter Hancock's 'Enterprise', which carried fourteen passengers at about ten m.p.h. But these vehicles were far too heavy for the roads that carried them. Turnpike companies, fearing damage to their roads, charged steam-coach operators such high tolls that they were mostly put out of business. Then, in 1865, Parliament passed the so-called **'Red Flag Act'.** It limited horseless carriages to four m.p.h. on country roads and two m.p.h. in towns. Also, they had to be preceded by a man carrying a red flag. This effectively ended the brief life of the steam carriage.

Motoring in Hampshire,
1907

The first really successful mechanical device for road travel was the **bicycle.** After becoming popular in France, bicycles were manufactured in Britain from 1869 onwards. On the earliest models the pedals were connected to the front-wheel axle. When it was found that greater speeds could be achieved with an enlarged front wheel, the famous 'penny-farthing' resulted. But the widespread popularity of cycling dates from the introduction of the modern 'safety bicycle' in the 1880s. Its wheels were almost equal in size and it had a rear-wheel chain-drive. In 1888 **John Boyd Dunlop** from Belfast produced a **pneumatic tyre,** with a separate, air-filled innertube. Bicycles were now both safe and comfortable, and cycling suddenly became a craze. Men and women from every walk of life invaded the countryside, especially at week-ends. Several discoveries prompted by the bicycle helped the later development of motoring, including steel spokes, roller bearings and, above all, the pneumatic tyre—the chief British contribution to the motor car.

The Motor Age really began in Britain in 1896, when Parliament repealed the Red Flag Act and raised the speed limit to fourteen m.p.h.

A Rolls-Royce 'Silver Ghost'

This was celebrated by an 'emancipation run' from London to Brighton; still commemorated in the annual 'vintage car' rally. In the same year **F. W. Lanchester** built the first British four-wheeled car; after which the manufacture of motor cars quickly became a thriving industry. One of the most famous companies in the early years was formed in 1906 by **Henry Royce,** a Manchester engineer, and **Charles Rolls,** one of the first racing motorists and airmen. Their forty to fifty horse-power 'Silver Ghost' was a magnificent piece of engineering. A year after it was finished it was driven 14,371 miles without mechanical trouble. In the next eighteen years, 'Silver Ghosts' were sold all over the world, remaining unequalled as luxury cars for the very rich.

In 1903, with the number of cars on British roads already approaching 20,000, Parliament compelled every motorist to obtain a 5s licence and registration number from his local authority. In the same Act, the speed limit was raised to twenty m.p.h. Most cars could comfortably go faster by this time. Thus carefree motorists on the country roads frequently found themselves caught in police 'speed traps' and fined. No doubt they could afford it, for a motor car was then a very expensive 'toy', beyond the reach of all but the wealthier middle and upper classes.

The earliest models were open-topped, so travellers needed weather-proof clothing. Fur coats, gloves and goggles were commonly worn; so were capes, as a protection against the clouds of dust stirred up by the wheels. Except for the larger towns, where streets were normally paved with stone blocks, the roads were most unsuitable for the new traffic. The iron-bound wheels of horse-drawn vehicles had helped to bind the loose stone surfaces, but soft rubber tyres sank into the cracks between the stones, loosening them and sucking out dust. The answer was to spray tar over the stones, or, better still, put down 'tarmacadam' (stones which are tarred *before* they are laid and rolled). Until these improvements were carried out, it was difficult to get through a day's motoring without at least one puncture.

Not all the early motor vehicles were built for pleasure. As early as 1905 the London General Omnibus Company, the largest owner of horse-drawn buses in Britain, decided to change to **motor buses.** After trying many different designs, they introduced the famous 'B-type' in 1910—a double-decker, seating thirty-four passengers. No fewer than 4'000 of them were built before they were withdrawn from service in 1925–6. Other towns were slow to follow suit, mainly because many of them had recently introduced electric trams. They were reluctant to change again after all the expense of laying tracks and installing overhead wires. Not until the 1920s and 1930s were motor buses in general use. Even then trams lingered on in some areas until the 1950s; or were partly replaced by electric trolley-buses which, being trackless, did not block the streets.

By the 1930s increasing numbers of buses and lorries had Diesel 'heavy oil' engines, invented by a German, **Rudolph Diesel,** in 1892. Combustion was produced not by a spark but by compressing the air in the cylinder so tightly that it became hot enough to ignite the heavy oil fuel the moment it was sprayed in. The Diesel was the most powerful internal combustion engine and the cheapest to run. But it needed cylinder walls of great strength, which made it too heavy to be fitted in motor cars. The earliest models were very large and were used to power ships and factory machines.

Meanwhile, private motoring gradually became more than just a

An Austin Seven

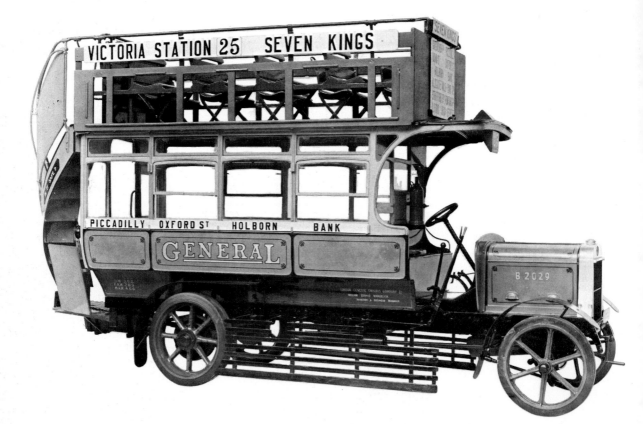

sport for the rich. The thing that brought motor cars within the reach of a larger section of the population was the beginning of **mass production methods,** pioneered by an American **Henry Ford** of Detroit. Using assembly lines to bring the cars and the necessary tools to each workman in turn, Ford produced a strong, reliable 'family car' at a remarkably low price. Worldwide sales of his 'Model T' (1909) reached 15 million in eighteen years. As more were made, production costs grew less and Ford was able to reduce his price further. In 1915, when a twelve horse-power car cost more than £350, a twenty horse-power Ford could be bought for £115. His first British factory was opened in Manchester (1911).

Taxes on petrol and licences began in 1910, and a Central Road Board used most of the revenue for tarring main roads. The new Ministry of Transport took over in 1919 and made roadbuilding grants to local authorities, out of motor taxation. At this stage, the amount of tax paid depended on engine size, so designers set out to get more power from smaller engines by making them work faster. The result was the popular **'baby cars'** of the 1920s and 1930s. When the Austin Seven appeared (1922) it was the smallest four-seater car ever made. It cost £165. In the same price range was the Morris Minor. Its maker, William Morris, later **Lord Nuffield,** was the first Englishman to take up Henry Ford's mass production methods. Having started in business as a cycle-repairer at the age of sixteen, he eventually became the richest man in Britain.

By the 1930s, when a Ford, Morris Minor or Austin Seven could be bought for little over £100, payable in instalments, cars were within the reach of the higher-paid working-classes. In 1939 there were nearly 2 million private cars licensed—one to every twenty-five persons. Traffic jams were already common in the towns.

William Morris's motor body shop at Oxford (1913)

Left: A 'B-type' bus

Total number of motor vehicles in Britain (all kinds)

1914	*1920*	*1930*	*1939*
400,000	650,000	2,300,000	3,000,000

The speed limit was abolished in 1930, but, following a rapid increase in accidents, a thirty m.p.h. limit was introduced in 'built-up areas' (1934).

Motor vehicles had far-reaching effects on life and work. Two deserve special mention. First, they brought together the town and the countryside; ending the isolation of remote villages. Second, they freed industry from dependence upon rail and water transport. New light industries developed alongside the main roads leading out of towns.

The conquest of the air

Before the invention of the internal combustion engine, the only successful human flights were in **balloons;** filled with hot air or a gas like hydrogen which is 'lighter than air'. But balloons cannot be properly controlled in flight. They are at the mercy of the wind and air-currents. Not until man had invented a powered, 'heavier than air' machine could he claim to have conquered the skies. Steam-engines were often tried in the nineteenth century, but they were much too heavy in relation to the power they produced. It was the lighter, more compact petrol engine that held the key to success.

Wilbur and Orville Wright were bicycle-makers from Dayton in the State of Ohio. In 1903, after carefully studying the problems of flight, they fitted a wooden glider with a twelve horse-power petrol engine and two propellers driven by bicycle chains. Then, on a cold morning in December at Kitty Hawk, North Carolina, they became the first men to fly a 'heavier than air' machine. The longest 'hop' made that day lasted only fifty-nine seconds, but it was enough to open a new chapter in the history of transport.

The British were slow to respond to the new invention. Five years went by before the first powered flight was made in England. In 1909, when the *Daily Mail* offered £1000 for the first man to fly the Channel, it was won by a Frenchman, **Louis Blériot.** It took him $35\frac{1}{2}$ minutes, from Calais to Dover Castle. Over 120,000 people saw Blériot's wood and sailcloth machine on exhibition in London. However, when the First World War broke out, five years later, the vast majority of the population had not yet seen an aeroplane. The military possibilities of aircraft were quickly realised, so the war led to a rapid development of aviation. For the first time planes were mass produced from standard parts. They were mainly used for reconnaissance, although fighters and bombers had been developed by 1918, when the **Royal Air Force** was formed.

The extent of the progress made during the war was shown in 1919, when two R.A.F. officers, **John Alcock** and **Arthur Whitten-Brown,** made the first flight across the Atlantic. They covered the 1890 miles from Newfoundland to Ireland at an average speed of 118 m.p.h., battling all the way against fog, ice and storms. At one point, Brown had to climb on the wings to hack away ice with a knife. In August of

the same year, the world's first daily air service began, carrying goods and passengers between London and Paris. By 1923 Croydon Airport, in Surrey, was handling up to thirty cross-Channel flights a day. A high standard of safety and reliability was achieved, although the journey was slow and bumpy and the passenger compartment noisy and cramped.

Services to other continental cities were soon introduced; but they failed to pay their way, despite high fares and freight charges. Foreign airlines were given financial assistance by their Governments, in the form of subsidies or grants. In 1924 the British Government did the same. A single company was formed—**Imperial Airways**—which took over all existing routes and began many new ones. By 1939 regular flights were being made to Australia (via India and Malaya), South Africa (via Egypt), Canada and many other Commonwealth countries. Air-mail was carried at ordinary rates of postage, often in flying-boats, since smaller territories lacked airport facilities. A transatlantic air-mail service began in 1939. Shortly afterwards, in April 1940, the Government merged Imperial Airways with a rival company, British Airways, which had enjoyed a monopoly of routes to Berlin and Scandinavia since 1935. The result was the state-aided **British Overseas Airways Corporation** (B.O.A.C.).

Kitty Hawk, 1903: the first flight in a 'heavier than air' machine. Orville Wright is at the controls

All these developments were on a very small scale in comparison with the progress of civil aviation since 1945 (see Chapter 25). The number of passengers carried was relatively small and the luxurious conditions of present day air travel were unheard of. The most comfortable (and costly) way to fly in this period was by **airship,** containing giant gas-filled balloons and powered by internal combustion engines. Airships were first built in Germany by **Count Zeppelin.** They carried out air raids in the First World War; but their great size made them more suitable for passenger services. All the comforts of an ocean liner, including separate cabins, lounges and dining-rooms, were provided on 'ships' like the German 'Graf Zeppelin', which flew round the world in twenty days (1928). But airships were liable to catch fire and explode, and a series of disasters soon put an end to their use. After 1930, when the great 'R.101' burst into flames over France, no more were built in Britain.

More railways and ships

Almost all the main **railway network** was laid by the 1850s (see Chapter 13). Although thousands of miles of track were later added (using mass produced steel rails from the 1870s onwards) most of the new routes were branch lines. At the end of the nineteenth century Britain's railway system was roughly what it is today. By this time a few long-distance expresses had achieved *average* speeds of more than a mile a minute. Moreover, following the introduction of restaurant and sleeping-cars (1870s) and corridor carriages (1890s), the highest standards of comfort were not far removed from those of the mid twentieth century.

Most railway companies had little interest in suburban services, regarding them as something of an interference with the free passage of long-distance expresses and coal trains. Thus travellers *within* London and other large towns mostly relied on horse-drawn buses and cabs. In 1863, however, the first **underground railway** was opened—the London Metropolitan—running almost four miles, from Paddington to Farringdon Street in the City. The Metro, like several others after it, was a 'shallow underground', only a few feet below the surface. The first deep 'tube', the City and South London Railway (1890) was forty feet down. It was also electrified; a great improvement on previous undergrounds, in which passengers endured the choking smoke of steam-engines. 'Tubes' quickly gained great popularity. Within twenty years, they reached Hampstead, Shepherd's Bush, Finsbury Park and Clapham. Only two other cities provided an alternative to surface transport—Liverpool, with an overhead electric railway on viaducts (1893–6) and Glasgow, with tube trains operated by cable haulage (1896).

The ordinary railway companies, 123 of them, were amalgamated into four large systems in 1921—the L.M.S. (London Midland Scottish), L.N.E.R. (London North Eastern Railway), G.W.R. (Great Western Railway), and S.R. (Southern Railway). It was now easier to finance large projects, like the electrification of suburban services south of London (which began in 1898). Nevertheless railways suffered a serious decline after the First World War, largely due to **growing competition from road transport.** While cars and cheap motor coaches took away passenger traffic, lorries had the advantage of being able to deliver goods door-to-door. They rivalled railways on all but the longest hauls and in handling all but the heaviest freight. For every ten railway passengers carried in 1920, only six were carried in 1938. Freight traffic fell by seventeen per cent in the same period. Railways tried to hit back with more return-ticket reductions and faster services, for example the L.N.E.R. 'Silver Jubilee Express' (1935) which ran from London to Newcastle in four hours. But most of them had ceased to pay their way, an important factor in their eventual nationalisation (see Chapter 25).

Top left: The 'Graf Zeppelin' flying over Wembley Stadium during the 1930 Cup Final.

Bottom left: Underground railway carriages (1902)

Below: The L.N.E.R. 'Silver Jubilee Express'

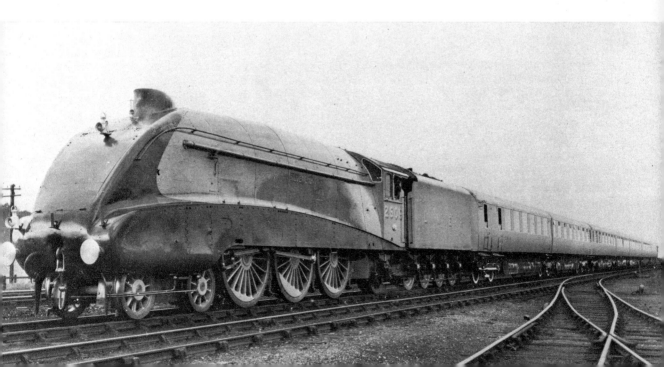

In 1882 the British Register of **Shipping** contained more steam-ships than sailing vessels for the first time. This trend was accelerated when the steam-engine reached its final stage of development in the **turbine** of 1884 (see Chapter 15). The steam turbine was first used for driving generators in electric power stations, but its inventor, **Sir Charles Parsons,** soon realised that its spinning motion made it ideal for driving the screw-propellers of ships. The superiority of the new engine was demonstrated beyond doubt in 1897, when Parsons went uninvited to the Naval Review at Spithead. His turbine-driven yacht, aptly named *Turbinia,* reached thirty-four and a half knots (almost forty m.p.h.) which was then a world record. The whole fleet had suddenly become obsolete. From 1905 all warships were fitted with turbines, and in 1907 the newly-built Cunarders *Mauretania* and *Lusitania* became the first big ocean liners to be powered by turbine engines.

Another important development was the introduction of **oil fuel** instead of coal. Oil could be used for firing the boilers of steam piston-engines and turbines; as well as for driving Diesel engines, which were first used for shipping in 1912. Oil was cleaner, easier to load and store, and produced more steam than the equivalent weight of coal. The Admiralty began using oil before 1914, but it was not in general use until the 1920s and 1930s. These years also saw the building on Clydeside of the two great Cunard liners, *Queen Mary* (81,000 tons) and *Queen Elizabeth* (85,000 tons). The former

The *Queen Mary* under construction on Clydeside

went into service on the Atlantic route in 1936, but the latter was still under construction when war broke out (1939). Her maiden voyage, to New York, was made in secret in 1940.

A London telephone exchange in 1883

The telephone, wireless and the B.B.C.

The first method of rapid communication over long distances was the electric telegraph (see Chapter 13). By the 1870s, when telegraph cables already carried Morse Code messages across continents and below oceans, a second great advance was made — the transmission of speech by **telephone.** This was first achieved by **Alexander Graham Bell,** an American teacher born in Edinburgh. It was a highly complicated apparatus, in which vibrations made in the air by the speaker caused variations of electric current (supplied from a battery) in an electro-magnetic coil. These were transmitted along the connecting wire, at the end of which the same process happened in reverse. The electric vibrations created sound waves on the same frequency as those of the speaker.

No special training was required to use a telephone, thus its effects on business and social life were much greater than those of the telegraph. The first British telephone exchange opened in 1879 in London. At the start, private companies operated under licence from the Government, but by 1912 the Post Office had taken control of the country's telephone services. There were already 700,000 receivers. The first automatic exchange was built in the same year. Nevertheless, progress was slow in comparison with the U.S.A. In 1920, when twelve per cent of Americans had a telephone, only two per cent of the British had one. However, in 1939 there were 3,235,000 receivers in the United Kingdom, roughly one to every fourteen persons.

Even before the invention of the telephone, scientists had begun to consider methods of transmitting sound *without* wires. In 1864 **James Clerk Maxwell,** a British physicist, proved (by mathematics) the existence of electro-magnetic 'waves', and showed that they obeyed the same natural laws as light. Just over thirty years later, the first public demonstrations of wireless communication were made by **Guglielmo Marconi** (1874–1919) an Italian who came to England in 1896. After successful transmissions in London, on Salisbury Plain and across the Bristol Channel, he established communication with the French coast (1899). But the experiment that aroused most interest was in December 1901. At St John's, Newfoundland, Marconi picked up the 'dot, dot, dot' of the Morse letter S from a transmitting station in Cornwall, nearly 2000 miles across the Atlantic.

The value of wireless for communication with shipping had already been realised, and Marconi's own company soon established a chain of coastal stations for this purpose. In 1912, when the giant British liner *Titanic* sank in the North Atlantic after hitting an iceberg, its wireless distress signal brought other vessels to the scene to pick up survivors. In the First World War, wireless was used by the armies and navies of both sides, and air-to-ground communication was introduced for aircraft. At the same time, rapid progress was made in the wireless transmission of speech. Keen radio amateurs began to build their own wireless transmitters and receivers and make private 'broadcasts'.

In response to the growing demand for a service of broadcast radio entertainment, the **B.B.C.** (British Broadcasting Company) was established by radio manufacturers in 1922. Within a few years, millions were 'listening in' to music, talks and news on homemade crystal sets with earphones. Later, large horn-shaped loudspeakers replaced headphones. The powerful position of the B.B.C. was demonstrated in 1926, when its news bulletins kept the nation informed of the latest developments during the General Strike (see Chapter 23). In the same year, the B.B.C. became the British Broadcasting *Corporation,* a public body, financed from licence fees paid by listeners. By 1939 very few homes were without a radio set.

Number of radio licences in Britain

1923	1927	1939
80,000	2,300,000	8,900,000

In 1922, the year in which wireless was established as a means of public entertainment, a Scotsman named **John Logie Baird** (1888–1946) began to tackle the problem of transmitting *pictures* by electro-magnetic waves. Just as newspaper illustrations consist of large numbers of dots, almost disappearing in some places and forming dark patches in others, so **television** pictures have to be broken down into dots and built up again on the screen. After two years of experiments, using odds and ends like a tea-chest, biscuit-tin and secondhand radio parts (he had very little money), Baird succeeded in transmitting the flickering outline of a Maltese Cross over a distance

Broadcasting Shakespeare in 1923

John Logie Baird and the apparatus with which he first televised a human being

of a few feet. In the following year (1925) he first televised a human being. However, others improved on Baird's invention, and when the B.B.C. began a regular television service (1936) it chose an alternative system developed by Electrical and Musical Industries. The first TV studios were at Alexandra Palace in North London. By 1939 there were about 80,000 television sets in use; all of them in the London area. Services were suspended during the Second World War and resumed in 1946 (see Chapter 25).

Just before the war broke out **Sir Robert Watson-Watt** and a team of British scientists developed **radar** (radio detection and ranging). It enabled objects within a certain distance (roughly thirty miles at ground level) to be located by the echoes or rebounds from radio waves. Radar was put to immediate use in detecting approaching aircraft during the Battle of Britain (1940). It soon proved to be of great value in all kinds of sea and air travel, for darkness or fog make no difference to its ability to detect moving objects and measure their distances and speeds.

Timeline
1863   London Metropolitan underground railway.
1865   'Red Flag Act'.
1875   Alexander Graham Bell invents the telephone.
1876   Nikolaus Otto's 'four-stroke compression engine'.
1887   First petrol-driven four-wheeled car (Gottlieb Daimler).
1888   John Boyd Dunlop's pneumatic tyre.
1892   Rudolph Diesel's 'heavy oil engine'.
1896   'Red Flag Act' repealed.
1896   Guglielmo Marconi's first wireless demonstrations in England.
1897   Sir Charles Parsons's *Turbinia* at the Spithead Naval Review.
1903   First powered flight (Wright brothers).
1921   Amalgamation of railway companies.
1922   B.B.C. established.
1924   Imperial Airways formed.
1924   First television picture transmitted (John Logie Baird).
1936   B.B.C. Television Service begins (London area).

Further study

Advances in transport and communications since the Second World War are described in the latter sections of Chapter 25.

Visits

Many museums all over Britain have exhibits illustrating the history of transport and communications. London's Science Museum contains sections on internal combustion engines and road vehicles (ground floor); telephony (first floor), radio, radar and television; aeroplanes and aero-engines—including over twenty full-size aircraft (third floor). The National Motor Museum, Beaulieu, Hants, has well over 200 exhibits from the history of road transport since 1895. The London Transport Museum, Syon Park, Brentford, has a collection of buses and trolley buses, trams and tube trains. Veteran cars, trams and coaches can be seen in the Old Corn Exchange, Hull. Railway museums are listed on p. 159.

General accounts

G. C. Allen, *Railways* (Blackwell) Ch. 4–5
M. N. Duffy, *Flight* (Blackwell, Twentieth Century Topic Books)
R. A. S. Hennessey, *Transport* (Batsford, Past-into-Present series)
L. Snellgrove, *From Rocket to Railcar* (Longmans) Ch. 10–13
L. Snellgrove, *From Steamcarts to Minicars* (Longmans) Ch. 1–9
L. Snellgrove, *From Kitty Hawk to Outer Space* (Longmans) Ch. 1–11
D. St J. Thomas, *The Motor Revolution* (Longman's Then and There series)
From Place to Place (Ginn's History Bookshelves, Grey Shelf)

Special topics

L. Reade, *Marconi and the Discovery of Wireless* (Faber)
J. Rowland, *The Radar Man* (Lutterworth Press), the story of Sir Robert Watson-Watt.
H. Thomas, *The Wright Brothers* (A. and C. Black, Lives to Remember)
The Bodley Head Men of the Modern Age series includes:
L. Meynell, *Rolls—Man of Speed*
C. Caldwell, *Henry Ford*
J. Leasor, *Wheels to Fortune* (Lord Nuffield)
O. J. Stevenson, *The Talking Wire* (Alexander Graham Bell)
J. G. Crowther, *Six Great Engineers* (Hamish Hamilton) includes Rudolph Diesel.
Transport (Longman, Secondary History Packs) Packs 17–20
D. Nye, *Carl Benz and the Motor Car* (Priory Press)
J. F. Moon, *Rudolf Diesel and the Diesel Engine* (Priory Press)
A. McElroy, *Alexander Graham Bell and the Telephone* (Priory Press)

Filmstrips

History of Road Transport, Part 3: The Motor Age (Common Ground)
The Story of the London Bus (British Transport)
The Story of the Bicycle (Basic Films)
History of Aviation, Parts 2–4 (Common Ground)
Milestones of Aviation, 1903–53 (Hulton)

22 War and Depression

The First World War and its effect on industry, agriculture and foreign trade (1914-39)

For a century following the Battle of Waterloo (1815) Britain was not involved in a major war. Peace was interrupted only by distant campaigns like the Crimean War against Russia (1854—6) and the Boer War of 1899—1902. Neither of these was fought against a neighbouring country. In fact, by the late nineteenth century Britain had ceased to have much influence on continental affairs. In the famous phrase of Lord Salisbury (Prime Minister 1895—1901) the country was in *'splendid isolation'*; concentrating its energies upon empire-building, notably in Africa (see Chapter 19). However, events in Europe led to a change of policy in the early years of the twentieth century.

The end of isolation

In 1871 a new and powerful **German Empire** was created out of a number of individual states. The military strength of the new nation had already been demonstrated when the armed opposition of Austria (1866) and France (1870) was overcome by crushing German victories. Having unified the separate states, Otto von Bismarck (Chancellor of Germany 1871—90) tried to re-establish peace in Europe. He regained the friendship of Austria and signed an alliance in 1879. This became the **Triple Alliance** (1882) with the addition of Italy. But France and Russia were suspicious and fearful of their new neighbour. In 1893 they formed a **Dual Alliance** for mutual help and protection. Thus Europe was divided into two 'armed camps'.

A growing number of British politicians were soon expressing concern at their country's isolation from the continental alliances. They urged the Government to 'come down off the fence' on one side or the other. If and when this happened, it seemed likely that Germany would be the natural ally of Britain. Wilhelm II, the German Kaiser (Emperor) was a nephew of King Edward VII (1901—10), and the two peoples had a long history of goodwill and co-operation. But friendly approaches to Germany—made secretly by Joseph Chamberlain, the Colonial Secretary, in the years 1898—1901— came to nothing. The two countries were beginning to drift apart. The Kaiser's decision to build a powerful navy alarmed the British, for it seemed to be intended for use against them. When they replied by strengthening their own fleet, a 'naval race' developed which seriously harmed Anglo-German relations.

Meanwhile, Britain and France, 'the traditional enemies', drew closer together. In 1904 they signed the **Entente Cordiale** (Friendly Understanding) recognising each other's areas of influence in North Africa. Three years later Britain made a similar agreement with Russia, France's ally, which settled their colonial differences in

Triple Alliance and
Dual Entente

Asia. The **Triple Entente** to which Britain now belonged was *not* an alliance. In other words, Britain was not legally bound to aid either France or Russia against an enemy. But it was now very likely that Britain would favour the Dual Alliance rather than the 'Central Powers' (as Germany and its allies were called) in the event of a European war. This likelihood increased when British and French naval chiefs began to hold secret talks.

Britain's vague policy of *semi*-commitment to the Dual Alliance was most unsatisfactory. If war broke out, France and Russia would expect assistance; yet, because there was no definite alliance, Britain could not hope to influence the actions of its friends when they looked like getting into trouble. The disadvantages of this position became clear in the summer of 1914. Britain was a helpless spectator while a quarrel between Austria and Russia developed into a world war.

The First World War, 1914–18

On June 1914 **Archduke Ferdinand,** the heir to the Austrian throne, was shot dead by a Serbian student. The Austrians had long been looking for an excuse to crush neighbouring Serbia (part of present day Yugoslavia) in order to expand into south-eastern Europe. Now was their chance. By the end of July the two countries were at war. The speed of events now quickened. Russia mobilised forces in Serbia's defence; determined to resist any extension of Austrian territory. Germany immediately supported its ally and declared war on Russia (1 August) and France (3 August). It was the start of the greatest bloodbath the world had seen, costing 10 million lives in just over four years.

Faced by enemies on two fronts, the Germans put into operation the **Schlieffen Plan,** prepared by a former Chief-of-Staff in 1905.

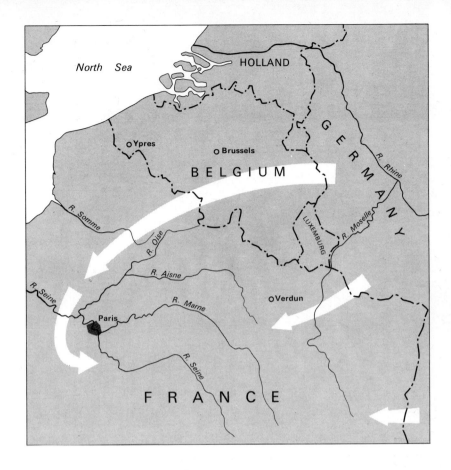

Their main attacking force was concentrated for a quick thrust against the French; hoping to knock them out of the fighting before Russia could fully mobilise on the Eastern Front. The German right wing aimed to sweep through Belgium and across the northern frontiers of France, the weakest point in the enemy's defences. Paris could then be attacked from the rear and the French army would be encircled.

Sir Edward Grey, Britain's Foreign Secretary, feared that if France was crushed the Germans would be able to dominate Europe. In his view, Britain was in duty bound to fight simply to preserve the *balance of power* on the Continent. But several members of the Cabinet disagreed at first. It was the German invasion of Belgium which enabled Grey to get the unanimous support of his colleagues and the nation for British entry into the war (4 August). Britain and the other great powers had signed a treaty in 1839 promising to defend Belgian independence. The German Chancellor now referred to it as a 'scrap of paper'. In any case, Britain could not stand by and see Belgium overrun, for fear that it might provide a springboard for an invasion across the Channel.

The Belgians resisted bravely, slowing down the German advance. By the time Brussels, the Belgian capital, fell (20 August) the first British troops had arrived to assist France. Nevertheless the Schlieffen

Plan came very near to succeeding. By 5 September the Germans were within striking distance of Paris. The Allies, aided by reinforcements rushed to the front in taxis, rallied just in time. During the next seven days, the invaders were pushed back from the river Marne to the river Aisne. After the vital **Battle of the Marne,** the greatest crisis was over and the character of the war changed. Swift movements in the open ceased as both sides dug themselves into **trenches,** protected by barbed-wire and machine-guns. In the next three and a half years, the trench lines, extending from the Channel to the Swiss frontier, never varied by more than twenty miles. Repeated efforts to achieve a breakthrough led to some of the bloodiest and most futile battles in history. Artillery and machine-gun fire gave defenders a clear advantage against troops advancing across the 'no-man's-land' between the trenches.

At the beginning of the war, cheering crowds had gathered in the streets of London, and young men had eagerly enlisted 'to fight for King and Country'. But the mood of the people quickly changed from cheerful optimism to grim acceptance of the horrors of trench warfare. **Lord Kitchener** became Minister of War (until his death at sea, 1916). He made a nationwide appeal for army recruits, and a million men came forward by the end of 1914. Conscription (compulsory enlistment) was not introduced in Britain until 1916—so successful was the campaign for volunteers. Meanwhile the civilian population concentrated on supplying the armed forces. Women workers played a vital part in the factories, the transport services, and on the land. Although there was no fighting on British soil, the people at home were given a taste of the war. Towns on the east coast were bombarded by the German navy, and occasional raids by aeroplanes and

Volunteers for Lord Kitchener's Army (1914)

Gallipoli

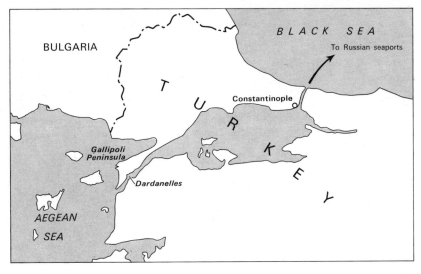

Zeppelins (airships, or powered balloons) claimed 1400 victims.

To the great disappointment of Britain and France, the Russians failed to break through on the Eastern Front. They were heavily defeated at **Tannenberg** in East Germany (August 1914) and never fully recovered. Russia was desperately short of military supplies, but it was difficult for Britain and France to make contact with their ally, especially after Turkey joined the Central Powers (October 1914). However, in the spring of 1915 the Allies began an offensive against Turkey, attempting to force a passage through the Dardanelles and attack Constantinople. A naval bombardment was tried first, but this gave the Turks warning and time to prepare their defences. When troops landed on the **Gallipoli** peninsula they suffered heavy losses and the campaign was abandoned after a few months. Thus

Allied troops landing on the Gallipoli peninsula (1915)

1915 was a disappointing year for the Allies, even though the Western Front held firm and they were joined by the Italians (who refused to support the Central Powers on the grounds that they were the aggressors). But Italy had little effect on the outcome of the war, being hard pressed to hold its own against Austria.

Meanwhile the deadlock in the West continued. Both sides sacrificed hundreds of thousands of lives in hopeless attacks on enemy entrenchments. In 1915 Germany tried poisonous gas, but it was soon countered by the use of gas-masks. In the following year, German forces gathered for an all-out attack at **Verdun.** The French suffered appalling casualties, but held on by the skin of their teeth. To relieve pressure on them, the British staged a mass offensive on the **Somme.** Their losses were immense—20,000 were killed on the first day (1 July). After four months a few miles of shell-torn countryside had been gained at the expense of 420,000 British casualties. There was great disillusionment at home, and this contributed to a change of leadership. **Lloyd George,** who distinguished himself while Minister of Munitions (1915–16), replaced Herbert Asquith as Prime Minister in December 1916. He formed a small War Cabinet of five members.

Like the fighting on land, the **war at sea** was a slow wearing-down process. With the Royal Navy in control of the oceans, the German battle fleet rarely ventured out of the Baltic. The only time the fleets came within striking distance of each other was in May 1916, off **Jutland** (mainland Denmark). But the Germans avoided a full-

The British battleship *Queen Mary* blowing up at the Battle of Jutland

German U-boats in Kiel harbour (1917)

scale battle and disappeared in the evening mist, having sunk fourteen British ships and lost eleven themselves. Both sides were reluctant to risk defeat, especially the British, who needed command of the seas in order to supply the army, feed the people and blockade German shipping.

The naval blockade deprived the Germans of vital supplies, including food. They replied by attacking British merchant shipping with **U-boats** (submarines). Early in 1917 the German High Command decided its best chance of victory was to starve Britain into surrender by *unrestricted* submarine warfare. From 1 February *all* ships approaching Allied ports were liable to be torpedoed, even if they belonged to neutral countries. The Germans realised that the U.S.A. would now almost certainly join the war against them, but they gambled on defeating the Allies before America could mobilise its troops. The plan almost succeeded. By April, when the United States declared war on Germany, over 1000 ships had been torpedoed in three months, and Britain had only six weeks' supply of food left. There were long queues outside the shops, and the Government introduced rationing to ensure fair distribution. After April, however, shipping losses were greatly reduced. Merchant vessels began to sail in *convoys,* escorted by destroyers equipped with depth-charges.

American support was especially welcome to Britain and France because Russia withdrew from the war soon after the Communists came to power in the Revolution of November 1917. Everything now depended on the Western Front. Another British offensive failed in the summer and autumn of 1917. They gained only five miles of muddy wilderness and the village of **Passchendaele,** near Ypres, at a cost of 300,000 casualties. Nevertheless, Germany, in the grip of the naval blockade, was now drastically short of food and raw materials. Austria and Turkey were also in trouble. In December 1917 the Turks lost Jerusalem to Britain's General Allenby, who was ably assisted by **T. E. Lawrence** ('Lawrence of Arabia') leading the tribes of the Arabian desert.

Germany's only hope was an all-out attack in the West before United States forces arrived in full strength. With troops transferred from the Russian frontier, the Germans began their great **Spring Offensives** in March 1918. They broke through the Allied defences in several places. At one time Paris was again in danger and a second Battle of the Marne was fought to save France's capital. But by June the Allies, strengthened with American troops and under the single command of the French **Marshal Foch,** began to drive the Germans back. A series of attacks all along the line soon led to its collapse. British tanks played a decisive part for the first time since their introduction in 1916. The Germans were too exhausted to rally. The Kaiser fled to Holland, and the long-awaited **armistice** came on 11 November at 11 o'clock. In London and all the Allied capitals, people rushed into the streets, dancing and cheering. There were plenty of tears also. Britain and the Empire alone had lost over a million men killed and more than twice as many wounded.

Nine weeks later representatives of thirty-two countries attended the Peace Conference in Paris. The Germans were deprived of some European territory and all their colonies; their army was reduced almost to nothing and their armaments manufacture strictly controlled. In addition, Germany was expected to pay large sums of money to the Allies as reparations (damages). **President Woodrow Wilson** of the U.S.A. asked the Conference to accept his *Fourteen Points,* containing a recipe for world peace. He had to give way on many of them, but his chief hope was realised — the creation of a **League of Nations,** to meet regularly and discuss world problems. But Wilson's political opponents at home kept the U.S.A. out of the League, thus reducing its effectiveness from the start.

The depression; industries old and new

For a short time after the war, exports soared and British industry prospered. Everywhere there was a great demand for manufactured goods that had been scarce during war-time. By 1920 the army was demobilised, most of the 3 million munitions workers were re-employed in peace-time industries, and everyone talked of 'business as usual'. But then, suddenly, this brief period of prosperity came to an end. In the winter of 1920–21, when more normal trading conditions returned, British exports fell and there was a consequent rise in **unemployment.** By June 1921, 2 million men were out of work —one in every seven of working age! There was no immediate panic, for everyone expected the situation to improve quickly, as it usually had done in trade 'slumps' of the past. But this time there was no immediate recovery. British foreign trade was entering a period of serious decline, and, from 1921 to 1940, the numbers of unemployed never fell below a million.

The First World War was partly to blame. While British industry

Above: British machine-gunners manning shell-holes near Passchendaele (1917)

Right: A wool combing shed in the West Riding of Yorkshire

concentrated on supplying the armed forces, many former markets overseas were lost for ever. Foreign customers either increased their own production of goods they had previously bought from Britain, or they found other sources of supply; for example, South American countries turned to the U.S.A. Naturally, when peace returned, these countries found they could manage with less British goods than they had bought before 1914.

Britain's share of world trade had been decreasing slowly for half a century, as other nations developed their own industries. But the war greatly *accelerated* this trend. Mass unemployment was unavoidable, for until Britain could find new customers, or recover lost markets with new products, there was simply not enough work to go round. The effects of the depression were not evenly spread over the whole country. The areas which suffered most—North-East England, Lancashire, South Wales and Clydeside—were the centres of the **old-established industries**: textiles (especially cotton), coal, iron and steel, heavy engineering and shipbuilding. Few of these industries regained the high level of output they had reached before 1914 and all of them failed to recapture fully their pre-war export trade.

The **cotton** industry was the hardest hit by the war, mainly because of its dependence on overseas markets. In 1914 there began a decline in the fortunes of the industry from which it never recovered. Like Britain during the Industrial Revolution, newly developing countries turned to cotton very early in their industrialisation. For instance, Japan and India gradually ceased to buy from Britain and became competitors instead. By 1935 the Japanese dominated Asian and Far-Eastern markets and were already exporting greater quantities of cotton goods than Britain. **Woollen textiles** fared much less badly.

New carding machinery
in the woollen cloth
industry

They had been in great demand for military uniforms during the war, and, in peace-time, a large proportion of the output of woollen cloth continued to be sold at home.

Coal-mining came under direct government control during the war, along with railways and munitions factories. When peace returned, the industry suffered a steady decline, in both its labour force and its output. The production figures for 1913 have never been equalled since.

British Coal Production (in millions of tons)

1913	1931	1938
287	207	227

Coal exports also fell, partly because continental countries increased their output. Technically, several of them were in advance of Britain, making greater use of mechanical cutters and conveyers. Meanwhile the growing use of electric power in industry reduced the demand for coal. It was still required to drive the generators in the power stations (see Chapter 15) but it was used more economically than in the days of steam-powered factories. Furthermore, shipping was rapidly changing over from coal to oil fuel.

Iron, steel and engineering experienced varying fortunes. New iron ore fields were developed in North Lincolnshire and Northamptonshire, leading to the growth of iron and steel towns like Scunthorpe and Corby. Nevertheless, an increasing proportion of Britain's iron ore had to be imported, while exports of pig iron to Europe dropped sharply. Steel and heavy engineering were hit by the depression, but revived in the late 1930s, stimulated by rearmament. Steel output in 1937 was more than a third above that of 1929. But **shipbuilding** suffered disastrously from the decline in the volume of international trade which, in turn, reduced the demand for new merchant vessels. In 1933 nearly two-thirds of Britain's shipbuilding workers were unemployed and many yards were being dismantled.

In contrast to this gloomy picture, a wide range of **newer industries** grew and prospered in the inter-war years (1918–39). There was a steady rise in the output of motor cars, aeroplanes, electrical equipment, chemicals, rubber goods, fertilisers, medicines, cosmetics, packaged foods and other products of light industry. Most of these were manufactured in the South Midlands and the South-East—for electric power encouraged the growth of factories away from the coalfields, in pleasanter surroundings. As George Orwell, the novelist, observed: 'The typical post-war factory is not a gaunt barrack or an awful chaos of blackness and belching chimneys; it is a glittering white structure of concrete, glass and steel, surrounded by green lawns and beds of tulips.'

In the early 1930s, when unemployment reached thirty to forty per cent in many coal-mining, cotton or shipbuilding towns, only about six per cent of workers in the 'lucky South' were without jobs. In fact, despite the depression, a *majority* of the people enjoyed an improvement in wages and living standards in the inter-war years. The main

Feeding a furnace with coal

centres of **motor-car manufacture**—Coventry, Birmingham, Oxford, Bedford and Dagenham—were among the most prosperous towns in Western Europe. Between 1929 and 1937, when old-established industries felt the worst effects of the trade slump, the output of motor vehicles more than doubled. Similarly, the **electrical industry** was little affected by the depression. Production of dynamos, electric motors, light bulbs, radio sets, cookers and vacuum cleaners rose steadily. The manufacture of **chemicals** was one of the few expanding industries partly located in the 'depressed areas'— notably Merseyside and the North-East. In 1926 four large firms came together to form I.C.I. (Imperial Chemical Industries Ltd), the largest industrial concern in the British Empire. The chemical industry played an important part in the development of **rayon,** made from cotton and cellulose (obtained from wood-pulp).

Most of the newer industries catered for the home market. Britain failed to capture a sufficiently large share of world trade in goods like cars, radio sets and rayon cloth to make up for the losses of the older industries.

State aid for agriculture

Farming, the oldest industry of all, enjoyed a brief period of prosperity during the First World War. U-boat attacks on merchant shipping, at a time when Britain imported about two-thirds of its food, made it essential to increase home production. The Government encouraged the ploughing-up of grassland in order to grow more cereals, and secured the co-operation of farmers by giving them guaranteed prices (1917). At the same time, agricultural labourers were granted a reasonable minimum wage. With additional help from the Women's Land Army and prisoner-of-war labour, the wheat harvest was increased by sixty per cent, and there was a substantial rise in the production of potatoes, barley and oats.

But agriculture slumped again soon after the war. The average price of wheat halved in the years 1920–22. Farmers were no longer guaranteed against losses after 1921, so they were forced to return to the pre-war practice of converting arable land into pasture (see Chapter 14). However, livestock- and dairy-farming requires fewer workers than arable cultivation, so this trend increased the numbers of unemployed. The Government felt compelled to take fresh action, to help farmers and to restore the balance between the different branches of agriculture. **State subsidies** (money grants) were paid to growers of wheat (1932), barley and oats (1937), as well as to meat-producers (1934). After 1933 **import quotas** limited purchases of foreign food to fixed quantities. Meanwhile central **Marketing Boards** were established (1931–3) to control sales of milk, bacon, pork, hops and potatoes, at guaranteed prices. The influence of government policy was well illustrated in the case of sugar-beet. Sugar was entirely imported before 1914, yet, by the early 1930s, heavy state subsidies had led to the development of a home industry, supplying a quarter of the country's sugar needs.

The combined efforts of the Government and the farmers resulted in a slight recovery of agriculture in the 1930s. This was aided by greater

A new development in farming: large pneumatic tyres fitted to a plough tractor

use of **machinery,** especially for threshing and milking. Combine harvesters were used on some larger farms. Motor tractors, which were almost non-existent in Britain before 1914, numbered 50,000 in 1939. Nevertheless the drift from the land was unchecked. Roughly a quarter of a million labourers left the countryside between 1918 and 1939. Thus the decline of village life continued and Britain remained dangerously dependent on foreign agriculture, as was shown in the Second World War.

The crisis of 1931 and the end of 'free trade'

In October 1929 there was a sudden fall in the value of shares on Wall Street (the New York Stock Exchange). Investments became almost worthless as thousands of speculators panicked and tried to sell in a market where there were no buyers. The **Wall Street Crash** began a worldwide financial crisis and a consequent slump in international trade which seriously affected Britain and other industrial nations. British exports almost halved in value in the next two years (1929–31) while the total of unemployed reached nearly 3 million (roughly one worker in five).

Faced with the worst depression in history, the Prime Minister, **J. Ramsay MacDonald** (1866–1936) formed an all-party **National Government** in 1931, splitting with Labour, his former party, in the process (see Chapter 23). The National Government assisted manufacturers as well as farmers. For example, loans were given to certain industries to help finance worthwhile projects. One result of this policy was the completion of *Cunarder 534* (renamed *Queen Mary*) which lay half-built on Clydeside. Four of the most depressed regions – the North-East, South Wales, the Scottish Lowlands and West

Cumberland—became **Special Areas** (1934) and industries were encouraged to move to them.

Above all, the National Government decided to abandon free trade (see Chapter 14). Since the mid nineteenth century, foreign manufactured goods had entered Britain free of customs duties, even though other nations imposed duties (tariffs) to protect their own industries from outside competition. Back in 1903, however, **Joseph Chamberlain** had resigned from the Conservative Government to launch a nationwide **Tariff Reform Campaign.** He proposed that Britain should give up free trade and impose tariffs which allowed for *imperial preference* (lower duties on Empire goods than on imports from other countries). His main aim was to strengthen the Empire, but he won support from many people who felt that Britain's rivals had an unfair advantage and that the Government should introduce tariffs which were equivalent to those placed on British goods abroad. But Chamberlain's scheme required substantial duties on *food* imports from countries outside the Empire. When his policy was put to the test of a general election (1906) the prospect of higher food prices caused most voters to reject it. Chamberlain immediately retired from politics and the campaign against free trade was not seriously revived until the coming of the depression.

In 1915 war-time duties were placed on non-essential imports like cars, clocks and musical instruments. When peace returned they were not repealed, even though this had been promised. Then, in 1921, Parliament imposed a few more duties to protect from foreign competition some small industries that had arisen during the war. This was 'the thin end of the wedge', but the decisive change came,

Cartoon showing Joseph Chamberlain searching for the remains of the Tariff Reform campaign after the 1906 election

HERE DISAPPEARED
TARIFF REFORM
IN THE GREAT STORM OF
THE GENERAL ELECTION
JANUARY 1906
SNOWED UNDER

in the depths of the depression, with the **Import Duties Act 1932.** The National Government decided that while it was powerless to prevent the slump in international trade, it could at least preserve the *home* market for British producers. Therefore a ten per cent customs duty was placed on a majority of imports. The only goods exempted were most foodstuffs and some raw materials like rubber, cotton and wool. Later in the same year, most duties were raised to twenty or even thirty-three and a third per cent. The Act did not apply to Empire products, so the way was clear for the immediate introduction of 'imperial preference' similar to that suggested by Joseph Chamberlain.

Despite the National Government's policies, recovery from the depression was painfully slow. It took the Second World War (1939–45) to bring mass unemployment to an end; although the numbers out of work fell gradually during the 'rearmament drive' of the late 1930s.

Timeline

1903–6   Joseph Chamberlain's Tariff Reform Campaign.
1904   'Entente Cordiale'.
1907   Anglo-Russian 'Entente'.
1914–18 First World War.
1920–21 Start of the depression.
1929   Wall Street 'crash'.
1931–5 National Government (state aid for industry and agriculture).
1932   Import Duties Act.

Further study

For developments in British industry and agriculture since 1939 see the first four sections of Chapter 25.

Visit
The Imperial War Museum, Lambeth Road, London SE1.

General accounts
S. R. Gibbons and P. Morican, *World War One* (Longman's Modern Times series) with optional L.P. record.
D. Lindsay and E. S. Washington, *A Portrait of Britain, 1851–1951* (O.U.P.) pp. 230–38 on industry and agriculture, 1919–39.
J. Roberts and A. Rowe, *Making the Present, 1918–72* (Hutchinson)
R. R. Sellman, *The First World War* (Methuen's Outlines series)

Special topics
Ships in Peace and War and *The Soldier and the Airman* (Ginn's History Bookshelves, Grey Shelf) contain brief background material on the armed services.
The Somme (Cape, Jackdaw series no. 111)
C. Hill, *Joseph Chamberlain* (Shire Publications, Lifelines series)

Filmstrip
Twentieth Century Britain, Part 1: the Economic Scene (Educational Publications)

23 The Troubled Years

Working-class movements and social conditions (1918-39)

At the end of 1918, when peace returned at last, the British people looked forward to the future with high hopes. Lloyd George promised to make Britain 'a fit country for heroes to live in', and few doubted his ability to do it. After all, if the Government could find £7 million a day to pay for the war, it seemed reasonable to suppose it could now finance a campaign against poverty and bad living conditions.

Even before the peace treaty was signed, the right to vote was extended to all men over twenty-one and to most women over thirty. A general election was held almost immediately, and Lloyd George's war-time **Coalition Government** was returned to power with an enormous majority (December 1918). Unfortunately, many of the easy promises made in the hour of victory could not be fulfilled in the difficult years which lay ahead.

Industrial unrest

The mass strike action on the eve of the First World War was halted by an 'industrial truce' between employers and trade unions which continued until 1918 (see Chapter 17). There were still a few strikes —for example among shipbuilding workers on Clydeside and miners in South Wales—but in general the unions co-operated with employers and the Government. Because of this inactivity, they emerged from the war with greatly increased funds. Furthermore, the number of trade union members almost doubled between 1913 and 1919. The unions had never been better equipped to do battle on the 'industrial front'.

They soon had plenty to fight for. Steeply rising prices immediately after the Armistice led to hundreds of claims for higher pay, and, where these were rejected, many bitter strikes. On average, more than 100,000 men were on strike every day throughout 1919. In some cases, however, workers achieved their aims without strike action. The Government set up an **Industrial Court** where both sides in a dispute could state their case and obtain a settlement. Early in 1920 dockers gained a substantial wage increase in this way. Their arguments were skilfully put by **Ernest Bevin,** a remarkable union leader who left school at the age of eleven and rose from farm-labouring to become a Cabinet minister in 1940. Bevin was largely responsible for the amalgamation of a number of separate unions into the great Transport and General Workers Union (1921) which he served as General Secretary. There were many other amalgamations in the post-war years, each of them resulting in more powerful organisations, such as the Amalgamated Engineering Union (1920).

Although many wage increases during 1919–20 were wiped out by the higher cost of living, the unions felt triumphant at having won a

Dockers on strike in the
post-war years

succession of victories over employers. But the coming of mass
unemployment in 1921 (see Chapter 22) caused a sudden reversal of
fortunes. Employers now held the upper hand, for whenever there
are more men than jobs those who strike may be threatened with
dismissal. The trade slump caused employers to press for *lower*
wages and *longer* hours. Unions were forced on the defensive.
Instead of asking for more, they had to struggle to keep what they
had got. This problem was greatest in old-fashioned industries, like
coal-mining, which were the hardest hit by the depression.

The miners' grievances and the General Strike (1926)

During the war, the coal industry was temporarily *nationalised* (taken
under direct government control). Wages were increased and they
no longer varied from one district to the next. Miners were more
contented than they had been under private employers, so when
peace came their union, the **Miners' Federation of Great
Britain,** demanded that nationalisation should continue. The
Government, under pressure from the coal-owners, refused the
demands of the union, even though a Royal Commission (1919)
declared itself in favour of state control. Needless to say, the miners
were very angry, especially as the Government had promised to
abide by the decision of the Royal Commission 'in the spirit and in
the letter'. The question of nationalisation remained a basic cause of
discontent in the coal industry for almost thirty years.

By the time nationalisation came to an end (March 1921) the
depression had begun. The export price of coal fell from 115*s* a ton
in the summer of 1920 to 24*s* in the spring of 1921. Mine-owners
gave advance warning that when they resumed control of their pits
they would make drastic wage cuts, and these would vary from region
to region, because some mines were more profitable than others.

Employers' view of the Triple Alliance, as shown in a *Punch* cartoon, April 1921

Stanley Baldwin in 1920

The Miners' Federation refused to accept the new terms and gained the support of the railwaymen and transport workers, their partners in the **Triple Industrial Alliance** of 1914 (see Chapter 17). A massive strike was arranged for 15 April, but when the day arrived the other unions withdrew their support. Trade unionists called it **'Black Friday'**, for the Triple Alliance had collapsed and the miners were left to fight alone. They eventually returned to work on 1 July, having gained very little improvement on the terms offered in March.

After a slight recovery, coal prices again fell sharply in 1925. Employers proposed immediate wage cuts and an increase of one hour in the working day. But the Miners' Federation protested that it was already 'stripped to the bone'. The Triple Alliance was revived and this time it held firm. The Prime Minister, **Stanley Baldwin** (1867–1947) saw that the only way of preventing a nationwide stoppage was for the Government to intervene and make up miners' wages to their previous level. Therefore, on 31 July, miners were offered a state subsidy of £24 million to offset the owners' wage cuts. It would last for nine months. The unions called their success **'Red Friday'**, but in fact it settled nothing. Both sides realised there would be a showdown if they still failed to agree when the subsidy ended.

As expected, neither the miners nor their employers were prepared to give way. The coal-owners continued to demand substantial wage cuts and longer working hours, and the miners replied with the slogan 'not a penny off the pay; not a minute on the day'. By the time the subsidy was withdrawn (1 May 1926) the Trades Union Congress had agreed to support the miners. Its members voted by an overwhelming majority for a **General Strike,** beginning on Tuesday, 4 May.

It was not necessary for all union members to strike. The country could be paralysed if workers came out in a few key industries. Therefore only railwaymen and transport workers, dockers, builders, iron, steel and chemical workers, printers, and gas and electricity workers supplying power for industry came out, in addition to the miners. Sanitary services continued and health and food services were not interfered with. There were altogether about 3 million men on strike (one in every five adult males). They formed the backbone of British industry.

It was the quietest Tuesday morning in living memory. Factories were deserted; there were no buses, trams or trains, and no newspapers. However, the 'great silence' was soon broken, for non-union business attempted to carry on as usual. In London crowds of people set out to walk from the suburbs to their offices in Town. Bowler-hatted businessmén were seen on bicycles, while thousands of motor cars, crammed with hitch-hikers, caused enormous traffic jams on main roads leading to the City. Many motorists were still trying to reach their destinations at midday!

The Government had made careful plans for dealing with the strike. Troops were sent to work in the docks and power stations and to accompany food convoys in the towns. In London, Hyde Park became a vast milk depot. Most important of all, a voluntary **Organisation for the Maintenance of Supplies** (O.M.S.) had for months been training ordinary citizens to drive buses and trains and to act as

A food convoy leaves London docks on the fifth day of the General Strike

special constables. Within a week, nearly 3000 trains were operating with amateur crews, and fairly regular bus services were running in many areas. There were more than the usual number of crashes, but few of them were serious.

Despite the printers' strike, Winston Churchill (the Chancellor of the Exchequer) and a band of willing helpers managed to produce a government daily newspaper—*The British Gazette*—from 5 May onwards. It accused the strikers of 'a direct challenge to ordered government', and 'a hold-up of the nation to ransom'. The T.U.C. (Trades Union Congress) replied with a paper called *The British Worker*, which denied the Government's charges and emphasised that the strike was simply 'an industrial dispute, *not* an attack upon Parliamentary government'. Most of the regular daily papers, like *The Times* and the *Daily Mirror,* were reduced to single sheets. The B.B.C. tried to make up for the newspaper shortage by putting out five news bulletins a day. Mr Baldwin made several broadcasts to the nation, but his Cabinet prevented both the T.U.C. and the Leader of the Labour Party from speaking on the radio.

Some of the strikers occupied their time trying to wreck vehicles driven by members of the O.M.S. As a result, many buses had windows boarded up against stone-throwers and barbed-wire across the bonnet to protect the engine from sabotage. In Northumberland a gang of wreckers managed to derail the 'Flying Scotsman' by removing a length of the railway track! But incidents of that kind were rare. Considering the serious nature of the dispute, most people were remarkably peaceful and good humoured. At Plymouth, for instance, a team of strikers played the local police at soccer. All over the country, entertainments and sports, including county cricket, helped to take people's minds off the crisis. Foreign observers were greatly impressed by the sensible behaviour of the British people. *The Philadelphia Record,* an American newspaper, pointed out on 11 May that after a week of the greatest industrial dispute in the nation's history 'not a single life has been lost, not a single shot fired'.

As the strike entered its second week, all seemed to be going well for the unions. But suddenly, on 12 May, the T.U.C. called it off, after only nine days. They said they had been given 'assurances that a settlement of the mining problem can be secured', but the Miners' Federation was dismayed to find that nothing *definite* had been promised by either the Government or the mine-owners. The T.U.C. leaders seemed to be afraid of the great weapon they had created and unwilling to be branded as revolutionaries. Thus the miners were left to fight alone, until near-starvation forced them to return to work, on the owners' terms, *six months later.* The Government pressed home its victory with a **Trade Disputes Act, 1927,** which made most kinds of 'sympathetic' strike illegal.

Some mining districts never recovered from the effects of the great coal strike. After standing idle for six months or more, many smaller pits were forced to close down, their workers swelling the already high numbers of unemployed. In the summer of 1927 a quarter of a million miners were out of work. Few of them had any immediate prospect of finding a job.

A Strike Edition of *The Times* compared with an ordinary alarm clock.

Ramsay MacDonald,
pictured after his victory in
the 1929 election

The mixed fortunes of the Labour Party

The General Strike cost the unions involved about £4 million. In the next few years, while their funds recovered, strikes were fewer and generally short. Meanwhile, working men took a greater interest in politics. If they could not get their way by withdrawing their labour, the best alternative was to support candidates who would further their aims in Parliament. It was, therefore, no coincidence that the defeat of the General Strike was followed by a rise in the fortunes of **Labour,** the only major political party which claimed to put the interests of the working-class uppermost (see Chapter 17).

The strength of the Labour Party had grown rapidly since the war. In the 1923 election it won 191 seats and took office for the first time (January 1924). But the Labour Government, headed by **Ramsay MacDonald,** depended on Liberal support, for the Conservatives were the largest single party. It only lasted ten months; yet in that time MacDonald and his Cabinet did much to convince the nation that Labour was 'respectable' and fit to govern. In the first election after the General Strike (1929) Labour won 287 seats, more than any other party. However, Liberal support was again required to give it an overall majority in the Commons.

The second Labour Government had the misfortune to encounter the great financial crisis which followed the collapse of the American stock market in 1929 (see Chapter 22). It broke up when MacDonald proposed cuts in government spending on the social services, notably a reduction in unemployment benefit (1931). This was against the principles of a party which claimed to protect the 'underdog'. MacDonald was regarded as a traitor, and, when he formed an all-party **National Government,** the bulk of Labour M.P.s would have nothing more to do with him. The party was divided and its strength in Parliament dwindled.

The 'dole' and the 'means test'

For unemployed workers and their families, life was a grim struggle. Debts piled up; furniture, clothing and personal possessions were taken to the pawnbroker; men searched for coal in slag-heaps and railway sidings, and thousands of families went short of food. But things would have been even worse without weekly unemployment benefits and allowances paid by the state. The original unemployment scheme in the National Insurance Act of 1911 only covered about 3 million workers in a small range of industries (see Chapter 20). However, by November 1920 everyone earning less than £5 a week was brought in, with the exception of farm labourers and domestic and civil servants. In return for weekly subscriptions of a few pence, benefits of 15s for men and 12s for women could be claimed for up to fifteen weeks in any year. In 1921 allowances for 'dependents' were added—5s for a wife and 1s for each child.

The new insurance scheme was worked out just before the start of the depression. Almost as soon as it came into operation it was out of date. Calculations had been based on an unemployment rate of no more than four per cent of the working population; but, in fact, it hardly ever fell below ten per cent for almost twenty years. Hundreds of thousands of workmen used up their fifteen weeks of benefit without there being any sign of a job. 'Extended benefits' (nicknamed the **'dole'**) were introduced; but there was a time limit on them. When they finished the only alternative was Poor Relief. In 1929, however, the whole system of Poor Law Guardians and workhouses was abolished. Responsibility for the jobless who exhausted their insurance benefits eventually passed to a new **Unemployment Assistance Board (1934).** It had offices all over Britain (thus relieving the overworked Labour Exchanges) and was financed out of national taxation.

Meanwhile, the numbers out of work rose above 2 million in 1931, and remained at this high level for three or four years. As part of its 'economy drive', the National Government cut benefits for the insured by ten per cent (1931) and introduced a **means test** for the long-term unemployed. This meant that the amount of financial assistance each man received depended on his family's total income, including pensions and savings. Even if his son had a paper round he had to declare it and his 'dole' was adjusted accordingly. The means test saved the Government several million pounds a year, but only at the cost of greater misery and discontent. It was hated by the unemployed, who resented officials enquiring into their family affairs. Worst of all, it caused bitterness between parents and children. If sons and daughters had regular jobs, father was 'knocked off the dole' and had to be supported by them. Nothing could be more damaging to a man's self-respect.

Most of the time the unemployed suffered in silence. But occasionally public demonstrations and 'hunger marches' were organised, to draw attention to the plight of the depressed areas. In 1936, for example, 200 men from Jarrow in County Durham marched nearly 300 miles to London to present a petition to the Prime Minister. Because of the dismantling of the town's shipyard, almost three-quarters of its working population was idle. The **Jarrow Crusade** stirred the conscience of the nation. So did a B.B.C. broadcast in 1934, when a group of men and women were invited to describe their experience of 'life on the dole':

'When there is a job going, anything up to twelve are sent for it,' said an ex-metal turner, who had served a seven-year apprenticeship. 'That means eleven of us are disappointed; and when this happens over and over again one gets real fed up.'

'My husband has worked about one year out of twelve and a half,' said a mother of four children. 'His face was lovely when I married him, but now he's skin and bones.' Housekeeping was a nightmare. 'I can't manage more than one box of matches a week,' she explained. 'Our kettle's got about six patches on it, made . . . from cocoa tins.'

Although the worst was over by about 1934, unemployment figures remained high for the rest of the 1930s. Families that were lucky enough to have a little savings could afford to move to one of the centres of the newer light industries, where chances of a job were good. Hence there was a rapid growth of population in south-eastern England during this period. For the remainder who stayed in the depressed areas, often the only hope was to obtain a place in a

The Jarrow marchers on their way to London

special government training centre, which prepared workers for new trades. Retraining was especially important for young men, many of whom had reached their mid-twenties without ever having a job. Older men, with little chance of finding work, were often given allotments of land where they could grow vegetables and fruit and rear poultry or rabbits for their families. They found this a great release from boredom and worry.

No 'homes for heroes'

Next to unemployment, **housing** was the greatest social problem of the inter-war years. Even under normal conditions house-building had always lagged behind the growth of population, but, during the First World War, building and repairs stopped almost completely for four years. Consequently, by 1918 there was a shortage of over half a million houses. Moreover, many rows of dismal terraced houses in the towns or crumbling country cottages were unfit to be lived in. At the end of the war, Lloyd George declared that the slums would be swept away and replaced by 'homes fit for heroes'. But this promise, like many others made at the time, proved unduly optimistic.

The full effects of the housing shortage were felt by the poorest sections of the community. As is nearly always the case, those who could afford to pay more got what they wanted. George Orwell put it in a nutshell: '"Housing shortage" . . . means very little to anyone with an income of more than £10 a week, or even £5 a week for that matter.' Even before the war builders were unable to construct houses at rents lower-paid workers could afford (see Chapter 16). The latter mostly had to make do with one or two rooms. But after 1918 a rise in the cost of materials made this problem worse and brought greater overcrowding in the slum areas.

Pre-war governments had done little to increase the supply of houses. They were always reluctant to interfere with private property unless it was an urgent matter of public health. But after the war-time standstill and Lloyd George's rash promise in 1918, direct government action was essential. Beginning with the **Housing Act, 1919,** the Government offered subsidies to local councils to help them provide decent homes for families with low incomes. Private builders could also qualify for financial assistance if they built houses which could be let at low rents. Up to the early 1930s, when subsidies were ended in the National Government's economy drive, estates of **council houses** sprang up all over Britain. They were very plain and rather dull in appearance, but they were far superior to many previous working-class houses, having gardens, inside toilets and bathrooms.

However, despite subsidies, councils still found it difficult to keep rents low enough. Most of their houses were let to higher-paid workers in fairly 'safe' jobs, while the poor and the unemployed had to be satisfied with what they had got. To make matters worse, two-thirds of all houses built in the inter-war years were *sold* to

An early council estate in York

owner-occupiers with comfortable incomes. By the 1930s there were *more than enough* houses in the middle and upper price ranges. The shortage was entirely confined to cheap, rented accommodation for the lower working classes.

In 1930 a special subsidy was offered to local authorities for **slum clearance.** The aim was not just to pull down slums but to rehouse their inhabitants as well. Thus the payment was only made if occupants of the demolished houses were given alternative accommodation at rents they 'could reasonably be expected to pay'. In 1933 councils were asked to prepare five-year programmes for the abolition of slums. But, despite great activity in many areas, only just over half the work was done by 1939 — when war interrupted and put the clock back by several years.

A fuller life

Although the depression cast a shadow of unemployment across many parts of Britain, most people outside the depressed areas enjoyed higher living standards and a fuller life than their fathers and grandfathers had done. Families were smaller, due to the spread of birth control; yet wages were generally better. Working hours had been reduced from about fifty-four to between forty-four and forty-eight a week since the turn of the century. Holidays with pay were introduced by many firms. On the whole the British were healthier than they had ever been. Better food and improved sanitation helped to prevent disease, so that the annual death-rate nearly halved between 1900 and 1939. At the same time, social services like National Insurance, pensions, subsidised housing and education (including milk and meals for needy children) helped to reduce the amount of poverty and ignorance.

In the Victorian Age, most of the working-classes had little energy for anything besides drinking. But by the 1920s and 1930s they enjoyed a wide range of leisure activities and entertainments.

A West End cinema in the 1930s

Most towns had sports clubs and swimming-baths, as well as dance-halls, theatres and music-halls. **Cinema-going** became a national habit in these years. Its popularity was firmly established during and after the First World War, when American 'stars' like Charlie Chaplin, Mary Pickford and Rudolph Valentino became household names. At first films were silent and required captions to give necessary details of the action. A continuous musical background was provided; usually by a pianist. The introduction of the sound-track (1927) transformed the cinema. Natural acting and more complicated and realistic plots were made possible. By the late 1930s, about a quarter of the population went to the films twice a week or more.

For those who wanted to get out and about, there were cheap railway excursions, and many working-class families could now afford motor cars, in which they set off for days in the countryside and holidays by the sea. The first of Billy Butlin's famous holiday camps was opened in 1937, at Skegness. Cycling was still popular, particularly among younger people. The Y.H.A. (Youth Hostels Association) was formed in 1930 to provide simple, inexpensive accommodation for cyclists and hikers.

The **radio** provided families with entertainment in their own homes (see Chapter 21). So did public libraries, which reflected the progress of education by lending a steadily increasing number of books each year. There was also a rapid rise in **newspaper** sales, particularly 'popular' dailies like the *Mirror, Mail, Express* and the

Herald. They set out to appeal to the masses by including strip cartoons, competitions, racing and sports pages and plenty of news about royalty. Large headlines and photographs helped to give these papers an eye-catching appearance.

Timeline

1919　Housing Act begins new policy of state subsidies.
1921　'Black Friday': failure of the Triple Industrial Alliance.
1924　First Labour Government.
1925　'Red Friday': nine month subsidy for the coal industry.
1926　General Strike, followed by great coal strike.
1927　Trade Disputes Act.
1927　First 'talkie' pictures.
1931–5　National Government (Ramsay MacDonald Prime Minister).
1931　Means test.
1934　Unemployment Assistance Board.
1936　'Jarrow Crusade'.

Further study

The growth of social services since 1940 is dealt with in the next chapter. For a general account of life and leisure in modern Britain see: Britain–'the Endless Middle' in Chapter 26.

General accounts
I. Doncaster, *Social Change in Twentieth Century England* (Longman)
D. Lindsay and E. S. Washington, *A Portrait of Britain, 1851–1951* (O.U.P.) pp. 220–9, 238–56
A. Robertson, *The Trade Unions* (Hamish Hamilton) pp. 80–94

Special topics
R. J. Cootes, *The General Strike, 1926* (Longman's Then and There series) traces the background to the dispute from the formation of the Miners' Federation of Great Britain (1889).
B. Barker and R. Boden, *General Strike* (Longman, History Games)
The General Strike (Cape, Jackdaw series no. 105)
Towards Democracy (Longman, Secondary History Packs) Pack 24
R. J. Cootes, *The Making of the Welfare State* (Longman's Modern Times series, pp. 48–63) with optional L.P. record.
On the growth of the cinema and other aspects of entertainment, see:
L. W. Cowie, *Social and Economic History from 1900* (Hamish Hamilton) Chapter 13
D. Kennedy, *Entertainment* (Batsford, Past-into-Present series)
The plight of the unemployed is the subject of several novels of the period, notably:
George Orwell, *The Road to Wigan Pier* and *Down and Out in Paris and London,* Part 2 (both Secker & Warburg and Penguin)
Walter Greenwood, *Love on the Dole* (Cape)

Filmstrip
Twentieth Century Britain, Part 2: Political, Social and Cultural Aspects (Educational Publications)

24 War and the Welfare State
The Second World War and the new social services

In the autumn of 1918, when the guns stopped firing and the nations of Europe counted their dead, most people felt they had witnessed 'the war to end all wars'. It was difficult to believe that statesmen and generals would ever again be capable of such madness and destruction. Yet, only twenty-one years later, Europe and most of the world was engulfed in another violent and bloody struggle.

No easy explanation can be offered, but undoubtedly part of the cause of the Second World War was the **Treaty of Versailles (1919)** which followed the first great conflict. The peace terms imposed on the Germans were unnecessarily harsh. They lost large slices of territory and were ordered to pay enormous reparations (damages) to the Allies. Although these were never paid in full, they did much to prevent the defeated nation from making a genuine recovery from the war. Germans felt humiliated and many of them became bitter and revengeful.

Adolf Hitler and German aggression

The disastrous slump in international trade after 1929 (see Chapter 22) added the suffering and discontent of **mass unemployment** to the already strong political grievances of the German people. By 1930, 6 million Germans were out of work, more than double the British total. Such conditions explain (but do not excuse) the sudden popularity of the National Socialist or **Nazi Party,** led by **Adolf Hitler** (1889–1945), a former house-painter and ex-army corporal. Hitler declared that most of Germany's troubles stemmed from the peace treaty of 1919 and the activities of Jews and communists within the country. He promised social reforms, measures to cure unemployment, and a recovery of German national pride and prestige. The latter was to be achieved by overthrowing the terms of the Treaty of Versailles and bringing all people of German nationality within the frontiers of a restored German Empire.

In 1932 the Nazis became the largest party in the Reichstag (Parliament). Within a year Hitler was Chancellor of Germany. He quickly set out to silence all opposition and to make himself a dictator. Concentration camps were established for the torture and extermination of his political opponents. The minds of the people, especially the youth, were filled with evil doctrines of German racial superiority. Jews, gipsies and other 'racially impure' elements in the population were cruelly persecuted. Meanwhile a recovery of industrial production, assisted by rearmament and public works like road-building, greatly reduced unemployment.

In March 1936 Hitler sent troops into the **Rhineland** area of Germany, which bordered France. It had been declared a demilitarised zone in the Treaty of Versailles, yet, as Hitler expected, Britain and

Hitler speaking at a Nazi Youth rally in 1938

France took no action against him. Their peoples were sick of war and wanted at all costs to avoid a repeat of the horrors of 1914–18. This suited Hitler's plans. Early in 1938 he occupied **Austria** and absorbed it into his new German Empire. **Czechoslovakia** was next on his list, for its population included 3 million Germans (see map on page 297). In September 1938, at a meeting in Munich, **Neville Chamberlain,** Britain's Prime Minister, got Hitler to agree to occupy only Sudetenland, the portion of Czechoslovakia containing people of German nationality. Furthermore, Hitler promised he would attempt no more territorial gains.

Chamberlain returned to London and announced to cheering crowds that he had achieved 'peace in our time'. But not everyone was so sure. Men like Winston Churchill and Duff Cooper (who resigned from the Government at this time) had long warned that there was no limit to Hitler's ambitions. It seemed they were right when, in March 1939, Hitler invaded the rest of Czechoslovakia and began to threaten **Poland.**

Although Britain promised to help the Poles if they were attacked only Russia was close enough to give them immediate support. But the Russians were unprepared for war. In August they signed a treaty of friendship with Germany, leaving Hitler free to attack Poland, which he did on 1 September. Britain and France could stand by no longer. With the deepest regret, they declared war on Germany **(3 September).** Crowds thronging the streets in London and Paris showed none of the excitement and enthusiasm which had marked the beginning of war in 1914.

Chamberlain's triumphant return from his meeting with Hitler at Munich

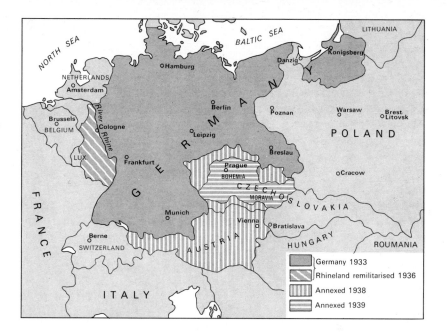

German expansion
1933–39

	Germany 1933
	Rhineland remilitarised 1936
	Annexed 1938
	Annexed 1939

The Second World War, 1939–45

British cities prepared for immediate bombing and poisonous gas attacks. Children were evacuated into the countryside; gas-masks were issued; and all house, shop and office windows were blacked out at night to make it difficult for enemy bombers to find their targets. But the hurry was unnecessary. Throughout the winter of 1939–40 so little happened that the Americans called it **'the phoney war'**. Germany and Russia divided Poland between them (part of their August agreement) but, in the West, the rival armies stayed behind their fortifications. The British spent their time clearing the seas of German merchant shipping and establishing an army in France. Conscription had already been introduced in May 1939.

The phoney war ended suddenly in April 1940, when Germany occupied Denmark and invaded **Norway**. A British naval squadron and a few Anglo-French troops were powerless to resist the German advance. Within a few weeks Norway was in enemy hands. At home, Chamberlain was accused of being half-hearted in his conduct of the war. He resigned, and an all-party **Coalition Government** took over, led by **Winston Churchill**. He was the ideal man for the job. As Britain prepared to face the greatest challenge of modern times, the courage and confidence revealed in Churchill's leadership and in his stirring speeches proved a constant source of inspiration, not only to his own people but to the forces of freedom everywhere.

On the day Churchill became Prime Minister (10 May) Hitler launched his long-awaited offensive in the West. There was no repeat of the deadlock of 1914–18. With great superiority in tanks and other armoured vehicles the Germans swept all before them. As in 1914 they by-passed the main French defences and attacked from the north. Holland and Belgium were soon overrun, and the

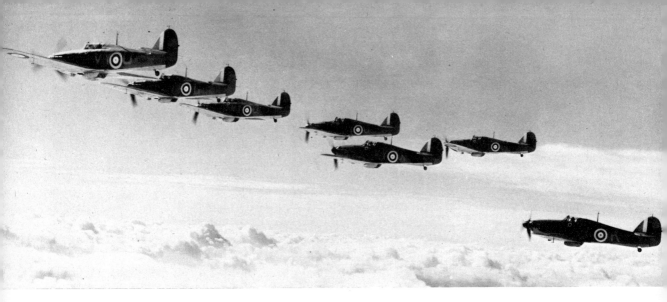

R.A.F. fighters during the Battle of Britain

British army was cut off and forced to retreat to the coast. From 24 May–4 June, 320,000 British and French troops were evacuated from **Dunkirk** and nearby beaches, The Royal Navy was assisted by hundreds of small craft, including ferry boats, pleasure steamers, tugs, yachts and trawlers. Churchill called it 'a miracle of deliverance'; but all the tanks and artillery were lost.

The French army swiftly collapsed and surrendered on 25 June. A fortnight earlier the Italian dictator, **Benito Mussolini,** had brought his country in on what he thought was the winning side. The British Empire stood alone, while Hitler prepared a cross-Channel invasion. Some Englishmen regarded the situation as hopeless; but not Churchill. 'We shall defend our island, whatever the cost may be,' he said, 'we shall *never* surrender.' The beaches were covered with barbed-wire and land-mines, and church bells were silent, reserved to sound the alert. However, before Hitler's invasion fleet could safely put out to sea, he had to gain superiority in the air. Goering, in command of the *Luftwaffe* (air force) assured his master that all he needed was 'five days of fine weather'. They were both due for a surprise.

Early in August the Luftwaffe began its task of destroying the R.A.F. and the airfields of southern England. But for the first time it met highly efficient opposition, equipped with coastal radar stations and spearheaded by Spitfire fighters, which were slightly superior to the German Messerschmitts. Although greatly outnumbered, British pilots inflicted such heavy losses on the enemy that by mid September the invasion plan was postponed indefinitely. The **Battle of Britain** was over. Hitler's plans had been upset by the skill and courage of a few hundred R.A.F. fighter pilots, nearly all of them under twenty-five. 'Never', said Churchill, 'was so much owed by so many to so few.' The Luftwaffe switched to night raids on London and other major cities, hoping to cripple British war production. **The Blitz,** as it was called, lasted into the spring of 1941. Night after

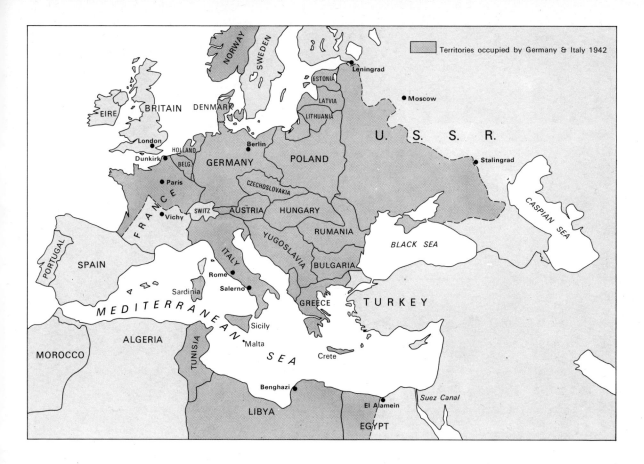

night, sirens warned families to take cover—in cellars, specially built air-raid shelters or, in London, Underground Railway stations. Despite widespread destruction, British resistance was unshaken.

Meanwhile the entry of Italy into the war threatened Britain's position in the Mediterranean. Tanks and troop reinforcements were sent to **Egypt,** to protect the Suez Canal and the vital oil supplies of the Middle East. At the end of 1940, when the Italians advanced from their colony of Libya into Egypt, British troops forced them back to Benghazi. But early in 1941 the German 'Afrika Korps' arrived under General Rommel. The British were themselves driven back into Egypt. Germany also rescued its ally in south-eastern Europe, conquering Greece, Yugoslavia and Crete (April–May 1941) after the failure of an Italian attack on Greece. However, **Malta,** Britain's 'unsinkable aircraft carrier', managed to survive heavy air attacks from enemy bases in Sicily.

In June 1941 Hitler broke his treaty of friendship and attacked **Russia,** the only possible military rival left on the Continent. An enormous army, supported by the Luftwaffe, met little resistance as it advanced along a 1500-mile front, stretching from the Baltic to the Black Sea. But as the Russians retreated across the plains they deliberately burnt towns, villages and farms. Short of food and deprived of buildings in which to quarter their troops, the German generals met a similar fate to that of Napoleon 130 years before.

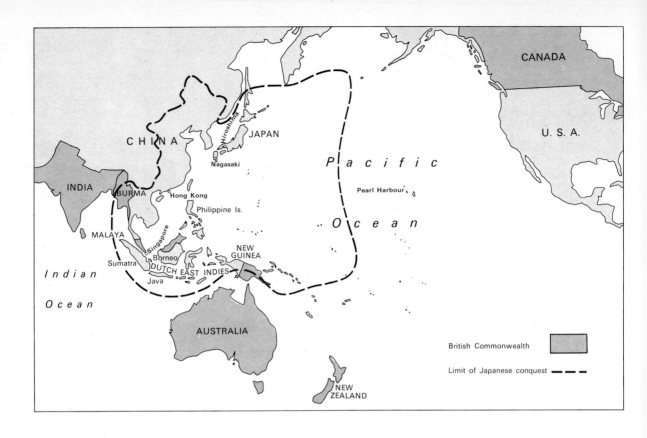

They were unprepared for a winter campaign, and their soldiers suffered terribly from the bitter weather and the Russian counter-attacks. Instead of gaining a quick victory, Hitler merely sacrificed hundreds of thousands of troops and masses of equipment. In the following year advances made in good weather were again checked when winter set in.

The war became truly worldwide in December 1941, when Japanese aircraft made a surprise attack on the U.S. Pacific fleet at **Pearl Harbour** in Hawaii. While European countries with posses-sions in the Far East were fully occupied, the Japanese aimed to acquire an empire in South-East Asia. They realised America would try to stop them, so they struck the first blow. Within six months, they had conquered the whole of the Far East, including the British territories of Malaya and Burma, the Dutch East Indies and the Philippines. But in the end Pearl Harbour proved as decisive as Hitler's attack on Russia. Britain gained as an ally the most powerful nation on earth. Henceforward U.S. forces not only set out to crush Japan but also led a counter-offensive in North Africa and Western Europe.

The turning of the tide in Africa came in October 1942, when the British Eighth Army, commanded by General Montgomery, defeated Rommel at **El Alamein.** The Afrika Korps retreated across Libya into Tunisia where it was trapped by Anglo-American forces under the U.S. General Eisenhower. In May 1943 over 250,000 German

The Second World War in the Far East

War in the desert (1942)

The Japanese attack on
Pearl Harbour.

and Italian soldiers were captured and Africa was cleared of the enemy. The Allies could now concentrate on freeing Europe from the grip of the Nazi dictator.

In the summer of 1943 Anglo-American forces captured Sicily and invaded **Italy.** Mussolini was overthrown before they arrived and the new Italian Government gave up the struggle; but German troops quickly occupied the country and put up a stiff resistance. Elsewhere, things were going badly for Hitler. Allied bombers were reducing many German cities to ruins. The Russians had won a great victory at **Stalingrad** early in the year and were now on the attack. Even the menace of German submarines in the Atlantic was being mastered. During 1941–2, British merchant ships suffered terrible losses; but by 1943 U-boats were being hunted successfully with long-range aircraft using searchlights and radar.

Meanwhile the Allies made plans to recover a foothold in Western Europe. On 6 June 1944 Anglo-American forces, commanded by Eisenhower, landed on the beaches of **Normandy.** After three months of hard fighting, France and Belgium were recovered, making possible the destruction of many launching sites for Hitler's 'new weapons',

the V1 flying-bomb and the V2 long-range rocket. By March 1945 Allied forces crossed the Rhine and struck into the heart of Germany. The Russians were closing in on the other flank. As they entered the suburbs of Berlin, on 30 April, Hitler shot himself. An armistice was signed on 8 May—**V.E.** (victory in Europe) **Day**—which was marked by scenes of great rejoicing in Britain. Japan held out for another three months, until August, when America dropped the first **atomic bombs** on Hiroshima and Nagasaki. Over 100,000 people died, and countless thousands were scarred and disabled in the terrible blast of heat, fire and radiation. The Japanese surrendered almost immediately (14 August).

In the end, British and Commonwealth forces lost about 400,000 dead, less than half the total of 1914–18. A further 60,000 British civilians were killed in air-raids. On the other hand, the Russians, who withstood the full force of the German onslaught, lost no less than 6 million soldiers and almost as many civilians. Europeans had suffered terribly under Hitler, especially the Jews, 6 million of whom were exterminated in gas chambers. Yet the Western Allies tried to avoid repeating the mistakes of 1919. Some of the Nazi ringleaders were tried and executed, but the rest of the German people were encouraged to get their country back on its feet as soon as possible so that it could take its proper place in a peaceful world. However, the attitude of the Russians proved a stumbling-block. They were unwilling to move out of East Germany; with the result that the country had to be divided into eastern and western occupied zones. The **Cold War** against the Communist World had begun.

In October 1945 the **United Nations Organisation** (U.N.O.) was created, with its headquarters at New York. It aimed to succeed where the earlier League of Nations had failed, by getting nations to settle their differences without the use of force.

Allied troops landing on
the Normandy beaches, 6
June 1944

The 'home front': warfare and welfare

Although there was no fighting on British soil, the menace of the
Luftwaffe and the shortages resulting from U-boat attacks on shipping
affected the lives of every man, woman and child. The Government
quickly realised that the safety and welfare of civilians was no less
important than the need to supply the armed forces.

Even before war was declared **evacuation** began. From the
1 to the 3 September 1939 well over a million people, mostly children,
were evacuated into the countryside from areas close to probable
air-raid targets. Further movements brought the total of evacuees up
to about 3 million by 1941. **Food rationing** began in 1940, and
became increasingly strict as time went by. Everyone had a ration
book containing coupons which were given up each time certain
basic foods were purchased. In this way the Government hoped to
ensure a fair distribution. Most important of all, the Government
found it necessary to expand existing **social services,** including
infant and child welfare, medical care, pensions and other forms of
financial assistance. Help was urgently required by growing numbers
of bombed-out families, wives of dead servicemen, old people cut
off from their relations, young children whose mothers were working
in essential industries, and many others.

An **Assistance Board** was created (1940) out of the old Unemployment Assistance Board. It aided bombed-out families and
others in distress, provided home-helps for the sick and elderly, and
distributed cash where necessary. For instance, supplementary
(extra) pensions were paid to over a million old people and widows.
The shortages, mishaps and dangers of war were shared by the whole
population. Consequently the Government set out to provide social
services for all who had need of them, not just the poor. In the
process, it took a vital step towards the modern idea of a *Welfare
State.*

High priority was given to the health and nourishment of infants
and young children. During the Blitz, the Ministry of Health began

Young evacuees talk to the
stationmaster at Euston
before leaving London for
the Midlands

a campaign to have children immunised against **diphtheria,** a killing disease which was likely to spread rapidly among families crowding in air-raid shelters. It was a wise decision. While war-time deaths from diphtheria rose alarmingly in most other European countries, in Britain they fell to a quarter of the pre-war figure by 1945.

A **National Milk Scheme** was introduced in 1940. All children under five and expectant and nursing mothers were entitled to a pint a day for 2*d* (free in some cases) instead of the full price of 4½*d*. In the following year, cod-liver oil and blackcurrant extracts (later replaced by orange juice from America) were provided for expectant mothers and young children. These *vitamin foods* were free at first, but a small charge was soon introduced. After the war the Welfare Foods Service continued, along with cheap milk for young children.

Up to July 1940 **school meals** were a form of Poor Relief, provided only for undernourished children. But then came a complete change of policy. With so many mothers working in war-time industries, the Government encouraged Local Education Authorities to provide subsidised meals for as many children as possible, regardless of their parents' incomes. Similarly, from September 1941, **school milk** was provided for all children at a subsidised price, or free if necessary. There could be no going back on these great advances when the war ended. School meals were provided for all who wanted them, at a reduced price or free in cases of need; and ⅓ pint of milk was given free to every child. (Free milk was restricted to primary schools in 1968 and to infants, aged 5–7, in 1971.)

The Beveridge Report (1942)

In the past, schemes of social security had been introduced from time to time without any overall plan. Thus there were different rates of benefit for the sick and the unemployed, even though their needs were similar; more than one contribution card was necessary, and a number of government departments controlled separate funds for similar purposes. With this in mind, the Government appointed a Committee of Inquiry (1941) to investigate 'existing national schemes of social insurance' and to suggest improvements. Its Chairman, who had sole responsibility for the contents of the report, was a senior civil servant, **Sir William Beveridge.** He was ideally suited to the task, having a greater knowledge and experience of social insurance than any other man of his time.

In his Report (November 1942) Beveridge proposed that all the bits and pieces of insurance and pensions should be replaced by *one* scheme, covering *all* citizens whatever their income. People of working age, together with their employers, would pay a weekly contribution, recorded by a stamp on a single card. In return, benefits would be paid on 'interruption of earnings'—sickness, unemployment, retirement or widowhood—for 'as long as the need continues'. All citizens would be equal members of the scheme, therefore no means test would be necessary. The actual rates of benefit would be based on a minimum standard of living 'below which no one should be allowed to fall'. There would be special allowances to cover extra expenditure, including maternity and funeral grants.

Sir William Beveridge explains his Plan

In addition to the insurance scheme, Beveridge urged the Government to pay weekly *family allowances* to parents for each dependent child. These were needed because a man's wages did not increase as his family grew in size.

The insurance scheme was not a complete system of social security. It dealt only with *want,* and, as Beveridge said, 'Want is only one of the five giants on the road of . . . social progress.' The other 'giants' were *Disease,* which could be overcome by a new health service 'for all citizens'; *Ignorance,* which would have to be attacked with 'more and better schools'; *Squalor,* which could be avoided with 'more and better houses', and *Idleness* or unemployment. The latter could only be kept in check by greater government control of industry.

The Beveridge Report was the greatest single influence on the making of the Welfare State. The public received it like a new gospel. Long queues formed outside His Majesty's Stationery Office, where the Report was on sale, and a special pamphlet on it was circulated among soldiers overseas. At first the Government refused to commit itself to the Beveridge plan. It was anxious not to raise false hopes, remembering the failure of the bright promises of 1918. But eventually, in 1944, a new **Ministry of National Insurance** was set up to prepare a scheme of social security along the lines proposed by Beveridge.

Secondary education for all

During the 1920s and 1930s, many new schools had been built. The curriculum had been widened to include science, more handicrafts and physical training, and an increasing number of able children from poor families had gained free places in secondary schools. But serious inequalities remained. If they were not particularly clever, working-class children remained at elementary schools until they left at fourteen. On the other hand, unless they were very stupid, children from wealthy homes were sent to grammar schools or some other kind of fee-paying school until they were sixteen or eighteen.

In 1926 a special Committee under Sir Henry Hadow recommended secondary education for all. The **Hadow Report** criticised 'all-age schools', where children spent their entire school life in the same buildings. It proposed a separate infant and junior school, from which pupils would be transferred at eleven to either grammar or senior elementary school, according to their 'different interests and abilities'. The Hadow Committee accepted the views of a few *psychologists* that intelligence could be measured by special tests, on the basis of which children could be selected for different types of education. But this practice was based on the belief that a child's achievement in school always corresponds with its inherited ability. In recent years this has been shown to be a false assumption—by *sociologists* and others studying the influence on school achievement of the child's home, its parents and its ambitions. Nevertheless, the Hadow Report was accepted without question by most Local Education Authorities. The reorganisation it suggested was about two-thirds completed by 1939.

Under the guidance of R. A. Butler, President of the Board (soon to be the Ministry) of Education, all the war-time plans for reform were brought together in the **Education Act of 1944.** (It applied only to England and Wales. The Scottish system continued to develop independently and required separate Acts of Parliament.) '*Free* secondary education for all' was to be the basis of the post-war system. The reorganisation suggested by the Hadow Report would be completed, with some important differences, notably the abolition of fee-paying in practically all grammar schools. It was the intention of the Government to remove wealth as a direct influence on state education, although fee-paying schools continued to flourish outside the state system.

The idea of 'elementary' education disappeared completely. In future there would be three successive stages—primary, secondary and further. The earliest leaving age was to be raised to fifteen almost immediately (it was done in 1947) and to sixteen as soon as possible after that. Physically and mentally handicapped children were not left out. It was the duty of each Local Education Authority to provide suitable schools for all children according to 'age, ability and aptitude', and also milk, meals and dental services.

A great expansion of universities and colleges of advanced technology (C.A.T.s) was also planned; together with more grants to enable pupils to study full-time for degrees without financial support from their parents. It was also intended to provide three years of part-time further education for early leavers at *county colleges.* But lack of money, teachers and buildings meant this plan was pushed into the background. Instead, 'day release' classes at colleges of further education and technical colleges were expanded, giving young people a chance to study while they were in a regular job.

Practically all children now took the 'eleven plus' examination to decide whether they should go to a grammar or technical school, with an 'academic' curriculum, or to a *modern school,* where the

R. A. Butler—architect of the 1944 Act

A modern classroom

A school of the present— and future

emphasis was on practical subjects. This system of selection was soon widely criticised. Many doubted the wisdom of making decisions about a child's future at such an early age, especially as the exam itself was not always reliable. Before long, newspapers carried stories of 'eleven plus failures' obtaining university degrees. All three types of secondary school were supposed to be equal in prestige, but this was just wishful thinking. Grammar schools were the objective of most parents and children, for they provided the surest route to higher education and the best-paid jobs.

To give their children greater opportunities, modern schools developed extended courses to sixteen, entering their most capable pupils for the **G.C.E.** (General Certificate of Education) which replaced the old School Certificate in 1951. As the numbers staying on an extra year in the secondary modern increased, the **C.S.E.** (Certificate of Secondary Education) was introduced in 1965, to cater for most of them. By this time many local authorities had modified the 'eleven plus' or scrapped it altogether in favour of **comprehensive schools.** These took children of all abilities at eleven and provided the whole range of courses for them. Comprehensive schools had been gaining in popularity for many years before they were made official policy by the new Labour Government in 1965. From then on, massive schemes of 'secondary reorganisation' began, often involving the amalgamation of former grammar and modern schools into single units.

Meanwhile, the shortage of teachers and suitable buildings

continued to hold up other necessary reforms. Twenty years after the war, seventy per cent of all primary schools and forty per cent of modern schools were in buildings more than fifty years old! Not until 1964 did the Government decide to raise the leaving age to sixteen. Even so, this did not come into operation until 1973.

Social security: the attack on want

Churchill's Coalition Government began the attack on the first of Beveridge's five giants—*Ignorance*—with the war-time Education Act. But the task of tackling the remaining giants fell, somewhat unexpectedly, to a Labour ministry led by **Clement Attlee** (1883–1967). In the **1945 election,** Labour won 393 seats out of 639, thus gaining an overall majority for the first time. It had been generally expected that Churchill's war record would ensure victory for his party, the Conservatives. But many voters blamed them for the miseries of the depression, the 'dole' queues and the means test. To break with the past they turned to the Labour Party, which had only held power for a total of three years before 1945. The new Government faced a mammoth task. Britain was almost bankrupt, many towns had suffered appalling bomb damage, and food, clothing and fuel were in short supply and still strictly rationed. Yet the people demanded 'social security from the cradle to the grave' and they would accept no excuses or delay.

Clement Attlee

Family allowances had already become law in 1945, before the election, although the first payments were not made until August 1946. Five shillings a week was paid for each child *after the first* up to the age of sixteen (now eighteen) or the start of full-time employment, whichever came first. They were increased in 1952, 1956 (when third and additional children received more than the second), and 1967–68, but each time they failed to catch up with the rising cost of living. All families could qualify for allowances, so no means test was necessary. But in 1967, when higher rates were fixed, the Government decided to take back this extra allowance from better-off families by raising their income tax.

The chief proposals of the Beveridge Report formed the basis of the **National Insurance Act, 1946.** It made insurance compulsory for everyone of working age, except married women. In return for a single weekly contribution (4s 11d for employed persons when the scheme started in 1948) there were sickness and unemployment benefits, retirement and widows' pensions, guardians' allowances, maternity benefits and a funeral grant. It was, in the words of James Griffiths, Minister of National Insurance, 'the best and cheapest insurance policy offered . . . to any people anywhere'. A separate, but linked, scheme was introduced by the **Industrial Injuries Act, 1946.** It provided compensation for those injured, disabled or killed at work.

These Acts remain the basis of present day social insurance, with one major change of principle. By the late 1950s, wages were rising so rapidly that National Insurance benefits could not keep in step, despite regular increases. Consequently, **graduated pensions** were introduced (1961). The majority of employees who did not already belong to a private pension scheme paid a little extra each week for

An employment exchange, opened in 1949. Notice the padded chairs and comfortable benches. It makes an interesting comparison with the 1910 Labour Exchange, shown on page 250

a larger pension on retirement. The higher their earnings, the greater both the contribution and the resulting pension would be. In 1966 the same principle was applied to sickness and unemployment benefits and widows' pensions **(wage-related short-term benefits)**. For an extra graded contribution, benefits from the third to the twenty-sixth week were substantially increased and scaled in relation to the normal income of each applicant.

To round off the system of social security, a new **National Assistance Board** was established (1948). It catered for those who needed help even though they had not paid for it through insurance. These included the blind, deaf, crippled and insane, the homeless, deserted or unmarried mothers and the wives and children of criminals. In addition, National Assistance provided a 'safety-net' for people whose needs were not fully met by National Insurance benefits. These were mostly old people who found that as prices rose pensions became insufficient. They were encouraged to apply to the Assistance Board for Supplementary Pensions. In 1966 National Assistance and National Insurance were put together under a new Ministry of Social Security (merged with the Health Ministry in 1968 to form the **Department of Health and Social Security**).

Post-war Governments took positive steps to prevent a return of

Aneurin Bevan

mass unemployment, the 'giant *Idleness'*, which could wreck all the schemes of social security. To maintain almost **full employment**, they tried to control things like the distribution of industry and the retraining of redundant workers for new jobs. As it turned out, post-war unemployment figures were even lower than planners like Beveridge had hoped. This was largely due to a steady expansion of international trade, which provided plenty of work for the vital exporting industries.

Health and housing

The attack on the two remaining giants, *Disease* and *Squalor,* was the special task of **Aneurin Bevan,** who, as Minister of Health (1945–50) was responsible for both health and housing policy. The creation of a free health service for all was one of his great ambitions. It was achieved, like most of the other post-war reforms, on the basis of war-time experience and planning. In making arrangements for the reception of air-raid casualties, Chamberlain's Government had discovered alarming shortages of hospital beds, nursing staff and medical equipment of all kinds, including such essentials as operating theatres. Equally serious was the small number of doctors practising in industrial towns, especially in the 'depressed areas'. Because state health insurance only covered wage-earners, not their wives and children, many doctors were reluctant to practise in the poorer districts for fear that their bills would not be paid. Most of them lived and worked in pleasant residential areas where patients were normally quite well off.

Realising the urgent need for reform, the Coalition Government produced a plan for a free state medical service (1944). Labour made some important changes in it before the **National Health Service Act** was passed in 1946. The whole range of medical treatment, including the services of dentists and opticians, was provided for every citizen, financed out of national taxation. To ensure a more even distribution of G.P.s (general practitioners) the Medical Practices Committee drafted new applicants to 'undoctored areas'. Hospital services were also remodelled. All but the teaching hospitals were *nationalised* (taken into public ownership) under the Ministry of Health. England and Wales was divided into fourteen sections (now fifteen) each under a Regional Hospital Board. In addition, County and County Borough Councils provided midwives, home nurses and health visitors, as well as ambulances. None of these had previously been compulsory. A completely new idea was the creation of local authority *Health Centres,* where family doctors could work together, with the latest equipment, and call on the skills of specialists when required.

The National Health Service came into operation on the same day as National Insurance and National Assistance—5 July 1948—the so-called **Appointed Day** for the official beginning of the Welfare State. Immediately, family doctors' surgeries were invaded like bargain sales, and dentists and opticians were booked solid for months ahead. Critics of the scheme said taxpayers' money was being squandered on people whose only aim was to get something

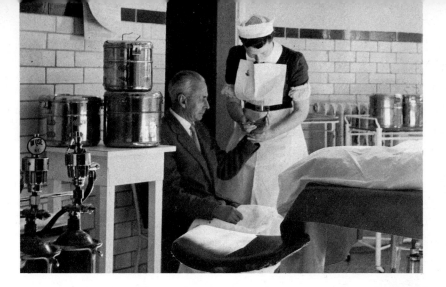

for nothing. But the Government pointed out that much of the early pressure on the health services was the result of previous neglect. Millions of people who needed spectacles did not have them, and millions more had allowed their teeth to decay rather than pay for dental treatment.

Although some private medical practice continued, well over ninety-five per cent of all doctors and patients joined the scheme. In terms of money and manpower, it was the second largest undertaking in the country, next to the armed forces. Nevertheless shortages of money, staff and equipment continued. Health Centres, which were intended to be the heart of the new service, did not exist in many areas twenty years or more after the Act was passed. Without them, hospitals were burdened with an increasing number of outpatients. The great cost of National Health soon resulted in **charges** being made on patients. Part of the cost of prescriptions, spectacles and dental treatment had to be paid, starting in 1951. Bevan, then the Minister of Labour, resigned from the Government. He protested that charges were against the principle of a *free* health service. The earliest contributions were small, but twenty years later they had grown large enough to deter some patients from seeking treatment.

During the Second World War, almost a third of Britain's houses were damaged or destroyed by enemy action. At the same time, building almost ceased. The result was a desperate **housing shortage**—far worse than that of 1918. An emergency house-building drive was essential; but, in the meantime, temporary accommodation had to be found for the homeless. Army huts and aeroplane factories were converted into dwellings, and colonies of 'pre-fabs' were built from factory-made sections bolted together on concrete bases. Even then, many small houses had two families living in them.

The Government concentrated on building estates of subsidised **council houses** and flats for renting. The construction of private houses for sale was severely restricted. Despite acute shortages of raw materials and skilled tradesmen, Britain produced more new

Part of Harlow New Town in Essex

houses in the first five years after the war than any other European country. A **New Towns Act, 1946,** combined the need for more homes with the task of reducing overcrowding in the main centres of population. Aided by government subsidies, these new communities were established close to London and other great cities to take their 'overspill'. The first twelve were begun by 1950, among them Crawley, Stevenage, Corby and Peterlee. In the next twenty-five years, twenty-one more were designated—bringing the total to twenty-three in England and Wales, six in Scotland and four in Northern Ireland. These developments gave planners the chance to try new ideas, such as traffic-free shopping centres and the separation of industrial zones from residential areas.

In the first ten years after the war, three-quarters of all new dwellings were council houses. They had previously been intended for the working-classes, but now they became more classless, like the other social services. Many council tenants had well-paid jobs and expensive cars. There were frequent objections to this, on the grounds that it was senseless to subsidise the houses of families that could afford the full rent. By the mid 1950s, although the overall shortage seemed never-ending and many condemned houses were still occupied, some of the worst problems had been overcome. In 1956, government subsidies to local councils were discontinued— except those for slum clearance. From then on, **private house-building** accelerated. More and more people borrowed money from building societies to buy their own homes. But high prices put house-purchase beyond the reach of millions of families.

Timeline
1919   Treaty of Versailles.
1926   Hadow Report (proposes secondary education for all).

1933	Hitler comes to power in Germany.
1939–45	The Second World War.
1942	The Beveridge Report.
1944	Education Act (free secondary education for all).
1945	Family Allowances.
1946	New Towns Act.
1948	Appointed Day—5 July—official beginning of the Welfare State. Start of National Insurance, National Assistance and the National Health Service.
1961	Graduated Pensions introduced.
1966	Wage-related short-term benefits.
1968	Department of Health and Social Security.

Further study

There have been a number of changes in the social services since this book was written. To obtain up-to-date information, consult the local offices of government ministries such as the Department of Health and Social Security.

Visit
The Imperial War Museum, Lambeth Road, London SE1.

General accounts
C. Bayne-Jardine, *World War Two* (Longman's Modern Times series)
R. J. Cootes, *The Making of the Welfare State* (Longman's Modern Times series). Chapters 9–13, 15. With optional L.P. record.
R. R. Sellman, *The Second World War* (Methuen's Outlines series)
Peter Lane, *A History of Post-War Britain* (Macdonald). Chapters 3, 4 and 10 on the Welfare State.
J. Roberts and A. Rowe, *Making the Present, 1918–72* (Hutchinson)
Series Two of Longman's Social Science Studies includes:
David Whittaker, *The Social Services*
Alan O'Donnell, *Education and Society*

Special topics
Britain at War, 1942 (Cape, Jackdaw series, no. 66)
N. D. Smith, *The Battle of Britain* (Faber, Men and Events)
N. Longmate, *How We Lived Then* (Hutchinson, Arrow Books) History of everyday life during the Second World War.
Social Welfare (Longman, Secondary History Packs) Packs 14, 15
On *Sir Winston Churchill* there are several short biographies to choose from, including those by
David Dilks (Hamish Hamilton, Men and Movements)
Alan Farrell (Faber, Men and Events)
N. D. Smith (Methuen's Outlines series)

Filmstrips
Sir Winston Churchill (Hulton, Pictorial Biographies)
Parts of 'Education' (Educational Productions)

25 Towards Automation

Modern industry, agriculture, transport and communications

Throughout the war years, the Government controlled almost every aspect of national life, including industry and agriculture. Factories were converted for the production of shells, bombs and guns, parachutes and uniforms, army lorries and tanks, R.A.F. fighters and bombers. Farmers were paid subsidies to plough up grassland and grow more grain. In these and many other ways, state control was far more extensive than it had been in 1914–18. When peace returned, the Government could hardly withdraw its guiding hand completely, especially in view of the lessons learned during the depression.

Public ownership

A sudden ending of state controls was all the more unlikely after Labour's victory in the election of 1945. The Labour Party had long been in favour of **nationalisation**—the compulsory transfer of industries from private ownership to state management. In particular, it believed that things like fuel, power and transport services, which everyone needed, should not be run for private profit. Therefore, between 1946 and 1949, coal, railways and many other transport services, electricity and gas were taken into public ownership and thoroughly reorganised.

Nationalisation of the coal industry had been recommended by a Royal Commission back in 1919 (see Chapter 23). If its advice had been taken, the General Strike would probably have been avoided. Relations between miners and their employers had long been clouded by distrust and suspicion, so Labour's Coal Nationalisation Act (1946) received the wholehearted support of the National Union of Mineworkers. Compensation amounting to £164,660,000 was awarded to the coal-owners, and on 1 January 1947 the **National Coal Board** took over the industry and began a vast modernisation scheme. Exactly a year later, the **British Transport Commission** was set up. It took control of the four railway companies (merged into *British Railways*) along with the canals, docks and steamers they owned, all long-distance road haulage (which became *British Road Services*) and London's buses and Underground trains. Shortly afterwards, the production and distribution of **electricity** was nationalised (1948) and, in the following year, all private and municipal **gas-works** were purchased by the state.

So far, opposition to the Government's policy was fairly mild. In almost every case, private owners had been unable to finance the extensive improvements that these services required. But the nationalisation of the principal **iron and steel** firms (1951) met stiff resistance. These companies were modern and profitable manufacturing concerns in which large sums of money had recently been invested. The Conservatives, who came back to power in 1951, returned iron and steel to private ownership (1953) and also most road haulage business, another aspect of the previous Government's policy to which they were opposed. Not to be outdone, Harold Wilson's Labour ministry re-nationalised the iron and steel industry in 1967.

Fuel and power

Coal is still Britain's main source of power, despite the growing use of fuel-oil, natural gas and, to a lesser extent, nuclear energy. The main uses of coal are in the production of electricity, gas, iron and steel. It is also a domestic fuel, and a raw material in the manufacture of chemicals, artificial fibres and plastics. To compensate for the continuing decline in the number of miners, the National Coal Board has invested millions of pounds in labour-saving machinery, much of it in the great Yorks-Derby-Notts coalfield, which now produces almost half the country's total output. In the first ten years after the war, coal production increased, but now it is on the decline and unprofitable pits are being closed down in large numbers. Many of the best and most convenient deposits were exhausted long ago, so every year coal has to be mined from deeper and thinner seams.

British coal output (in millions of tons)

1945	1954	1964	1974
175	223	193	107

It has been estimated that Britain's reserves of coal will last another 200 years at the present level of output.

Over half of the country's coal output is consumed by electric power stations. But even in the production of electricity its supremacy is beginning to be challenged by the growing use of **atomic**

Bevercotes Colliery in Nottinghamshire—Britain's first automated pit. All operations are linked to a central control room

Bradwell nuclear power
station, on the Essex coast

energy, a development in which Britain led the world. An *atom* is
a small particle of a chemical element. Its *nucleus* (central core) is
held together by very powerful forces. Scientists have found that the
fission (splitting) of the uranium nucleus releases immense heat
which can be used to raise steam for driving the turbines of electricity
generators. Britain's first nuclear power station was opened in 1956
at Calder Hall, on the Cumberland coast. By 1973 nuclear power
stations provided nine per cent of Britain's electricity supply—about
one-sixth of the world total of nuclear generation.

Meanwhile, British consumption of **petroleum** has increased by
leaps and bounds. Different kinds and grades are required as fuel for
aeroplanes, cars, diesel lorries and railway engines, ships and
furnaces; and a wide range of lubricating oils is used for everything
from the engines of an ocean liner to the moving parts of a watch.
In 1939 three-quarters of Britain's supply of petroleum was refined
before it was shipped (all but a tiny fraction is imported). Since the
war many large refineries have been built in the United Kingdom,
notably at Fawley, near Southampton, Stanlow, in Cheshire, Milford
Haven, in West Wales, and along the Thames estuary. Industries using
petroleum by-products have grown up alongside the refineries. They
include paint, synthetic rubber and plastics (together known as
'petro-chemicals').

In 1973 over 104 million tons of oil were refined in Britain, compared with only 4 million tons in 1948. All this time Britain depended on imported supplies. But vital discoveries of oil in the British sector of the North Sea, from 1970, promised to make the U.K. a major oil producer within a few years. The first North Sea oil was brought ashore in 1975, when it was estimated that Britain would be able to supply all its own needs by the early 1980s.

Part of the Esso Refinery at Fawley, near Southampton

Manufacturing industries

The gradual decline of long-established industries like shipbuilding and cotton and woollen textiles, which began with the First World War, continued after 1945. But the gap was filled by a newer range of manufactures, including motor vehicles and aircraft, electronic equipment, plastics and artificial fibres like nylon and terylene. Largely because of these developments, Britain gained many new export markets and was able to recover from the war without experiencing a return of mass unemployment.

The **motor industry** continued to develop in the Midlands and the South-East, although in recent years manufacturing and assembly plants have been opened in South Wales, the Scottish Lowlands and on Merseyside. As a result of a series of amalgamations, production became concentrated in the hands of a few large firms. Four of them—

the British Leyland Motor Corporation, Ford, Chrysler and Vauxhall —produced over ninety-five per cent of Britain's motor vehicles in the early 1970s. The United Kingdom is one of the world's major exporters of cars and commercial vehicles.

The manufacture of **aircraft and aero-engines** was one of the most prosperous export industries after the war. Scores of new factories sprang up in places like Bristol, Coventry and Hatfield. Planes like the Comet and the Viscount, which went into service in 1952 and 1953, demonstrated Britain's world leadership in jet aircraft design. At the same time, Rolls-Royce jet engines became as internationally famous as Rolls-Royce cars. But by the 1960s, a serious falling off in sales of military aircraft in particular led to a major setback for the industry. British producers had to rely increasingly on sales of aero-engines. However even this branch of the industry seemed far from healthy when Rolls-Royce went bankrupt and had to be taken over by the Government in 1971.

Many aspects of modern industry—and of the modern world in general—cannot be explained in straightforward language to the non-expert. **Electronics** is a good example, particularly the production of *computers*. These were first used, shortly after the war, to work out complicated mathematical problems in science and engineering. Computers cannot think for themselves, but they can make calculations and perform routine tasks at incredible speeds. By the 1950s they were being used in many large offices, handling orders or compiling pay-slips by the thousand. More recently they have been introduced into factories to control and check manufacturing processes automatically. When this latest development in computers becomes normal practice, we will have *automation*. Many of the hardest and most repetitive jobs will disappear, and the

Top left: The start of the final assembly line in Ford's paint, trim and assembly building at Dagenham

Above: Computers at work

majority of factory workers will be programmers, electronic engineers, maintenance technicians and 'machine monitors'.

Modern scientific research has led to changes not only in manufacturing processes but also in industrial materials. Numerous metal alloys have been created, together with a whole new range of **plastics**. The latter, made by complicated chemical processes, provide a cheap and strong alternative to metal and wood, with the added advantage of being easy to mould into the required shape. Plastics can be used for almost anything from radio cabinets and furniture to pens and toothbrushes. Chemical research has also resulted in the growth of a new **man-made fibres** industry. The first fibre to be made entirely from chemical substances was *nylon,* which was developed in the U.S.A. and first produced in Britain in 1941. It combines lightness with great strength and can be used for the finest stockings or the toughest rope. *Terylene,* which was developed in Britain around the same time, has many similar uses to nylon. It is light, strong and hardwearing and creases or pleats in terylene clothes can be 'heat-set' for life.

Iron and steel remain the basic materials in all kinds of engineering. For this reason the iron and steel industry has been the only one of the old-established industries which has continued to expand in recent years. Britain's output of steel doubled between 1945 and 1960, almost half of it produced in two areas, South Wales and north-eastern England. Many plants have been reconstructed with up-to-date equipment, and massive new steelworks have been built, especially in South Wales, the Scottish Lowlands and on Tees-side. In the early 1970s Britain was the world's fifth largest steel-producing nation.

Just as in the average High Street supermarkets have captured much of the trade of small 'family grocers', so in industry, large concerns like I.C.I., British Leyland Motor Corporation, Unilever and General Electric have taken over or put out of business many lesser firms. Enormous companies like these are able to finance large-scale research and modernisation, thus making themselves more efficient. Every British citizen depends on such developments, especially in the export industries. Foreign earnings have to pay for most of the country's food and four-fifths of its raw materials. If British firms cease to be competitive in overseas markets, exports will decline and so will the people's standard of living.

The revival of agriculture

At the start of the Second World War, about two-thirds of the country's food was imported. Thus when German submarines began to sink merchant ships by the hundred, agriculture became as important to Britain's survival as the manufacture of armaments. The greatest need was for more home-produced grain, therefore the Government paid a subsidy of £2 per acre to farmers who ploughed up grassland and sowed corn crops. As a result, the total acreage of arable land increased by a half. In the emergency, wasteland was cleared with bulldozers, playing-fields were ploughed up and even roadside verges were planted with rows of potatoes. To make way for the change, the Government encouraged farmers to reduce stocks of poultry, sheep and pigs—but not cattle, for these were necessary to maintain milk supplies.

In peace-time the Government continued to give massive support to agriculture. War-time subsidies were retained, and additional grants were paid for things like improved land drainage and the reconstruction of farm buildings and workers' cottages. The **Agriculture Act, 1947,** set the pattern for the future. It gave farmers real security by laying down guaranteed prices for a wide range of produce. From 1950 to 1957, more state Marketing Boards were created, to control the sale of wool, cheese, eggs, fatstock and tomatoes. Meanwhile farmers' incomes rose dramatically, especially among larger employers. Even the wage rates of labourers were substantially increased, although they failed to catch up with the earnings of factory workers.

British farming now became the most highly mechanised in the world. In 1939 there were 50,000 tractors in use; fifteen years later there were 400,000. The numbers of combine harvesters and milking machines rose in even greater proportions. More and better fertilisers and improved varieties of seeds both helped to raise the crop yield per acre. By 1957 the average dairy cow was producing thirty per cent more milk than in pre-war years. Never since the days of Robert Bakewell and Thomas Coke (see Chapter 4) had there been such rapid progress in British farming. It almost amounted to a second Agricultural Revolution.

There was even a check in the 'drift from the land'. As piped water

A new diesel locomotive

supplies, electric power, television, school buses and travelling libraries reached into the remotest areas of Britain, the discomforts of country life were greatly reduced.

British railways, roads and shipping

When the railways were nationalised (January 1948) the Government realised that vast sums of public money would have to be spent on re-equipping them. Locomotives and rolling stock had deteriorated through lack of maintenance during the war, and many bridges, stations and sections of track were in a shocking state of repair.

A new series of British Railways *Standard* steam locomotives was introduced (1951). But by the time the last of them was built—a goods engine named 'Evening Star' (March 1960)—**diesel and electric locomotives** were taking over from steam. In 1955 there were 19,000 steam-engines in operation, yet eight years later numbers had dropped below 7000. Many that were scrapped had years of useful life left in them. However diesel and electric trains were cleaner, more efficient and required much less servicing between runs. Electric trains in particular can start and stop very quickly. This made them a great asset on the crowded Southern Region suburban services, which were largely electrified by 1939. Only the great cost of electrification prevented other regions from following the example of the Southern much earlier than the 1950s and 1960s.

Road transport continued to capture traffic from the railways, especially freight. To enable railways to compete on more equal terms, a massive **Modernisation Plan** was introduced in 1954. The building of diesel and electric engines was speeded up; stations and marshalling yards were remodelled, and local passenger services that lost money were reduced or discontinued. Britain's railway network, which reached a peak of 20,405 route miles in 1930, had come down to 17,000 miles by 1963. In that year further drastic cuts were proposed by a special Committee of Inquiry under **Dr Reginald Beeching.** To reduce British Rail's enormous losses (£87 million in 1962) Beeching advised that a further 5000 miles of unprofitable lines should be closed. At the same time, traffic would be built up on well-loaded routes; mainly long-distance freight and passenger runs and the daily suburban services of large towns. The Government stopped the full swing of the 'Beeching Axe', in the interests of country areas where railways were the main contact with the world. Even so, the railway network was down to 11,000 miles by 1970.

Meanwhile, the rapid growth of **motor traffic** caused serious congestion on the roads. From 1951 to 1960, the number of road vehicles doubled and it doubled again before the end of the 1960s! Britain had more cars per mile of road than any other country. Consequently parking in towns became a greater problem every year. 'No Waiting' signs multiplied in busy streets, and coin meters were introduced to discourage motorists from parking for long periods. But the greatest need was for more underground and multistorey car parks, to take stationary vehicles off the roads. Despite elaborate 'one-way' systems, more traffic lights, warning signs and special pedestrian crossings, the number of accidents soared. In 1966 road

Harvesting on a modern farm

deaths reached nearly 8000—an average of almost twenty-two a day. Faced with the problem of reducing this appalling slaughter, the Government introduced new laws against drunken drivers (October 1967) involving the use of preliminary 'breathalyser tests'.

The difficulty of driving in heavy traffic and parking in confined spaces led to a growing demand for **small cars,** which had the added advantage of being cheaper to run. 'Bubble cars' appeared in the early 1950s, and the popular 'Minis' in 1959. The latter were only 10 feet long and 4 feet 7 inches wide, yet they allowed reasonable head and leg room for four adults. The engine was mounted sideways to occupy less space, a technique which B.L.M.C. also use in larger family saloon cars.

But the best way of reducing traffic congestion was to improve the highways. Unfortunately, for many years after the war the increase in cars far outpaced the construction of roads. Not until 1959 was the first of Britain's **motorways** opened—the M1—a six-lane dual carriageway running for seventy miles between London and Birmingham. No cyclists or pedestrians were allowed on it, and instead of crossroads there were flyover bridges to ensure an uninterrupted flow of traffic. By 1974 well over 1000 miles of motorway had been completed throughout England and Wales. Yet Britain was a long way behind countries like the U.S.A., Germany and Italy, where roads of this kind had been built since the 1920s and 1930s.

The M1—Britain's first motorway

Motorways are improving Britain's long-distance communications, but a greater problem remains unsolved, that of **traffic in towns.** This is the title of an alarming Report produced in 1963 by a special Committee under **Professor Colin Buchanan.** He found it 'difficult to avoid the conclusion that, for a long period ahead, traffic will increase faster than we can hope to cope with it'. If the present trend continued, said the Report, towns would cease to be reasonable places to live in. It recommended a whole new approach to the problem. Simply widening streets and building larger roundabouts will tear the heart out of towns. Therefore, in certain cases, it may be necessary to abandon altogether the traditional side-by-side arrangement of streets and buildings.

In the early 1970s Britain's **merchant fleet,** most of it diesel-driven, was the world's third largest in active employment, after those of Liberia and Japan. By then giant oil tankers were the largest ships afloat. Many were too big for the Suez Canal (which was closed in any case from 1967 to 1975) and had to sail via the Cape. The volume of freight carried by sea has increased steadily since the war, but passenger services have suffered in competition with airlines. Lack of customers on transatlantic crossings led to the sale of the great *Queens, Mary* and *Elizabeth,* and their withdrawal from service (1967–8). The Cunard Company planned to replace them partly with the smaller *Queen Elizabeth 2,* which went into service in the summer of 1969.

An outstanding technical advance was the invention of the **hovercraft** by a British engineer, **C. S. Cockerell.** It hovers over water or land on a cushion of compressed air. The first experimental model, the SR-N1, crossed the Channel in 1959 at an average speed of twenty-

five knots. By 1965 regular passenger services had begun around Britain's coasts, to places like the Isle of Wight, and, in 1966, across the Channel to France.

Flight in the Jet Age

The Second World War, like the First, brought rapid developments in aviation. Radar navigational aids led to greater safety and regularity, and aero-engines were improved—particularly with the introduction of the gas-turbine or **jet engine,** invented by **Frank Whittle,** an R.A.F. officer. Air was sucked in at one end and compressed by a rotating fan before passing into a combustion chamber, where liquid fuel was sprayed in and the mixture ignited. The resulting gases expanded violently and were forced out of a rear nozzle with such power and speed that the aircraft was driven forward. Although very expensive on fuel, its continuous rotary motion caused less rubbing and vibration than pistons in cylinders, so it could run for a much longer period without needing an overhaul.

Whittle had taken out his first patent in 1930, being already convinced that the piston-engine could not provide the answer to flight at greater speeds. But the difficulty of finding metal alloys capable of withstanding immense heat held up progress and prevented the Air Ministry from giving its official backing until 1939. An experimental aircraft—the **Gloster E.28**—was fitted with Whittle's turbo-jet engine and successfully completed its trials in May 1941, achieving a speed of 370 m.p.h. (faster than the Spitfire). By the end of the war, jets had fought on both sides—the 'Gloster Meteor', designed by Whittle, and the German 'M.E. 262'. Both proved deadly in air combat.

B.E.A. (British European Airways) was set up by the Government in 1946, to operate routes at home and to the Continent. By 1949 all British routes were controlled by two state corporations, B.E.A. and B.O.A.C.—later to be merged as **British Airways** (1972). Meanwhile, British manufacturers took a lead in the development of jet propulsion. The world's first turbo-jet airliner, the De Havilland **Comet,** went into regular service with B.O.A.C. in 1952. It was followed, a year later, by the Vickers **Viscount,** fitted with *turbo-prop* engines (gas turbines drove ordinary propellers). Around this time, jet-powered military aircraft, like the Hawker Hunter, were beginning to reach the speed of sound (about 750 m.p.h. at sea-level). Swept-back delta (triangular) wings helped to reduce wind resistance. In 1956 the world's air speed record, held by Britain, had reached 1132 m.p.h. Two years later, the Comet 4 airliner began the first regular transatlantic jet service. Already more people were crossing the Atlantic by air than by sea.

In December 1962 the British and French Governments agreed to share the cost of producing the world's first supersonic airliner, **Concorde.** Work was shared between the British Aircraft Corporation at Bristol and a French company. The delta-winged Concorde was designed to fly at speeds of up to 1450 m.p.h., at a height of more than ten miles. But its immense cost, and concern about its noise at ground level, led many foreign airlines to withdraw their

The British Hovercraft Corporation's SR-N6, on trials in Sweden (1966)

advance orders—despite successful trial flights. The introduction of Concorde into regular service, early in 1976, was awaited with mixed hopes and fears for its future.

Into space

Even the wonders of jet aircraft have become commonplace now that the conquest of space has begun. The Space Age really dates from 4 October 1957, when a giant three-stage rocket carried the first Russian **sputnik** (artificial earth satellite) into orbit. Scientists all over the world picked up the *bleep-bleep* of its radio signals as it transmitted information about the upper regions of the atmosphere. *Sputnik II* carried a dog in an air-conditioned container. Observers on the ground recorded its breathing and its heartbeats and kept a check on its eating habits. When the first American satellite was launched (January 1958) the 'space race' between Russia and the U.S.A. began in earnest.

In 1959 a Russian rocket, *Lunik III,* sent back television pictures of the far side of the moon, the side man had never seen. A still greater milestone came in April 1961, when a Russian, **Yuri Gagarin,** became the first man to go beyond the pull of the earth's gravity into free orbit. His space capsule, *Vostok I,* circled the earth in 100 minutes at a maximum speed of 18,000 m.p.h. Even then the Americans were not far behind. In February 1962 **John Glenn** went into orbit and 'splashed down', according to plan, in the Atlantic Ocean. The first vital steps towards space travel had been taken. By the end of 1968 the U.S.A. took the lead in the 'space race', when a three-man *Apollo* spececraft orbited the moon and safely returned to earth. Seven months later, on 21 July 1969, the American astronauts **Neil Armstrong** and **'Buzz' Aldrin** became the first men to walk on the moon!

So far the British have taken little part in the progress of manned space travel, being unable to afford the enormous cost of research. But they have co-operated with the United States in the development of **communications satellites.** Since 1962, when a special earth station was opened at Goonhilly Downs in Cornwall, television pictures have been relayed across the Atlantic via satellites like *Telstar* (1962), *Early Bird* (1965) and *Ariel 3* (1967).

Timeline

1941   Successful trials of Whittle's jet-powered Gloster E.28.
1946–9   Nationalisation of Coal, Transport, Electricity and Gas.
1947   Agriculture Act.
1952   De Havilland Comet, the world's first jet airliner.
1954   Railways Modernisation Plan.
1956   First nuclear power station opened at Calder Hall.
1957   First *sputnik.*
1959   M1 opened, Britain's first motorway.
1959   C. S. Cockerell's SR-N1 hovercraft.
1962   First transatlantic television pictures via *Telstar.*
1967   Nationalisation of Iron and Steel (second time).
1969   American *Apollo* spacecraft lands on the moon.
1972   Formation of British Airways.
1975   First North Sea oil brought ashore.

Further study

To keep up to date with things like atomic power and the conquest of space it is necessary to read the newspapers regularly and watch news and current affairs programmes on television.

Visit

London's Science Museum contains modern mining machinery (lower ground floor); sections on rail and road transport—including electric and diesel locomotives, and Jet 1, the first gas-turbine car, made by the Rover Company in 1950 (ground floor); agricultural machines and implements (first floor); a section on industrial chemistry (second floor); and recent developments in aviation, including Whittle's Gloster E.28 and present day turbo-jet and turbo-prop engines (third floor).

General accounts

G. C. Allen, *Railways* (Blackwell), Chapter 6
R. A. S. Hennessey, *Transport* (Batsford, Past-into-Present series)
J. Roberts and A. Rowe, *Making the Present, 1918–72* (Hutchinson)
L. E. Snellgrove, *From Kitty Hawk to Outer Space* (Longmans)

Special topics

J. G. Crowther, *Six Great Inventors* (Hamish Hamilton) includes Sir Frank Whittle.
J. O'Connell, *Science and Industry*: one of a set of five booklets in *Making the Modern World: 1. Britain* (Longman)
P. Lane, *A History of Post-War Britain* (Macdonald). Chapters 2, 11 and 20 deal with nationalisation, new industries and modern developments in communications.
Transport (Longman, Secondary History Packs) Packs 17–20 deal largely with earlier developments, but some items are relevant to the post-war period.
Britain—An Official Handbook (H.M.S.O.) is published yearly and contains the latest facts and figures on industry, transport and a wide range of other subjects. Start by looking up 'Fuel and Power' and making a map of Britain's atomic power stations.

Above: A 'Concorde' prototype taking shape

Left: A successful launching on the Woomera Rocket Range in Australia

26 Sunset on the Empire

The Commonwealth and the 'Affluent Society'

In the late nineteenth century half a dozen European nations, including Britain, extended their rule over millions of people in the 'undeveloped areas' of the world. It was an Age of Imperialism (see Chapter 19). In contrast, the mid twentieth century became an **Age of Decolonisation,** when the great European empires were broken up and their subject peoples achieved self-government. From the end of the Second World War to the mid 1960s, almost the whole of Africa and southern Asia, along with many smaller regions, became independent of foreign rulers.

The British Empire, by far the largest, was the first to undergo decolonisation. During the war, when British statesmen declared their willingness 'to guide colonial people along the road to self-government', there were many foreign leaders, including America's President Roosevelt, who disbelieved them. Yet in the space of twenty years practically all Britain's former colonies were given their freedom. Independence did, of course, carry with it the right to end all connections with the United Kingdom. This was the immediate choice of Burma, Somaliland, Sudan and South Cameroons. But the great majority of countries newly independent of Britain preferred to remain partners in the *Commonwealth.*

Thus the old Victorian view of empire, consisting of a Queen Empress ruling over subject peoples, gave way to the idea of an international 'community of equals'.

Canada, Australia and New Zealand

The modern idea of the Commonwealth as a *partnership* of self-governing states had first been applied to the former dominions— Canada, Australia, New Zealand and South Africa—which were populated largely by British and other European settlers. After the First World War, in which the dominions lost nearly 200,000 men, each of them had their own representatives at the Peace Conference and signed the Treaty of Versailles separately. In these circumstances it seemed reasonable for Britain to recognise them as fully independent countries. This was done eventually in the **Statute of Westminster (1931),** an Act of Parliament which declared the dominion territories to be equal partners with the United Kingdom in a free 'Commonwealth of Nations'. They were no longer bound by any laws passed by the British Parliament, unless they agreed to them. However, legal freedom did not prevent these countries from coming to Britain's assistance in the Second World War. The ties that really mattered were those of friendship, reinforced by trading connections and a shared language and culture.

Of all the former dominions, **Canada** has the richest natural resources and the largest population. It has plentiful supplies of gold, uranium, copper and iron ore, and experts estimate that there is more oil and natural gas in the State of Alberta than in the Middle East. But many branches of mining and manufacturing are only just beginning to be developed. Even in the 1960s Canada's main export was still wheat. Its future as an industrial nation depends largely on a continuing flow of immigrants from Europe. The population rose from 7 million in 1911 to 22 million in 1973, yet Canada could comfortably support two or three times that number. Its high standard of living is mainly due to the influence and assistance of the U.S.A., particularly the investment of American dollars. For instance, the great **St Lawrence Seaway,** which enables ocean-going ships to reach ports on the Great Lakes, was a joint enterprise between Canada and the United States (1954–9). By the mid 1960s, Americans controlled seventy per cent of Canada's oil companies and sixty per cent of its manufacturing industry.

Up to the Second World War, **Australia** and **New Zealand** traded mostly with Britain and, unlike Canada, had no close relationship with any other country. But in recent years ties with the United Kingdom have loosened. British forces no longer provide military protection in the Far East, so both Australia and New Zealand joined the United States in a defence agreement called **A.N.Z.U.S.** (1951). They also began to trade more and more with the countries of Asia and the Pacific. Britain bought two-thirds of all New Zealand's

The Cornwall Dam, Ontario—part of the St Lawrence Seaway project

exports in 1950, yet only half in 1966. In the same year Japan replaced Britain as Australia's best customer. Apart from its large production of wool and meat, Australia has resources of coal, iron ore, copper, oil, tin and uranium. Its industries are developing rapidly, even though its population is still quite small. Between 1945 and 1973 it rose from $7\frac{1}{2}$ to $13\frac{1}{4}$ million, with the help of state-assisted immigration from Britain and Europe. In New Zealand efforts to increase mining and manufacturing have been less successful. Its 3 million people still depend mainly on exports of meat and dairy produce.

India—independence and partition

With the exception of the 'white Commonwealth', the earliest demands for freedom from British rule came in India. After the First World War, the cause of Indian independence came under the influence of **Mohandas Karamchand Gandhi** (1869–1948). Although he had studied at London University and been for many years a successful barrister in South Africa, he lived with the simplicity of a peasant and refused to adopt a Western way of life. His sincerity and his saintly qualities greatly impressed the Indian people, who called him *Mahatma* (Holy One). Gandhi hated violence. He believed independence should be achieved by a policy of 'non-violent non-co-operation', involving strikes, demonstrations and a boycott of British goods.

To give Indians less cause for complaint, the British granted them a greater share in governing themselves and promised independence some time in the future. By 1935 **provincial councils,** dealing with matters like health, education and agriculture, were entirely under Indian control. But nothing short of 'immediate self-government' would satisfy the **Congress Party,** led by Gandhi. Real power was still in the hands of the British Viceroy and his ministers, and the U.K. Parliament could overrule the decision of any Indian assembly.

During the Second World War, Gandhi refused to co-operate with the Allies, despite the Japanese conquest of neighbouring Burma. He ran a 'Quit India' campaign against the British, which infuriated Churchill and made him even more determined to resist Indian demands. But the post-war Labour Government took a different view. In 1947 it decided to make India self-governing. This was easier said than done, for there were deep religious divisions within the country. The Muslims, who were outnumbered three to one by Hindus, feared that when British rule came to an end they would be unfairly treated. For some years their leader, **Muhammed Ali Jinnah,** had been demanding independence not only of Britain but of the Hindus as well. He wanted a separate state, to be called **Pakistan** ('land of the pure'). The Hindu Congress was completely opposed to the idea, but riots and disturbances convinced the British Government that *partition* (separation) might be the only way to prevent civil war.

Therefore, when the British withdrew (15 August 1947) *two* independent states—India and Pakistan—came into being. Pakistan was itself divided into two parts, the larger in the North-West, containing the capital, Karachi, and the smaller in the North-East*. Great move-

Above: Gandhi, pictured during a visit to Britain (1931)

Opposite above: Mrs Indira Gandhi

Opposite below: Modern street scene in Srinagar, Kashmir

---

* After a civil war in 1971, East Pakistan broke away from the West and renamed itself Bangladesh.

ments of population were necessary to get the two religious groups mainly within their own borders. In the confusion, riots broke out and at least 200,000 people were massacred. There was even a full-scale war in **Kashmir,** a mainly Muslim area, when its Hindu ruler tried to join it to India. It has been divided and a cause of dispute ever since. In 1965, after years of border disturbances, the two countries again went to war over Kashmir, and again failed to settle their differences.

Right from the start, both new nations had to fight an enormous amount of poverty and ignorance. They were overpopulated and their agriculture was backward. If the Monsoon rains failed to arrive on time, food production suffered and many people starved to death. The population of India alone rose from 360 million in 1951 to 548 million in 1971. Three-quarters of them could not read or write. **Pandit Nehru** (1889–1964) who became India's ruler when Gandhi was assassinated in 1948, was determined to lead his country out of what he called 'the cowdung age'. He wanted new industries, mechanisation of agriculture, more scientific research and a campaign to encourage birth control. But lack of success in the last of his aims hindered progress in other directions. When his daughter, **Mrs Indira Gandhi,** became Prime Minister (1966) she faced much the same problems.

'Wind of change' in Africa

The story of African independence really began after 1945, when there were only four self-governing states in the whole continent. Two world wars had seriously weakened the colonial nations of Europe. Moreover, in each colony there was by this time a group of educated Africans who, as students or soldiers, had become familiar with Western political ideas. Like the Indians, they demanded self-rule and declared that if Europeans believed in freely elected governments for themselves they could hardly object when others wanted the same.

The British had long claimed that their colonial rule was designed to benefit the native peoples and would be given up when these were ready to govern themselves. But they refused to be hurried, preferring to introduce self-government gradually, as they had done in India. In some colonies this policy began in the 1930s, with the creation of regional councils to which a few educated Africans were appointed. But even at the end of the war most colonies were still very backward.

With the exception of Egypt, which gained control of its own affairs in 1936, the first African states to become independent of Britain were in the old slave-trading areas of **West Africa.** Here, owing to the hot climate, there were relatively few white settlers to oppose majority rule. The Gold Coast was the first to gain independence, as **Ghana,** in 1957. **Nigeria,** the largest and most highly populated colony, became a federation containing three separate regions in 1954 and achieved independence six years later. **Sierra Leone** was the next to get its freedom (1961). Finally, when the tiny colony of **Gambia** became self-governing (1965) Britain's empire in West Africa was at an end.

Not all these changes worked out as well as had been hoped. Ghana's leader, **Dr Kwame Nkrumah,** soon forgot the principles of free choice he had been preaching at the British in the years before independence. He gradually took on the powers of a dictator, out-lawing all political parties except his own. It came as no surprise when he was overthrown in an army revolt (1966). In Nigeria the separate regions and tribes never fully accepted the idea of unity under a federal government. In 1967 the Eastern Region broke away and declared itself independent as the republic of Biafra. But after three years of bloodshed, Biafra was crushed and Nigerian unity restored.

In **East Africa** the move to independence was often complicated by the presence of quite large minorities of white settlers who clung to their privileged position under colonial rule. The granting of self-government went fairly smoothly in Tanganyika (1961) and **Uganda** (1962). The former became **Tanzania** in 1964, when it was united with the off-shore island of Zanzibar. However, in **Kenya** there was a background of fierce racial clashes. About 40,000 whites controlled the local Assembly and owned a quarter of all arable land, leaving the remainder for several million Africans. The Kikuyu tribe, led by **Jomo Kenyatta,** complained bitterly at this injustice. Beginning in 1952, a secret terrorist organisation called *Mau Mau* carried out a series of murderous attacks on settlers. Britain declared a state of emergency, flew in troops and imprisoned Kenyatta, although his part in terrorist activities was not proved. After order had been

Dr Kwame Nkrumah

restored, around 1956, the Africans were gradually given a greater share in government. Kenyatta was finally released and became the first Prime Minister of an independent Kenya (1963).

Further south, troubles were less easily solved. In 1953 Northern and Southern Rhodesia and Nyasaland were joined together in a Central African Federation. But, from the outset, black Africans in Northern Rhodesia and Nyasaland opposed union with Southern Rhodesia. There, 200,000 Europeans controlled the Government almost completely and owned two-thirds of the land, while 4 million Africans were treated as second-class citizens. They were denied proper voting rights and forced to live in special 'reserved areas'. In 1962 an extreme party called the *Rhodesian Front* gained power, with the aim of achieving independence under white rule. Discontent grew, until Britain was forced to break up the Federation (1963) and allow Northern Rhodesia and Nyasaland to become self-governing, as **Zambia** and **Malawi** (1964).

The white Government of **Southern Rhodesia** also demanded independence. But Britain wanted assurances that black Africans would receive full voting rights within a reasonable period and, in the meantime, would be given opportunities to prepare themselves for future responsibility. These terms proved unacceptable to the Rhodesian Front. **Ian Smith,** who became leader of the party in 1964, made it clear that he intended to preserve white rule far into the future.

Rhodesian Prime Minister, Ian Smith, signs the declaration of independence in Salisbury, Rhodesia (11 November 1965)

When talks with Britain reached deadlock, his Cabinet made a *unilateral* (one-sided) declaration of independence—**U.D.I.** (November 1965). Harold Wilson's Government immediately banned all British trade with Rhodesia, hoping to paralyse the rebellion. When talks again failed (1966) he took the matter to the United Nations. A world boycott on all trade with Rhodesia was declared; but many businessmen found ways of avoiding the ban, thus reducing its effectiveness. Rhodesia declared itself a republic in 1969.

Like their Rhodesian neighbours, Europeans in **South Africa** resisted the wave of freedom sweeping across the continent, the 'wind of change', as Harold Macmillan, Britain's Prime Minister, called it in 1960. Most of the country's 3 million whites are Afrikaaners, descendants of the Boers, who founded Cape Colony in the seventeenth century. To them Africa is home and they are determined to stay. Their high standard of living depends on the 'cheap labour' of 15 million black Africans. By denying them voting rights, higher education and other 'privileges', Afrikaaners hope to keep control of the government and the country's industry and agriculture. As a further precaution against black domination, the extreme Nationalist Party, which gained power in 1948, introduced **Apartheid,** or separation of the races. Black Africans were forced to live in special suburbs and reserves; mixed marriages were forbidden; separate schools were built, and the races were kept apart in public buildings, on beaches, buses and trams. Those who opposed *Apartheid* were severely punished. Clearly, there was no place for such views within the multiracial Commonwealth. In 1961 South Africa broke away and became a republic.

When **Botswana** (formerly Bechuanaland), **Lesotho** (formerly Basutoland) and **Swaziland** became independent members of the Commonwealth (1965–68), British rule in Africa had come to an end. Most of the new states were backward, disunited and heavily dependent on foreign aid. Moreover, the political principles they had learned from Europe proved to be unworkable. Constitutions prepared in Western capitals were soon replaced by one-party systems and military dictatorships. In fact, no black African government has so far been *voted* out of office. The idea of a permanent 'alternative government' in the form of an opposition party proved too great a temptation to those eager for power.

The 'wind of change' was not only felt in Africa. Apart from a few scattered islands, mostly in the Pacific, almost the entire British Empire had been dissolved by the mid 1960s. In the **West Indies,** a Federation of British islands was formed in 1958, but it only lasted four years. There were too many rivalries between the members. Jamaica and Trinidad and Tobago became independent in 1962, followed by Barbados and Guyana (formerly British Guiana) in 1966. On the other side of the world, North Borneo, Sarawak, Malaya and Singapore were formed into the self-governing **Federation of Malaysia** (1964). Singapore broke away in the following year. Finally, in the Mediterranean, **Cyprus** (1960) and **Malta** (1964) became independent of Britain, the former after years of civil war between Greek and Turkish Cypriots. In complete contrast, **Gibraltar,**

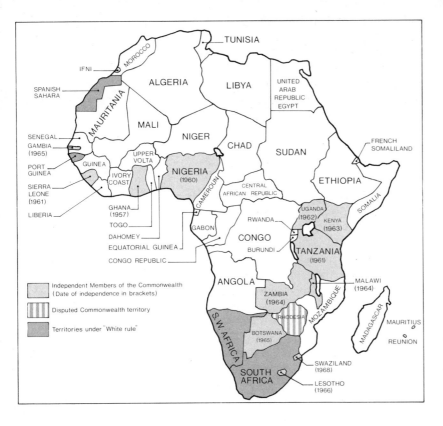

Left: Africa 1975

Below: Harold Macmillan Conservative Prime Minister, 1957–63

fearing Spanish threats to take over the rock, voted by an over-whelming majority in 1967 to *remain* a British dependency.

Britain – 'the endless middle'

While the newly independent countries struggled to overcome poverty and backwardness, the average British citizen enjoyed the highest standard of living the country had ever known. By the mid 1950s, when war-time shortages had finally disappeared, most Western countries, including Britain, entered upon a period of *affluence* (wealth or abundance) which, for the first time, affected all social classes.

In the reign of Victoria, Britain had the greatest empire and was the supreme manufacturing and trading nation, yet millions of ordinary people lived in poverty. But in the reign of Elizabeth II (1952–   ) even though British supremacy was a thing of the past, nearly all the worst poverty had been eliminated. In general, people were taller, heavier, better fed, better housed, better clothed, better educated and had a longer expectation of life. In the words of Harold Macmillan, they had 'never had it so good'.

All this was the result of full employment, higher productivity in industry, and a *redistribution of wealth* from richer to poorer. The services of the Welfare State, including subsidies to reduce the cost of essential foods and housing, together with high taxes on the wealthy, had narrowed the immense gulf in living standards between the upper and lower classes. Moreover, in the period 1951–63, average wages rose by seventy-two per cent. After allowing for the declining value of the pound, this was still a substantial gain, especially among less-skilled workers. It reflected the great power of **trade unions,** whose total membership increased by a half in the decade 1938–48. Although much of the atmosphere of 'class war' against 'the bosses' had gone, strikes were hardly ever out of the news. Many were 'unofficial', and unions were criticised for failing to discipline members. In the mid 1960s, however, trade unionists showed willingness to act in the national interest. They accepted temporary Government control of wages in 1966–7, owing to the country's financial difficulties. But industrial unrest soon returned, and in 1970 there was an all-time record number of strikes — 3906. In an attempt to curb industrial disputes, especially unofficial strikes, the Conservative Government passed an Industrial Relations Act (1971). This was bitterly resented by trade unionists, and the next Labour Government repealed it in 1974. By then *inflation* (rapidly rising prices and incomes) was Britain's major economic problem. It was clear that to curb inflation a new spirit of co-operation between unions, employers and the Government was required.

Manual workers, backed by powerful unions, were now better off than most clerical workers. The lower middle classes looked back longingly to 'the old days' before the war, when there was a clear division in income and status between 'white collar' and manual jobs. Craftsmen suffered a similar fate to clerical workers. As the demand for their skills fell, so did the higher wages they once commanded. Many tradesmen abandoned their crafts to earn more money doing repetitive jobs on 'assembly lines'. Meanwhile, able young men from all walks of life obtained university degrees and rose to senior positions in industry, commerce and the professions. At many levels the old class structure seemed to be breaking down into an 'endless middle'.

This change was reflected in people's **clothing.** Women of all classes now looked very much alike in simple dresses, skirts and sweaters; while fewer workmen wore the traditional cloth cap, muffler and heavy boots. There was less need for special 'working clothes' now that technological changes in industry were taking much of the dirt and sweat out of people's jobs. Dockers began to use fork-lift trucks, railway engine-drivers left the footplate for upholstered seats in electric or diesel locomotives, and more and more factory workers became button-pushers or dial-watchers.

'Tough' jobs like mining, quarrying and 'navvying' became increasingly difficult to fill. So did lower-paid positions in public services like railways and buses, the G.P.O. and the hospitals. These began to employ large numbers of **Commonwealth immigrants,** most of them from the West Indies, India and Pakistan. By the 1950s they were flocking to Britain in their thousands, eager to find work and to benefit from the educational and welfare services. They gathered in places like London, Birmingham and the West Midlands, where jobs were usually plentiful. Unfortunately they often lived together in overcrowded conditions, partly due to the housing shortage, combined with a lot of racial prejudice on the part of landlords. Advertisements for rented accommodation frequently ended with the words 'No Coloured'—until such discrimination was made illegal by the Race Relations Acts (1965, 1968). The flow of immigrants was restricted after 1962, when it became necessary for them to have a job waiting. Even so their total numbers reached a million by 1967.

Despite the difficulties facing Commonwealth immigrants most of them enjoyed a standard of living far beyond that in their own countries. In Britain, full employment and rising wages meant even lower-paid workers were able to buy expensive goods like television sets, vacuum cleaners and washing machines, with the aid of **hire purchase.** When all that was needed was a small deposit, luxuries were somehow turned into necessities. By the 1960s, motor cars accounted for more than half the nation's H.P. debt; and many of the new owners were manual workers. Even continental holidays could be paid for in instalments. In 1973 over 8 million people took foreign holidays—compared with $1\frac{1}{2}$ million in 1950. Many were teenagers, some in school parties, others paying for themselves out of regular earnings. Before the war, young people at work had counted their spending money in shillings and pence, now they counted it in

Commonwealth immigrants on arrival at London airport

pounds. Industries like clothing, cosmetics, motor cycles and scooters depended heavily on teenage buyers.

Inside a bingo hall

While teenagers enjoyed a new-found freedom, many parents became slaves to the **television** screen. The 'telly' moved into the centre of the family circle, reorganising people's lives around it. Yet as recently as 1949, three years after the B.B.C.'s Alexandra Palace service reopened, two-thirds of the population had never seen a television programme. It was not until the opening of regional transmitters, beginning with Sutton Coldfield, near Birmingham (1950), that the rush to buy sets became nationwide. The **Independent Television Authority** was set up in 1954, to promote a new service financed by advertising. In the following year the public had its first taste of television commercials. The B.B.C.'s new rival quickly captured a majority of the viewing audience which, by 1958, numbered half the total adult population at a 'peak period' like Sunday evening. The opening of *B.B.C.2* (1964) had little immediate effect on the popularity of independent television. Colour transmissions began on *B.B.C.2* in 1967 and on the other channels in 1969.

No other invention in history had such an impact on social life. Television was held responsible for broken marriages, the continuing decline in church-going, children's nightmares, typists' bad spelling, declining football crowds and, of course, juvenile delinquency. It was certainly to blame for the decline of sound radio and the cinema. *The wireless* still had an average audience of 9 million in 1954, yet this fell to $3\frac{1}{2}$ million only three years later. However, in the mid 1960s, the appearance around Britain's coasts of 'pirate' radio stations, illegally financed by advertising, led to a revival of interest in 'steam radio'. Parliament banned the pirates (1967) but a new B.B.C. 'popular music' station—Radio One—was provided in their place. Although radio suffered in competition with television, the **cinema** fared worse. Between 1954 and 1959, over 800 picture houses were closed or converted into bingo halls and ten-pin bowling alleys. As cinema attendances dropped film-makers tried, with limited success, to recapture lost audiences with big screen 'epics' and thrillers.

Critics of television claimed it discouraged people from **reading.** No doubt this was often true, nevertheless yearly sales of 'paperbacks' rose from 10 million just before the war to over 60 million in 1960, and continued to climb steeply. Magazine and newspaper sales increased too. In the 1950s and 1960s half the nation's families took either the *Daily Mirror* or the *Daily Express,* and altogether the British purchased more papers per head than the people of any other country.

Overtures to Europe

By the 1960s, as Commonwealth ties loosened, it seemed that Britain's high standard of living might in future depend upon a closer relationship with the countries of Western Europe, particularly the six members of the **European Economic Community** (E.E.C.). Although a third of Britain's foreign trade was still carried on within the Commonwealth, European markets were becoming increasingly important as outlets for the more advanced industries. Not only the country's future prosperity, but also its opportunity to play a major part in world affairs, might depend on 'going into Europe'.

E.E.C., otherwise known as the *Common Market,* was founded in 1957, when France, West Germany, Italy, the Netherlands, Belgium and Luxembourg ('The Six') signed the **Treaty of Rome.** They agreed to form a customs-free area by gradually removing all tariffs on trade among themselves; although they kept an *external tariff* on trade with countries outside the Community. But it was more than just a trading arrangement. Members agreed to adopt common policies in agriculture and transport, and to prepare for eventual political unity. It was felt that only a truly united Western Europe could deal on equal terms with the U.S.A. and Russia. However political unification progressed very slowly, largely because the French President, General De Gaulle (1958–69), was not prepared to give up national independence.

At first it was thought that membership of E.E.C. would interfere with Britain's 'special relationship' to the U.S.A. and, above all, with its position as the centre of the Commonwealth and of a vast international network of trading and financial interests. However, Britain did join six other nations—Austria, Sweden, Switzerland, Norway, Denmark and Portugal—in a **European Free Trade Association** (E.F.T.A.) which came into operation in 1960. Members agreed to promote the maximum amount of free trade among themselves and to remove tariffs on industrial goods completely. But E.F.T.A. was not a real alternative to the Common Market. It was only a customs union, and, in any case, it could not provide Britain with a sufficiently large market for manufactured

'The Six' and 'The Seven' —before the entry of the United Kingdom, Eire and Denmark into the E.E.C. (1973), thus making it 'The Nine'

goods. Therefore, in 1961, the Government applied for membership of the Six. Long and detailed talks were held until January 1963, when General De Gaulle suddenly called a halt. He said links with the U.S.A. and the Commonwealth would make it impossible for Britain to be loyal to the Six.

The other five members of E.E.C. were in favour of British entry and strongly criticised De Gaulle. Their continued support, together with a growing acceptance in Britain of the need for closer links with Europe, encouraged the Labour Government to reapply for membership in 1967. Little progress was made until after De Gaulle's fall from power in 1969. Talks began in earnest following the Conservative victory in the British election of 1970. By autumn 1971 terms of membership had been agreed between the United Kingdom and the E.E.C. countries. Britain finally turned the tide of history and 'went into Europe' (along with Eire and Denmark) on 1 January 1973.

A majority of the Labour Party opposed British entry into the Common Market on the terms accepted by the Conservatives. And they claimed that the British people had not been consulted. So after the return of a Labour Government under Harold Wilson in 1974, the terms of entry were 're-negotiated' and the whole question of British membership of the E.E.C. put to a nationwide *referendum* (a form of secret ballot in which each voter is asked to answer 'yes' or 'no' to a specific question). Following a lively campaign, in which the main political parties were divided amongst themselves, the E.E.C. Referendum was held on 5 June 1975. The result was a two-thirds majority in favour of continued membership. Britain's new ties had been cemented.

Edward Heath, Britain's chief representative in the first unsuccessful bid to join the Common Market. He became Prime Minister in June 1970, and his Government negotiated British entry to E.E.C. in the following year

Timeline

1931   The Statute of Westminster.
1947   Independence of India and Pakistan.
1952–6 *Mau Mau* troubles in Kenya.
1953–63 Central African Federation.
1954   Independent Television Authority established.
1957   Ghana becomes the first black African state to gain independence from Britain.
1957   Treaty of Rome—E.E.C. created.
1960   European Free Trade Association (E.F.T.A.).
1961   South Africa leaves the Commonwealth.
1965   U.D.I. in Rhodesia.
1967   First colour television transmissions.
1968   Swaziland independent—end of British rule in Africa.
1973   Britain a member of the E.E.C.
1975   E.E.C. Referendum

Further study

To keep in touch with the development of the Common Market and with changes in the Commonwealth, it is essential to follow the news in the press and on television.

Special topics
Taya Zinkin, *Gandhi* (Methuen's Story Biographies)

K. Savage, *The History of the Common Market* (Longman)

B. Williams, *Modern Africa* (Longman's Modern Times series)

P. Squibb, *Britain Today*, and other titles in *Making the Modern World: 1. Britain* (Longman)

S. Wilmott, *Fashion and Dress* (Blackwell, Twentieth Century Topics)

P. Lane, *A History of Post-War Britain* (Macdonald). For the Commonwealth, E.E.C., industrial relations, immigration and many other aspects of post-war British history.

A. Walker, *Modern Commonwealth* (Longman's Modern Times series)

Making the Modern World: 6. Africa and the Middle East (Longman) includes the following:

P. Ripley, *Kenyatta*

B. Williams, *South Africa*

Longman's Social Science Studies includes useful items on life in modern Britain, including:

Richard Cootes, *The Family* (Series One)

Susan Dickinson, *Leisure* (Series Two)

Filmstrip

Twentieth Century Britain, Part 3: The Empire, the Commonwealth and the World (Educational Publications)

Index